Mark and Paul

Beihefte zur Zeitschrift für die
neutestamentliche
Wissenschaft

Edited by
James D. G. Dunn, Carl R. Holladay,
Matthias Konradt, Hermann Lichtenberger,
Jens Schröter and Gregory E. Sterling

Volume 199

Mark and Paul

Comparative Essays Part II
For and Against Pauline Influence on Mark

Edited by
Eve-Marie Becker, Troels Engberg-Pedersen
and Mogens Müller

DE GRUYTER

ISBN 978-3-11-055274-4
e-ISBN 978-3-11-031469-4
ISSN 0171-6441

Library of Congress Cataloging-in-Publication Data
A CIP catalog record for this book has been applied for at the Library of Congress.

Bibliographic Information published by the Deutsche Nationalbibliothek
The Deutsche Nationalbibliothek lists this publication in the Deutsche Nationalbibliografie; detailed bibliographic data are available in the Internet at http://dnb.dnb.de.

© 2017 Walter de Gruyter GmbH, Berlin/Boston
This volume is text- and page-identical with the hardback published in 2014.
Druck: Hubert & Co. GmbH & Co. KG, Göttingen

♾ Printed on acid-free paper
Printed in Germany

www.degruyter.com

Preface

This volume aims to take up and continue the scholarly discussion of the relationship between Mark and Paul that has recently become a "hot topic" in New Testament exegesis: was the evangelist directly influenced – in spite of writing in a completely different literary genre – by Paul, the writer of letters? Or should we rather refer any similarities to the fact that both belonged to and articulated the broader traditions of what we might best call "earliest Christianity"?

This is the set of questions that was put on the agenda when the two New Testament departments at Denmark's universities of Aarhus and Copenhagen decided to engage in a joint research venture a few years ago. We organized our work around two conferences. In September 2010, the Danish participants in the project met in Aarhus for a two-day session where we presented first drafts of papers on the topic. During these two days we also discussed how the joint research project might be continued in and beyond the Danish universities.

In August 2011 we met again, this time in Copenhagen and this time with a number of international participants as presenters of papers and/or respondents: John Barclay (Durham, UK), Ismo Dunderberg (Helsinki), Elizabeth Struthers Malbon (Virginia Tech), Joel Marcus (Duke), Margaret Mitchell (Chicago), Gerd Theissen (Heidelberg) and Oda Wischmeyer (Erlangen). Since then the various papers offered by both New Testament scholars teaching in Denmark and the global experts have been carefully revised for publication in the present volume.

At the same time, on the initiative of Oda Wischmeyer this volume was related to a publication project on "Paul and Mark: Two Authors at the Beginnings of Christianity" (BZNW 198), so that it now forms part two of a shared publishing venture. It is our hope that the appearance of these two volumes will help to place the question of the Paul/Mark and Mark/Paul relationship on a new scholarly level.

We cannot end this preface without commemorating a much-missed contributor, Anne Vig Skoven. Vig Skoven began to study theology after a rich and varied career, eventually becoming, until her much-too-early death in spring 2013, a PhD. student at the University of Copenhagen in a research project devoted to the Mark/Paul project. All who knew her remember her as a stimulating, insightful and kind person, someone whom we deeply miss. We are sad that she could not see the final result of the shared project in which she showed such a keen interest.

It remains to thank the editorial board of BZNW for accepting our project for publication in this series, and especially Dr. Albrecht Döhnert, Dr. Sabine Krämer and Sophie Wagenhofer for their cooperation, patience and support during the process of publication. We also thank Aarhus University, the University of Copenhagen and the Danish Research Council for the Humanities (FKK) for financial support for our meetings in Aarhus and Copenhagen and for the publication of the volume. We thank stud. theol. Anna Bank Jeppesen (Aarhus) for producing the indices.

Last but not least, we would like to thank all contributors and respondents – in Denmark, as well as colleagues from abroad – for their work together in moving into the centre of the New Testament, where we find Paul and Mark. If we definitely knew how these two authors are related, we would finally have unraveled how the Jesus tradition, the Christian kerygma and Hellenistic literacy met and set the agenda for the written "gospel proclamation" in and beyond the first century CE.

Eve-Marie Becker, Troels Engberg-Pedersen and Mogens Müller
Aarhus and Copenhagen, 1st November 2013

Table of Contents

Eve-Marie Becker, Troels Engberg-Pedersen and Mogens Müller
Mark and Paul – Introductory Remarks —— 1

I. Histories and Contexts

Anne Vig Skoven †
Mark as Allegorical Rewriting of Paul: Gustav Volkmar's Understanding of the Gospel of Mark —— 13

Joel Marcus
Mark – Interpreter of Paul —— 29

Heike Omerzu
Paul and Mark – Mark and Paul
   A Critical Outline of the History of Research —— 51

Gerd Theissen
„Evangelium" im Markusevangelium
   Zum traditionsgeschichtlichen Ort des ältesten Evangeliums —— 63

Eve-Marie Becker
Earliest Christian *literary activity:* Investigating Authors, Genres and Audiences in Paul and Mark —— 87

Mogens Müller
In the Beginning was the Congregation
   In Search of a *Tertium Comparationis* between Paul and Mark —— 107

II. Texts and Interpretations

Oda Wischmeyer
Romans 1:1–7 and Mark 1:1–3 in Comparison
   Two Opening Texts at the Beginning of Early Christian Literature —— 121

Jan Dochhorn
Man and the Son of Man in Mark 2:27–28
An Exegesis of Mark 2:23–28 Focussing on the Christological Discourse in Mark 2:27–28 with an Epilogue Concerning Pauline Parallels —— 147

Kasper Bro Larsen
Mark 7:1–23: A Pauline Halakah? —— 169

Troels Engberg-Pedersen
Paul in Mark 8:34–9:1: Mark on what it is to be a Christian —— 189

III. Topics and Perspectives

Gitte Buch-Hansen
The Politics of Beginnings – Cosmology, Christology and Covenant: Gospel Openings Reconsidered in the Light of Paul's Pneumatology —— 213

Ole Davidsen
Adam-Christ Typology in Paul and Mark: Reflections on a *Tertium Comparationis*
Preliminary Remarks —— 243

Jesper Tang Nielsen
The Cross on the Way to Mark —— 273

Finn Damgaard
Persecution and Denial – Paradigmatic Apostolic Portrayals in Paul and Mark —— 295

List of Contributors —— 311

Index of Subjects and Names —— 313

Index of References —— 319

Eve-Marie Becker, Troels Engberg-Pedersen and
Mogens Müller
Mark and Paul – Introductory Remarks

In Paul and Mark we meet *the* two basic figures in earliest Christian theology and literature. In principle, we might consider both authors and theologians more or less independently from one another. In so doing, we might soon agree on stating that the impact of Paul's letter-writing activity cannot be underestimated – neither in a theological nor in a literary sense[1] – and the same is also true for 'Mark', the initiator if not the actual inventor of the narrative genre. In separating Paul and Mark, we might relate these two authors and theologians to different generations within earliest Christianity and qualify their writings differently in terms of genre – as being either epistolary or narrative in nature. However, the question would remain to what extent Paul and Mark also share common materials – Jesus traditions like the *paradosis* concerning the last supper (1 Cor 11:23– 26; Mark 14:22–25) or kerygmatic formulas (1 Cor 15:3b-5; Mark 8:31) – and how and why they do so. In other words, the quest for a theological and literary interrelation or dependency will not be long in emerging.

On second thought, therefore, the need to consider Paul and Mark comparatively imposes itself. There are various ways of doing so. First, we may discuss on the level of tradition history how Paul might have had access to a number of Jesus traditions which we also know from the Synoptic tradition – and thus from Mark.[2] Secondly, in connection with Ferdinand Christian Baur's interest in differentiating the various theological movements in earliest Christianity by profiling a basically Pauline and an anti-Pauline group, we might read the Markan Gospel as a response to Paulinism in the last third of the 1st century.[3] Thirdly, we might consider comparatively central lexemes, syntagms, propositions and

---

[1] Cf. most recently: F. W. Horn (ed.), *Paulus Handbuch* (Tübingen: Mohr Siebeck, 2013); *Paulus – Werk und Wirkung. FS für A. Lindemann zum 70. Geburtstag*, eds. P.-G. Klumbies et al. (Tübingen: Mohr Siebeck, 2013).
[2] Cf., e.g. recently: J. Schröter, "Das Verhältnis zum irdischen Jesus und zur Jesusüberlieferung." In F. W. Horn (ed.), *Paulus Handbuch*, 279–285; E.-M. Becker, "2 Corinthians 3:14, 18 as Pauline Allusions to a Narrative Jesus Tradition." In *"What Does the Scripture Say?": Studies in the Function of Scripture in Early Judaism and Christianity*, LNTS 470, eds. C. A. Evans and H. D. Zacharias (London/New York: T & T Clark International, 2012), 121–133.
[3] Cf. in general: J. Wischmeyer, "Paul and Mark in Nineteenth Century Scholarship." In *Paul and Mark: Two Authors at the Beginnings of Christianity*, BZNW 198, eds. O. Wischmeyer, D. Sim, I. Elmer (Berlin/Boston: Walter de Gruyter, 2014) (forthcoming).

theologumena (such as εὐαγγέλιον or πίστις etc.)[4] or narrative patterns in Paul and Mark and discuss in what sense and to what extent the Markan Gospel might be seen as a theological and/or literary successor of Paul – or whether what they share was simply property common to all in earliest Christian times. Finally, we might directly take Mark and his gospel narrative as our point of departure and analyze how far the earliest gospel writer might have had access to Pauline traditions, or even to the Pauline letters themselves.

But even if we try to sharpen our approach and our methodological instruments, we may still expect the Paul and Mark/Mark and Paul relationship to be quite complex and to elude any simple solution. This means that in this field, where we can only work with historical and literary hypotheses, focus on the task of comparison becomes particularly important.[5] It is against this background that the Paul and Mark/Mark and Paul project – now brought together in two BZNW volumes – has its special profile.

The contributions in *Paul and Mark* (BZNW 198) serve the purpose of giving a comprehensive overview of the historical, literary and theological track that might lead from Paul to Mark. Here, the history of research on the question is recalled from the 19th century onwards and historical issues such as the connection of both authors to Rome are addressed. In addition, various theological concepts, narrative shapings and cultural issues are discussed in comparative form. A fourth section in the first volume points to the interrelation of Paul and Mark in reception history up to Papias' time.[6]

The contributions in *the present* volume, *Mark and Paul*, to some extent continue this debate, but several of them also suggest a change in perspective by focusing on one or the other of the two specific queries or approaches that were adopted at the two conferences underpinning the volume. The first query specifically addresses the issue of genre and asks how an apostolic letter and a gospel narrative might be compared. Are Paul's and Mark's theologies and ways of thinking confined by the needs of the literary genre they are using? Or – the other way round – is their use of literary genre dependent on their theological concepts? Or, finally, are there ways of overcoming the genre differences

---

[4] See the various contributions in: *Paul and Mark* (see n. 3).
[5] Cf. on similar projects: *Mark and Matthew, Comparative Readings I: Understanding the Earliest Gospels in their First-Century Settings*, WUNT 271, eds. E.-M. Becker and A. Runesson (Tübingen: Mohr Siebeck, 2011); *Mark and Matthew II, Comparative Readings: Reception History, Cultural Hermeneutics, and Theology*, WUNT 304, eds. E.-M. Becker and A. Runesson (Tübingen: Mohr Siebeck, 2013).
[6] Cf. more extensively: O. Wischmeyer's introduction, in: *Paul and Mark* (see n. 3).

without playing them down? How far does the 'letter-gospel-divide' illuminate these two theological and literary profiles in earliest Christianity?

The second query specifically takes Mark and his gospel narrative as its point of departure and asks, from a reception perspective, what kind of evidence we find for or against a Pauline influence on Mark if we, as it were, start out from Mark. A third query that was also constantly present at the two conferences is the methodological question that was raised, in the history of scholarship, by Martin Werner in his 1923 reaction to Gustav Volkmar's nineteenth-century interpretation and again more recently by Joel Marcus in reaction to Werner. Marcus' essay is reprinted in this volume in an extended version, and is referred to numerous times in the other essays of the volume.

All three questions – of genre, reception and previous scholarship – are variously addressed in the essays throughout the volume, though with different emphases. The volume is organized in three sections, reflecting on the three approaches from partly historical, partly exegetical and partly conceptual perspectives.

The first section is entitled "Histories and Contexts" and leads back to the beginnings of the current Mark/Paul debate. At the same time, it reflects upon how we may define the crucial literary and social contexts in which both authors should be placed. This section to some extent continues the approach of the first volume. It begins with an essay by *Anne Vig Skoven* on "Mark as Allegorical Rewriting of Paul: Gustav Volkmar's Understanding of the Gospel of Mark". Here the reader is brought back to the founding work on the Paul/Mark relationship that set the scene for the following 150 years of scholarly discussion – to the extent that this issue was discussed at all after Martin Werner's frontal attack on Volkmar's thesis in 1923. Vig Skoven's essay serves the purpose of describing what Volkmar actually said and meant, and she copiously quotes from Volkmar himself in a manner that considerably deepens the picture of Volkmar's ideas in comparison with how they have been received. In a brief account of Werner's reaction to Volkmar, Vig Skoven perceptively suggests that his rejection of Volkmar was so influential not so much because of the quality of his individual arguments as because of the rise of form criticism, which sidetracked the line of inquiry that Volkmar had initiated. Vig Skoven ends by noting a number of features where Volkmar in fact anticipated much later developments in biblical scholarship. She concludes by suggesting that rather than trying to prove, against Werner, that Mark is a Pauline gospel, it might be better to ask, more modestly, whether Paul can shed light on certain Markan phenomena which continue to puzzle New Testament exegetes.

In his seminal essay, "Mark – Interpreter of Paul", *Joel Marcus* brought the Mark/Paul debate to scholarly attention once again. In constant dialogue with

Werner, he lists a number of topics where Mark agrees with Paul more than any other New Testament writer. Both place emphasis on the εὐαγγέλιον as a central aspect of their theology. Both see Jesus' crucifixion as the apocalyptic turning-point of the ages. Both celebrate Jesus' victory over demonic powers. Both see Jesus as a new Adam. Both emphasize the importance of faith in Jesus. Both have negative things to say about Peter and about members of Jesus' family. Both claim that Jesus came, not for the righteous, but for ungodly sinners, on whose behalf he died an atoning death, and that he came for the Jews first, but also for the Gentiles. And more. The same convergence is then found in their treatment of the topic on which Marcus spends most of his time, namely, the idea of the cross. Against Werner, Marcus also advances the argument that a 'Paulinist' need not take over everything in Paul – as we already know from Colossians and Ephesians and from the Pastoral letters. For the present publication Marcus has developed his 'Pauline' understanding of Mark 7 in a careful discussion of Daniel Boyarin's recent proposal, which finds a much more Jewish Mark here.

Heike Omerzu, in "Paul and Mark – Mark and Paul. A critical outline of the history of research", covers some of the same ground as Marcus, but adds to his discussion in two respects. First, she goes into slightly more detail about work done on the issue since Werner, even including some treatments that have appeared since Marcus' essay was first printed. Secondly, she raises some critical questions that come out of this whole scholarly discussion. The most important of these is probably the need for clarification of the contentious notion of 'Paulinism', 'Pauline thought' and 'Pauline theology', an issue that has recently been much debated both within Pauline studies themselves and also in relation to the supposed 'Paulinism' of the Acts of the Apostles. Towards the end of her essay, Omerzu points to a renewed focus on "the actual textual relations between Paul and Mark" as a possible way forward "instead of recovering assumed pre-Markan and pre-Pauline material in the context of tradition-historical studies". But she also rightly notes the risk one thereby runs of constructing an authoritative image of Paul that does not fit the historical situation in antiquity itself.

In his wide-ranging essay, "'Evangelium' im Markusevangelium. Zum traditionsgeschichtlichen Ort des ältesten Evangeliums", *Gerd Theissen* begins from a careful analysis of the meaning and use of the term εὐαγγέλιον in Paul and Mark. He shows that the two authors are closer to one another than to any other New Testament writers in their handling of the concept. And he develops the political content of this notion, which combines input both from the Old Testament and from Hellenistic royal rhetoric and which is shared by both authors. Going carefully through all occurrences of the term in Mark (1:1, 1:14–15, 8:35, 10:29, 13:10, 14:9), Theissen also shows how Mark continues to develop an initially 'Pauline' use of the term that Mark has presented first, thereby enlarging and changing it for his own purposes. Theissen argues that Mark's knowledge of Paul goes back to the Antiochene period, and he situates Mark in the context of Syrian Christianity, to which Paul and Peter, Barnabas and Mark all at one time belonged. Theissen supports this view by noting (among other things) that *all* statements about the historical Jesus made by Paul in his letters are supported by Mark. Theissen still sees Mark as articulating an 'intermediary' position in the understanding of Jesus, one which rather goes back to Peter and Barnabas. Mark does know (early) Paul; but while not being a direct spokesman for Peter, he rather represents the Antiochene position in early Christianity that we should connect with Peter and Barnabas.

Following on from these discussions of the state of the art and its origins, Eve-Marie Becker and Mogens Müller refer to two further kinds of 'histories' that need to be taken into consideration in investigation of the Paul/Mark and Mark/Paul debate: the literary-historical setting of both authors in the Hellenistic-Roman period, and the quest for the 'Sitz im Leben' within congregational life. Becker and Müller end, however, by suggesting two different perspectives.

In "Earliest Christian *literary activity:* Investigating Authors, Genres and Audiences in Paul and Mark", *Eve-Marie Becker* aims to contextualize Paul and Mark within the broader framework of Hellenistic literary culture in the early Principate. Becker specifically looks for a "'Pauline' and... 'Markan' cluster of *literary activity*" in order to envisage what "the earliest processes of literary production among Christ believers between ca. 50 and 70 CE" might have looked like. By referring to the phenomenon of *recitatio* she underlines that in antiquity author, audience and genre were inseparably interrelated so that the quest for the author immediately implies observations about genre as well as audience, and *vice versa*. On the basis of her provisional conclusion that "literary *genres* are nothing less than a communicative link between author and *audience*", Becker next examines Paul's epistolography and Mark's gospel-writing comparatively. Finally she makes the following claims regarding their different literary concepts: "it is mainly the divergence of literary activity behind Paul and Mark – implying different kinds of literary authority as well as the shift in audience and genre expectation – that stimulates conceptual differences; either epistolary or pre-historiographical literature points to a diversification of literary milieu(s), already in earliest Christian times". This conclusion makes evident that the Paul/Mark and Mark/Paul debate sheds light on the very beginnings of Christian literary history.

In his programmatic essay, "In the Beginning Was the Congregation: In Search of a *Tertium Comparationis* between Paul and Mark", *Mogens Müller* focuses the understanding of the two very different literary genres of the apostolic letter and the evangelist's gospel onto a single point which Müller locates in the use of both genres in the communal life of the earliest Christian congregations. For: "In the beginning was the congregation." Setting out from Paul, Müller stresses the role of the paraenetic passages in the letters, claiming that when Paul relates what is basic in Christianity, it is the new conduct of life which is emphasized as what counts. He also shows how central theologoumena – like that of a 'New Covenant', of the role of the Spirit, of baptism and other motifs with their roots in the Old Testament – are picked up by Paul to support the new life of the congregation. Next Müller turns to Mark, in whom he finds an attempt to produce 'Scripture' along the lines of the Old Testament, but again for direct and immediate use in congregational service, possibly in the form of a 'lectio sollemnis im Gottesdienst'. Here, too, Müller finds an emphasis on the implicit paraenetic implications of the Jesus story. Müller ends up suggesting that the shift from the letter form of Paul to the narrative gospel form of Mark had a kind of *tertium comparationis* in the change in the reader's consciousness that both aimed to create, a change that may be summarized under the heading of a "new creation (καινὴ κτίσις)".

In *the second section* – "Texts and Interpretations" – the Mark/Paul debate is approached through examples of concrete, comparative textual interpretation that take their point of departure from Mark in accordance with the overall profile of the volume. In this way, central passages in the Markan Gospel, such as the *initium* and parts of the so-called controversy stories in Mark 2–3, as well as sections in Mark 7 and 8, are related to equivalent passages in Paul in order to discuss the affinity or diversity of the Markan and Pauline ideas.

In her essay on "Romans 1:1–7 and Mark 1:1–3 in Comparison: Two Opening Texts at the Beginning of Early Christian Literature", *Oda Wischmeyer* points to an affinity between the two texts that exceeds any simple quest-for-genre debate. After stating that "Romans 1 and Mark 1... can be regarded... as important theological statements at the outset of early Christian literature", Wischmeyer undertakes exegetical analysis from various perspectives including, first, describing the textual dimension of both texts comparatively. In a second and third step she focuses on the 'literary dimension', addressing genre-criticism as well as the socio-religious setting and function of both texts. Finally, Wischmeyer analyses how Paul and Mark make similar use of biblical quotations and references, and how the term εὐαγγέλιον in a specific sense appears to be a 'key term' behind the literary conceptualization of both opening texts. It is particularly here that Wischmeyer not only develops Becker's comparative view on earliest Christian literary activity, but also qualifies that picture: Paul and Mark, she writes, "introduced a literature of their own for the early Christian communities. The overall purpose was not to establish a 'Christian' literary culture, but to better communicate the εὐαγγέλιον". For Wischmeyer, the "configuration as the twofold 'origin' of Christian literature and theological culture" in Paul and Mark will also reveal important insights into "the question of early Christian *identity*".

In his essay, "Man and the Son of Man in Mark 2:27–28: An Exegesis of Mark 2:23–28 Focussing on the Christological Discourse in Mark 2:27–28 With an Epilogue Concerning Pauline Parallels", *Jan Dochhorn* argues for a pre-Markan source behind Mark 2 as a whole, and then detects a 'high' Christology in Mark 2:27–28 that has its roots long before Mark. This high Christology is both a 'Son of Man Christology' and a 'New Adam Christology'. The fact that this type of Christology may also be found in Romans 1 and Hebrews 1:1–2:9 does not reflect any direct influence from Paul on Mark. Rather, as Dochhorn claims, we have good reason to assume that many basic Christological concepts were generated quite early on, including Christological claims that even ascribe to Jesus the position of God. It is true that Mark and Paul may be found to have many special elements in common, but Dochhorn points to something more general: that Mark and Paul share Christological ideas because they are witnesses to Early Christian theology that precedes them both. What they have in common may simply be very old.

Kasper Bro Larsen, in "Mark 7:1–23: A Pauline Halakah?", goes through a text in Mark that might seem an obvious candidate for tracing direct Pauline influence on Mark. Starting from Werner's and Marcus' opposing positions on Mark's 'Paulinism', Bro Larsen ends up suggesting that his chosen Markan text points toward a *via media* between the two scholars as the most reasonable path to tread. Thus the pericope of Mark 7:1–23 is neither 'ecumenical' (Werner) nor necessarily Pauline (Marcus): it legitimizes the dietary practices of Gentile Christ believers – whether Pauline or not – by means of the Jesus tradition. Bro Larsen concludes that while this result may appear disappointing to scholars in a search of Pauline-Markan connections, it is as far as one may go on the basis only of Mark 7:1–23. Still, as a test case the analysis of Mark 7:1–23 cannot stand alone but must be compared with other test cases in order to construct a full scenario both in terms of quantity (i.e. the number of parallels) and quality (i.e. the specificity of any supposed parallels). Thus the search must go on, until "the next Werner" will pick up his battered gauntlet and present an up-to-date synthesis.

Troels Engberg-Pedersen, in "Paul in Mark 8:34–9:1: Mark on what it is to be a Christian", belongs to those who see a direct influence of Paul on Mark. In a fairly classical, redaction critical analysis of Mark 8:34–9:1 he argues that this passage is tightly constructed by Mark on the basis of 'Q-material' that is found in both Matthew and Luke outside their parallels with the Markan text itself. The changes incorporated by Mark, however, that help to give his text its tight inner logic are drawn from passages in the Pauline letters that are distinctly Pauline inasmuch as they describe – in Paul's almost inimitable way – Paul's own 'conversion' to a 'directedness' towards Christ that excludes all other concerns. Mark, however – so Engberg-Pedersen claims – does attempt to imitate Paul here. He takes over specific phrases and ideas used by Paul to describe his own 'conversion', applies them to all Christ-believers and puts that application into the mouth of the earthly Jesus himself. Engberg-Pedersen's interpretation is that Mark's aim was to have his Jesus identify the essence of 'what it is to be a Christian'. In this, Engberg-Pedersen claims, he was directly helped by Paul.

In *the third and last section* – "Topics and Perspectives" – the volume presents various contributions in which the Mark/Paul affinity is looked at from the point of view of fundamental literary and theological and/or religious concepts such as cosmology, myth, 'cross' and apostleship. Again, the contributors do not agree on how closely Mark should be placed in the context of the Pauline tradition. Rather, the purpose of this section is to reflect upon how the Mark/Paul debate appears when seen in the light of a number of broader interpretive constructs.

Gitte Buch-Hansen, in "The Politics of Beginnings – Cosmology, Christology and Covenant: Gospel Openings Reconsidered in the Light of Paul's Pneumatology", addresses the Christologies with which Paul begins his letter to the Romans and Mark his gospel in the light of the role played by the πνεῦμα ('spirit') in Paul's overall theology and ethics. In an extended discussion of the way Paul handles the issue of ethnicity in relation to the Christ event in Galatians 3, she develops the concrete, quasi-biological sense in which Paul employs the notion of the resurrected Christ as πνεῦμα as a tool through which Gentiles were literally grafted into Judaism and the heritage from Abraham. Turning then to the gospel openings, she shows that the Christology of Mark 1 – particularly as implied in the account of Jesus' baptism – lies midway between Paul's literal understanding of Christ as πνεῦμα (which links believers directly with Judaism) and Luke's Christology in the annunciation scene (which completely separates Jesus' origin from anything concretely Jewish). Though Mark, by contrast, may well have been inspired in the baptism scene by Paul's understanding of the πνεῦμα, unlike Paul, he does not describe Jesus as the first-born among others with the πνεῦμα acting as a link between Jesus and believers. Rather, by understanding Jesus as the unique son of God, he moves in the direction of Luke's Christology. This move shows that Mark has in fact moved away from the central Pauline idea of the unity of Jews and Gentiles in Christ.

A different type of overall view of the Mark/Paul relationship is given by Ole Davidsen and Jesper Tang Nielsen. Both situate their analysis in the semiotic and narrative tradition of A. Greimas. Interestingly, however, they reach rather different results concerning the Mark and Paul debate. The difference between Tang Nielsen's tentatively positive and Davidsen's more sceptical conclusion concerning the Mark/Paul relationship may be due to a divergent view of narrative structures: while Davidsen focuses on certain fundamental or deep structures, Tang Nielsen has his eye on narrative features that lie more on the literary surface.

In his essay, "Adam-Christ Typology in Paul and Mark: Reflections on a *Tertium Comparationis*", *Ole Davidsen* engages in a discussion with Joel Marcus by articulating a number of different possible relationships between (a) pre-Pauline traditions, (b) Paul and (c) Mark that need to be distinguished before addressing the question whether Mark was "an interpreter of Paul". We may be able to detect 'intertextual relations' between Paul and Mark, but that is no argument for mutual *influence* either way. Rather than looking for similarities in order to detect particular Pauline traits in Mark, we should focus, so Davidsen claims, on similarities in order to detect general features pointing to a shared primal tradition. Davidsen develops this understanding in an analysis of the 'Adam-Christ typology', which he considers to be of paramount importance in Paul, but also implicitly present in Mark. This correspondence, however, should not be taken as a sign of Pauline influence on Mark. Rather, the Adam-Christ typology as an organizing narrative structure points to a pre-Pauline narrative tradition which Mark could well have learned from some other source.

In "The Cross on the Way to Mark", *Jesper Tang Nielsen* reaches a "tentative conclusion" to the effect that Mark does build on and continue Paul's specific interpretation of the earliest traditions about Jesus' death, one which focuses on a special understanding of the meaning of the cross. Searching for distinct narrative structures of the Jesus story – first in the pre-Pauline traditions that may be gathered from Paul himself, then in Paul's own theological elaborations of this material and finally in Mark's rendering of that story – Tang Nielsen identifies a number of specific narrative features in Paul's elaborations that can be found again in Mark. Whereas in the earliest ascertainable material the main focus was much more on Jesus' relationship with God than on its implications for believers, Paul works hard to bring these two aspects together. In this, moreover, Paul developed a set of coherent ideas that were intended to spell out the meaning and wider implications of the notion of Christ's having died on the cross. This special focus, as Tang Nielsen goes on to show in an overall reading of Mark, is also found in the first evangelist.

Finn Damgaard, in "Persecution and Denial – Paradigmatic Apostolic Portrayals in Paul and Mark", sees a more direct, literary relationship between Paul and Mark. Damgaard relates Mark's ambiguous portrayal of the apostle Peter to the Pauline letters in an unexpected way. While many scholars like Joel Marcus who argue for Markan dependence on Paul often assume that

Mark's negative portrait of Peter is in some way influenced by Paul's attitude to Peter in the letters, Damgaard suggests that Mark created his ambiguous portrayal of Peter in imitation of Paul's *own* biography of reversal. Paul's autobiographical remarks not only exerted an influence on how later Christians wrote his biography: they had an impact on the way Peter was portrayed in Mark. By imitating Paul's popular biography of reversal, Mark created a paradigmatic portrayal of Peter. In particular, Damgaard suggests that Mark constructed his portrait of the tearful Peter on the basis of Paul's autobiographical remarks in 1 Corinthians.

It will be obvious from this summary of the essays that the contributors do not come to a final agreement on how to answer the question about the Mark/Paul relationship. We do believe, however, that taken together the essays contribute considerably to clarifying the issue, both through explicit methodological reflections and through actual exegetical practice. We also note not only that different methodological approaches in many cases yield different results – but also, and rather more interestingly, that different approaches may in some cases yield closely similar results. This highlights the insight that further progress with regard to the question about the Mark/Paul relationship will have to rely, not on scholars' imaginative powers or on their capacities for reading the texts, but on their achieving the utmost clarity concerning the theoretical and methodological framework with which they as scholars approach the issue.

This volume – like the previous one (BZNW 198) – cannot therefore be understood as the 'last word' on the Paul/Mark and Mark/Paul debate. Further steps still have to be taken. Rather, we consider this collection of essays to be a reminder of a crucial issue in New Testament studies. Indeed, the Paul/Mark and Mark/Paul debate is and will continue to be indispensable. This is true in at least two ways: The Paul/Mark and Mark/Paul debate sheds light simultaneously on the literary and theological roles of the two main authors at the origins of Christianity and on their mutual affinity, closeness and influence. And it reminds us to see an eminent tool of exegetical work more clearly: any hypothetical (re)construction of interrelatedness in theological or literary terms must always reflect the methodological awareness that is part and parcel of a well-founded comparative reading.

I. Histories and Contexts

Anne Vig Skoven †
Mark as Allegorical Rewriting of Paul: Gustav Volkmar's Understanding of the Gospel of Mark

> "Ganz geschichtlich und ganz Poësie,
> Beides in Einem"
> (Gustav Volkmar, 1857)

Introduction: The beginning of the Mark/Paul-connection in the scholarly debate

Unlike exegetes of the patristic tradition and also unlike most of 20th century scholarship, biblical scholars of the 19th century were not foreign to the idea that Paulinism was to be found in the Gospel of Mark. The founder of the so-called Tübingen School, Ferdinand Christian Baur (1792–1860), for instance, regarded the Gospel of Mark as a synthesis of Petrine and Pauline traditions.[1] Baur argued that Mark was based on Matthew and Luke and composed in the 2nd century. According to the Tübingen School, the Gospel of John was the final synthesis of the antitheses between Jewish Christian orthodoxy and the Pauline spirit – and Mark was one step on that way.

In 1857, the German exegete Gustav Hermann Joseph Philipp Volkmar (1809 – 93) characterized the Gospel of Mark as a Pauline gospel. Although Mark's story was concerned with Jesus' life and death, it was also, so Volkmar argued, permeated by Pauline theology. During his lifetime, Volkmar remained a solitary figure, and David Friedrich Strauss (1808–1874) once considered him a "närriger Kauz".[2] Nevertheless, at the end of the 19th century knowledge of Volkmar's the-

---

[1] F. C. Baur, "Das Evangelium des Marcus. " In *Kritische Untersuchungen über die kanonischen Evangelien, ihr Verhältnis zu einander, ihren Charakter und Ursprung* (Tübingen: Ludw. Fr. Fues Verlag, 1847), 535–67.
[2] In English: a ludicrous little owl. In a letter to Wilhelm Vatke from 1861, Strauss describes Volkmar as … "ein närriger Kauz, der aber nicht ohne einzelne Lichtblicke ist … es ist Tollheit, was er vorbringt, doch nicht ohne Methode … leider ist diese Methode zum Theil die Baur'sche," quoted from Adolf Jülicher, "Volkmar, Gustav." In *Allgemeine Deutsche Biographie* (herausgegeben von der Historischen Kommission bei der Bayerischen Akademie der Wissenschaften, Band 54, 1908), 764–775 (771).

sis and writings was widespread among German speaking scholars. His thesis drove a wedge into German biblical scholarship; Adolf Jülicher (1857–1938) and William Wrede (1859–1906) both appreciated Volkmar's work, Albert Schweizer (1875–1965) and his student Martin Werner (1887–1964) did not.

Since Gustav Volkmar is rather unknown to contemporary biblical scholarship, I shall here provide a short biography.[3] Volkmar studied theology and philology in Marburg in 1829–32 and obtained his dr. phil. in 1838. From 1833 to 1852, he taught in various *Gymnasien*, in which he primarily worked within the field of philology and classical studies. In 1850 he published a book on Marcion and the Gospel of Luke, in which he claimed against Baur and Albrecht Ritschl (1822–1889) that Marcion's gospel was a rewriting of Luke.[4] According to Adolf Jülicher, Volkmar had deserved a chair for this – today widely accepted – thesis. However, a series of dramatic events prevented that. Due to church political controversies, Volkmar was arrested in the classroom in 1852 and charged with lesemajesty and dismissed from his job. In 1853, he was called to Zürich where he was finally appointed professor of New Testament studies in 1863.[5] In Zürich he published the works which are of special relevance to the present study:[6]

- *Die Religion Jesu und ihre erste Entwickelung nach dem gegenwärtigen Stande der Wissenschaft* (Leipzig: F. A. Brockhaus, 1857); a popular work, which introduced Volkmar's thesis of Mark as a Pauline gospel.
- *Die Evangelien, oder Marcus und die Synopsis der kanonischen und ausserkanonischen Evangelien nach dem ältesten Text mit historisch-exegetischem Commentar* (Leipzig: Ludw. Fr. Fues Verlag, 1870); a scholarly commentary on the Gospel of Mark, in which Volkmar, against Baur, forwarded his thesis that Mark was the first gospel, Luke the second and Matthew only the third. The commentary was republished in a slightly edited second edition with a new title in:

---

[3] Volkmar's commentary on Mark is, for instance, not included in the otherwise encompassing and impressive bibliography in Adela Yarbro Collins, *Mark: A Commentary*, Hermeneia (Minneapolis MN: Fortress Press, 2007).

[4] The title was: *Das Evangelium Marcions: Text und Kritik mit Rücksicht auf die Evangelien des Märtyrers Justin, der Clementinen und der apostolischen Väter; eine Revision der neuern Untersuchungen nach den Quellen selbst zur Textesbestimmung und Erklärung des Lucas-Evangeliums* (Leipzig: Weidmann, 1852).

[5] Volkmar was appointed "ausserordentlicher Professor" in Zürich in 1857/58 and "ordentlicher Professor" in 1863.

[6] Volkmar's list of publications also includes works on classical issues (for instance Sophokles' *Antigone*, 1851), heretical Christianities, Jewish apocalyptic writings (for instance on *4 Ezra, 1 Enoch* and *Assumption of Moses*, 1860–63) and commentaries on *Revelation* (1862) and *Romans* (1875).

– *Marcus und die Synopse der Evangelien nach dem urkundlichen Text und das Geschichtliche vom Leben Jesu* (Zürich: Verlag von Caesar Schmidt, 1876).[7]

In addition to Volkmar's traditional commentaries on the Markan text, the books from 1870/76 offer an early reception history of the Markan narratives. Volkmar traces the stories through nine subsequent gospels or gospel fragments in – what he believes to be – the right chronological order.[8] According to Jülicher, this was a learned, outstanding and original enterprise.[9] However, we must leave this volume from Volkmar's hand aside for the present purpose.

In his biographical sketch of Gustav Volkmar from 1908, Adolf Jülicher characterizes Volkmar as an exegete whose work was framed to the one side by Baur's *Tendenztheorie* and to the other side by Strauss' scepticism (772f). Yet, he differs from both schools on two important issues: historicity and Markan priority. With regard to Strauss, Volkmar welcomes his critique of the rationalistic and harmonizing exegesis of early 19th century scholarship.[10] But he is also critical of Strauss' concept of the gospel narratives as *mythoi*, instead he prefers the term "Poësie". Unlike Strauss Volkmar emphasizes the historicity of the gospel narratives.[11] Yet, his understanding of historicity, as well as his method are clos-

---

7 Relevant to our history of research is also *Jesus Nazarenus und die erste christliche Zeit mit den beiden ersten Erzählern* (Zürich: Verlag von Caesar Schmidt, 1882), a popular work, which was the basis of Albert Schweitzer's negative review of Volkmar's thesis, set out in *Von Reimarus bis Wrede* (1906). I thank Professor (MSO) Heike Omerzu for the reference.
8 Volkmar's sequence was Genealogus Hebraeorum (80 AD) (The Gospel of the Hebrews); Evangelium Pauperum, Essenorium (80 AD) (The Gospel of the Ebjonites); The Gospel of Luke (100 AD); The Gospel of Matthew (110 AD); The Gospel of Peter (130 AD); The Gospel of Paul according to Marcion; The Gospel of the Nazarenes (150 AD); The Logos Gospel (The Gospel of John) (155 AD) and The Gospel of the Egyptians (160–70 AD) (Volkmar 1870, viii).
9 "Das Vollständigkeit, mit der Volkmar hier das gesammte Evangelien- und evangelisch-historische Material der ersten 2½ Jahrhunderte verarbeitet hat, ist seitdem von niemandem erreicht worden." "Ein originellerer Commentar als der Volkmar's zu Marcus wird nie geschrieben werden; ich meine aber, er kann sich auch an gelehrter Gediegenheit mit jedem messen" (Jülicher 1908, 770f).
10 Set out in David Friedrich Strauss, *Das Leben Jesu, kritisch bearbeitet I-II* (Tübingen: Osiander, 1835–36).
11 "Die Nachbildung des A.T.'s ist freilich nirgends mechanisch, oder gar nach einem schon feststehenden Messias-Schema, das Strauss unterstellte, sondern *überall hat sie in dem geschichtlichen und weltgeschichtlichen Leben Jesu ihren Grund, was Str. noch nicht sah*" (Volkmar 1876, 645, emphasis added). "Nur war sein [Strauss'] positiver Versuch, die evangelischen Erzählungen als Niederschlag dunkler Traditionen oder Mythen aufzufassen, so haltlos unbegründet, dass der Fortschritt nothwendig war, die Natur und Komposition der einzelnen Evangelienschriften in's Auge zu fassen, und ihnen das Geheimnis ihrer Conception abzulocken" (Volkmar 1870, xi).

er to those of 20th century redaction criticism than to the *Leben Jesu Forschung* of his own century. With regard to the Tübingen School, Volkmar treats the early Christian literature as *Tendenzschriften*. His overall project was to reconstruct the history of the gospel traditions as a reflection of the developments in early Christianity. But unlike the Tübingen exegetes, he accepted, as already mentioned, the thesis of Markan priority. Consequently, he rejected the idea of an "Ur-Evangelium" which was needed for the Tübinger explanation of the gospel relations. Likewise he rejected the idea of a *Spruchbuch* or *Schriftquelle* (1870, viii-xi; 1876, 646) – later identified as Q. According to Volkmar, Mark's only sources were: the Old Testament writings, four Pauline letters (Romans, Galatians, 1 and 2 Corinthians), the oral tradition of early Christian communities – and, surprisingly, Revelation.

In this essay, I shall offer a thorough presentation of Volkmar's thesis about Paulinism in Mark. In the first part, I discuss the alleged relationship between Revelation and the Gospel of Mark. I also account for Volkmar's considerations of the composition and genre of Mark. In the second part, I go into more detail concerning the relationship between Mark and Paul. Here I first provide a summary of the general thesis as set out in 1857, which reflects Volkmar's view of the Markan Jesus. Next, I give an example from his 1870/76 commentary on Mark, which demonstrates the literary character of the relationship between the Jesus traditions and the Pauline gospel in the Markan text. In the third part, I return to the reception of Volkmar's work among his contemporary colleagues and elaborate on the criticism to which his work was exposed around the *fin de siècle*. Finally, I discuss the relevance of Volkmar's thesis for 21st century New Testament studies.

1 Gustav Volkmar's Understanding of the Gospel of Mark

Redating Mark

According to Volkmar, Revelation – or the apocalypse of Jesus Christ as he calls it using the self-designation of the text (Rev 1:1) – was the 'thesis' towards which the Gospel of Mark was the 'antithesis' and reaction (1876, 646). The apocalypse was, so Volkmar explains, the first narrative Christian text. It was written in 68 during the reign of Nero, presumably by John, the Zebedee son. It represented Jewish Christian orthodoxy and emphasized the exclusively future character of salvation which was to take place at the *parousia*. Within this worldview, there was no future and no salvation for the Gentiles. In contrast, the second narrative Christian writing, the Gospel of Mark, featured the (true) Pauline Christ who preached salvation for all, including the Gentiles (1876, 7–8).

Volkmar argues that Mark was written in the seventies, that is, a hundred years earlier than the Tübingen School presumed.[12] As for provenance, he seems to favour Palestine.[13] Volkmar believes the author of Mark to be a Hebrew-thinking, Greek-speaking Jew, who had spent some time in Galilee and Jerusalem, and who was acquainted with the Pauline gospel as well as with early oral traditions (1876, 647). He thinks very highly of the author: "er bleibt doch einer der geistvollsten und einflussreichsten Schriftsteller, die es nach Paulus gegeben hat" (1876, 647).

Character – composition – genre

Volkmar saw the Gospel of Mark as a didactic poem based on historical events: "ein selbstbewusstes Lehrpoesie auf historischem Grund" (1870, xx).[14] However, Mark's successors changed the original gospel in a more prosaic direction (*prosaïsieren*). In the Gospel of Mark, Revelation's apocalypticism and future *parousia* were transformed into a didactic narrative about the historical manifestations of the glory of the Pauline Christ: "Die visionäre Erzählung von künftigen Parusie ist hier [in Markus] zu einer lehrbildlichen Erzählung von der schon diesseitigen Herrlichkeit des Christus *Pauli* geworden" (1876, 646, emphasis added). Mark's Gospel had a distinctly *doctrinal* character which, from the very beginning, was polemically directed against Revelation. Consequently, his *evangelion* begins – not with the *parousia* – but with John the Baptist, who, as foretold by Isaiah, was to prepare the coming of the kingdom in *history*. The whole section in Mark 1:1–8 was a doctrinal discourse (*Lehrvortrag*) about the character of John's baptism. On the one hand, it was a divinely ordered and necessary preparation for

---

12 Earlier in 1857, Volkmar had dated Mark to 80 AD, that is, during the surprisingly mild reign of Titus – a dating that challenged the apocalyptic schedule of Revelation (the horns) (1857, 195). In 1870, he changed the date to 73 AD, claiming that the 40 days of temptation was an apocalyptic code for the years that had passed since Jesus' death (1870, 50).
13 In his 1857 book, Volkmar argued that due to the Markan text's Latinisms, Mark was probably written in Rome. But in 1870, he became sceptical of his former thesis. After all, the Latinisms were not sufficient reason for making Italy the place of provenance. If the same argument had been applied to the Talmud, these texts must also have been written in Rome or Italy (1876, 646).
14 Probably this understanding of the character of Mark's Gospel is indebted to the German idealist Friedrich Schiller and the philosophical and didactic aims of his dramas which transcended a merely sensuous understanding. I thank Professor Oda Wischmeyer for this reference.

the salvation through Christ (1:1–4). On the other hand, it was not sufficient, which the Baptist himself confirms: "I have baptized you with water, but he shall baptize you with Holy Spirit" (Mark 1:7–8) (1876, 31).

Unlike the later proponents of form criticism and their understanding of Mark's Gospel as a collection of traditional material, Volkmar believed Mark to have been carefully composed: "nach einer durchgreifendes" (1857, 206) and "wohl gegliederte Sachdisposition" (1876, 644). In the 1857 volume, he argued that Hebrew parallelisms shaped the structure of the gospel on every level. On the macro-level, Mark was divided into two major sections, 1:14–8:26 and 8:27–16:20.[15] Both of these sections could be divided into four subsections – and so on. Volkmar kept struggling with the Markan outline over the years. The exact number of subsections changed both in 1870 and again in 1876. Nevertheless, Volkmar maintained a certain doctrinal progression, which was important to his interpretation of Mark as a theological treatise. Part 1 (1:14–8:26) dealt with the Jewish beginnings (*die Anfänge*, 1:14–45) which were followed by the transcendence of old religious borders (*der Fortschritt*, 2:1–3:6) and the founding of a new community (*die Stiftung*, 3:7–4:34). Then Mark demonstrates the omnipotence of Jesus' ministry (*die Allgewalt*, 4:35–5:45) and the universal scope of his salvation (*das Allerlösen*, 6:1–8:26).

According to Volkmar, Mark's primary purpose was not to write a historical biography about Jesus, but to give an exposition of the true Christ: "eine Darstellung vom *wahren* Wesen Jesu Christi" (1857, 269). Consequently, Mark made every effort for his gospel *not* to be considered a biography of Jesus (1857, 263). Even the inclusion of Jesus traditions into the text does not make it a biography. Everything that is told in the gospel – including the historical details from Jesus' life – has the overall purpose of presenting Jesus as the already ascended Son of Man (1857, 269). Thus, the true protagonist of the gospel is not Jesus, but the risen Christ. Also when traditional material is included, the gospel narratives remain symbolic representations of Pauline theology. Volkmar explains: "Der Inhalt der Erzählungen ist durchweg *als sinnbildliche Darstellung paulinischer Lehre zu begreiffen, so viel Überlieferungsstof darein verwebt sein mag*" (1876, 644, emphasis added). Therefore Mark's Gospel belongs to the genre of epic. It is composed as an "Epos des Christenthums". It is, as Volkmar explains: "ganz geschichtlich und ganz Poësie, Beides in Einem" (1857, 276).

The conception of Mark as the epic of Christianity implies a two-level reading of the gospel, which, when these readings are juxtaposed, covers events right

---

15 Volkmar thinks that Mark 16:15–16,19–20 belonged to the original gospel. However, the present form of the verses is somewhat corrupted (1857, 205).

from the era of Jesus to the evangelist's own time.[16] Thus, Volkmar does not discharge the gospel as a source for the life of Jesus: "Es ist eine kostbare Quelle für das Leben Jesu, *aber auch solche für das Leben des Paulus und der Christenheit nach ihn*" (1857, 269, emphasis added). But above all, the Gospel of Mark is a didactic narrative, which presents (the true) Pauline Christianity in a new genre: "ein Darstellung echt christlicher Lehre paulinischen Sinnes in erzählender Form."

2 Mark as an Allegorical Rewriting of Paul

The Gospel of Mark as a didactic poem

In *Die Religion Jesu* from 1857, Volkmar drew attention to the Pauline *Tendenz* in Mark's arrangement of his gospel and he gives a clear, although – when compared to his later works – simplified, impression of his two-level reading and didactic understanding of the gospel. Right from the prologue, Mark portrays Jesus as "Christus des Geistes, wie er sich im Apostel [that is, in Paul] offenbart hat". However, this Paulinized version of Christ is connected to Judaism only in the respect that he emerged *from* it. The greatest person with*in* Judaism was John the Baptist, although his baptism only offered an external initiation into Christ. Nevertheless, Volkmar takes John's baptism of Jesus to be "das Vorbild für die Taufe Aller" (1876, 40). In this way, true (Pauline) Christianity is shown to be rooted in Judaism.

In the first part of Mark (1:14–8:26), Jesus continues the Baptist's call for repentance (1:14–15). While recognizing the pillars of the church and their status as Jesus' first disciples (1:16–20), Mark demonstrates how Jesus transcends Judaism in his authoritative teachings and also through the universal scope of his ministry, which is not directed to the Jewish world alone, but also to the Gentiles. Interestingly enough, Volkmar takes the unclean spirit in 1:21–28 to be the first representative of the Gentile world. It was unclean due to its worship of idols.[17]

---

[16] Volkmar explains: "Die Elemente dieses epischen Gemäldes von der ersten Parusie Jesu Christi als des Sohnes Gottes in geistiger Herrlichkeit, bestehen einfach in der gesamten christlichen Erfahrung von den ersten Zeiten an bis auf die Zeit des Verfassers, also aus wirklicher Ueberlieferung aus der Urzeit des Christenthums und aus alledem, was sich in der christlichen Gemeinde, im Besondern auch im Leben und Wirken des Apostels Paulus durch das Wirken des Auferstandenen Großes ereignet hat" (1857, 206).

[17] According to Volkmar, the terror of demons was especially prominent during the Roman Empire (1870, 86).

Proceeding from the original group of disciples (1:29–34) to wider areas (1:35–39), Jesus' ministry soon includes the outcasts among the Jews. But when Jesus cleanses the leper (1:40–45), he ignores the commandments of the Mosaic Law. Yet he does not demand of his fellow countrymen that they neglect it, too (1:44). This *transcendence of Judaism* – Volkmar repeatedly speaks about "*der Fortschritt*" – is illustrated and legitimized in the following chapter through the pardoning of sins (2:1–12), the acceptance of sinners (2:13–17) and changed habits (2:18–3:5). These new practices lead to persecution (3:6), but they also attract attention (3:7), and Jesus' popularity frequently disturbs and threatens his ministry. However, by calling the twelve, Mark's Jesus gives authority to the Jewish-Christian communities; Volkmar speaks of "die Judenapostel-Autorität". Nevertheless, these *sarkan* relations (3:20–35) have to be opened up towards the Gentile world (1857, 265).

Mark 4 addresses the greatest obstacle to Jesus' legitimacy, namely the continuing *sarkan* non-understanding which characterizes the Jewish Christian majority (4:1–34). Yet, no cosmic power – neither the storm (4:35–41), nor the satanic legion, nor Gentile uncleanness (5:1–20), nor even severe sicknesses or death (5:21–43) – can resist Jesus' power. Mark's Jesus/Christ has this *Alles überwindendes Wesen*, which also characterizes the Pauline Christ Jesus. Yet the fact that it is Jesus of Nazaret who possesses these powers puzzles the natives of his hometown (*Heimat*) (6:1–6). Just like the prophet Elijah, Jesus must leave his native land. Also in parallel with the Christ of Paul's letters, Mark's Pauline Jesus brings the *Liebesmahl des Abends* to the Gentiles (6:30–46). In this way, he overcomes the divide of the deadly sea (6:47–52). The introduction of a new principle of spiritual purity (*Geistesreinheit*) in Mark 7:1–23 implies that Gentiles far away (7:24–30) as well as nearby (7:31–37) come within Jesus' reach. But in spite of the repetition of the miraculous supper among the Gentiles (8:1–9), the Jewish pillars among the apostles still fail to understand that the gospel is not only to be taken *sinnlich* (8:14–21). Yet, Christ finally succeeds in opening their eyes to his true *Wesen* (8:22–26), and the reader proceeds to the second part of the gospel (8:27–16:20).

The first person in Mark's Gospel to realize that Jesus is the Christ is Peter, but the first *historical* person to understand what this meant was the apostle to the Gentiles. Paul understood *how* Jesus was the Christ – namely, through his suffering (cf. Mark 8:27–38) and subsequent resurrection. These are the two focal points in Paul's Christology: crucifixion and glorification. Although Jesus rebukes Peter for his lack of understanding of the Son of Man's inexorable fate (8:31–33), his confession leads to the transfiguration, which shows Jesus Christ in his – otherwise hidden – glory (9:2–13).

Through Jesus' instruction of his disciples on the way to Jerusalem, the reader is taught what proper discipleship and true faith imply: confidence in God's power (9:14–29) and the will to keep peace (9:3–50). Just like Jesus' first disciples the reader, too, must realize that the *true* law consists of higher, eternal and "*übermosaische*" commandments (10:2–12), the fulfilment of which presupposes the attitudes of true faith (10:13–16), true love (10:17–27) and true hope (10:28–31). On his way to his own suffering, Jesus makes it clear to his disciples that all apocalyptically inspired ambitions of ruling must be abandoned in favour of serving and (potential) suffering (10:35–45) (1857, 264–68).

The Markan Jesus according to Volkmar

I hope that it is obvious from the above summary why, according to Volkmar, the Gospel of Mark cannot be regarded as a Jesus biography. Mark's Gospel is to be seen as an odyssey in which the reader travels with the historical Jesus, with the apostle Paul and with the risen Christ (or the Christ-spirit). Volkmar explains: "... durch das ganze Ev. hin ist das Leben Jesu, wie das Leben, Wirken und Leiden Pauli mit im Auge" (1876, 645). Whereas the author of Luke and Acts chose to allocate these travel narratives to two separate volumes, Mark's single two-level story encompasses both. Volkmar regards the Markan Jesus as a literary character who is based upon several literary and historical figures – including, of course, the historical Jesus. However, when speaking of Christ the author often has Paul in mind. Apparently, Mark has projected Paul and his Gentile mission – as we know it from Paul's letters and from the Acts of the Apostles – back into Jesus' life. Volkmar also finds Pauline theological concepts expressed in the Markan Jesus' words and deeds (i.e. the above mentioned faith, love and hope in 10:13–31).

It is this procedure that I refer to as "an allegorical rewriting of Paul".[18] However, unlike his reviewers, Volkmar never employed the term "allegory" to describe his understanding of Mark's Gospel. Instead, he spoke of symbols (*Sinnbilder*) and of the "parabolic" nature of the gospel. In line with the prevailing understanding of allegory in German scholarship on literature and theology, Volkmar associated allegory with an unwarranted loss of historicity, which ear-

---

18 Employing the term "rewriting" in this context refers to the general inscription of Pauline matters into the setting of Jesus. However, it does not qualify as a rewriting in the narrow and technical sense in which rewriting meets specific criteria or depends on specific literary matrices. Volkmar's thesis does not rest on verbatim agreements.

lier had been the very reason for his criticism of Strauss' *mythos*.[19] The continuity between the historical Jesus and Paul's mission was essential to Volkmar's understanding of Mark. This important point is demonstrated in his 35 page analysis of the small story about the calling of Levi in Mark 2:13–17.

Mark 2:13–17 as an allegorical rewriting of Gal 2,11ff

Volkmar places Mark 2:13–17 in the subsection 2:1–17, which consists of two *Lehrstücken:* the first section, 2:1–12, concerns the healing of the paralyzed man and challenges the Jewish view of sin and sinners; the second section, 2:13–17, concerns the acceptance of these sinners as implied in Jesus' calling of Levi. In the larger context, this subsection belongs to 2.1–3.6, which Volkmar spoke of as "[der] Fortschritt über die jüdische Anschauung" (1876, 151; 1857, 136).[20]

In the tradition, the paralyzed man from 2:1–12 was understood as a symbolic representation of fallen mankind. He is, as Volkmar explains, "der von der Sünde gelähmte Mensch". In his own interpretation of the story, an ethnic dimension is added to the predicament, since it is especially characteristic of the Gentile world. After the healing of the (sinfully) paralyzed man, Levi – now the sinner is depicted as a tax collector – can be called upon in order to follow Jesus (2:14). That the calling is an invitation into community is demonstrated by the meal, when Jesus and his disciples eat together with tax collectors and sinners. However, this meal is – and I use a Pauline word – a *skandalon* to the Pharisean scribes (2:15–17). According to Volkmar, three groups are present at the meal: Jesus and his disciples, tax collectors and sinners – and then he adds: the Pharisaic scribes.[21] It is very likely, so Volkmar argues, that Hillel's dis-

---

[19] That allegory should imply a loss of historicity is deeply rooted in the Christian tradition. However, in the Hellenistic period we also find allegory practised *without* the exclusion of a literal, historical dimension. This is e. g. the case in Philo's work. See Henrik Tronier, "Philonic Allegory in Mark." In *Philosophy at the Roots of Christianity*, Working Papers 2, Biblical Studies Section, eds. Henrik Tronier and Troels Engberg-Pedersen (Copenhagen: University of Copenhagen, 2006), 9–48.

[20] Volkmar appears to be the first scholar who has seen the interrelatedness of 2:1–3:6, since he joyfully reports that Weiss and Holtzmann followed *him* in this respect.

[21] In Volkmar's reading, the Pharisaic scribes belong among the followers of Jesus. His punctuation of the Greek text differs from that of Nestle-Aland, *Novum Testamentum Graece*, 27 edition [= 28. edition]. According to Codex Sinaiticus (and P88) vv. 15–16 reads "for they were many, and they followed him, even (*kai*) the Pharisean scribes". Nestle-Aland reads with Codex Vaticanus: "for they were many and they followed him. And the Pharisaic scribes …"

ciples were also attracted to Jesus' teachings, yet unprepared for its radical consequences. It is in accordance with this reading, when Volkmar suggests that the narrated meal did not take place in Levi's home, but in the house where Jesus was staying – that is, in Peter's house.²² Otherwise it would not be possible for the Pharisaic scribes to be present. In this respect Mark differs from Luke and Matthew, who could not conceive of such a Pharisaic group being close to Jesus. But Mark could, since he, in Volkmar's view, only had in mind the episode in Antioch, which Paul described in his letter to the Galatians. Volkmar draws attention to the fact that unlike most of Mark's other stories, this incident has no Old Testament parallel. Even in 1 Kings 17:13f, where Elijah goes to a Gentile woman's house, he eats only *at* her house, not *with* her. Instead, the parallel case is to be found in the Antioch meal practice *before* the delegation from James arrived (Gal 2:11–14). The disciples who are called first in Mark include the pillars mentioned in Gal 2:9 (Peter and John). Levi, who is called next, fills in the place of the sinful Gentile Christians in Antioch (Gal 2:12). The third party, the Pharisaic scribes from Mark, plays the same part at the common meal as "those from James" in Antioch in Gal 2:12. "Those from James", who have a Pharisaic orthodox interpretation of the Law, may very well have posed the same question to Kefas, Barnabas and the other Jews as the scribes do in Mark: Are we to eat with sinners? Volkmar concludes that both texts deal with an *inner* Christian conflict between Jews and Gentiles, with Paul and Mark on the one side and James and the author of Revelation on the other.

According to Volkmar, the Jewish doctrine of Israel's election, which separates the *dikaioi* from the *hamartôloi*, constitutes the theological background for the Markan story. He draws attention to the fact that Paul addresses the same issue repeatedly in his letters: in Gal 2:15 he refers to the common understanding among Jews that Gentiles were born sinners; in 1 Cor 9:21 he speaks about the *anomos* and *ennomos*; and in Romans 1:18–3:20 he engages in a comparison of Jews and Gentiles without and within Christ. In the Gospel of Mark, the tax collector Levi has come to represent the whole category of sinners being accepted at Christ's table. According to Volkmar, the break with this conception of sinners had its source in the life and practices of the historical Jesus. Volkmar explains: "Dieser Fortschritt über die jüdische Anschauung ist ohne Frage von Jesus selbst ausgegangen, oder Paulus ist auch dabei nur von seinem Vorgang und Wesen begeistert worden" (1876, 151; 1857, 136). Mark was probably aware of that. Compared to the conflict between the Jewish Christians from James and Paul, Mark's achievement was to bring to mind Jesus' historical prac-

---

22 The referent of the pronouns in 2:15 (twice *autos*) is not obvious.

tice and, in addition, to breathe the Pauline Christ-spirit into the Markan Jesus' words. Volkmar describes Mark's contribution to the development of Christianity in this way: "den grossen Grundsatz des paulinischen Christenthums als Jesu Stimme zu zeigen, und die Erinnerung an sein eignes Leben mit Zöllnern zu erneuen" (1876, 146). But after all, Paul's mission fulfilled the potential of the historical Jesus' practices. Consequently, Mark's Gospel remains: "Ganz geschichtlich und ganz Poësie, Beides in Einem."

Paul's description of the Antioch episode in Galatians makes Volkmar wonder whether Kefas was at all present at the meal(s) to which Mark's narrative refers, and whether he ever understood the Pauline scope of Jesus' words about the righteous and sinners. Obviously James and the author of Revelation did not.[23] But the story about Levi in Mark and the Antioch episode in Galatians certainly have the opposite point – namely, in my paraphrase of Volkmar's point: *Nicht heraus, sondern herein!*

3 Reception and Criticism

As mentioned in the introduction, Volkmar's commentary was appreciated by a number of contemporary scholars. Although Jülicher found several weaknesses in Volkmar's work, he also spoke of it as "ein zu früh vergessenes Buch" and of Volkmar as "einer der bedeutendsten Bibelkritiker der letzten hundert Jahre" (1908). Wrede was even more enthusiastic and described Volkmar as: "unzweifelhaft ... das geistreichste und scharfsinnigste und m. E. überhaupt das bedeutendste, das wir über Markus besitzen."[24] Scholars like Adolf von Harnack, Johannes Weiss and Heinrich Julius Holtzmann likewise appreciated Volkmar's work. In spite of resistance from scholars such as Schweitzer, Werner and Paul Wernle, the idea of Paulinism in Mark eventually became so widespread in German scholarship that Martin Werner felt the need to write an entire monograph, *Der Einfluss paulinischer Theologie im Markusevangelium*, published in 1923, to refute Volkmar's thesis.[25]

---

23 The author of Revelation most emphatically demands the Nikolaites who eat meat sacrificed to idols to leave the community (Rev 2:15).
24 William Wrede, *Das Messiasgeheimnis in den Evangelien. Zugleich ein Beitrag zum Verständnis des Markusevangeliums* (Göttingen: Vandenhoeck & Ruprecht, 1901), 283.
25 Martin Werner, *Der Einfluß paulinischer Theologie im Markusevangelium: eine Studie zur neutestamentlichen Theologie*. Beihefte zur ZNW 1 (Berlin: de Gruyter, 1923). Werner's monograph was dedicated to Albert Schweitzer.

In the preface to his book, Werner explains his worries about the consequences of Volkmar's line of thought. Werner perceived Volkmar's work to be in line with other recently published books which treated Jesus as a purely mythical figure. Werner foresaw that this tendency would have serious consequences for the *Leben Jesu Forschung*. His criticism was based upon the claim that Volkmar was guilty of *allegoresis*. In Werner's view, Volkmar was not dealing with the Markan gospel itself, but with an allegorical reading of it. This allegorical reading, so Werner claimed, was the vehicle by means of which Volkmar imported the so-called Pauline features into Mark. His attack was directed against the very premises on which Volkmar's reading rested. As mentioned above, Volkmar never employed the term allegory himself. Instead, he argued for a *parabolic* reading of the gospel, and he made a list of ten features in Mark's Gospel that legitimized his hermeneutical approach, among these the *symbolism* involved in the cursing of the fig tree (11:12–14); the glorification or *spiritualization* of Christ that took place in the transfiguration (9:2–8); and the *two-step* healing of the man born blind (8:22–26) (1876, 644f). Werner attacked the most widespread of these arguments. He either rejected or shed doubt upon them through references to established scholars like Julius Wellhausen and Wernle. Werner concluded that *allegoresis* was unnecessary to explain Mark's Gospel and he insisted on a literal reading of the gospel, which he generally believed to be more Petrine than Pauline. Having questioned the legitimacy of doing *allegoresis* in a reading of Mark, Werner systematically compared Mark's and Paul's views on a vast number of issues: Christology, the law, gospel, faith, Jews and Gentiles, sacraments etc. He found some common traits, but more often serious differences, e.g. the often-claimed incompatibility between Mark's horizontal Jesus and Paul's vertical Christ. Werner's conclusion was that the common material was not distinctively Pauline, but belonged to the mainstream tradition of early Christianity.

In my view, a systematic comparison like the one undertaken by Werner also has some flaws. Firstly, it fails to pay sufficient attention to the differences of genre. Secondly, it rests on a traditional view of Pauline theology as a static enterprise. Thirdly, Werner's insistence upon a literal reading seems somewhat strained and it is hard to avoid the impression that it is rooted in apologetics with the aim of protecting the historical Jesus from dogmatic, Pauline fetters. Yet, Werner's thorough analysis and strong criticism of Volkmar's work convinces a present-day reader that a different procedure is needed in order to reopen the case.

Of course, Volkmar's interpretation of Mark is open to critique. His project was probably as rooted in apologetics as was Werner's. In Volkmar's case, Pauline theology was brought to the fore at the expense of the *Leben Jesu Forschung*. Firstly, Volkmar's view of the didactic nature of Mark (especially the sketch from

1857, summarized above) seems exaggerated and his exegesis sometimes strained. Secondly, the Pauline Gentile mission, which he finds almost everywhere in the gospel, overshadows other important aspects in Mark's narratives. Thirdly, his Tübinger scheme of early Christian tendencies was too narrow. Fourthly, Volkmar's claim that the replacement of the *particularistic* Judaism with the *universalism* of Christianity constituted a *"Fortschritt"* cannot be accepted today, but reflects the ideological landscape of the 19th century. But still other aspects of Volkmar's reading of Mark's Gospel appear surprisingly acceptable to modern scholarship, and many of his insights anticipated 20th century biblical scholarship. I mention the most important issues:

- The hypothesis of Markan priority.
- The insight of redaction criticism that the Markan Jesus was a reflection of the proclaimed Christ of this community.
- The focus on ethnicity in the New Perspective on Paul according to which Paul's theologizing was seen as a response to his work among Jews and Gentiles.
- The approach to the gospel as a piece of literature and the evangelist as an author which narrative criticism made mainstream exegesis.

It has been suggested that Werner's monograph put an end to the idea of Paulinism in Mark. I would argue that it was not so much Werner's refutation itself as the rise of form criticism that sidetracked the line of inquiry that Volkmar had initiated. As we know, form criticism concentrated on the individual pericopes and traced their history backwards in search for their *Sitz-im-Leben*, but it took no interest in the gospels as complete works. It is quite telling that the interest in the relationship between Paul and Mark surfaces again with redaction criticism. Anglo-American scholars inclined toward literary readings like Joel Marcus and William Telford have long advocated for ideas that resemble Volkmar's readings.[26] So maybe the literary turn in exegesis has finally paved the way for a comeback for the latter's thesis. Maybe the task is not so much to refute Werner by *proving* that Mark constitutes *the* Pauline gospel, but to ask, more modestly, whether Paul can shed light on certain Markan phenomena which keep puzzling New Testament exegetes.[27] Can the Messianic secret, for instance, be seen as a parallel to the hidden mystery of 1 Cor 2:7? Should we understand the lack of understanding among the disciples in Mark in light of the divine strat-

---

[26] Joel Marcus, "Mark – Interpreter of Paul." *NTS* 46 (2000), 473–487; William R. Telford, *The Theology of the Gospel of Mark* (Cambridge: Cambridge University Press, 1999), 164–169.

[27] This approach is taken by J. C. Fenton in "Paul and Mark." In *Studies in the Gospels: Essays in Memory of R. H. Lightfoot*, ed. D. E. Nineham (Oxford: Blackwell, 1955), 89–112.

egy of hardening in Rom 9–11? The answers to these and other questions may well receive stimulating input from the work of Gustav Volkmar.[28]

---

[28] The author of this essay, Anne Vig Skoven, was PhD student at the University of Copenhagen until her tragic, premature death in March 2013. The essay has been prepared for publication by Gitte Buch-Hansen and Mogens Müller.

Joel Marcus
Mark – Interpreter of Paul[1]

In recent years the question of the relation between Mark and Paul has been reopened. This contrasts with the situation that prevailed during most of the twentieth century. After the publication of Martin Werner's 1923 monograph, *Der Einfluss paulinischer Theologie im Markusevangelium*,[2] most scholars had treated the question as closed, accepting Werner's arguments (or, more often, other scholars' acceptance of them) that the first Gospel was uninfluenced by the Apostle to the Gentiles.[3] Such has been the impact of Werner's work that even some of those who have pointed out similarities between Mark and Paul have been reluctant to posit a direct connection.[4]

---

[1] The title, of course, plays upon Papias' famous description of Mark as the interpreter of *Peter* (Eusebius, *Church History*, 3.39.15). There may be something to the suggestion of Rudolf Pesch, *Das Markusevangelium*, HTKNT 2 (Freiburg: Herder, 1976), 1.8–9, that Papias' description, like the pseudonymous ascription of 1 Peter to Peter, is an attempt to reconcile the Pauline and Petrine wings of the church by attributing to Peter a work that highlights Pauline theology.– The present essay was originally published under the same title in *NTS* 46 (2000): 473–487. The new version incorporates some changes in the footnotes and a new appendix on a recent reading of Mark 7.

[2] Martin Werner, *Der Einfluss paulinischer Theologie im Markusevangelium: eine Studie zur neutestamentlichen Theologie*, BZNW 1 (Giessen: Töpelmann, 1923). The primary target of Werner's polemic was the nineteenth-century monograph by Gustav Volkmar, *Die Religion Jesu* (Leipzig: Brockhaus, 1857), which claimed that Mark was an allegory in which Jesus stood for Paul, the family of Jesus stood for the Law-observant Jerusalem church led by James, the Pharisees stood for Paul's Pharisaic Christian opponents, etc.; cf. Volkmar's restatement of his position in Gustav Volkmar, *Die Evangelien oder Marcus und die Synopsis der kanonischen und ausserkanonischen Evangelien nach dem ältesten Text mit historisch-exegetischem Commentar* (Leipzig: Fues's Verlag (R. Reisland), 1870). The manifest weaknesses of Volkmar's monograph provided Werner with a perfect foil. But cf. the more positive, though balanced, assessment of William Wrede, *The Messianic Secret*, reprint, 1901, Library of Theological Translations (Cambridge: James Clarke & Co., 1971), 284: "The sum total of what is false and impossible in his work is great in things both great and small... [Yet] without a doubt Volkmar's book is the most perceptive and shrewd, and to my mind altogether the most important, that we possess on Mark."

[3] Exceptions have included Benjamin W. Bacon, *The Gospel of Mark: Its Composition and Date* (New Haven/London: Yale University Press/Oxford University Press, 1925) and John C. Fenton, "Paul and Mark." In *Studies in the Gospels: Essays in Memory of R. H. Lightfoot*, ed. D. E. Nineham (Oxford: Basil Blackwell, 1957), 89–112.

[4] See e.g. C. Clifton Black, "Christ Crucified in Paul and in Mark: Reflections on an Intracanonical Conversation."In *Theology and Ethics in Paul and His Interpreters: Essays in Honor of Victor Paul Furnish*, eds. E. H. Lovering and J. L. Sumney (Nashville: Abingdon, 1996), 80–104

But now the ground appears to be shifting, and several scholars have recently contended that Mark should be situated in the Pauline sphere of activity,[5] though without in the main attempting to respond to Werner's arguments. The republication of this essay in a volume devoted to the Mark/Paul question is a further sign of this shift.[6] This renewal of the theory of Markan Paulinism reflects developments both in Synoptic criticism and in Pauline study. In the Synoptic area, redaction criticism's stress that Mark was not just a collector of traditions but also a theologian in his own right has led to a renewed attempt to situate him within the spectrum of first-century Christian theology, and this has naturally resulted in comparisons with his great predecessor, Paul.[7] In the area of Pauline studies, one important trend in scholarship since World War II has been the re-emergence of Ferdinand Christian Baur's thesis that Paul was a polemical theologian, and that his opinions about subjects such as the Law and the theology of the cross were not consensus positions but embattled outposts.[8] If Paul was a lonely and contentious figure rather than a universally approved one, it is more remarkable than it would otherwise be that Mark frequently agrees with him.

---

who prefaces his fine article on the canonical interplay between Paul and Mark with a ritual invocation of Werner (p. 185). Similarly, Ulrich Luz, "Theologia Crucis als Mitte der Theologie im Neuen Testament." *EvT 34* (1974): 120–21 n. 11, who disagrees with Werner's thesis that the similarities between Mark and Paul stem from their common access to pre-Pauline traditions, but still thinks that the thesis of direct contact between the two "nach wie vor unwahrscheinlich bleibt".

5 E.g. Michael D. Goulder, "Those Outside (Mk. 4:10–12)." *NT* 33 (1991): 289–302; John R. Donahue, "The Quest for the Community of Mark's Gospel." In *The Four Gospels 1992: Festschrift Frans Neirynck*, ed. Frans Van Segbroeck, et al., BETL 100 (Leuven: Leuven University Press, 1992), 2.817–38; Wolfgang Schenk, "Sekundäre Jesuanisierungen von primären Paulus-Aussagen bei Markus." In *The Four Gospels 1992: Festschrift Frans Neirynck*, ed. Frans Van Segbroeck, et al., BETL 100 (Leuven: Leuven University Press, 1992), 2.877–904; John R. Donahue, "Windows and Mirrors: The Setting of Mark's Gospel." *CBQ* 57 (1995): 1–26; and Heikki Räisänen, "Jesus and the Food Laws: Reflections on Mark 7.15." In *Jesus, Paul and Torah: Collected Essays*, reprint, 1982, JSNTSup 43 (Sheffield: Sheffield Academic Press, 1992), 127–48.
6 See also Oda Wischmeyer and David Sim, eds., *Paul and Mark: Two Authors at the Beginnings of Christianity*, BZNW 198 (De Gruyter, 2014).
7 Cf. Black, "Christ Crucified", 187–88.
8 See especially the works of Ernst Käsemann, e.g. Ernst Käsemann, *New Testament Questions of Today*, reprint, 1957, The New Testament Library (London: S.C.M. Press, 1969); Ernst Käsemann, *Commentary on Romans* (Grand Rapids: Eerdmans, 1980). See also Gerd Lüdemann, *Opposition to Paul in Jewish Christianity* (Minneapolis: Fortress, 1989); J. Louis Martyn, *Galatians: A New Translation with Introduction and Commentary*, AB 33 A (New York: Doubleday, 1997); J. Louis Martyn, *Theological Issues in the Letters of Paul*, SNTW (Edinburgh/Nashville: T. & T. Clark/Abingdon, 1997).

Mark, too, has been portrayed in post-war scholarship as a polemical writer,[9] and it is natural that sooner or later the attempt would be made to compare and even to draw lines of influence between these two contentious theologians.[10]

And, indeed, there are on the face of it a number of similarities between Paul and Mark. Both, for example, make the term εὐαγγέλιον a central aspect of their theology (e. g. Mark 1:1; Gal 1:6–9; Rom 1:16–17).[11] Both stress the significance of Jesus' crucifixion as the apocalyptic turning point of the ages (see below), although neither ignores the resurrection either.[12] Both highlight Jesus' victory over demonic powers (the Markan exorcisms; Rom 8:38–39; 1 Cor 15:24 etc.) and see his advent as the dawn of the age of divine blessing prophesied in the Scriptures (e. g. Mark 1:1–15; Rom 3:21–22). Both portray Jesus as a new Adam.[13] Both emphasize the importance of faith in Jesus and in God, sometimes picturing this faith in a dualistic way as a new mode of seeing that God grants to his elect people while condemning outsiders to blindness (Mark 4:10–12; Rom 11:7–10; 1 Cor 2:6–16).[14] In both cases, however, such dualism sometimes yields

---

9 See e.g. Willi Marxsen, *Mark the Evangelist* (Nashville: Abingdon, 1969); Theodore J. Weeden, *Mark: Traditions in Conflict* (Philadelphia: Fortress, 1971); and Etienne Trocme, *The Formation of the Gospel According to Mark*, reprint, 1963 (Philadelphia: Westminster, 1975).
10 On Mark and Paul as polemical theologians, see Luz, "Theologia Crucis", 118.
11 Cf. Marxsen, *Mark*, 117–50. See also the essays in this volume by Gerd Theissen and Oda Wischmeyer.
12 On the resurrection see e.g., on the Pauline side, Rom 1:3–4 and 1 Corinthians 15, and, on the Markan side, Mark 9:9 and the Markan passion predictions (8:31; 9:31; 10:34), all of which end with a reference to the resurrection.
13 With regard to Paul, see Rom 5:12–21; 1 Cor 15:21–22, 45–49. With regard to Mark, it is commonly recognized that his temptation narrative has background in the Adam story; see e.g. Hermann Mahnke, *Die Versuchungsgeschichte im Rahmen der synoptischen Evangelien: ein Beitrag zur frühen Christologie*, BBET 9 (Frankfurt am Main/Bern/Las Vegas: Peter Lang, 1978), 28–38. The Adamic background is more pronounced in Mark than in the Matthean/Lukan (Q) parallels, where a Mosaic/exodus typology predominates; see Dale C. Allison, *The New Moses: A Matthean Typology* (Edinburgh: T & T Clark, 1993), 165–72. But it is not only the temptation narrative but also the entire sequence of which it is part, 1:9–15, that has Adamic background; see Ulrich Meli, "Jesu Taufe durch Johannes (Markus 1:9–15) – zur narrativen Christologie vom neuen Adam," *BZ* N.F. 40 (1996): 161–78. The Markan transfiguration narrative also has Adamic features; in contrast to Matthew and Luke, for example, it is Jesus' *clothes* rather than his *face* that shines. This motif of radiant clothing corresponds to a widespread emphasis in early Judaism and Christianity on Adam's "garments of glory"; see e.g. *Targum Yerusalmi* on Gen 3:7, 21; *Gen. Rab.* 18:56; 20:12; *Pirqe R. El* 14; but cf. already Ezek 28:13. On these elements, see Joel Marcus, "Son of Man as Son of Adam," *RB* 110 (2003), passim. For Adam and Christ in both Paul and Mark see also Ole Davidsen's essay in this volume.
14 Cf. Kazimierz Romaniuk, "Le probleme des paulinismes dans l'Evangile de Marc." *NTS* 23 (1976–77): 266–74.

to a universalistic perspective (e.g. Mark 10:45; Rom 11:25–32). Both Mark and Paul have negative things to say about Peter and about members of Jesus' family (e.g. Mark 3:20–21, 31–35; 8:31–33; Galatians 2). Both assert that Jesus came not for the righteous but for ungodly sinners (e.g. Mark 2:17; Rom 4:15; 5:18–19), on whose behalf he died an atoning death (Mark 10:45; Rom 3:25; 5:8), and that he came for the Jews first (πρῶτον) but also for the Gentiles (Mark 7:27–29; Rom 1:16; cf. Romans 11). And both think that the widening of God's purposes to incorporate the Gentiles was accomplished by an apocalyptic change in the Law that had previously separated Jews from Gentiles, a change that included an abrogation of the OT food laws; in the new situation that pertains since Jesus' advent, all foods are pure (Mark 7:19; Rom 14:20).[15]

Werner, however, had already weighed many of these points in the balance, and had found them wanting. On the penultimate page of his monograph (209), he summarizes his conclusions succinctly in three points:[16]

1. Where Mark agrees with Paul, it is always a matter of *general* early Christian viewpoints.
2. Where in Paul's letters special, characteristically Pauline viewpoints come to the fore, either Markan parallels are lacking or Mark represents exactly contrary standpoints.
3. Therefore there cannot be the least influence of Pauline theology on the Gospel of Mark.

I disagree with this conclusion. In this essay, however, I do not intend to enter into an extended debate with Werner or to try to answer all of his points in detail. But I *would* like to engage him on one of the most important issues that he raises, namely the comparison between Markan and Pauline Christology. This area of Christology is crucial for Werner's argument, as is indicated not only by the amount of space he devotes to it (nearly a quarter of his monograph) but also by the fact that he places it in the first position after his introduction.

Even within this Christological area, however, my aim is not primarily to provide a point-by-point rebuttal of Werner, although many of his specific assertions will be engaged. What I am aiming at, rather, is a new look at the two most im-

---

15 For Daniel Boyarin's challenge to this contention, see the APPENDIX at the end of this essay. For Mark 7 see also Kasper Bro Larsen's essay in this volume.
16 The translation is mine.

portant issues that he discusses, namely the earthly career of Jesus and the theology of the cross.[17]

A general point

First, however, a general point:[18] a large part of Werner's monograph is devoted to showing that there are differences between Paul's theology and that of Mark, often on matters of fine detail. On the basis of these differences, Werner draws that conclusion that Mark is not a Paulinist. But does the conclusion necessarily follow? Are there not differences between Paul and the *other* Paulinists we know about from the early church? Luke, for example, considers himself to be a Paulinist, but there are enough differences between his theology and Paul's to have encouraged Philipp Vielhauer to write a largely persuasive essay about Luke's misunderstanding of Paul.[19] Similar remarks could be made about the author or authors of Colossians-Ephesians, assuming those letters are Deutero-Pauline, and of the Pastorals. Scholars have detected significant theological differences between these writers and Paul, and those differences have been an important part of the case against Pauline authorship. Yet the authors of these letters were Paulinists; indeed, they felt so Pauline that they signed Paul's name to their own compositions. Later Paulinists such as Ignatius of Antioch, too, do not agree with Paul in every particular, or put the emphasis in exactly the same places that Paul does. Ignatius, for example, is like Mark in that he puts more emphasis on the Jesus tradition than does Paul.[20] So even if there are dif-

---

[17] Besides these two topics, Werner treats one other in considerable detail, namely the Christological titles in Paul and Mark respectively. Since this treatment, however, is largely an exercise in hair-splitting, I will relegate discussion of it to a section at the end.

[18] This point was made to me independently by three readers of an earlier version of this study: Dale Allison, John Barclay, and David Sim.

[19] Philipp Vielhauer, "On the 'Paulinism' of Acts." In *Studies in Luke-Acts*, eds. L. E. Keck and J. L. Martyn, reprint, 1963 (Philadelphia: Fortress, 1980), 33–50. Some aspects of Vielhauer's theses have been successfully attacked by Werner Georg Kümmel, "Current Theological Accusations Against Luke." *ANQ* 16 (1975): 131–45 and Joseph A. Fitzmyer, *The Gospel According to Luke,* AB 28 & 28 A (New York: Doubleday, 1981–85), 1.18–29. But the basic thesis, in my view, remains valid.

[20] See the listing of Gospel traditions in Ignatius in the publication of the Committee of the Oxford Society of Historical Theology, *The New Testament in the Apostolic Fathers* (Oxford: At the Clarendon Press, 1905), 77–83. On Ignatius' use of Paul and of Gospel traditions, see Christine Trevett, *A Study of Ignatius of Antioch in Syria and Asia,* Studies in the Bible and Early Christianity (Lewiston/Queenston/Lampeter: Edwin Mellen Press, 1992), 15–23.

ferences between Paul and Mark, that does not necessarily mean that Mark is un-Pauline.

The earthly career of Jesus

One of the discrepancies that is most stressed by Werner and his followers is the different importance ascribed to the earthly Jesus by Paul and by Mark, as is illustrated by the fact that Mark gives a detailed account of certain incidents in Jesus' life whereas Paul does not.[21] In fact, however, there might be good reasons why a later Paulinist such as Mark might want to anchor Pauline theology in traditions about the earthly Jesus. As the continuation of this study will emphasize, Paul's theology was controversial; Mark, therefore, may have been trying to defend it against its detractors by demonstrating its conformity with the authoritative Jesus tradition. Other possible motivations, such as an attempt to combat incipient docetism, have been advanced in the scholarly literature.[22] My intent here is not to argue strongly for any particular explanation, but merely to suggest that a Pauline disciple might have had plausible reasons for doing what Paul did *not* do, namely to incorporate the Jesus tradition into his kerygma.

For Werner, however, the problem is not only that Mark writes a Gospel while Paul does not, but that the decision to do so supposedly reflects such a different notion of Jesus' earthly life (pp. 51–60). The defining characteristic of the earthly Jesus in Mark, according to Werner, is the strength of the πνεῦμα, whereas the defining characteristic of the earthly Jesus in Paul is the weakness of the σάρξ (citing Phil 2:7–8; Rom 8:3; 2 Cor 8:9).

Werner achieves this contrast, however, only by concentrating one-sidedly on the picture of Jesus' miracles in the first half of Mark and ignoring the passion narrative's extraordinary emphasis on Jesus' suffering and weakness. These two Markan elements are, to be sure, in tension with each other, but as William Wrede already recognized, the discrepancy between them has to do with the conflicting aims of the Markan narrative,[23] and is to some degree endemic to the Gospel genre itself. On the one hand, Mark wants to express the conviction, which he shares with Paul and other early Christians, that Jesus' death and res-

---

[21] Werner, 51–60; cf. also the influential treatment by Martin Dibelius, "Evangelienkritik und Christologie." In *Zur Formgeschichte des Evangeliums,* ed. Ferdinand Hahn, reprint 1935, Wege der Forschung 81 (Darmstadt: Wissenschaftliche Buchgesellschaft, 1985), 53–54.
[22] See Eduard Schweizer, "Mark's Theological Achievement." In *The Interpretation of Mark,* ed. W. Telford, reprint 1964, IRT 7 (Philadelphia/London: Fortress/SPCK, 1985), 42–63.
[23] See Wrede, *Messianic Secret,* 124–29.

urrection were the turning point of the ages, the beginning of the messianic aeon of revelation and spiritual power. On the other hand, Mark is making these points through a narrative about the earthly Jesus, and his picture of that *einmalig* figure cannot help but be coloured by his convictions about who Jesus *presently* is.[24] So there are revelations of messiahship and spiritual power within the narrative (e.g. the miracles); but usually these revelations are qualified by commands to silence or by incomprehension that point to the death-and-resurrection as the moment of unveiling.[25]

The truth is that, if the Pauline gospel is to be expressed in narrative form, that narrative *has* to be one that combines strength and weakness, glory and abasement, life and death in its picture of the earthly Jesus. A Gospel that only emphasized Jesus' lowliness, humanity, and suffering would not be good news, and it would not be true to Paul.[26] For Paul the word of the cross is not only foolishness; it is also the power of God (1 Cor 1:18). And since Mark does not go down the Lukan route of appending a history of the post-Easter church to his account of Jesus' life, he has no choice but to portray both the strength and glory of the risen Jesus, on the one hand, and the weakness of the earthly Jesus, on the other, through a narrative that is ostensibly set in Jesus' lifetime.

---

24 For the *einmalig* terminology and the general point, see J. Louis Martyn, *History and Theology in the Fourth Gospel*, 3rd ed., reprint 1968 (Louisville/London: Westminster John Knox, 2003).
25 On this "history of revelation" interpretation of the messianic secret motif, see the description by H. Räisänen, *The "Messianic Secret" in Mark's Gospel*, SNTW (Edinburgh: T&T Clark, 1990), 68–71 of the views of Ernst Percy, Georg Strecker, and others; cf. the treatment of the same view in Christopher M. Tuckett, ed., *The Messianic Secret*, IRT 1 (Philadelphia: Fortress, 1983), 15–17.
To take up Werner's two premiere examples of Markan revelation scenes that supposedly would be impossible for Paul, namely the baptism and the transfiguration: already at his baptism Jesus is proclaimed Son of God by a heavenly voice (1:11). But no one except Jesus hears the voice, and it thus remains within the realm of narrative silence that scholars term "the messianic secret"; only at Jesus' death does a human being say with comprehension, "Truly this man was the Son of God" (15:39). Similarly, at the Transfiguration Jesus appears as a being of shining glory, and is proclaimed Son of God in the hearing of the disciples; but the latter do not appear to comprehend what is going on (9:6), and the whole experience is placed under a ban that will only be lifted at the resurrection (cf. 9:9).
26 One suspects, however, that Werner may have had a theological investment in precisely this sort of Christology; see e.g. his statement on p. 56: "It is precisely in his existence κατὰ σάρκα [according to the flesh], and only so, that the earthly Jesus of Paul fulfills the soteriological goal of his appearance on earth." This emphasis on the salvific nature of Christ's incarnation apart from any miracle strikes a modern and in some ways un-Pauline note (see e.g. the positive evaluation of miracles in passages such as 1 Cor 2:4 and Gal 3:4).

The theology of the cross

Having advanced the general point that a later Paulinist does not have to present his theology in a way that is *identical* to the manner in which Paul presents his, and having shown that the supposed differences between Paul and Mark on the question of the earthly Jesus are not as radical as has sometimes been urged, let me now turn to the crucial test case of my thesis, a comparison of the theology of the cross in Paul and Mark. Even Werner has to acknowledge that the similarity between the two authors on their soteriological evaluation of Jesus' death is one of the strongest arguments for the theory of Markan Paulinism, although he goes on to try to undermine that argument (pp. 60–72). Perhaps unsurprisingly, Werner does not go into the details of this similarity, but I will do so here.

Both Paul and Mark lay *extraordinary* stress on the death of Jesus. This theme dominates Paul's Christological affirmations. Similarly, Mark's whole narrative, at least from 2:20 and 3:6 on, points toward the crucifixion scene that is its climax. So Martin Kähler was exaggerating a truth when he called Mark and the other Gospels "passion narratives with extended introductions"[27] – but the description applies pre-eminently to Mark. In both Paul and Mark the death of Jesus on the cross is understood as an apocalyptic event, the turning point of the ages; this has been demonstrated recently by Clifton Black, who points to the apocalyptic metaphors "this age," "in a mystery," "that which has been hidden" and "revealed" in 1 Corinthians 1–2, and the cosmic darkness and rending of the Temple curtain in Mark 15. We may also note Gal 6:14, in which the cross of Jesus is the means for the crucifixion of the old world, and the fact that Mark 15:33 echoes Amos 8:9, in which the sun will go down at noon "on that day" of God's judgment.[28] Jesus' subsequent resurrection *confirms* this eschatological change, but does not supersede it. Paul, consequently, can sum up his whole gospel as "the word of the cross" and remind the Corinthians that he had decid-

---

27 M. Kähler, *The So-Called Historical Jesus and the Historic Biblical Christ,* reprint 1892 (Philadelphia: Fortress, 1964), 80 n. 11.
28 Cf. Black, "Christ Crucified", 201. On Paul's apocalypticism in general see J. Christiaan Beker, *Paul the Apostle: The Triumph of God in Life and Thought* (Philadelphia: Fortress, 1980) and J. Louis Martyn, *Theological Issues;* on Mark's, see Joel Marcus, "Mark 4:10–12 and Marcan Epistemology." *JBL* 103 (1984): 557–74 and Joel Marcus, *Mark: A New Translation with Introduction and Commentary,* AYB 27/27 A (New Haven/London: Yale University Press, 2000–2009), Introduction.

ed to "know" nothing in their midst except "Jesus Christ and him crucified" (1 Cor 2:2).[29]

Mark is similarly focused on the cross. He prescinds from describing resurrection appearances[30] because for him, as J. Christiaan Beker puts it, "The cross...is itself both the judgment of the world, and the victory over the world".[31] He shapes his narrative in such a way that it climaxes with the point of apocalyptic revelation at which a human being for the first time recognizes Jesus' divine sonship – which is precisely the moment of his death (15:39).[32] Furthermore, the continuing reality of Jesus' crucifixion for both Paul and Mark is expressed in a shared grammatical feature: both use the perfect passive participle ἐσταυρωμένον to remind their readers that the Risen Jesus continues to be the Crucified One (1 Cor 1:23; 2:2; Mark 16:6).

Yet both Paul and Mark recognize that another reaction to this revelation, one that rejects the folly of a Messiah "crucified in weakness" (2 Cor 13:4), is not only possible but inevitable. Both writers acknowledge that the proclamation of a crucified Messiah is scandalous and contrary-to-sense because it calls on human beings to see God's eschatological power, life, and glory displayed in a scene of the starkest human weakness, degradation, and death. Paul forthrightly terms the content of his proclamation τὸ σκάνδαλον τοῦ σταυροῦ ("the *scandal* of the cross": Gal 5:11; cf. 1 Cor 1:23), and by his addition to the Christ-hymn in Philippians 2 of the phrase θανάτου δὲ σταυροῦ ("even death on a cross"), he highlights "the unusual degree of suffering and humiliation that was bound up with this death",[33] which was considered to be a form of death appropriate only for slaves.[34] Furthermore, in a deliberately provocative way, Paul emphasiz-

---

29 See Ernst Käsemann, "The Saving Significance of the Death of Jesus in Paul." In *Perspectives on Paul* (Philadelphia: Fortress, 1971), 59: "The theology of the resurrection is a chapter in the theology of the cross, not the excelling of it."
30 On the question of the Markan ending, see the works cited below, n. 45.
31 Beker, *Paul*, 201.
32 See Black, "Christ Crucified", 198 n. 48. As Black notes, at this point in their narratives both Matthew (27:54) and Luke (23:47) "in different ways ease the Markan paradox that revelation is mediated through *concealment* (4:11–12, 21–25)". See also Luz, "Theologia Crucis", who asserts that it is only in Paul and Mark that a *theologia crucis* opposes a a *theologia gloriae;* cf. William Telford, *The Theology of the Gospel of Mark,* New Testament Theology (New York: Cambridge University Press, 1999), 167.
33 Ernst Käsemann, "Significance", 36.
34 Black, "Christ Crucified", 196 n. 44 appositely cites Cicero, *In Verrem* 2.5.66 (LCL 293:654–57), on the crucifixion of Gavius of Messana: "He hung there [to] suffer the worst extremes of the tortures inflicted upon slaves. To bind a Roman citizen is a crime, to flog him is an abomination, to slay him is almost an act of murder: to crucify him is – what? There is no fitting word that can possibly describe so horrible a deed."

es that Jesus died a death cursed by the Law (Gal 3:13; cf. Deut 21:23), one "declaring him to be unclean and outside the divine covenant".³⁵

Mark does not accentuate in the same direct way the violation of Torah involved in Jesus' manner of death, but he does something analogous when he has the Temple curtain rip apart at the moment of Jesus' decease, thus proleptically symbolizing the end of the central institution of Judaism (15:38). And in a way similar to Paul's accent on the humiliation of the θανάτου δὲ σταυροῦ, he greatly stresses the elements of torture (14:65; 15:15,19–20), disgrace (14:65b; 15:24),³⁶ mockery (14:65a; 15:16–19), and God-forsakenness (15:34) in the crucifixion.³⁷ Both writers deliberately highlight these negative elements in Jesus' death and thus require from their readers, and intend to induce in them, the adoption of a new epistemology that sees the power of God to be revealed nowhere else than in this seemingly God-deserted landscape.³⁸

Peculiar emphases

But are these emphases peculiar to Paul and Mark? Recall that Werner claims that, whenever the two agree, it is not a matter of special Pauline themes but of general early Christian viewpoints. But is that really the case?

It is of course a problem to try to compare Paul with his contemporaries. His are the earliest Christian writings, and we know of no others that can be dated

---

35 Ernst Käsemann, "Significance", 36.
36 In 14:65 even the *servants* (ὑπηρέται) abuse Jesus. In 15:24 he is stripped naked.
37 Beker, *Paul,* 201 asserts that there is a contrast between Paul and Mark in that Paul is a theologian of the *death* of Jesus whereas Mark is a theologian of Jesus' *sufferings*. But Paul discusses Jesus' sufferings in two important passages (2 Cor 1:5–7; Phil 3:10), linking them both with Jesus' death and with the sufferings of Christians. And in Mark, on the other hand, the dramatic point of apocalyptic revelation is not Jesus' sufferings but his death. It is then that the world is symbolically exorcised in Jesus (φωνῇ μεγάλῃ), the Temple curtain is ripped apart, and the divine glory hidden behind it begins to flood the world; as a result of that effluence, a human being for the first term discerns Jesus' true identity as Son of God (15:37–39). On Jesus' death as an exorcism, see below, "Werner's Argument".
38 For Paul the divine wisdom of this paradoxical concept is hidden from "the rulers of this age" who are responsible for crucifying Jesus (1 Cor 2:7–8). This is similar to the way in which, in Mark, the blinded populace and leaders who have driven Jesus to the cross join in mocking his powerlessness in terms that recall the sentence of imperception enunciated earlier in the Gospel (ἵνα ἴδωμεν καὶ πιστεύωμεν, 15:32; cf. ἵνα βλέποντες βλέπωσιν καὶ μὴ ἴδωσιν, 4:12).
On Pauline and Markan epistemology, see J. L. Martyn, "Epistemology at the Turn of the Ages." In *Theological Issues in the Letters of Paul*, SNTW (Edinburgh/Nashville: T. & T. Clark/Abingdon, 1997), 89–110; Marcus, "Epistemology"; Black, "Christ Crucified", 203.

with any confidence until we reach Mark. It impossible, then, to determine with certainty the extent to which Paul's theology of the cross was controversial. Still, there *is* some indirect evidence that suggests that it was a matter of intense debate.

The first sort of indirect evidence is polemics in Paul's letters against opposing theological positions. This does indeed imply that Paul's cross-centered theology was controversial among Christians, at least in some localities. In the Corinthian correspondence, for example, passages such as 1 Corinthians 4:8–13 point to Paul's opponents as people who take their cues from the glory and strength of the resurrected Christ rather than from the lowliness and weakness of the Crucified One. In the same letter, Paul embraces the adjective "fool" and the noun "foolishness" – surely polemical terms that were hurled at him in disparagement by his Corinthian Christian opponents. And this he does in passages close to those in which he affirms the "foolish" preaching about Christ crucified (1 Cor 4:10; 1:18, 23; cf. 2 Cor 11:1). This suggests that his cross-centered proclamation brought him into disrepute. Similarly, in Galatians Paul presents the preaching of the cross as intrinsically scandalous (Gal 5:11). And in Philippians he refers to "enemies of the cross of Christ" (Phil 3:18), who are probably Christians.[39]

Another sort of indirect evidence for the controversial nature of Paul's theology of the cross is his apparent redaction of pre-Pauline traditions, such as the addition of θανάτου δὲ σταυροῦ to the Philippians hymn.[40] Of course, this sort of analysis is necessarily speculative, and some exaggerated claims have been made for it.[41] Still, it is significant that Paul's distinctive "cross/crucify" terminology, though not overwhelmingly frequent in his letters,[42] is absent in the reconstructed pre-Pauline traditions and is usually used by him polemically.[43]

---

39 Cf. Gordon Fee, *Paul's Letter to the Philippians*, NICONT (Grand Rapids: Eerdmans, 1995), 76–100.

40 On this phrase as a Pauline addition to a pre-Pauline hymn, see Ralph P. Martin, *Carmen Christi: Philippians 2:5–11 in Recent Interpretation and in the Setting of Early Christian Worship*, Rev. ed., reprint 1967 (Grand Rapids: Eerdmans, 1983), passim.

41 See for example Ernst Käsemann, "Significance", 57, who contends that "before Paul, the cross of Jesus formed the question which was answered by the message of the resurrection". But earlier in the same article (p. 45) Käsemann contradicts this blanket assertion when he acknowledges that "long before Paul, theological reflection and the liturgical creeds emphasize the death of Jesus as saving event".

42 Rom 6:6; 1 Cor 1:17,18; 2:2; 2 Cor 13:4; Gal 2:19; 3:1, 13; 5:11; 6:12,14; Phil 2:8; 3:18.

43 See however the summary and careful qualifications of Charles B. Cousar, *A Theology of the Cross: The Death of Jesus in the Pauline Letters*, Overtures to Biblical Theology (Minneapolis: Fortress, 1990), 21–24.

Certain aspects of Paul's thought on Jesus' death, therefore, do seem to set him apart from other contemporary Christians, and to have made some of them angry.

As for the question of Mark's distinctiveness, he is not alone among the Gospel writers in devoting attention to the passion and death of Jesus. All the others do the same. Furthermore, all the evangelists regard Jesus' death as the apocalyptic turning point, and Matthew even emphasizes this conception more dramatically than Mark by adding an earthquake and a series of resurrections to his death-scene (Matt 27:51–53). But the other Gospels do not concentrate on the cross as single-mindedly as Mark does. Nor do they share to the same extent the Markan emphasis that this apocalyptic demonstration of divine power took place in an arena of stark human weakness.

In none of the other Gospels, for example, is the revelation of Jesus' divine sonship to human beings withheld until the precise moment of his death by crucifixion.[44] Furthermore, all the other Gospel writers depart from Mark's concentration on the cross by describing resurrection appearances.[45] And Luke (but not Matthew) strikes from Mark 16:6 the perfect passive participle ἐσταυρωμένον, which suggests the continuing relevance of Jesus' crucifixion.

In their different ways, moreover, both Matthew and Luke attenuate the Markan emphasis on the weakness and abandonment experienced by Jesus in the Passion Narrative. In the Gethsemane scene, for example, Luke eliminates Jesus' depression entirely, while Matthew retains it but changes Mark's graphic ἐκθαμβεῖσθαι ("he became depressed," Mark 14:33) to the less colorful λυπεῖσθαι ("he became sad," 26:37). In Mark (followed by Matthew), Jesus seems overwhelmed at the threat of death and *falls* to the ground to pray; in Luke, by way of contrast, he *bends his knees* and prays in a dignified and exemplary manner (Luke 22:41). Luke spares Jesus both of the beating scenes that follow his two

---

44 In Matthew Peter proclaims "the Christ, the Son of the living God" at Caesarea Philippi (Matt 16:16); in John a similar acclamation happens even earlier, at Nathanael's first encounter with Jesus (John 1:49); and in Luke it is already revealed to Mary before Jesus' birth that he will be the Son of the Most High, the Son of God (Luke 1:32, 34).

45 I am assuming that Mark was originally intended to end at 16:8. On the question, see Kurt Aland, "Der Schluss des Markusevangeliums." In *L'evangile selon Marc. Tradition et redaction*, ed. M. Sabbe, reprint, orig. 1974, BETL 34 (Leuven: Leuven University Press, 1988), 435–70; Andreas Lindemann, "Die Osterbotschaft des Markus. Zur theologischen Interpretation von Mark. 16.1–8." *NTS* 26 (1980): 298–317; and J. Lee Magness, *Sense and Absence: Structure and Suspension in the Ending of Mark's Gospel*, SBLSS (Atlanta: Scholars, 1986). Since this article was first published, N. Clayton Croy, *The Mutilation of Mark's Gospel* (Nashville: Abingdon, 2003) has argued strongly for the thesis that the original ending of Mark has been lost; for critique, see Marcus, *Mark*, 2.1091–96.

trials in Mark, and his Jesus tells the daughters of Jerusalem that they should weep for themselves rather than for him (Luke 23:27–31). Nor is he totally abandoned on the cross, mocked even by his fellow victims of capital punishment, as in Mark (and Matthew); one of the brigands crucified with him becomes his adherent (Luke 23:39–43). Most strikingly, in the death scene Luke changes Jesus' last cry from "My God, my God, why have you forsaken me?" to "into your hands I commit my Spirit" (Luke 23:46).

Matthew is less radical in his retouching of Mark, but he still qualifies Mark's *theologia crucis* somewhat. In the scene of Jesus' arrest, for example, he introduces a saying in which Jesus stresses that he could if he wanted to, even at this moment, escape arrest by appealing for heavenly intervention (Matt 26:53–54). Although he retains the cry of dereliction, there is more of an element of control in his version of Jesus' decease than there is in Mark's; the Matthean Jesus *gives up* (ἀφῆκεν) his spirit (Matt 27:50), rather than simply expiring (ἐξέπνευσεν), as in Mark 15:37.[46] Matthew also dilutes the cross-centredness of the narrative by changing the motivation for the centurion's acclamation of Jesus' divine sonship from perception of Jesus' *death* to observation of the earthquake and the accompanying phenomena (Matt 27:54).

John has nothing like the Markan death scene either. Indeed, he goes in exactly the opposite direction, emphasizing that Jesus is in control all through the passion events.[47] In John, Jesus does not even give up the ghost until he has decided that "all has been accomplished", and at the end he says "I thirst" not so much because he is prey to this human emotion as in order to fulfill the scripture (John 19:28–30). One would be hard-pressed, then, to affirm of the Johannine Jesus, as one can affirm of the Markan one: μορφὴν δούλου λαβών ("he took the form of a slave": Phil 2:8).

Mark, then, *is* distinctive among the Gospel writers in his treatment of Jesus' suffering and death. And this distinctiveness overlaps with Paul's peculiar emphasis on the cross as the paradoxical instrument for the revelation of the apocalyptic power of God in a devastated landscape of human weakness and death.

---

46 In Mark, significantly, ἀφίημι is applied not to Jesus' spirit, as it is in Matthew, but to his death-scream.

47 See e.g. the way in which he "floors" those who come to arrest him and arranges for his disciples' escape (John 18:6–9), his assertion to Pilate that he would not have been delivered if his kingdom were of "this world" and that Pilate would have no power over him if it had not been given to him by God (18:36; 19:11), and his calm provision for the mutual care of his mother and the beloved disciple (19:26–27). See Donald Senior, *The Passion of Jesus in the Gospel of John* (Wilmington: Glazier, 1991), passim; Raymond E. Brown, *The Death of the Messiah: From Gethsemane to the Grave. A Commentary on the Passion Narratives in the Four Gospels*, ABRL (New York: Doubleday, 1994), passim.

Werner's argument

Werner's main counter-argument is that Mark and Paul have a different conception of the *nature* of Jesus' saving death. Although both authors attest the idea that that death was a vicarious sacrifice for human sin (Mark 10:45; 14:24; Rom 3:25; 5:9; 1 Cor 5:7; 11:25; 15:3), according to Werner this idea is far more prominent in the thought of Mark than it is in that of Paul. Paul merely takes it up from tradition. The "Kardinaldogma" of Paul is rather that Jesus' death represented his triumph over the demonic powers that were responsible for crucifying him (1 Cor 2:8).[48] This idea leaves absolutely no trace in Mark, despite the fact that it is strongly present in two of the other Gospels (Luke 22:3; John 6:70; 12:31; 13:2, 27; 14:30).

But both the Pauline and the Markan sides of this contrast are exaggerated. As far as Paul is concerned, it may well be that he takes up from tradition the idea of Christ's death as a vicarious sacrifice, but he *does* take it up, and relatively frequently. Why would Paul appropriate it so often if he disagreed with it?[49] Mark doubtless inherited the idea from tradition too, as is shown by its appearance in his Last Supper story (14:24). Here he is obviously using a tradition, as is shown by the parallel with 1 Cor 11:23–26. Moreover, Mark does not introduce the idea into the death scene itself,[50] where, as we have already seen, the same sort of apocalyptic context dominates as in Paul's letters.

Werner, moreover, exaggerates and distorts when he contrasts the supposed Pauline "Kardinaldogma" of demonic responsibility for Jesus' death with the supposed Markan view that Jesus' human enemies were culpable. First Corinthians 2:8 is the only passage that Werner cites for the Pauline "Kardinaldogma" of demonic responsibility for Jesus' death,[51] and he acknowledges that elsewhere Paul attributes Jesus' death to the enmity of human beings (for example, 1

---

48 These emphases on the merely traditional nature of the notion of vicarious atonement in Paul and on Paul's greater interest in the idea of Jesus' death as an apocalyptic triumph anticipate two of the major themes of Ernst Käsemann, "Significance".
49 See Cousar, *Theology*, 16–18.
50 See Black, "Christ Crucified", 200 n. 55.
51 Since Werner's subject is Paul, he does not mention Deutero-Pauline passages that have themes similar to the ones he is in discussing. In the Deutero-Pauline (?) Colossians (2:14–5), Jesus triumphs over "the principalities and powers" (ἀρχαὶ καὶ ἐξουσίαι) through the cross, whereas in Ephesians (1:21) he defeats them at his resurrection. In the authentically Pauline 1 Corinthians (15:24), however, the final defeat of the powers is reserved for the parousia. On the tension between Paul's different statements about the defeat of evil powers, see Martinus C. de Boer, *The Defeat of Death: Apocalyptic Eschatology in 1 Corinthians 15 and Romans* 5, JSNTSup, vol. 22 (Sheffield: Sheffield Academic Press, 1988).

Thess 2:15).⁵² It may be true, as Werner claims, that Paul would have seen those human beings as the tools of the demons, but this is probably Mark's view as well. As James M. Robinson has shown in an important monograph, and as Susan Garrett's insightful recent study confirms, the evangelist portrays the human opposition to Jesus, which is visible for example in the controversy stories, as an extension of the cosmic opposition, which is visible especially in the temptation narrative (1:12–13) and the exorcisms.⁵³

This intertwined demonic/human opposition culminates in Jesus' crucifixion. Mark probably means his readers to understand that the Jewish leaders' conspiracy to liquidate Jesus (3:6; 11:18) reflects the demons' fear that he will liquidate *them* (1:24); the verb ἀπολέσαι is used in both cases and resurfaces in the description of a demon's intention to destroy a human being in 9:22. Various features of the Markan passion narrative imply that the climax of this reciprocal hostility is Jesus' death. Mark portrays the latter as a scene of cosmic darkness (15:33), and darkness suggests demonic powers elsewhere in the NT (e.g. Eph 6:12) and in Jewish sources (e.g. 1QS 3:15–4:26). Mark himself, moreover, links an apocalyptic darkening of the sun with the disturbance of cosmic (demonic?) powers in 13:24–25. And at the climax of the Passion Narrative Mark uses exactly the same phrase to describe Jesus' death-scream (φωνὴ μεγάλη, 15:34, 37) as he has employed previously to describe the screams of demoniacs who are in the process of being exorcised (1:26; 5:7), thereby suggesting that Jesus' death is equivalent to an exorcism.⁵⁴

Conclusion

Thus Werner fails in his attempt to drive a wedge between Paul and Mark on the subject of Jesus' death. Both portray the death of Jesus in similarly overlapping ways. It is at the same time a defeat of the devil, a vicarious sacrifice for human

---

52 Indeed, many recent interpreters have asserted that 1 Cor 2:8 itself speaks of human beings rather than demonic powers as the culpable parties in Jesus' death, an exegesis that would destroy Werner's contrast totally; see e.g Mario Pesce, *Paolo e gli arconti a Corinto. Storia aella ricerca (1888–1975) ed esegi di I Cor 2,6–8* (Brescia: Paideia, 1977). But in a good review, George B. Caird, "Review of M. Pesce, *Paolo e gli arconti a Corinto*", JTS 29 (1978), asserts that the passage has in view *both* human *and* demonic ἄρχοντες.
53 James M. Robinson, *The Problem of History in Mark and Other Marcan Studies* (Philadelphia: Fortress, 1982; orig. 1957); Susan R. Garrett, *The Temptations of Jesus in Mark's Gospel* (Grand Rapids/Cambridge: William B. Eerdmans Publishing Company, 1998).
54 In 1:26 the demon cries with a loud voice (φωνῇ μεγάλῃ) as it *comes out of the* demoniac; cf. 9:26.

sins, and the beginning of the new age in a scene of humiliation, weakness, and death whose true significance is accessible only to those who have learned to see in a radically new manner.⁵⁵ Because some of these themes are especially prominent both in Paul and in Mark, the thesis that Paul influenced Mark receives important support from the comparison of the two authors' theology of the cross.

Let me conclude simply with a claim that I will not now try to substantiate in detail: a similar demonstration to the one I have just made could be constructed about other aspects of Pauline and Markan theology. Not everyone agreed with Paul that the Law was passé for Christians – but Mark did. And he even expressed this point in terms that are remarkably similar to those of Paul in Romans 14 (καθαρίζων πάντα τὰ βρώματα, Mark 7:19; compare πάντα μὲν καθαρά, Rom 14:20).⁵⁶ Not everyone was as negative as Paul about Peter and Jesus' family – but Mark was. And only Mark among the NT writers gives to one of his stories, that of the Syrophoenician woman, an interpretation that echoes Paul's formula "to the Jew first, but also to the Gentiles".⁵⁷

---

55 On the complementarity of these different ways of describing the death of Jesus in Paul and in Mark respectively, see Cousar, *Theology*, passim and Garrett, *Temptations*, 104–15.
Black, "Christ Crucified", 204 suggests that Mark portrays Christ's death in an even starker fashion than Paul does: "So muted is God's presence in Mark 15 (N.B. 15:34) that, even with the passion predictions in Mark 8–10 but lacking Paul's more explicit treatment in 1 Corinthians 1– 2, Christian theology would be hard-pressed to discern *God's* wisdom within the centurion's cryptic comment." To the extent that this is true, it is a reason for concluding that Mark's Gospel presupposes Paul's preaching, not only on a canonical level (as Black argues) but historically as well, since it is unlikely that an ancient audience would have read Mark as a manifesto for nihilism. But Black's suggestion perhaps underplays the revelatory import of the events described in 15:37–39: Jesus *dies*, the curtain of the Temple is *ripped apart* – not only to symbolize the Temple's approaching destruction but also to enable the divine glory concealed behind the curtain to escape – and as the initial effect of that illumination, a human being for the first time in the Gospel realizes Jesus' divine sonship.
56 See Heikki Räisänen, "Jesus and the Food Laws". See also Kasper Bro Larsen's essay in this volume.
57 As Sharyn Dowd pointed out at the SBL meeting in Orlando, November 1998, where I delivered a version of this study, both Paul and Mark also *undermine* this "to the Jew first" scheme. Paul qualifies it by his olive tree metaphor, in which Jewish branches are cut off from the *heilsgeschichtlich* tree in order for Gentile branches to be grafted in, so that in the end the Jewish branches may be grafted back in also; thus, in a sense, the Gentiles precede the Jews into the kingdom, although *in principle* the Jews come first. Similarly, in Mark the Syrophoenician woman's reply in 7:28, although in principle accepting the idea of Jewish priority ("Yes, Lord..."), ends up asserting the *simultaneity* of Jewish and Gentile "feeding". The Parable of the Vineyard in 12:1–9 undermines the notion of Jewish priority even more radically; see Joel Marcus, "The Intertextual Polemic of the Markan Vineyard Parable., In *Tolerance and Intolerance in Early*

If these are coincidences, they are amazing coincidences. If not-and I think not-they provide further evidence of Pauline influence on Mark.

APPENDIX: DANIEL BOYARIN ON MARK 7:1–23

Although this essay concentrates on the overlaps between Mark and Paul in the area of Christology, it does in its introduction and its end mention other overlaps such as their shared attitude towards Torah-observance. Since it was first published, however, this commonality has been indirectly challenged by Daniel Boyarin, who describes Mark as a "Jewish Gospel".[58] By this Boyarin means, not only that the author of the Gospel was ethnically Jewish, that his thought was decisively shaped by Judaism, and that his Christology followed Jewish patterns, but also that he and the Jesus he pictured operated within recognizable Jewish parameters of Torah-observance: "Mark was a Jew and his Jesus kept kosher."[59]

If Boyarin is right that Mark endorses keeping kosher, the thesis of this essay is wrong.[60] Although Paul was ethnically Jewish, he did *not* keep the kosher food laws, at least not consistently.[61] Indeed, in his famous self-portrait in 1 Cor 9:19–22, Paul depicts his *modus operandi* vis-à-vis Torah observance in remarkably flexible terms: sometimes he becomes "as a Jew" (ὡς Ἰουδαῖος) or "as one under the Law" (ὡς ὑπὸ νόμον), but only in order to win Jews to Christian belief; at other times, when he is preaching to "those not under the Law", he becomes "as a lawless one" (ὡς ἄνομος). He quickly adds, to be sure, that he is not lawless before God (μὴ ὢν ἄνομος θεοῦ) but one who lives in the Law of Christ

---

Judaism and Christianity, eds. Graham N. Stanton and Guy G. Stroumsa (Cambridge: Cambridge University Press, 1998), 211–27.

58 Daniel Boyarin, *The Jewish Gospels: The Story of the Jewish Christ* (New York: The New Press, 2012). It will be more directly challenged by Boyarin in a forthcoming essay, Daniel Boyarin, "Moses and Jesus Against the Pharisees: Or, Why Mark Isn't (Always) Paul." In *The Christian Moses, from Philo to the Qur'an,* eds. Janet Timbie and Philip Rousseau (2014).

59 Boyarin, *Jewish Gospels,* 126.

60 In "Moses and Jesus" (n. 3), Boyarin prescinds from drawing general conclusions about the question of Markan dependence on Paul: "As Marcus has noted, Mark could easily have been a dissenting follower of Paul, after all." But for me it is hard to imagine Mark as a follower of Paul in any significant sense if he differed from him on the all-important issue of Torah-observance – any more than one could be deemed a follower of Daniel Boyarin if he believed in a sharp and non-permeable divide between Judaism and Christianity in the early centuries of the Common Era.

61 Boyarin acknowledges and even emphasizes this aspect of Paul's thought in Daniel Boyarin, *A Radical Jew: Paul and the Politics of Identity,* Contraversions 1 (Berkeley/Los Angeles/London: University of California Press, 1994), 55, 112–14.

(ἔννομος Χριστοῦ) – a statement that is elucidated by the reduction of Torah to love of neighbour in Gal 5:14 and Rom 13:8–10. For Paul, therefore, "the Law of Christ" does not seem to entail *kashrut*, any more than it does circumcision. In Galatians 2:11–14, for example, Paul recalls his rebuke of Peter for withdrawing from table-fellowship with Gentiles, and in Romans 14:14–23 he expresses his basic agreement with Roman Christians who believe that all foods are "clean". If Boyarin, then, is right that Mark endorsed *kashrut*, this is a fundamental issue on which Mark and Paul disagreed.

But such disagreement is hard to locate within the crucial passage, Mark 7:1–23. Indeed, Mark here seems to echo Pauline terminology when he explicates Jesus' reiterated saying that nothing from outside a person can defile him (δύναται…κοινῶσαι, 7:15,18; cf. 7:20, 23) with the clause καθαρίζων πάντα τὰ βρώματα ("thereby purifying all foods," 7:19c). A decade or so earlier, in the context of a similar discussion of permissible and impermissible foods, Paul had spoken equally emphatically, and in similar terms: "I know and am convinced in the Lord Jesus that nothing is unclean in itself" (οἶδα καὶ πέπεισμαι ἐν κυρίῳ Ἰησοῦ ὅτι οὐδὲν κοινὸν δι' ἑαυτοῦ, Rom 14:14), and "all things are pure" (πάντα μὲν καθαρά, Rom 14:20).[62]

Boyarin is aware of this problem for his understanding of Mark's attitude towards *kashrut*, and in response he offers a revisionist reading of καθαρίζων πάντα τὰ βρώματα in Mark 7:19. This interpretation restricts the issue to extensions of biblical purity rules, such as the Pharisaic requirement that the hands be washed before eating, rather than viewing the phrase as an attack on the biblical food laws themselves:

> [W]hen Mark wrote the words καθαρίζων πάντα τὰ βρώματα "purifying all foods," there is little reason to believe that it meant "thus he permitted all foods," but rather, "thus he purified all foods," meaning that he rejected the extra-stringent laws of defiled foods to which the Pharisees were so devoted –not the kosher rules. [The Markan] Jesus was certainly not sanctioning here the eating of bacon and eggs; rather, exactly as the text says, he was permitting the eating of bread without ritual washing of hands, quite a different matter. The controversy ends where it began, in a contest over the question of bodily impurity caused by the ingestion of impure foods.[63]

Now, it is certainly true that the discussion in Mark 7 *begins* with the issue of handwashing (7:1-5) – but does it stay there? For Boyarin, it does, more or

---

[62] On these overlaps, see Heikki Räisänen, "Jesus and the Food Laws", 145.
[63] Boyarin, *Jewish Gospels*, 121. Cf. p. 125: "When Jesus speaks of the purity or impurity of foods, he is not speaking about the kosher system at all, but about the pharisaic understanding of purity practices."

less; the question throughout the chapter is only the technical one of whether or not impurity, either of hands or of food, is transmitted to the eater. This is not, for Boyarin, equivalent to the question of whether non-kosher foods may be eaten; presumably all religious Jews – including, for Boyarin, Mark – would have agreed that they should not. But that is not the question being engaged here, which in Boyarin's view is restricted to the ritual physics of what happens if such foods *are* consumed. Does eating unclean food, or eating with unwashed hands, render the person of the eater *unclean*?[64]

With all due respect for Boyarin's erudition and ingenuity – and his explanation is ingenious – I do not find this a convincing description of what is going on in Mark 7:1–23.[65] The discussion there, which *begins* with the Pharisaic handwashing rules, morphs into an exploration of the question of whether or not all foods – not the *people* who have consumed them – are clean. To be sure, rabbinic discussions referred to by Boyarin, which deal with the question of the circumstances under which impurity can be transferred to people, may be helpful for understanding the terminology of 7:15,18, 20, and 23, which speak of what defiles a *person*. But they do not seem to me to be helpful for interpreting the key Markan addition in 7:19c, which speaks of purifying *foods*.[66]

For by saying that Jesus purified all foods, or declared them clean, Mark places him on a collision course with Leviticus 11:46–47, which definitely presents certain foods as impure, and therefore as things that should not be eaten (see also Deut 14:3–20). And this discussion occurs in one of the characteristic Markan scenes in which Jesus takes the disciples aside and explains to them the sig-

---

[64] Boyarin, *Jewish Gospels*, 117–19. Boyarin here draws on Yair Furstenberg, "Defilement Penetrating the Body: A New Understanding of Contamination in Mark 7.15." *NTS* 54 (2008): 176–200, who in turn draws on Menahem Kister, "Law, Morality, and Rhetoric in Some Sayings of Jesus." In *Studies in Ancient Midrash*, ed. James L. Kugel (Cambridge MA: Harvard University Center for Jewish Studies, 2001), 150–54. Unlike Boyarin, however, Kister and Furstenberg do not try to relate their revisionist interpretations of Mark 7:15 to 7:19c, realizing the problem that καθαρίζων πάντα τὰ βρώματα poses for it; see Kister, p. 154 n. 33 and Furstenberg, pp. 179–80.
[65] It may, however, tell us something about the background and prehistory of that section. Particularly interesting is the comparison, which Boyarin develops further in "Moses and Jesus", between 7:15 and the understanding of ritual contamination present already in the Old Testament: people are normally rendered unclean by things that come *out* of them (genital blood, semen, and gonnorheal fluxes), not by things that go *into* them. As Boyarin points out, this comparison was already made by Matthew Henry in the eighteenth century (see Matthew Henry, *An Exposition on the Old and New Testament*, reprint 1708–10 [London: J. Stratford, 1793], on Mark 7:17, citing Lev 15:2 and Deut 23:13 [a mistake for 23:10?]).
[66] In "Moses and Jesus" Boyarin, apparently aware that 7:19c is the weak spot in his analysis, suggests that the phrase may very well be a scribal gloss by a Gentile Christian committed to the notion that all foods may be eaten.

nificance of a saying he was remembered as having uttered (cf. 4:10–20; 9:28–29; 13:3–37). Scholars rightly identify these scenes as attempts by the later church to reactualize the tradition about Jesus in view of later issues that have arisen – such as the question of permissible foods.[67] This is the reason that Matthew, who, unlike Mark, probably *is* Torah-observant, gets rid of καθαρίζων πάντα τὰ βρώματα in his editing of Mark 7:19 (see Matt 15:17) and, at the end of the passage, adds a coda that restricts the whole discussion to the question of handwashing (Matt 15:20b). Boyarin, then, may unwittingly have supplied an accurate description of Matthew's version of the story rather than Mark's.[68]

Boyarin, however, wants to separate the question of the purity of foods from that of whether or not they may be eaten. He acknowledges, to be sure, that the Torah conflates these two questions, and indeed the evidence is striking, since Lev 11:47 uses "pure" (καθαρῶν) and "impure" (ἀκαθάρτων) for animals that may or may not be eaten (τὰ ἐσθιόμενα.,.τὰ μὴ ἐσθιόμενα). But Boyarin argues that "the later tradition" (by which he apparently means the rabbis) clearly distinguishes the two issues.[69] In Boyarin's rendering, then, the Markan Jesus, by "purifying all foods," is *not* saying that all foods may be eaten, but only that the (kosher) foods under discussion, whose consumers have not washed their hands, do not transmit impurity to their eaters. But nothing in the immediate Markan context suggests such a restrictive interpretation of "purifying all foods", and the categorical nature of Mark's diction, especially the use of "nothing" (οὐδέν) in 7:15 and the repeated use of "all" (πᾶν) in 7:18,19, and 23, tell against it.[70] The Markan Jesus says that *all* foods are pure, that *nothing* from outside of a person can pollute him – and *prima facie* that would seem to include non-kosher foods.

Boyarin fails to show, moreover, that the distinction he posits between pure foods and permissible ones had come into being by the first century, and Rom 14:20 and Acts 10:11–15, which use terminology very similar to that in Mark 7, offer strong counter-evidence. In the Acts passage, the voice from heaven tells Peter to kill and eat the forbidden, non-kosher foods he has seen lowered down from heaven in a sheet. He replies, "But I have never eaten anything common and unclean!" (οὐδέποτε ἔφαγον πᾶν κοινὸν καὶ ἀκάθαρτον). The heavenly voice responds, "What God has purified (ἐκαθάρισεν), don't you declare com-

---

[67] See Marcus, *Mark*, Subject Index s.v. "Two-level narratives".
[68] In "Moses and Jesus", Boyarin argues that Matthew does not distort Mark's meaning but brings out its implications.
[69] Boyarin, *Jewish Gospels*, 181 n. 9.
[70] It is noteworthy that Matthew, who evidently wants to turn the Markan story in a more nomistic direction, gets rid of the οὐδέν in 7:15 and the πάντα in 7:19, 23.

mon" (σὺ μὴ κοίνου). The language is very reminiscent of Mark 7, the issue is whether or not Levitically forbidden foods may be eaten, ἀκάθαρτον ("impure") is used for these foods, and καθαρίζειν ("to purify") is used for the position that they may be consumed. Similarly, in Rom 14:20, Paul uses καθαρά ("pure") for foods that may be eaten (cf. 14:14).

Moreover, it is not even clear that rabbinic texts themselves consistently make the distinction Boyarin advocates between pure foods and those that may be eaten. For example, in passages such as *m. Hul* 8:4, (cf. *t. Hul.* 8:11) and *m. Bek.* 1:2 (cf. *t. Bek.* 1:6), בהמה טהורה ("clean animal") seems to mean an animal that may be eaten. In these passages, the Mishnah and Tosefta simply adopt the terminology of Lev 11:47, which equates "clean" with "permissible", in an attempt to adjudicate liminal cases such as a kosher animal cooked in the milk of a non-kosher one or a kosher animal that resembles a non-kosher one in some ways. For this reason, Marcus Jastrow, the compiler of the standard lexicon of rabbinic literature, gives "permitted to eat" as one of the meanings of טהור.[71] The Tannaim, then, do not seem to have forgotten the Leviticus passage, which equates "clean" with "permissible to eat" and "unclean" with "forbidden to eat."

All of this strongly suggests that, for first-century Christians, καθαρίζων πάντα τὰ βρώματα in Mark 7:19c meant "declaring all foods kosher—including non-kosher ones."

---

[71] Marcus Jastrow, *A Dictionary of the Targumim, the Talmud Babli and Yerushalmi, and the Midrashic Literature,* reprint, 1886–1903 (New York: Judaica, 1982), 520.

Heike Omerzu
Paul and Mark – Mark and Paul
A Critical Outline of the History of Research

Not yet two decades ago, in 1996, C. Clifton Black could summarize the state of research on the question of a connection between Paul and Mark as such: "[I]f some conjunction of Paul and Mark once appeared to open up a *Hauptstrasse* [highway] for exegetical traffic, now more than ever their intersection looks like a *Sackgasse* [dead end]."[1] However, this situation was about to change at the very time Black made his observation because from the early 1990s on scholars such as Michael D. Goulder[2], John R. Donahue[3] or Wolfgang Schenk[4] have proposed to locate Mark within the Pauline tradition. A similar claim was made by Joel Marcus in his seminal essay "Mark – Interpreter of Paul" published in 2000.[5] Since then a fresh debate of the so-called Paulinism of Mark has emerged that the current volume attests to. Before I will further engage in that debate I shall briefly sketch the history of research on the relation between Paul and Mark that Black designated as a development from an exegetical "highway" to a "dead end".

---

1 C. Clifton Black, "Christ Crucified in Paul and in Mark: Reflections on an Intracanonical Conversation." In *Theology and Ethics in Paul and his Interpreters: Essays in Honor of Victor Paul Furnish*, eds. Eugene H. Lovering and Jerry L. Sumney (Nashville: Abingdon, 1996), 184–206, 186.
2 Cf. Michael D. Goulder, "Those Outside (Mk. 4:10 –12)." *NT* 33 (1991): 289–302.
3 Cf. John R. Donahue, "The Quest for the Community of Mark's Gospel." In *The Four Gospels 1992. Festschrift Frans Neirynck*, vol. 2, eds. Frans van Segbroeck, Christopher M. Tuckett, Gilbert van Belle and Joseph Verheyden, BEThL 100 (Leuven: Leuven University Press/Peeters, 1992), 817– 38.
4 Cf. Wolfgang Schenk, "Sekundäre Jesuanisierungen von primären Paulus-Aussagen bei Markus." In *The Four Gospels 1992* (see n. 3), vol. 2, 877–904. Schenk states: "Es handelt sich bei der Frage nach der Rezeption von Material der Paulusbriefe durch Mk nur um ein scheinbar erledigtes Problem." (879)
5 Cf. Joel Marcus, "Mark – Interpreter of Paul." *NTS* (2000): 473–87. Reprint with a new appendix in this volume.

1 History of Research[6]

In the 19th century the main motivation for the quest for Mark's connection to Paul was of a historical nature, either related to the notion of Paulinism as developed by the Tübingen school or connected to source criticism. The most drastic proposal was probably Gustav Volkmar's attempt in 1857 to interpret the Gospel of Mark as "an allegorization of Pauline teaching,"[7] in other words as a life of Paul rather than one of Jesus.[8] He was followed by, for instance, Carl Holsten[9] and Moritz Herman Schulze,[10] who approached the issue from different angles but agreed with Volkmar on the idea that the second Gospel is an apology for Paul by transferring Pauline theology "back" into the sayings and doings of Jesus.[11] Others were more careful as regards hypothesising about Mark's intentions but assumed at least a certain degree of Paulinism in Mark.[12] At the beginning of the 20th century, scholars such as Johannes Weiß[13] and Alfred Loisy[14]

---

[6] I am grateful to the late Anne Vig Skoven († 27.03.2013) for giving me access to the sketch of her PhD-project on "Paul and Mark" which was very helpful regarding Danish contributions to the topic. In addition, the following paragraph draws especially on Schenk, "Jesuanisierungen"; William R. Telford, "The Interpretation of Mark: A History of Developments and Issues." In *The Interpretation of Mark*, ed. idem (Edinburgh: T&T Clark ²1995), 1–61; idem, *The Theology of the Gospel of Mark*, New Testament Theology (Cambridge: Cambridge University Press, 1999).
[7] Black, "Christ Crucified", 185.
[8] Cf. Gustav Volkmar, *Die Religion Jesu* (Leipzig: Brockhaus, 1857); cf. for further references Schenk, "Jesuanisierungen", 879 note 11. See also Anne Vig Skoven's essay in this volume.
[9] Cf. Carl Holsten, *Die drei ursprünglichen, noch ungeschriebenen Evangelien* (Karlsruhe: Reuther, 1883); idem, *Die synoptischen Evangelien nach der Form ihres Inhalts* (Heidelberg: Groos, 1885); cf. Schenk, "Jesuanisierungen", 879 note 13.
[10] Cf. Moritz Hermann Schulze, *Evangelientafeln* (Dresden: A. Dieckmann, 1861, ²1886); cf. Schenk, "Jesuanisierungen", 879 note 12.
[11] Cf. Martin Werner, *Der Einfluß paulinischer Theologie im Markusevangelium. Eine Studie zur neutestamentlichen Theologie*, BZNW 1 (Gießen: Töpelmann, 1923), 2–3; Schenk, "Jesuanisierungen", 879 with notes 13 and 14. More recently Goulder, "Those Outside", has argued that Mark is a Pauline Christian on account of the controversy stories between Jesus and the Pharisees. According to Goulder these stories reflect debates between Paul and the Jerusalem church. In order to legitimise the view of the apostle "the Marcan Jesus speaks with the voice of Paul" (295). Cf. a restatement of this hypothesis in idem, "A Pauline in a Jacobite Church." In *The Four Gospels 1992* (see n. 3), vol. 2, 859–75.
[12] Cf. the examples given in Werner, *Einfluß*, 3 note 2.
[13] Cf. Johannes Weiß, *Das älteste Evangelium. Ein Beitrag zum Verständnis des Markus-Evangeliums und der ältesten evangelischen Überlieferung* (Göttingen: Vandenhoeck & Ruprecht, 1903), 94–95: "So sehr wir ablehnen müssen, dass unser Evangelist ein steifer, pedantischer Nachtreter des Paulus gewesen sei, der seine Darstellung in jedem einzelnen Punkte nach den Finessen der Paulinischen Lehre in fast spitzfindiger Weise gemodelt habe, so sehr müssen wir

took it for granted that Mark represented a Pauline interpretation of the "Urtradition".¹⁵

The turning point of this debate is marked by Martin Werner's study *Der Einfluß paulinischer Theologie im Markusevangelium* published in 1923. Werner tried to prove Volkmar's assumption wrong that Mark was a Paulinist by concluding that:

> 1. Where Mark agrees with Paul, it is always a matter of *general* early Christian viewpoints. 2. Where in Paul's letters special, characteristically Pauline viewpoints come to the fore, either Markan parallels are lacking or Mark represents exactly contrary standpoints. 3. Therefore there cannot be the least influence of Pauline theology on the Gospel of Mark.¹⁶

With only few exceptions¹⁷ Werner's conclusions as well as his general approach determined critical scholarship for several decades.¹⁸ Methodologically this implied a focus on the examination of (assumed!) characteristics of Pauline theology and of Pauline vocabulary.¹⁹ Developments in both Synoptic and Pauline

---

doch auch die Baur'sche These von der blassen Neutralität des Markus für unrichtig halten. Wenn man unser Evangelium auffasst, wie es sich gibt, als eine Niederschrift der apostolischen Verkündigung von Christus dem Gekreuzigten und Auferstandenen, wenn man es als ein lebensvolles Ganzes versteht, in der eigentümlichen Gliederung und Beseelung, die der Verf. ihm gegeben hat, so wird man darin die Ideen und Interessen des Paulinischen Kreises sich wiederspiegeln [sic!] sehen. " This statement is, of course, based on the assumption that John Mark is the author of the oldest Gospel.
14 Cf. Alfred Loisy, *Les Évangiles synoptiques. Traduction et commentaire* I (Haute-Marne: Ceffonds, 1907), 116–17.181; cf. Schenk, "Jesuanisierungen", 880 note 16.
15 Schenk, "Jesuanisierungen", 880.
16 Werner, *Einfluß*, 209; English translation by Marcus, "Interpreter", 476. Marcus remarks regarding Werner's long lasting impact: "The manifest weaknesses of Volkmar's monograph provided Werner with a perfect foil." (473, note 2).
17 Cf. for examples Marcus, "Interpreter", 474 note 3.
18 Cf., for instance, Rudolf Bultmann, *Die Geschichte der synoptischen Tradition. Mit einem Nachwort von Gerd Theißen*, FRLANT 29 (Göttingen: Vandenhoeck & Ruprecht, ¹⁰1995), 372 note 2: "Daß Mk nicht von der paulinischen Theologie getragen ist, hat M. Werner (...) richtig gezeigt." Werner Georg Kümmel, *Einleitung in das Neue Testament* (Heidelberg: Quelle & Meyer, ²⁰1980), 67: "So eindeutig Mk die palästinische Jesustradition von heidenchristlichen Voraussetzungen aus theologisch geformt hat, so wenig läßt sich irgendein Zusammenhang gerade mit Paulus oder der paulinischen Form des Heidenchristentums erweisen." Howard C. Kee, *Community of the New Age. Studies in Mark's Gospel* (Macon: Mercer University Press, 1977), 6, states that "none of the characteristic theological language of Paul appears in Mark, or if roughly similar terms occur, they are used in a significantly different conceptual framework".
19 Cf., for instance, Vincent Taylor, *The Gospel according to Mark* (London: Macmillan, ²1966), 126: "Whether Mark was familiar with the Pauline Epistles, and to what extent, if any, he was influenced by Pauline teaching, can be decided only by examining his vocabulary and the

studies have qualified Werner's arguments somewhat but for several decades these did not succeed to check the overall impact of Werner's study. William Telford appropriately points out that "the advent of redaction criticism[20] (...) has opened up the possibility of a more discriminating analysis"[21] and claims that "W. Marxsen, for example, has criticized Werner for comparing Pauline thought with the Markan Gospel *as a whole* and not with the Markan *redaction*, that is with the distinctively *Markan* contribution to the pre-Markan tradition".[22] Besides, Marxsen called attention to the fact that "the differences in the way each writer has chosen to express his theology – Paul in the *direct* form of an epistle, Mark in the *indirect* form of a story"[23] – had to be taken into account when discussing their relationship. Marxsen thus followed Rudolf Bultmann who agreed with Werner that Mark was not directly influenced by Paul but that the purpose of the Gospel was to establish "[t]he union of the Hellenistic *kerygma about Christ*, whose essential content consists of the Christ myth as we learn of it in Paul (esp. Phil. 2.6 ff.; Rom. 3.24), with the *tradition of the story of Jesus*."[24] Although Bultmann's idea of a Hellenistic Christ-myth in Mark could not stand, a connection between Markan (or pre-Markan) traditions and the Christology reflected in texts such as Phil 2:6–11; 1 Cor 2:8 or Rom 1:3–4 has repeatedly been proposed.[25] An important impetus for comparisons between

---

nature of the affinity between characteristic elements in his theology and distinctive ideas of Paul" (cited after Schenk, "Jesuanisierungen", 878). Taylor, *Gospel*, 127 concludes, however, on this basis that "Mark may have lived in a Pauline environment and possibly knew Romans and I Thessalonians".

20 Cf. Willi Marxsen, *Der Evangelist Markus. Studien zur Redaktionsgeschichte des Evangeliums*, FRLANT 67 (Göttingen: Vandenhoeck & Ruprecht, ²1959), 83–92; also Eduard Schweizer, "Die theologische Leistung des Apostels". *EvTh* 24 (1964): 337–55, 346; cf. Schenk, "Jesuanisierungen", 881.

21 Telford, *Interpretation*, 31.

22 William R. Telford, *The Theology of the Gospel of Mark*, New Testament Theology (Cambridge: Cambridge University Press 1999), 169 (his emphasis) with reference to Willi Marxsen, *Mark the Evangelist: Studies on the Redaction History of the Gospel* (Nashville: Abingdon, 1969), 213.

23 Telford, *Theology*, 169.

24 Rudolf Bultmann, *The History of the Synoptic Tradition* (Oxford/New York: Blackwell, ²1968; English translation of *Die Geschichte der synoptischen Tradition* (see n.18); cited after Kee, *Community*, 6).

25 Cf., for instance, Johannes Schreiber, "Die Christologie des Markusevangeliums. Beobachtungen zur Theologie und Komposition des zweiten Evangeliums." *ZThK* 58 (1961): 154–83, 183, who claims that "die Christologie des Markusevangeliums dem heidenchristlichen hellenistischen Typus der paulinischen Sphäre zugehört". Ludger Schenke, "Gibt es im Markusevangelium eine Präexistenzchristologie?" *ZNW* 91 (2000): 45–71, 69, holds: "Dieses christologische Schema (scil. in Phil 2:6–11; Rom 1:3–4) steht als Voraussetzung zwar *hinter* dem MkEv. *In ihm* aber wird ein anderer Weg dargestellt". David C. Parker, "Et incarnatus est." *SJTh* 54 (2001):

Paul and Mark as the oldest Gospel is regularly derived from a *traditio-historical* quest for sayings of Jesus as retained in the synoptic Gospels and the Pauline Epistles respectively.[26] Besides, a special focus is placed on the question of the law as reflected in Paul and in Mark 2–3 and 7.[27]

This reveals, however, that the past decades have produced regular attempts to question Werner's assertion that the second Gospel is *completely uninfluenced* by Pauline theology and that these have eventually led to a re-visiting of the issue. The refutations of Werner are based on various arguments that partly overlap.

2 Paul and Mark – Re-visited

The main arguments in the debate can be arranged into two categories, namely agreements regarding themes and terminology on the one hand and a similar view on Christian communities and their contexts on the other hand:[28]

330–43, relates Mark to the kenotic Christology in Phil 2:6–11. Cf. also Siegfried Schulz, "Mark's Significance for the Theology of Early Christianity (1964)." In *Interpretation of Mark*, 197–206.

26 Cf. Schenk, "Jesuanisierungen", 877 with reference to Dale C. Allison, "The Pauline Epistles and the Synoptic Gospels. The Pattern of the Parallels." *NTS* 28 (1982): 1–32; Frans Neirynck, "Paul and the Sayings of Jesus." In *L'Apôtre Paul. Personnalité, Style et Conception du Ministère*, eds. Albert Vanhoye et al., BEThL 73 (Leuven: Peeters, 1986), 265–321.

27 Cf., for instance, Ulrich B. Müller, "Zur Rezeption gesetzeskritischer Jesusüberlieferung im frühen Christentum." *NTS* 27 (1981): 158–85, who reckons with an independent development of law critical traditions in Mark (and the Synoptics) and Paul while James D.G. Dunn, "Mark 2.1–3.6: A Bridge between Jesus and Paul in the Question of the Law." *NTS* 30 (1984): 395–415, 413, assumes on account of "the tradition behind Mark 2.15–3.6 (…) [a] development in Christian thinking on the law which must have prepared the way for the decisive contribution of Paul". Cf. to the contrary Heikki Räisänen, "Jesus and the Food Laws: Reflections on Mark 7:15." *JSNT* 16 (1982): 79–100, who argues for Mark's dependency on Paul rather than the apostle's taking up Jesus-traditions. Cf. similarly idem, *Paul and the Law* (Philadelphia: Fortress Press, 1983), 245–48.

28 Cf. for the following Marcus, "Interpreter", 475–76; John R. Donahue and Harrington, Daniel J., *The Gospel of Mark*, Sacra Pagina 2 (Collegeville, Mi.: Liturgical Press, 2002), 39–40; cf. also already Benjamin Wisner Bacon, *Is Mark a Roman Gospel?* HThS 7 (Cambridge, Ma.: Harvard University Press 1919), 66–75.

2.1 Similarities in themes and terminology

Several studies argue – against Werner – that significant similarities in theology, topics and terminology may be found between Mark and Paul.[29] Their observations include, for instance, the prominent use of the term εὐαγγέλιον by both authors (Mk 1:1.14; Gal 1:6–9; Rom 1:1.16–17; 15:16; 1 Thess 2:2.9) to describe the core of the Christian "kerygma".[30] They both reflect a theology of the cross[31] and stress Jesus' victory over demonic powers (Mk 1:23–28.32–39; 5:1–20; Rom 8:38–9:1; 1 Cor 15:24 etc.). Further similarities are Jesus' portrayal as a new Adam (Mk 1:9–15; Rom 5:12–21; 1 Cor 15:21–22.45–49)[32] as well as the emphasis on the faith in Jesus and God, often in a dualistic manner (Mk 4:10–12; Rom 11:7–10; 1 Cor 2:6–16).[33] They both stress that Jesus did not come for the righteous but for the sinners (Mk 2.17; Rom 4:15; 5:18–19) and have similar views of soteriology (Mk 10:45; Rom 3:24–25; 5:8)[34] and the primacy of the Gospel to the Jews (Mk 7:27; Rom 1:16).

Both Paul and Mark represent a negative view on Peter as well as Jesus' family (Mk 3:20–21.31–35; 8:31–33; Gal 2).[35] They both include catalogues of vices (Mk 7:21; Rom 1:29; Gal 5:19–21) and emphasize the "hardening of the heart" (Mk 10:5; Rom 2:5). Mark 10:10–12 as well as 1 Cor 7:10 attest to women's right to divorce, Mark 13:13 and Rom 2:7 stress the virtue of ὑπομονή prior to the end-time and the difference between hidden and revealed is highlighted in Mark 4:21–25 and Rom 2:28.

---

29 Cf. Schenk, "Jesuanisierungen", 882–902; Marcus, "Interpreter", 475–76; idem, *Mark 1–8*, Anchor Bible 27 (New York: Doubleday, 2000), 73–75. Cf. also Telford, *Theology*, 164–69.
30 Cf. Marxsen, *Evangelist*, 77–101; Pierre-Marie Beaude, *Qu'est-ce que l'Évangile?*, Cahiers évangile 96 (Paris: Cerf, 1996).
31 Marcus, "Interpreter", 475: "Jesus' crucifixion as the apocalyptic turning point of the ages"; cf. Black, "Christ Crucified", 201.
32 Cf. Marcus, "Interpreter", 475 with note 11 for further references.
33 Cf. Marcus, "Interpreter", 475.
34 David Seeley, "Rulership and Service in Mark 10:41–45." *NT* 35 (1993): 234–50, 247 claims that Mark's use of λύτρον in Mk 10:45 "is echoing Paul". His main hypothesis is, however, that the "stress of lowliness of service and death" (250) in Mk 10:41–45 was mediated via Cynic appropriation.
35 Thus Marcus, *Mark*, 74 – but does that for Paul also apply to Jesus' family? Cf. also David Wenham and A.D.A. Moses, "'There are some standing here …': Did they become the 'Reputed Pillars' of the Jerusalem Church? Some Reflections on Mark 9:1, Galatians 2:9 and the Transfiguration." *NT* 36 (1994): 146–63.

2.2 Community issues

Further similarities relate to community concerns,[36] such as the debate about clean and unclean food (Mk 7:14–23; Rom 14:1–23)[37] or a similarly conservative view of the state (Mk 12:13–17; Rom 13:1–7)[38] that is related to the love command (Mk 12:28–34; Rom 13:8–10). In addition, both authors do not use ἐκκλησία as a self-identification of the community but refer to houses, i.e. house churches (cf. Mark 10:30; Rom 16:1–16).

However, many of these alleged similarities are related to aspects qualified by Werner as "general Christian viewpoints". This is why Marcus decided to focus in his study – that explicitly seeks to disprove Werner – on the Christology of Paul and Mark. He thereby tries to designate ideas that are especially prominent in Paul and Mark and regards their respective "treatment of Jesus' suffering and death"[39] as adequate examples. Marcus concludes:

> Werner fails in his attempt to drive a wedge between Paul and Mark on the subject of Jesus' death. Both portray the death of Jesus in similarly overlapping ways. It is at the same time a defeat of the devil, a vicarious sacrifice for human sins, and the beginning of the new age in a scene of humiliation, weakness, and death whose true significance is accessible only to those who have learned to see in a radically new manner. Because some of these themes are especially prominent both in Paul and Mark, the thesis that Paul influenced Mark receives important support from the comparison of the two authors' theology of the cross.[40]

According to Black "Paul's theological method sharpens the disclosure point of 'the one crucified' along the horizon of God's eternity, [while] Mark's deepens its irrefragable 'thisworldliness,' as defined by Jesus Christ."[41] Neither Marcus' nor Black's observations seem to me sufficient to prove the hypothesis that Paul directly influenced Mark's view.

Other qualifications of Werner's rejection of a connection between Paul and the second Gospel focus either on the concept of "Paulinism" or on the different literary genres employed by Paul and Mark.

---

36 Cf. for the following Donahue/Harrington, *Mark*, 40.
37 Cf. Räisänen, "Food Laws", passim.
38 Cf. W.R. Herzog, "Dissembling. A Weapon of the Weak: The Case of Christ and Caesar in Mark 12:13–17 and Romans 13:1–7." *Perspectives in Religious Studies* 21 (1994): 339–60.
39 Marcus, "Interpreter", 484.
40 Marcus, "Interpreter", 486.
41 Black, "Christ Crucified", 206.

2.3 Defining Paulinism

Already Werner pointed to the lack of a sound definition of Paulinism[42] and referred to the related problems in assessing the relationship between Paul on the one hand and the Deutero-Pauline letters or the Acts of the Apostles on the other hand.[43] Although both corpora locate themselves in the tradition of Paul and include the apostle as a character in their writings, they significantly deviate from the authentic Pauline epistles with respect to, for instance, theology and language.[44] To Marcus such dissimilarities do not inevitably prove the independence of the two traditions since he assumes that "if there are differences between Paul and Mark – such as that Mark writes a story about the earthly Jesus whereas Paul seems to be relatively uninterested in him – that does not necessarily mean that Mark is unPauline."[45] However, this point still requires a critical consideration of what is meant by "Pauline" or "Paulinist" and how the "essence" of Pauline thought is to be established and distinguished. Is the evidence of one letter enough or is a broader base needed? When comparing Paul and Mark, should the Deutero-Pauline letters be included or not and why so? Should a comparison be restricted to the linguistic level or proceed beyond that? Any definition of "Paulinism", "Pauline thought" or "Pauline theology" will by nature be based on subjective decisions of the respective interpreter.

In a different context Stanley E. Porter recently raised the question: "Was Paulinism a thing when Luke-Acts was written?"[46] and came to the conclusion that "one should be sceptical about Paulinism being a thing at all, as there are a number of (…) problems with the notion of a developed and systematically defined sense of Paulinism (…) Therefore, it is worth considering whether the notion of Paulinism as traditionally defined should be abandoned in scholarship

---

[42] Werner, *Einfluß*, 29–30 complains that "jeder unter 'Paulinismus' wieder etwas anderes versteht" and demands a careful definition of "was überhaupt als Paulinismus zu gelten habe".
[43] The debate of the "Paulinism of Acts" has recently been addressed again; cf. Daniel Marguerat, ed., *Reception of Paulinism in Acts / Réception du Paulinisme dans les Actes des Apôtres*, BEThL 229 (Leuven: Peeters, 2009). Cf. also the epoch-making essay by Philipp Vielhauer, "On the 'Paulinism' of Acts." In *Studies in Luke-Acts*, eds. Leander E. Keck and J. Louis Martyn (Philadelphia, PA: Fortress, 1966) 33–50 (transl. of "Zum 'Paulinismus' der Apostelgeschichte." *EvTh* 10 [1950/1951] 1–15).
[44] Cf. Schenk, "Jesuanisierungen", 879; Marcus, "Interpreter", 476–77.
[45] Marcus, "Interpreter", 477.
[46] Cf. Stanley E. Porter, "Was Paulinism a Thing when Luke-Acts Was Written?" In *Reception of Paulinism in Acts* (see note 43), 1–13.

on Paul and Luke-Acts".⁴⁷ Ultimately one might have to add that it should be abandoned in scholarship on Paul and Mark, as well.

A third trend of investigating the relation between Mark and Paul is not so much interested in historical developments as in issues of literary criticism, intertextuality and constructivism aiming at a better understanding of Mark's text.⁴⁸

2.4 Literary considerations

While older scholarship often used the fact that Mark and Paul represent different genres as sufficient argument for their unrelatedness⁴⁹ and was more interested in the relation between Paul and sayings of Jesus (i.e. pre-Markan traditions), as discussed above, more recent debates have turned the attention to the relation between Paul and Mark in the wider context of postmodern theory. Such issues have not least been explored by different Danish scholars under the headings of "biografisering" and "narrativisering". Troels Engberg-Pedersen regards Mark as a biographical expression of central Pauline concepts.⁵⁰ He considers the Gospel of Mark to be a narrative construction "centred on the question of the adequate understanding of Jesus and his significance".⁵¹ According to Engberg-Pedersen Mark's "Kristuskonstruktion"⁵² bears considerable resemblance with Paul's, for example, regarding their respective employment of the cross for parenetical reasons. Where Paul addresses his audience directly, the narrative genre of the Gospel requires an indirect parenesis.⁵³ Henrik Tronier chooses a different approach, to some extent following in the footsteps of Volk-

---

47 Porter, "Paulinism", 13.
48 Cf. already John C. Fenton, "Paul and Mark." In *Studies in the Gospels. Essays in Memory of R. H. Lightfoot*, ed. Dennis Eric Nineham (Oxford: Blackwell, 1955), 89–112, 91–92: "Our aim here is not to make a diagram of the controversial positions in the early Church and locate Mark on it, but to enquire whether the Pauline Epistles help to bring out the meaning of Mark".
49 Cf., for instance, Martin Dibelius, "Evangelienkritik und Christologie (1935)." In *Botschaft und Geschichte* I, ed. idem (Tübingen: Mohr, 1953), 293–358.
50 Cf. Troels Engberg-Pedersen, "Biografisering: teologi og narration i Markusevangeliet kap. 8–10." In *Frelsens biografisering*, Forum for Bibelsk Eksegese 13, eds. Thomas L. Thompson and Henrik Tronier (København: Museum Tusculanums Forlag, 2005), 177–89, 180.
51 Engberg-Pedersen, "Biografisering", 184: "Markusevangeliet er centreret om spørgsmålet om den rette forståelse af Jesus og hans betydning", my translation above; H.O.
52 Engberg-Pedersen, "Biografisering", 182.
53 Cf. Engberg-Pedersen, "Biografisering", 186.

mar,⁵⁴ by suggesting an allegorical reading of Mark.⁵⁵ Tronier is not interested in a comparison of single traits or theological concepts but rather seeks for the hermeneutical and literary strategies deployed by Mark, for instance, in the use of literary moulds such as Homer or the Septuagint. According to Tronier Mark used the allegorical approach in order to "inscribe" Pauline Christology into circulating Jesus-traditions. He thereby perpetuated Paul's hermeneutical concerns regarding the Christ-figure and constructs Christian identity by breaking with Judaism and redefining traditional Jewish boundary and status markers. However, whether Mark actually broke with Judaism has now become controversial.⁵⁶

Instead of "biografisering" Wolfgang Schenk speaks of "Jesuanisierungen" of Pauline concepts in the second Gospel. Mark does not thereby pursue apologetic aims but wants to provide "eine Leseranweisung, die Paulusbriefe als 'Epistellesungen' auf der Basis seiner 'Evangoliumclocung' zu recipieren".⁵⁷ It is, however, questionable to what extent this idea is applicable for the first century CE and what the underlying implications of "Paulinism" are even though Schenk advocates a literary-historical or intertextual approach instead of a traditio-historical one.⁵⁸

3 Conclusions

To sum up my necessarily incomprehensive sketch of the history of research on the topic "Paul and Mark", I would like to stress that Werner's study definitely did not provide the "ultimate" answer to the question. Already early on but especially in the wake of redaction criticism his assumptions and conclusions were

---

54 Cf. also Telford, *Theology*, 169: "Volkmar's original suggestion that Mark's Gospel is an allegorical presentation of Pauline teaching in the form of a narrative may be due, therefore, for a comeback".
55 Henrik Tronier, "Markusevangeliets Jesus som biografiseret erkendelsesfigur." In *Frelsens biografisering* (see note 50), 237–71, 238–39.
56 Cf., for instance, for a different view Daniel Boyarin, *The Jewish Gospels. The Story of the Jewish Christ* (New York: The New Press, 2012).
57 Schenk, "Jesuanisierungen", 904.
58 Cf. Schenk, "Jesuanisierungen", 904: "Das der herrschenden synoptischen Traditionsgeschichte zugrundeliegende Modell von Geschichte ist zu einem guten Teil Ideologie, was sowohl am spekulativen Charakter ihrer vermeintlich realgeschichtlichen Basis wie an ihren inneren Widersprüchen deutlich wird. Daher ergibt sich auch forschungsgeschichtlich die Notwendigkeit, verstärkt die primär literarischen Vergleiche der frühen christlichen Texte literarhistorisch vor allem unter dem Aspekt ihrer möglichen und wahrscheinlichen Intertextualität zu analysieren."

criticized or at least refined and qualified. It is true, though, that Werner's study was the last monographic treatment of the issue. Besides, he was methodologically very influential in so far as he carefully defined concepts of Pauline theology or thought (and to a minor degree also Pauline vocabulary) that he subsequently compared with the second Gospel to demonstrate the dissimilarities between Paul and Mark. I have pointed out some of the problems underlying the notion of "Paulinism"; a related issue is the more general question how to define criteria for the relatedness or interdependence of traditions and texts beyond a mere lexical level. To my mind that is one of the great challenges of future research on "Paul and Mark" and it is therefore a welcome development that more recent studies have focussed on actual textual relations between Paul and Mark instead of recovering assumed pre-Markan and pre-Pauline material in the context of traditio-historical studies. However, this approach also runs the risk of limiting our view and awareness of the variety of Early Christianity and of inscribing an ahistorical, authoritative image of Paul.

The author is Research Associate at the Department of Biblical and Ancient Studies, University of South Africa, P.O. Box 392, UNISA 0003, South Africa.

Gerd Theissen

„Evangelium" im Markusevangelium

Zum traditionsgeschichtlichen Ort des ältesten Evangeliums[1]

Für den Begriff „Evangelium" werden zwei Ursprünge diskutiert. Die eine Traditionslinie führt zum Freudenboten Deuterojesajas, der Jerusalem Heil verkündet, und ist mit dem Partizip εὐαγγελιζόμενος verbunden (vgl. LXX Nahum 2,1; Jes 40,9; 52,7). Die andere führt zum hellenistischen Herrscherkult, in dem das Substantiv εὐαγγέλια (im Plural) zu Hause ist.[2] Beide Traditionen sind in ihrem Ursprung politisch: In der alttestamentlichen Tradition ist der Untergang Ninives bzw. das Ende des Exils aufgrund der Politik des Kyros die Nachricht des Freudenboten, in der hellenistischen Herrscherrhetorik sind es Nachrichten von Siegen oder Herrscherkarrieren. Beide Traditionslinien kommen im Urchristentum zusammen:[3] Das Verb εὐαγγελίζεσθαι begegnet einmal in der Jesusüberlieferung in Q (Mt 11,5/ Lk 7,22), nie im MkEv, häufig aber bei Paulus und im lk Doppelwerk. Das Substantiv εὐαγγέλιον findet sich dagegen im Singular fast nur im paulinischen Milieu (64 mal),[4] außerhalb paulinischer Schriften mit einer Ausnahme nur im MkEv (7 mal) und von ihm abhängig im MtEv (4 mal). Da es in den johanneischen Schriften fehlt, ist man versucht, es dem paulinischen Milieu zuzuschreiben, würde nicht in Apk 14,6 ein „ewiges Evangelium" verkündigt (vgl. das entsprechende Verb in Apk 10,7; 14,6). Die Übersicht zeigt: Der Begriff εὐαγγέλιον verbindet Paulus und das

---

[1] Den Teilnehmern des Kopenhagener Symposiums zum Thema Markus und Paulus danke ich für viele Anregungen, darüber hinaus aber vor allem Petr Pokorný (Prag) für einen Austausch über das Thema „Evangelium", über das er eine umfassende Arbeit inzwischen vorgelegt hat: *From the Gospel to the Gospels. History, Theology and Impact of the Biblical Term 'euangelion'* (BZNW 195. Berlin [u.a.]: de Gruyter, 2013.
[2] Vgl. die Kalenderinschrift von Priene [OGIS 458 bei Stefan Schreiber, *Weihnachtspolitik. Lk 1–2 und das Goldene Zeitalter* (NTOA 82. Fribourg / Göttingen: Academic Press / Vandenhoeck 2009), 122–127], dazu die beiden Notizen von den „Evangelien" vom Aufstieg des Vespasian (Jos. bell 4,618.656). Vgl. G.H.R. Horsley, New Documents Illustrating Early Christianity, 3 (Macquarie University 1983), 10–15. Für eine Herleitung des Substantivs „Evangelium" aus antiker Herrschaftsrhetorik plädiert Georg Strecker, „Das Evangelium Jesu Christi", in: *Jesus Christus in Historie und Theologie* (FS H. Conzelmann, Tübingen: Mohr 1975), 503–548, für eine Ableitung aus der alttestamentlichen Tradition Peter Stuhlmacher, *Das paulinische Evangelium* I (FRLANT 95, Göttingen: Vandenhoeck 1968).
[3] Sie begegnen nicht nur im Urchristentum: William Horbury, „'Gospel' in Herodian Judaea", in: ders., *Herodian Judaism and New Testament Study* (WUNT 193, Tübingen: Mohr 2006), 80–103.
[4] Εὐαγγέλιον begegnet 48mal bei Paulus, 13mal in den Deuteropaulinen, 3mal im paulinischen Einflussbereich in 1 Petr 4,17; Apg 15,7; 20,24.

MkEv in besonderer Weise. Es liegt daher nahe, mit seiner Hilfe den traditionsgeschichtlichen Ort des MkEv näher zu bestimmen.

Der Begriff hat außerhalb des Neuen Testaments ein breites Bedeutungsspektrum: Er steht für politische und private Nachrichten, bezeichnet aber auch den Botenlohn und die Opferfeiern, die man nach guten Nachrichten bringt. Wenn im paganen Sprachgebrauch der Plural dominiert, so hängt das damit zusammen, dass Feste in der Regel durch ein Neutrum im Plural bezeichnet wurden. Aus dem Athener Festkalender seien als Beispiele genannt die *Kronia, Panathenaia, Eleusinia, Thesmophoria, Anthesteria* usw.,[5] aus dem römischen Festkalender die *Liberalia, Cerialia, Vestalia, Neptunalia* usw.[6] Der Plural εὐαγγέλια weckte Assoziationen an die Feste, mit denen eine gute Botschaft gefeiert wurde, der Singular εὐαγγέλιον erinnerte eher an die gute Nachricht selbst. So wird z. B. das Hilfeersuchen der jüdischen Aristokratie gegen die Rebellen am Anfang des Aufstandes ironisch ein δεινὸν εὐαγγέλιον (Jos. bell 2,420) genannt – hier kann man kaum an Feste denken, mit denen diese Nachricht gefeiert wird. Die Nachricht vom Tod des Tiberius sind dagegen εὐαγγέλια für den gefangenen Agrippa, der auf Befreiung hofft. Hier liegt die Assoziation an Feste viel näher (ant. 18,229). Wenn das Urchristentum den Singular vorzieht, könnte zwar der Gegensatz zwischen den vielen „Evangelien" der Welt und dem einen „Evangelium" von Christus mitschwingen,[7] aber ein entscheidendes Motiv kann es nicht sein, sonst hätten die Christen ihre Evangelienschriften nicht εὐαγγέλια nennen können (Justin Apol I,66). Im Christentum liegt der Akzent eher auf der Botschaft selbst, wie die ältesten Belege bei Paulus zeigen.

Paulus hat den Begriff εὐαγγέλιον nicht ins Urchristentum eingeführt. Er bezeichnet mit ihm seine mündliche Missionsverkündigung, die seinen Briefen immer schon vorangegangen ist.[8] In 1 Kor 15,1ff erinnert er die Korinther an das „Evangelium", das er ihnen in Übereinstimmung mit allen Aposteln (15,11) als erstes (15,3) überliefert und selbst von anderen empfangen hat. Sein Inhalt ist Tod und Auferstehung Jesu (15,3–5). Weitere Formeln, die das Evangelium zusammenfassen, sind: Jesus wurde als Davidssohn geboren, zum Gottessohn aber nach

---

5 Vgl. O. Gigon, Art. Feste A. Griechisch, *dtv-Lexikon der Antike, Religion Mythologie* Bd 1, 1970, 250–253.
6 Vgl. H. Le Bonniec, Art. Feste B. Römisch, *dtv-Lexikon der Antike, Religion Mythologie* Bd 1, 1970, 253–255.
7 So Gerhard Friedrich, Art. εὐαγγελίζομαι, *ThWNT* 2 (1935), 705–735, dort S. 722: „Den vielen Botschaften setzt das NT das e i n e Evangelium entgegen, den vielen Thronbesteigungen die e i n e Proklamation der βασιλεία τοῦ θεοῦ."
8 Vgl. Michael Wolter, *Paulus. Ein Grundriss seiner Theologie* (Berlin: de Gruyter 2011), 52–71, dort S. 52.

seinem Tode eingesetzt (Röm 1,3f). Auch die in 1 Thess 1,5 genannte Verkündigung des „Evangeliums" wird wahrscheinlich in einer traditionellen Formulierung zusammengefasst, die von Jesu Auferweckung und seiner Parusie als Gottessohn sprach (1 Thess 2,9f).

Lk/Apk folgt der alttestamentlichen Tradition: Das Verb εὐαγγελίζεσθαι begegnet 25mal im lk Doppelwerk, das Substantiv τὸ εὐαγγέλιον dagegen nur zwei Mal in der Apg, freilich immer an wichtiger Stelle: auf dem Apostelkonzil im Munde des Petrus und im Testament des Paulus in Verbindung mit den typisch paulinischen Begriffen „Glauben" (15,7) und „Gnade" (20,24). Der Verfasser des lk Doppelwerks setzt paulinischen Sprachgebrauch voraus: Das εὐαγγελίζεσθαι begann für ihn vor Ostern, das εὐαγγέλιον erst nach Ostern, und es ist dort mit Petrus und Paulus verbunden – wie in vorpaulinischer Formulierung in Gal 2,7.

Der Mt-Evangelist benutzt zurückhaltend den Begriff εὐαγγέλιον. Er übernimmt ihn vier Mal aus dem MkEv und grenzt das Evangelium entweder als „Evangelium von der *Gottesherrschaft*" (Mt 4,23; 9,35; 24,14) oder als „*dieses* Evangelium" (Mt 24,14; 26,13) gegen eine andere „Evangeliumsverkündigung" ab, wahrscheinlich gegen das Evangelium des Paulus.[9]

Der Befund legt die Annahme nahe: Der Begriff stammt aus dem hellenistischen Urchristentum, das Paulus geprägt hat. Mk hat ihn hier kennen gelernt – offen ist, ob aus vorpaulinischen Traditionen, die er mit Paulus teilt, oder aus der mündlichen Pauluspredigt und ihren Nachwirkungen oder aus den paulinischen Briefen.[10] Relativer Konsens ist, dass das MkEv ihn zuerst in die Jesusüberlieferung eingeführt hat.[11] Aber auch das muss immer wieder neu nachgewiesen werden.

1 „Evangelium" als redaktioneller Begriff im MkEv

Erkennbar ist die redaktionelle Herkunft des Begriffs im MkEv immer dort, wo der Mk-Evangelist den Begriff εὐαγγέλιον so verwendet, dass er das Mk-Evangelium als Ganzes oder größere Teile von ihm im Blick hat, da erst er selbst das MkEv als

---

[9] Vgl. Gerd Theissen, „Kritik an Paulus im Matthäusevangelium? Von der Kunst verdeckter Polemik im Urchristentum", in: O. Wischmeyer / L. Scornaienchi (eds.), *Polemik in der frühchristlichen Literatur* (BZNW 170, Berlin: de Gruyter 2011), 465–490.
[10] Vgl. Eric Kun Chun Wong, *Evangelien im Dialog mit Paulus. Eine intertextuelle Studie zu den Synoptikern* (NTOA 89, Göttingen: Vandenhoeck 2012), 61–106.
[11] Vgl. Willi Marxsen, *Der Evangelist Markus. Studien zur Redaktionsgeschichte des Evangeliums* (FRLANT 49, Göttingen: Vandenhoeck 1956), 77–101. Zur Forschungsgeschichte der Beziehungen zwischen Paulus und den Evangelien vgl. E.K.Ch. Wong, *Evangelien*, 28–45.

Ganzes aus kleinen Einheiten und kleinen Sammlungen solcher Einheiten geschaffen hat. Der Mk-Evangelist benutzt den Begriff εὐαγγέλιον als „Überschrift" seines Buches (Mk 1,1), dann noch einmal als Überschrift zur gesamten Verkündigung Jesu (Mk 1,14 f), hat also immer größere Abschnitte im Blick, die mehrere Perikopen umfassen. Er markiert mit ihm zwei *Anfänge* und hat dabei ein Ganzes im Blick.

In der Mitte seines Evangeliums hat er das Wort „Evangelium" nach den ersten Leidensankündigungen (Mk 8,31; 9,12.31) zwei Mal mit der *Nachfolge* Jesu verbunden (Mk 8,35; 10,29) und stellt so über Perikopengrenzen hinweg eine sinnvolle Wiederholung her, die auf ihn zurückgehen muss. Da die Wendung „um des Evangeliums willen" in den Varianten dieser Worte außerhalb des MkEv fehlt, hat er sie ziemlich sicher selbst hinzugefügt.[12]

Gegen Ende des MkEv hat der Mk-Evangelist in der synoptischen Apokalypse mit der Weissagung: „Zuerst muss das Evangelium *allen Völkern* verkündet werden" (Mk 13,10), drei Logien zum Thema von Verfolgungen (Mk 13,9.11.12) unterbrochen. Wenn er dann in Mk 14,9 voraussagt, seine Salbung werde erzählt, wo das Evangelium *in der ganzen Welt* verkündigt wird, bezieht er sich wiederum über Perikopengrenzen hinweg auf Mk 13,10 zurück und indirekt auf seine eigene Schrift: Denn überall, wo das in ihr enthaltene Evangelium verbreitet wird, soll an die Frau erinnert werden, die Jesus gesalbt hat.[13]

Dem Anfang des „Evangeliums" in Mk 1,1 entspricht schließlich auch der Schluss. Das Kommen Jesu wird am Anfang durch einen Boten Gottes angekündigt, aber die von ihm angekündigte Taufe mit dem Geist wird im MkEv nicht mehr erzählt. Am Ende erscheint wieder ein Bote Gottes, der verheißt, dass die Jünger den Auferstandenen *sehen* werden (Mk 16,6 f). Aber auch das wird nicht mehr erzählt. Die Geschichte Jesu ist daher am Ende des MkEv noch nicht abgeschlossen. Da für den Mk-Evangelisten und seine Leser der Begriff „Evangelium" (Mk 1,1) das enthalten dürfte, was der Engel verkündigt, also Tod und Auferweckung Jesu (1 Kor 15,3),[14] ist „Evangelium" wahrscheinlich im MkEv wie bei Paulus vor allem die nachösterliche Verkündigung – also eine Größe, die vor allem nach

---

12 Mk 8,35 wird in Mt 16,25 und Lk 9,24 ohne „Evangelium" wiedergegeben: Mt und Lk haben übereinstimmend „und um des Evangeliums willen" gestrichen, weil ihnen das Wort ohne diese Wendung (Q Mt 10,39; Lk 17,33) vertraut war. – Im Wort vom Verlassen der Familie in Mk 10,29 hat Mt „wegen des Evangeliums" in „wegen meines Namens" verändert (Mt 19,29), Lk verändert es in „wegen der Gottesherrschaft" (Lk 18,29). Beide haben die Wendung bei Mk gelesen. Das verwandte Wort vom Hass der Familie in der Q-Überlieferung enthält sie nicht (vgl. Mt 10,37; Lk 14,26).

13 So Adela Y. Collins, *Mark* (Hermeneia, Minneapolis: Fortress 2007), 643 f.

14 E.K.Ch. Wong, *Evangelien*, 84, 172; Joel Marcus, *Mark 8–16* (AB 27B, New Haven/ London: University Press 2009), 1085.

dem im MkEv berichteten Geschehen die Geschichte bestimmt. Ein kurzer Überblick über die Stellen fasst unsere bisherigen Beobachtungen zusammen:

Am Anfang bezeichnet „Evangelium" die Verkündigung der Hoheit Jesu
und seine Proklamation der Gottesherrschaft in Judäa und Galiläa:
1,1: „Anfang des Evangeliums Jesu Christi"[15] (Evangelium + Genitiv).
 Der Anfang des Evangeliums beginnt mit dem Auftreten des Täufers:
 Er *verkündigt* die Taufe der *Umkehr*.
1,14f: Jesus *verkündigt* das „Evangelium Gottes" (Evangelium + Genitiv).
 Er fordert Aufforderung zur *Umkehr* und zum „Glauben an das Evangelium".

In der Mitte ist das Evangelium ein Motiv für die Nachfolge:
8,35: Die Nachfolger riskieren ihr Leben
 „*um meinetwillen* und um des Evangeliums willen".
10,29: Die Nachfolger verlassen Haus und Familie
 „*um meinetwillen* und um des Evangeliums willen".

Gegen Ende ist das Evangelium der Begriff für die weltweite Verkündigung nach Jesu Tod:
Es wird „unter allen Heiden" oder „in der ganzen Welt" *verkündigt*.
13,10: Mitten in Verfolgungen „um meinetwillen" muss (bis zum Weltende)
 „zuerst das Evangelium *allen Völkern* verkündet werden".
14,9: Wo das Evangelium *„in der ganzen Welt" verkündigt* wird,
 wird auch von der Salbung durch eine Frau erzählt „ihr zum Gedenken".

16,6: Der Engel fasst die Botschaft zusammen, die in der ganzen Welt verkündigt werden soll:
 Jesus, der Nazarener, wurde gekreuzigt (ἐσταυρωμένον) und auferweckt.
 Die Jünger und Petrus werden ihn sehen.

Wenn der Mk-Evangelist den Begriff „Evangelium" in die synoptische Tradition ca. 70 n.Chr. eingeführt hat, *kann* er vom (vor-)paulinische Sprachgebrauch beeinflusst sein. Dass dessen Einfluss *tatsächlich* vorliegt, zeigt die inhaltliche Nähe der im MkEv und von Paulus verarbeiteten Traditionen. Beide verraten m.E. den Einfluss hellenistischer Herrschaftsrhetorik.

---

15 Der zweite Genitiv, „des Sohnes Gottes", könnte textgeschichtlich sekundär sein. Vgl. A.Y. Collins, *Mark*, 130.

2 „Evangelium" als Herrschaftsrhetorik bei Paulus und im MkEv

Mk und Paulus verbinden mit dem Substantiv εὐαγγέλιον einen Herrschaftsanspruch. Das ist umso auffälliger, als der Begriff an und für sich mehrdeutig ist. Cicero benutzt εὐαγγέλια z. B. als „Fremdwort" für die Nachricht vom Freispruch eines Angeklagten oder von einer neuen politischen Konstellation (Cic. Att.2,3,1; 13,40,1; vgl. Att.2,12,1). Erst in Verbindung mit weiteren Begriffen antiker Herrschaftsrhetorik gewinnt der Begriff eindeutig politische Färbung im Sinne der Herrscherideologie.[16]

2.1 Evangeliumsbegriff und Herrschaftsrhetorik bei Paulus

In 1 Thess 1,5 spricht Paulus von „*unserem Evangelium*" und meint inhaltlich die Auferweckung Jesu und seine Wiederkehr (1,10). Politische Assoziationen durchziehen den ganzen Brief: Die Christen werden durch das „Evangelium" Gottes (2,9 vgl. 2,2.4) nicht nur in „sein Reich (βασιλείαν)" berufen (1 Thess 2,11). Jesu Kommen ist vor allem seine παρουσία (1 Thess 2,19; 3,13; 4,15–17). *Parusie* (oder Adventus) meint das Erscheinen einer Gottheit oder eines Herrschers.[17] Der Begriff stammt in dieser Bedeutung nicht aus der LXX, sondern aus der hellenistischen Herrscherrhetorik. Die Christen rücken dem Herrn entgegen, wie ein Herrscher „eingeholt" wird. „Einholung" ist ein charakteristischer Begriff für den Empfang eines Herrschers.[18] Falls Paulus in Thessaloniki so gepredigt hat, wie er im Thessalonicherbrief schreibt, wäre verständlich, dass ihm in Thessaloniki der Vorwurf gemacht wurde, er mache einen anderen als den Kaiser zum βασιλεύς

---

[16] Mit Recht weist M. Wolter, *Paulus*, 53, auf den breiten Sprachgebrauch von „Evangelium". Das schließt nicht aus, dass Paulus an den politischen Sprachgebrauch anknüpft, wie N.T. Wright, „Paul's Gospel and Caesar's Empire", in: R.A. Horsley (ed.), *Paul and Politics, Ekklesia, Imperium, Interpretation* (FS K. Stendahl; Harrisburg: Trinity Press 2000), 160–183, und U. Schnelle, *Paulus. Leben und Denken* (Berlin: de Gruyter 2003), 456–458, meinen.
[17] Das ist keine Alternative, da Herrscher als epiphane Götter galten. Vgl. Walter Radl, Art „παρουσία" (*EWNT* III, Stuttgart: Kohlhammer 1983), 102–105, bes. Sp. 103. Zur Sache Christian Gizweski, Art. Adventus, *DNP* 1 (1996), Sp. 135 f.
[18] Erik Petersen, „Die Einholung des Kyrios", *ZSTh* 7 (1929/30) 682–702; Ute Eisen, „Die imperiumskritischen Implikationen der paulinischen Parusievorstellung", in K.-M. Bull und E. Reinmuth (eds.), *Bekenntnis und Erinnerung* (FS H.-F. Weiß, Rostocker Theologische Studien 16, Münster 2004), 196–214.

(Apg 17,7): Er kündigt das Kommen Jesu so an, dass man ihm leicht unterstellen konnte, Jesus sei ein zu seinem Advent kommender neuer Herrscher.

In 1 Kor 15,3–4 zitiert Paulus ein „Evangelium", das er als Tradition empfangen hat. Diese Tradition spricht von Χριστός ohne Artikel, als liege hier ein Eigenname vor, verwendet den Begriff aber danach als Titel (vgl. den Artikel in 15,15.22.23b). Wenn von diesem Christus gesagt wird, er komme zur *Parusie* (15,23) und übergebe danach seine Herrschaft (βασιλεία) an Gott (15,24), wird er als Herrscher vorgestellt.

Eindeutige politische Konnotationen finden sich in Röm 1,3: Das „Evangelium" verkündigt Jesus als Nachkommen aus davidischem Königshaus, der aufgrund seiner Auferstehung Sohn Gottes wurde. Paulus hat den Auftrag, seine Weltherrschaft unter allen Völkern zu proklamieren. Möglicherweise formuliert Paulus in Widerspruch zur umstrittenen Apotheose des Kaisers Claudius nach dessen Tod am 13.10.54. Im Unterschied zu Claudius wurde Jesus postmortal „wirklich" (ἐν δυνάμει) zum Sohn Gottes eingesetzt, während Claudius nur durch ein fiktives Staatsritual in den Himmel aufgenommen wurde.[19] Erst nach dem Tod des Claudius, der ca. 49 n.Chr. alle Unruhe stiftenden Judenchristen aus Rom ausgewiesen hatte, konnte der notorische „Unruhestifter" Paulus es wagen, nach Rom zu reisen. Er war ziemlich sicher über den Tod des Claudius, möglicherweise auch über dessen (umstrittene) Apotheose informiert.

Wo Paulus den Begriff εὐαγγέλιον aus vorpaulinischen Formeln übernimmt, wird also im paulinisch formulierten Kontext antike Herrschaftsrhetorik erkennbar – sei es durch Verbindung mit παρουσία und βασιλεία, sei es durch Erwähnung der königlichen Abstammung Jesu. Diese Herrschaftsrhetorik klingt auch an, wenn Paulus sein Evangelium oft das „Evangelium *des* Messias" (εὐαγγέλιον τοῦ Χριστοῦ) nennt.[20] Der Messiasbegriff meint den jüdischen Heilskönig. Entscheidend ist für uns: Finden wir auch im MkEv vergleichbare politische Konnotationen, so dass der mk Sprachgebrauch traditionsgeschichtlich in die Nähe dieser (vor-)paulinischen Traditionen zu stehen kommt?

---

[19] Vgl. Gerd Theissen, „Auferstehungsbotschaft und Zeitgeschichte. Über einige politische Anspielungen im ersten Kapitel des Römerbriefs", in: *Auferstehung hat einen Namen* (FS H.J. Venetz, Luzern: Exodus 1998), 58–67. Seneca bestreitet in seiner Schrift *Apocolocyntosis*, dass Claudius in den Himmel aufgenommen wurde. Die Götterwelt sendet ihn dort in die Unterwelt. In dieser Satire nennt er die Nachricht von der Aufnahme der Drusilla in den Götterhimmel eine „gute Nachricht" (tam bono nuntio; Sen. Apocol. 1,3)
[20] εὐαγγέλιον τοῦ Χριστοῦ 8 mal: 1 Thess 3,2; Gal 1,7; 1 Kor 9,12; 2 Kor 2,12; 9,13; 10,14; Phil 1,27; Röm 15,19 vgl. noch 2 Kor 4,4, εὐαγγέλιον τοῦ θεοῦ 6 mal: 1 Thess 2,2.8.9; 2 Kor 11,7; Röm 1,1; 15,16.

2.2 Evangeliumsbegriff und Herrschaftsrhetorik im MkEv

Das in Mk 1,1 genannte „Evangelium von Jesus Christus" kündigt die Herrschaft Gottes an (Mk 1,14f). Das ist ein Herrschaftswechsel. In der Mitte der Evangelienschrift bekennt sich Petrus zu Jesus als irdischem „Messias" (Mk 8,29), dessen Leiden er ablehnt (Mk 8,33). Deshalb ruft Jesus ihn und seine Anhänger in die Leidensnachfolge: „Wer sein Leben um meinetwillen und um des *Evangeliums* willen verliert, der wird es gewinnen" (Mk 8,35). Jesus fordert hier wie ein Feldherr von seinen Anhängern den Einsatz des Lebens.[21] Gegen Ende des MkEv wird das „Evangelium" (Mk 13,10) Machthabern und Königen entgegengesetzt: Die Jünger werden sich (nach Jesu Tod) vor ihnen verantworten müssen „um meinetwegen" und „ihnen zum Zeugnis" (Mk 13,9). Das Evangelium Jesu steht hier in Opposition zu den Mächtigen dieser Welt. Dazu passt, dass die Salbung in Bethanien wahrscheinlich als Messiasweihe dargestellt wird. Wie bei der Königsweihe wird nämlich – anders als in Lk 7, 36 – 50 – der Kopf gesalbt (vgl. 1 Sam 10,1; 16,1f; 1Kg 1,39; 2 Kg 9,6).[22] Diese Salbung durch eine Frau gehört zum „Evangelium": „Wo immer das Evangelium in der ganzen Welt verkündigt wird, wird auch von dem geredet werden, was sie getan hat – ihr zum Gedenken" (Mk 14,9). Das wird plausibler, wenn die Salbung Herrschaftssymbolik ist. Denn am Ende wird Jesus als „König der Juden" hingerichtet (Mk 15,26) und als „Christus" und „König Israels" (15,32) verspottet. Das „Evangelium" im MkEv könnte zudem Gegenbotschaft zu den „Evangelien" des Vespasian sein:[23] Nicht der römische Kaiser bringt

---

21 Vgl. J. Marcus, *Mark 1 – 8*, 626.
22 Monika Fander, *Die Stellung der Frau im Markusevangelium. Unter besonderer Berücksichtigung kultur- und religionsgeschichtlicher Hintergründe* (MThA 8, Altenberge: Telos 1989), 127 – 130. A.Y. Collins, *Mark*, 65 Anm. 202, weist auf den Kontext: Auf die Salbung im MkEv folgt die Suche nach einem Raum, auf die Königssalbung in 1 Sam 10 folgt die Suche der Eselinnen. Sie betont eine Schwierigkeit: Bei der Königssalbung wurde „Olivenöl" (ἔλαιον) verwandt, nicht aromatisches Öl (μύρον) (A.Y. Collins, *Mark*, 641f). Erzählerisch ist μύρον mit erotischen Konnotationen (Hld 1,3 – 4 u.ö.) etwas interessanter und macht die Neudeutung der Salbung auf eine vorweggenommene Totensalbung (vgl. μύρον in Lk 23,56) leichter. Zu bedenken ist ferner: „(Oliven-)Öl" und „aromatisches Öl" stehen in Lk 7,46 fast synonym nebeneinander: Aromatisches Öl ist kostbarer als Olivenöl. Es soll Jesu Status gewiss nicht mindern, wenn er mit dem kostbareren Öl gesalbt wurde. Zu bedenken ist schließlich: Die Salbung in Bethanien war eine ursprünglich selbständige Erzählung. Von Bethanien brach Jesus auf, um in Jerusalem als König einzuziehen (Mk 11,1), dorthin kehrt er zurück (Mk 11,11). Die Salbung könnte die nicht-öffentliche Einsetzung zum messianischen König in Bethanien gewesen sein, der die öffentliche Akklamation beim Einzug entsprach (Mk 11,1– 11). Durch Lokalisierung in Bethanien stellt das MkEv auf jeden Fall einen konnotativen Zusammenhang mit der Einzugsgeschichte und ihrer Königsthematik her.
23 Vespasian war am 1. Juli 69 von Tiberius Iulius Alexander, den Neffen Philos, in Alexandrien zum Imperator proklamiert worden und wurde im Osten schnell anerkannt: „Schneller als der

das Heil, auch wenn er in der Welt Frieden geschaffen hat, sondern der gekreuzigte „König der Juden". Doch ist unsere Argumentation in diesem Aufsatz unabhängig von dieser These.

Sowohl bei Paulus als auch im MkEv klingt also in den von ihnen verarbeiteten Traditionen hellenistische Herrschaftsrhetorik nach – ebenso wie im einzigen Beleg außerhalb des paulinischen Milieus: Das von einem Engel in Apk 14,6 verkündigte „ewige Evangelium" ist eindeutig eine Gegenbotschaft zum römischen Reich (vgl. Apk 12–13; 14,8.9–12). Richtig ist, dass die Herrschaftskonnotationen bei Paulus oft verblassen. Sein Evangelium rettet aus Sünde und Tod (Röm 1,16f u.ö.). Daher fragen wir, ob und wie auch das MkEv den Evangeliumsbegriff abgewandelt hat.

3 Die Abwandlung des Evangeliumsbegriffs in den „Doppeltexten" des Markusevangeliums

Wir gehen dabei von folgender Beobachtung aus: Im MkEv gehören jeweils zwei Belege von εὐαγγέλιον inhaltlich und kompositorisch zusammen.[24] Daraus ergeben sich drei Doppelbelege. Dabei steht der jeweils erste Text der paulinischen Tradition nahe, der zweite Beleg modifiziert sie dagegen im Sinne der mk Redaktion.

Flug der Gedanken verkündigten die Gerüchte die Botschaft vom neuen Herrscher über den Osten, und jede Stadt feierte die gute Nachricht (εὐαγγέλια) und brachte zu seinen Gunsten Opfer dar" (bell. 4,618). Aus ganz Syrien kamen Gesandtschaften, um Vespasian zu huldigen. Auch die Nachricht von seiner Bestätigung in Rom am 22. Dez. 69 wird εὐαγγέλια genannt (bell 4,656). Vespasian erschien als Retter der *pax romana*. Dass auch jüdische und judentumsnahe Kreise diese Nachricht bewegt hat, ist wahrscheinlich: Ein Apostat vom Judentum hat Vespasian zum Kaiser ausgerufen. Er befand sich in einem Krieg gegen das aufständische jüdische Volk. Vgl. Gerd Theißen, *Lokalkolorit und Zeitgeschichte in den synoptischen Evangelien* (NTOA 8, Fribourg/ Göttingen: Vandenhoeck 1989), 270–284. – Meine These geht nicht dahin, dass das MkEv zum Widerstand gegen Rom aufruft. Das MkEv warnt nur vor der religiösen Verführungsmacht eines Kaisertums, das mit der Aura des Weltretters auftrat und auf das sogar Josephus messianische Erwartungen übertrug. Kritisiert wird die religiöse Herrschaftspropaganda der Flavier. Das ist Widerstand, aber kein Aufstand. Aufgenommen und weitergeführt wurde meine These von Martin Ebner, „Evangelium contra Evangelium. Das Markusevangelium und der Aufstieg der Flavier", BN 116 (2003), 28–42; Adam Winn, *The purpose of Mark's Gospel: an Early Christian response to Roman imperial propaganda* (WUNT II, 245, Tübingen: Mohr 2008); Karl Matthias Schmidt, *Wege des Heils. Erzählstrukturen und Rezeptionskontexte des Markusevangeliums* (NTOA 74, Fribourg/ Göttingen: Vandenhoeck 2010), 287ff.
24 E.K.Ch. Wong, *Evangelien*, 78f.

3.1 Der erste Doppelbeleg: „Evangelium" in Mk 1,1 und 1,14f

Die „Überschrift" in Mk 1,1 ist einerseits Titel, andererseits Beginn der Erzählung.[25] Man kann hinter: „Anfang des Evangeliums von Jesus Christus", einen Punkt setzen, aber auch 1,1 als ersten Satz der Erzählung verstehen: „[Der] Anfang des Evangeliums von Jesus Christus (Gottes Sohn) [geschah so], wie es im Propheten Jesaja geschrieben steht." Vergleicht man das zweite Vorkommen des Evangeliumsbegriffs in 1,14f, fallen zwei Akzentunterschiede auf.

Erstens wird aus dem Evangelium Jesu Christi, das von Jesus verkündigt (1,1), das Evangelium, das er selbst verkündigt (1,14f).[26] Mk 1,1 kann *Genitivus objectivus* oder *subjectivus* sein. Da aber der Täufer den Stärkeren weissagt, kommt inhaltlich nur die Bedeutung „Verkündigung von Jesus Christus" in Frage, wie es auch dem urchristlichen Sprachgebrauch entspricht (1 Kor 15,3; Röm 1,3f). In Mk 1,14f ist εὐαγγέλιον τοῦ θεοῦ formal ein *Genitivus subjectivus:* Gott ist Urheber des Evangeliums, das Jesus verkündigt. Anders als bei Paulus ist Jesus aber in Mk 1,14f Subjekt der Evangeliumsverkündigung. Das entspricht dem Inhalt des MkEv, der den irdischen Jesus als Verkündiger darstellt.

Ferner wird aus dem Evangelium von *Jesus Christus* das Evangelium von der *Gottesherrschaft*. Paulus bringt das „Evangelium" nur einmal indirekt mit der „Gottesherrschaft"[27] in Verbindung: Das Evangelium vom Gekreuzigten und Auferstandenen (1 Kor 15,1–5ff) wird in 1 Kor 15,24 zur Hoffnung auf seine „Herrschaft".[28] Im MkEv ist die Gottesherrschaft bis in die Passionsgeschichte hinein (Mk 14,25; 15,43) ein wichtiges Thema. Dabei schimmert immer wieder durch, dass das „Geheimnis der Gottesherrschaft" (Mk 4,11) Jesus selbst ist. Denn die Jünger, die vor ihrem Tod die *Gottesherrschaft* „sehen" sollen (Mk 9,1), sehen auf dem Berg der Verklärung *Jesus* an Stelle der Gottesherrschaft (Mk 9,2–10).

Die beiden Akzentverschiebungen zwischen Mk 1,1 und 13f lassen sich in dem Sinne deuten, dass der Mk-Evangelist beim zweiten Vorkommen des Begriffs spezifisch markinische Akzente setzt: Das „Evangelium" ist Jesu Verkündigung

---

25 Mk 1,1 ist ein Paratext und zugleich Teil des Textes. Eve-Marie Becker, *Das Markus-Evangelium im Rahmen antiker Historiographie* (WUNT 194, Tübingen; Mohr 2006), 112, deutet ἀρχή sowohl als Hinweis auf den Titel als auch auf den Beginn der Erzählung.
26 An beiden Stellen begegnet eine Genitivverbindung (Mk 1,1; 1,13f), einmal ohne Artikel in εὐαγγέλιον Ἰησοῦ Χριστοῦ, einmal mit Artikel in εὐαγγέλιον τοῦ θεοῦ.
27 Der Begriff der Gottesherrschaft war ihm aus der Tradition vertraut: 1 Thess 2,12; Gal 5,21; 1 Kor 4,20; 6,9.10; 15,50; Röm 14,17.
28 Das zweimalige ἔπειτα in 1 Kor 15,6.7, mit dem dort die alte Formel 15,3 erweitert wurde, findet sich noch einmal in 15,34. Damit soll nicht gesagt sein, dass das Traditionsstück in 15,4–7 in 15,23ff weiter zitiert wird, wohl aber, dass Paulus an dieses Traditionsstück anknüpft.

und ihr Inhalt die Gottesherrschaft. Mk 1,1 stimmt eher mit dem (vor-)paulinischen Sprachgebrauch überein, Mk 1,13f setzt eigene Akzente.

3.2 Der zweite Doppelbeleg: Evangelium in Mk 8,35 und 10,29

Der Doppelbeleg zum „Evangelium" in der Mitte der Evangelienschrift sagt an seiner ersten Stelle: Nachfolger Jesu müssen sich selbst verleugnen und ihr Kreuz auf sich nehmen, um Jesus nachzufolgen (Mk 8,34). Wenn sie bereit sind, um Jesu „und um des Evangeliums" willen ihr Leben zu verlieren, werden sie es retten (8,35). Dieselbe Wendung findet sich noch einmal in Mk 10,29: Jünger, die alles „um meinetwillen und um des Evangeliums willen" verlassen haben, werden hundertfach entschädigt werden.[29]

Es spricht viel dafür, dass der Mk-Evangelist an beiden Stellen redaktionell tätig war.[30] In dem Logion: „Wer sein Leben (ψυχή) retten will, wird es verlieren; wer bereit ist, es um meinetwillen und um des Evangeliums willen zu verlieren, der wird es gewinnen" (Mk 8,35),[31] hat er den Hinweis auf das Evangelium eingefügt (vgl. Mt 10,39/ Lk 17,33). Seine Vorstellung einer Leidensnachfolge steht dabei der paulinischen Vorstellung vom Erscheinen des Gekreuzigten im Leben des Apostels (2 Kor 4,10 – 12) nahe. Dem Gegensatz von „Leben retten" und „Leben verlieren" in

---

29 Man mag unsicher sein, ob in den ursprünglichen Worten nur ein „um meinetwillen" stand, das der Mk-Evangelist durch ein „und um des Evangeliums" willen ergänzt hat, oder ob beide Elemente mk Zusatz sind (A.Y. Collins, *Mark*, 409).
30 Troels Engberg-Pedersen, „Paul in Mark 8:34 – 9:1" (in diesem Band), hat mit Recht die große Nähe zwischen den Logien Mk 8,34 – 38 und der paulinischen Theologie herausgearbeitet. Der Mk-Evangelist hat an dieser Stelle redaktionell eingegriffen. In Varianten zu Mk 8,34 fehlt der Hinweis auf eine Selbstverleugnung (vgl. Mt 10,28/Lk 14,27). Vielleicht hat der Mk-Evangelist das ἀπαρνησάσθω ἑαυτόν (8,34) eingefügt, um den Ruf in die Kreuzesnachfolge metaphorisch zu deuten. Lk unterstreicht das, wenn er sagt, „täglich" soll der Christ sein Kreuz auf sich nehmen (Lk 9,23). Dann aber zeigt sich hier eine Nähe zur paulinischen Vorstellung von einer Leidensgemeinschaft mit Christus (vgl. Gal 2,19; 6,14). Sie schließt reales Martyrium nicht aus. Mk schränkt Mk 9,2 den Adressatenkreis auf drei Jünger ein: Diese gelten als Märtyrer. Das belegt für die beiden Zebedaiden Mk 10,38, für Petrus Mk 14,31: Petrus will mit Christus sterben. Drei Märtyrer dürfen Jesus vor ihrem Tod in seiner Herrlichkeit auf dem Berge der Verklärung sehen. Sie sind Jesus in den Tod gefolgt.
31 Es kann offen bleiben, ob man ψυχή mit „Seele" übersetzen werden muss. Manchmal ist im MkEv das Leben gemeint (Mk 10,45), manchmal das Innere, wenn Jesus sagt: „Meine Seele (ψυχή) ist bis in den Tod betrübt" (Mk 14,34), oder wenn er auffordert, Gott mit ganzem Herzen, ganzer Seele (ψυχή), ganzem Verstand und aller Kraft zu lieben (Mk 12,30). Vielleicht will der Mk-Evangelist das Verständnis in beide Richtungen offen halten.

Mk 8,35 entspricht in 2 Kor 4,11 die Opposition von: „In den Tod gegeben werden" und „Offenbarwerden des Lebens".

Der Gedanke einer Nachfolge „um meinetwillen und um des Evangeliums willen" begegnet ein zweites Mal in Mk 10,28 – 31. Hier geht es nicht um den Verlust des Lebens im wörtlichen oder übertragenen Sinne, sondern um Sozialverluste: Die Jünger mussten ihre Familien verlassen, werden dafür aber durch eine neue *familia Dei* belohnt.[32] In Mk 10,29 hat der Mk-Evangelist dabei nachösterliche Gemeinden im Blick. Er denkt an Wandercharismatiker, die in vielen Gemeinden eine Heimat finden.[33] Man beachte die Asymmetrie zwischen den verlassenen und den neuen Sozialbeziehungen. Wer Jesus nachfolgt, verlässt Haus *oder* Brüder *oder* Schwester *oder* Mutter *oder* Vater *oder* Kinder *oder* Äcker (Mk 10,29). Nur wenige Nachfolger haben alles zusammen verlassen müssen. Aber alle erhalten hundertfach Häuser *und* Brüder *und* Schwestern *und* Mütter *und* Kinder *und* Äcker zurück (Mk 10,30). Diese Addition von (jeweils hundert) neuen Verwandten ist nur durch Aufnahme der Wandercharismatiker in mehreren Gemeinden möglich. Wieder ist die Variation des Nachfolgegedankens spezifisch markinisch. Paulus mahnt nicht zum *Verlassen* bestehender Sozialbeziehungen, im Gegenteil, seine Devise lautet: Jeder bleibe in den Verhältnissen, in denen ihn der Ruf Gottes getroffen hat (1 Kor 7,24).

Noch wichtiger ist ein zweiter Gegensatz zu Paulus. Paulus schreibt Jesus die Anordnung zu, dass die, „die das Evangelium (εὐαγγέλιον) verkündigen, sich vom Evangelium nähren sollen" (1 Kor 9,14). Er selbst sorgt wie Barnabas durch eigene Arbeit für sich und unterscheidet sich dadurch von *Petrus* und den übrigen Aposteln (1 Kor 9,5). In Mk 10,28 – 30 wird – unter Berufung auf das „Evangelium" – die Gegenposition vertreten: Wer um Jesu und des Evangeliums willen alles verlässt, soll in den Gemeinden alles erstattet bekommen. Er darf von den Gemeinden leben. Da Jesus diese Zusage dem *Petrus* gibt, könnte Mk 10,29 hier bewusst von Paulus abweichen.

3.3 Der dritte Doppelbeleg: Evangelium in Mk 13,10 und 14,9

Am deutlichsten sind Aufnahme und Abwandlung einer paulinischen Tradition in Mk 13,10 und 14,9. In Mk 13,10 scheint der Mk-Evangelist direkt von der weltweiten Verkündigung des Paulus zu sprechen: Das „Evangelium" muss *allen Völkern*

---

[32] Zu Mk 10,28 – 31 vgl. Taeseong Roh, *Die familia dei in den synoptischen Evangelien. Eine redaktions- und sozialgeschichtliche Untersuchung zu einem urchristlichen Bildfeld* (NTOA 37, Freiburg Schweiz / Göttingen: Vandenhoeck & Ruprecht 2001), 128 – 144.
[33] Vgl. A.Y. Collins, *Mark*, 482.

gepredigt werden. Die weltweite Verkündigung ist hier Aufgabe *aller* Jünger. Mitten in Verfolgungen durch Synhedrien und Synagogen, Statthalter und Könige soll das Evangelium allen Völkern verkündigt werden. Wenn die Jünger „meinetwegen ihnen zum Zeugnis" vor Statthaltern und Königen stehen (Mk 13,9), so erinnert ἕνεκεν ἐμοῦ εἰς μαρτύριον αὐτοῖς an die Wendung „um meinetwillen" in 8,35; 10,29. Die Leidensnachfolge, die in der Mitte des Evangeliums thematisiert worden war, wird mit dem Thema der „Verkündigung" vom Anfang des Evangeliums verbunden. Es gibt jedoch zwei Unterschieden zu Mk 1,1.14 f.

Der erste Unterschied ist: Das Evangelium wird nicht nur in Galiläa und Judäa verkündigt, sondern *weltweit* „unter allen Völkern" und „in der ganzen Welt" (Mk 13,10; 14,9). Paulus spricht oft von den Völkern, zu denen er gesandt ist, selten von „allen Völkern",[34] nie von einer Verkündigung „in der ganzen *Welt*". Diese Wendung findet sich nur im sekundären Mk-Schluss, vielleicht angeregt durch Mk 14,9: „Geht hin in alle *Welt* und predigt das Evangelium aller Kreatur" (Mk 16,15).

Der zweite Unterschied ist: Subjekt der Verkündigung sind nicht der Täufer und Jesus, sondern *Christen in der Zeit nach Ostern.* Damit hängt eine wichtige Akzentverschiebung zwischen Mk 13,10 und 14,9 zusammen: In Mk 14,9 wird in den Inhalt des Evangeliums die *Vergangenheit* einbezogen. Mit der Evangeliumsverkündigung ist „Erinnerung" verbunden: Die Salbungsgeschichte wird zum Gedenken an die anonyme Frau erzählt, wo immer das Evangelium verkündigt wird (εἰς μνημόσυνην αὐτῆς Mk 14,9). Auch Paulus kennt das Erinnerungsmotiv beim Abendmahl (εἰς τὴν ἐμὴν ἀνάμνησιν 1 Kor 11,24.25). Verkündigt wird in ihm Jesu Tod (1 Kor 11,26). Die Erinnerung umschließt im MkEv dagegen das ganze Wirken Jesu vom Täufer bis zu seinem Tod und umfasst auch Nebengestalten. Mk 14,9 entspricht dem Programm des MkEv, eine Darstellung des Wirkens Jesu zu geben. Das unterscheidet ihn von Paulus.

Der Mk-Evangelist hat den Evangeliumsbegriff drei Mal im Sinne seiner Intentionen abgewandelt. Bei den Doppelbelegen für „Evangelium" entspricht jeweils der erste der (vor-)paulinischen Tradition: Das Evangelium meint das Evangelium von Jesu Person (1,1), umschließt Leidensnachfolge (8,35) und wird unter allen Völkern verkündigt (13,10). Der jeweils zweite Beleg entspricht dem Programm des MkEv: Das Evangelium ist Verkündigung durch den irdischen Jesus (1,14 f), verlangt Nachfolge mit Unterhaltsverpflichtung der Gemeinden (10,28) und umfasst Erinnerungen an den irdischen Jesus, die auch Nebengestalten umschließt (14,9). Paulus und Mk greifen beim Begriff εὐαγγέλιον auf eine gemeinsame Tradition zurück, wandeln sie aber unabhängig voneinander in verschie-

---

34 Röm 1,5; 15,11 (= Ps 117,1); Gal 3,8 (= Gen 12,3) und in der sekundären Schlussdoxologie des Römerbriefs Röm 16,26.

dener Weise ab. Doch müssen wir an diesem Punkte noch genauer fragen: Knüpft das MkEv nur an vorpaulinische Traditionen an oder auch an die mündliche Überlieferung von Paulus oder sogar an seine schriftlichen Briefe?

4 „Der Anfang des Evangelium" und die Verkündigung am Grab – ein paulinischer Rahmen?

Erklärt sich vielleicht die Entsprechung von Anfang und Schluss des MkEv durch Rückgriff auf Paulus? Dem Boten Gottes (1,2–8), der dem Auftritt Jesu vorangeht und ihn deutet, entspricht am Ende der anonyme Bote, der das leere Grab interpretiert. So wie in Mk 1,1 eine Nähe zu Paulus bzw. der vorpaulinischen Tradition spürbar ist, so auch in der Engelbotschaft in Mk 16,6.[35]

4.1 Der „Anfang des Evangeliums" in Mk 1,1

Zum Vergleich für Mk 1,1 lässt sich der Anfang des Römerbriefs heranziehen.[36] Wie in Mk 1,1ff das „Evangelium" durch alttestamentliche Prophetentexte vorhergesagt wurde, so wird es auch in Röm 1,1 „vorher verkündigt durch die Propheten in heiligen Schriften". Deren Weissagungen werden im Röm 1,3 in zwei Stufen verwirklicht: zunächst durch die Geburt Jesu als Davidssohn, dann durch seine Einsetzung zum Sohn Gottes „in Macht" seit der Auferweckung von den Toten. Im MkEv gibt es ebenfalls Stufen, wobei wir über ihre Folge unsicher sind. Entweder ist die erste Stufe die Verkündigung des Täufers, die zweite die Einsetzung Jesu zum Sohn Gottes durch die Taufe (Mk 1,9–11). Oder die erste Stufe umfasst das ganze Evangelium, die zweite die nachösterliche Verkündigung. Es ist auf jeden Fall kein Zufall, dass die beiden ersten Werke an der Schwelle zur urchristlichen „Literatur", der Römerbrief und das MkEv, mit εὐαγγέλιον programmatisch den Inhalt ihrer Schriften bezeichnen. Sie begründen mit diesem Begriff den *öffent-*

---

35 Joel Marcus, „Mark – Interpreter of Paul", *NTS* 46 (2000), 473–487, gab mit seinem Aufsatz den Anstoß, das Verhältnis des MkEv zu Paulus neu zu bestimmen. Die Übereinstimmung in der *theologia crucis* ist für ihn das entscheidende Argument. Ähnlich schon Ulrich B. Müller, „Die christologische Absicht des Markusevangeliums und die Verklärungsgeschichte," *ZNW* 64 (1973), 159–193: Wenn im MkEv das Kreuz zum Vorzeichen aller Theologie wird, so sieht er darin eine Nachwirkung des Paulus.
36 Vgl. Oda Wischmeyer, „Romans 1–7 and Mark 1: 1–13 in Comparison" (in diesem Band).

lichen Anspruch ihrer Botschaft.[37] Das Besondere bei Mk ist, dass sie bis Ostern mit Geheimnis umgeben ist.

Die Betonung des „Anfangs" gehört zur hellenistischen Herrschaftsrhetorik.[38] Die Begriffe ἀρχή und εὐαγγέλια finden sich auch in der Inschrift von Priene (OGIS 458).[39] Diese Inschrift führt einen neuen Kalender ein, der mit der Geburt des Augustus beginnt. Zur Begründung wird gesagt, dass „mit dem Geburtstag dieses Gottes für die Welt die ganzen Nachrichten (τῶν δι' αὐτὸν εὐαγγελίων), die von ihm ausgehen, ihren *Anfang* nahmen (ἦρξεν)" (Z.40). In der Rahmenerzählung zur Geschichte dieses Beschlusses spielt der „Anfang" ebenfalls eine Rolle: Der Geburtstag des Kaisers gilt als der Tag, der „dem Beginn (ἀρχή) aller Dinge gleichkommt" (Z.5). Er ist für den Menschen *„Anfang* (ἀρχήν) seines Lebens und seines Daseins" (Z.10) und als dieser *„Anfang"* (ἀρχήν) Grund zur Freude (Z.20). Auch die Anfangsrhetorik am Anfang des MkEv sagt: Eine neue Weltepoche hat begonnen, die das Leben der Welt und der Menschen verändert, aber nicht der Kaiser, sondern Jesus selbst ist Anfang des Heils. Die Anklänge an biblische Anfänge in Gen 1,1 und Hos 1,2a (LXX) machen deutlich: Diesen Anfang hat Gott gesetzt. Durch sein Handeln beginnt eine neue Weltzeit.

Umrätselt ist bis heute, worin der Anfang im MkEv zu sehen ist. In der Priene-Inschrift ist es die Geburt des Kaisers – also ein Ereignis vor der Zeit, in der er Frieden schaffen konnte. Erst wenn er zur Herrschaft kommt, wird er die Welt verändern. Der „Anfang der Evangelien" bezieht sich in Priene also auf die Vorgeschichte vor der Wende zum Heil. Vermutlich ist es im MkEv ähnlich. Schon in alttestamentlichen Weissagungen (in Ex 23,20/Jes 40,3) war das Kommen Jesu und seines Vorläufers vorausgesagt. Mit dem Auftreten des Täufers begann die Erfüllung dieser Weissagungen. Der „Anfang des Evangeliums" ist also ein „Vorlauf" vor der Wende zum Heil: Diese könnte mit der Einsetzung Jesu zum Sohn Gottes beginnen (Mk 1,9 – 11). Aber auch das ist noch kein öffentlicher Anfang, er bleibt von Geheimnis umgeben, während „Evangelium" eine öffentliche Proklamation meint. Erst mit der Auferweckung von den Toten, darf überall verkündigt werden, dass Jesus der Sohn Gottes ist (Mk 9,10 – 11). In der Herrschaftsrhetorik beziehen sich „Evangelien" auf Ereignisse wie den Geburtstag, den Amtsantritt, die Hochzeit oder den Sieg des Kaisers, manchmal auch auf seinen Tod, wenn er mit Erleichterung aufgenommen wurde wie bei Tiberius (εὐαγγέλια Ant. 18,229) oder Domitian (εὐαγγέλια Philostrat, vita Apoll. 8,27,1). Vergleichbar ist das Evangelium im MkEv in einer Hinsicht: Das Stichwort *Evangelium* fällt immer dann, wenn Jesus

---

37 Vgl. Gerd Theissen, *Die Entstehung des Neuen Testaments als literaturgeschichtliches Problem*, Heidelberg 2007, 84 – 92: „Ein Bios mit öffentlichem Anspruch".
38 Vgl. E.K.Ch. Wong, *Evangelien*, 80.
39 Griechischer Text und deutsche Übersetzung in St. Schreiber, *Weihnachtspolitik*, 122 – 127.

einen Schritt weiter auf dem Weg zur vollen Offenbarung seiner Würde ist. Jesus verkündigt das *Evangelium* Gottes in 1,14–15, weil er vorher durch den Geist die Macht erhalten hat, über den Teufel zu siegen (1,9–13). Durch das Messiasbekenntnis des Petrus (8,26–32) wird Jesu Würde zum ersten Mal von den Jüngern erkannt. Jetzt wird ihnen gesagt, dass sie sich um seinetwillen und um des *Evangeliums* willen bewähren müssen. Die Salbungsgeschichte (14,3–9) ist Toten- und Messiassalbung zugleich. Von ihr erzählt auch das „*Evangelium*". Die öffentliche Evangelienproklamation beginnt zwar erst nach Ostern, aber schon im Leben Jesu haben wir von Geheimnis umgebene „Anfänge" des Evangeliums.[40] Das MkEv verleiht dabei Ostern durch die Auferstehungsbotschaft in Mk 16,6 einen besonderen Akzent.

4.2 Die Botschaft in Mk 16,6

Das MkEv beginnt mit einer Ankündigung, die erwarten lässt, sein Inhalt sei dem paulinischen Evangelium von Jesus Christus vergleichbar. Am Ende des MkEv steht noch einmal ein Summarium der Verkündigung von Jesus, das an das paulinische Kerygma erinnert, wie folgende Synopse zeigt:[41]

Das „Evangelium" des Paulus in 1 Kor 15,3b–5	Die Engelbotschaft in Mk 16,6–7
Christus starb,	Jesus von Nazareth wurde gekreuzigt.
wurde begraben,	Siehe der Ort, wo sie ihn hingelegt haben.
wurde auferweckt,	Er wurde auferweckt.
erschien	Ihr werdet ihn sehen,
Kephas und den Zwölfen	die Jünger und Petrus

---

40 Der „Anfang des Evangeliums" bezieht sich entweder auf das Auftreten des Täufers oder auf das Wirken Jesu, also das ganze Buch. Denn traditionell begann das Evangelium als Verkündigung von Kreuz und Auferstehung. Bestechend ist die Überlegung J. Marcus, *Mark 1–8*: „Interpreting 1:1 as the title of the book, therefore, helps make sense of the abrupt ending at 16:8 – the *beginning* of the good news is over on Easter morning; after that 'the good news of Jesus' will continue through the life of the church." Durch die Geheimnismotive kann der Mk-Evangelist dem Leser das Bewusstsein geben, dass er im Vorgriff schon im Leben Jesu mit diesem nachösterlichen Evangelium konfrontiert wurde.

41 Die Nähe zur urchristlichen Bekenntnisformulierung in 1 Kor 15,3 wurde schon oft registriert: Vgl. Rudolf Pesch, *Das Markusevangelium* II (HThK II,2, Freiburg: Herder 1977), 533; Joachim Gnilka, *Das Evangelium nach Markus* (EKK II,2, Zürich/Neukirchen: Benziger /Neukirchener Verlag 1979), 339.

Hier berühren sich MkEv und Paulus. Die urchristliche Bekenntnisformel spricht davon, dass Christus „gestorben" (ἀπέθανεν) ist, Paulus aber spricht betont vom Gekreuzigten als dem ἐσταυρωμένος im Perfekt Partizip (1Kor 1,23; 2,1; Gal 3,1) – genauso wie der Engel im MkEv: „Ihr sucht Jesus, den Nazarener, den Gekreuzigten (τὸν ἐσταυρωμένον). Er ist auferstanden. Er ist nicht hier" (Mk 16,6).[42] Verwandte Redeweisen im Urchristentum sind von Paulus oder Markus abhängig. Sicher gilt das für Mt 28,5, wahrscheinlich auch für das σταυρωθείς im Petrusevangelium (EvPetr 13,56). In der Bezugnahme auf den Gekreuzigten könnte ein Reflex der Botschaft des Paulus vorliegen. Wenn das MkEv in seiner Osterbotschaft freilich vom auferstandenen „Nazarener" spricht, verbindet er die Osterbotschaft mit der ganzen Geschichte Jesu und weicht dadurch in charakteristischer Weise von Paulus ab.[43]

5 Überlegungen zum traditionsgeschichtlichen Ort des MkEv

Sicher ist nach den bisherigen Ergebnissen: Es gibt traditionsgeschichtlich Zusammenhänge zwischen paulinischer Theologie und dem MkEv.[44] Beide knüpfen an vorpaulinische Traditionen an. Darüber hinaus könnte das MkEv in einem dialogischen Verhältnis zu Paulus stehen. Einige Züge wie die Rede vom „Gekreuzigten" in Mk 16,7, vielleicht auch die paulinische Stilisierung von Mk 8,34f weisen über eine gemeinsame Tradition hinaus.[45] Diese Berührungen sind auch ohne Kenntnis der paulinischen Briefe vorstellbar. Über Paulus kursierten ja viele mündliche Traditionen im Urchristentum. Das zeigt die Apg. Schon in der Zeit vor

---

[42] Theo K. Heckel, „Der Gekreuzigte bei Paulus und im Markusevangelium", *Biblische Zeitschrift* 46 (2002) 190–204.
[43] Vgl. J. Marcus, *Mark 8–16*, 1085: „... and so the combination *ton Nazarênon ton estaurômenon* reveals both similarity to and difference from Paul; like Paul, Mark concentrates on the continuing significance of Jesus' death, but unlike Paul, he also writes a Gospel that provides an extended introduction to the Nazarene's passion".
[44] Nicht alle gemeinsamen Traditionen konnten diskutiert werden. Die Abendmahlsworte in Mk 14,22–25 und 1 Kor 11,23–25 sind verwandt: Das MkEv feiert das Abendmahl als Bundesmahl (Ex 24,8), Paulus feiert es als Mahl des „neuen Bundes". Eine neue Beziehung hat Eve-Marie Becker, „2 Corinthians 3;14,18 as Pauline Allusions to a Narrative Jesus Tradition", in: *‚What does the Scripture say?' Studies in the Function of Scripture in Early Judaism and Christianity Vol.2. The Letters and Liturgical Tradition* (Library of NT Studies 470, London/New York: T&T Clark 2012), 121–133, zur Diskussion gestellt: Da 2 Kor 3,18 an den Auferstandenen denkt und Paulus vor Mk schreibt, wird hier an die vormarkinische Fassung der Verklärungsgeschichte angespielt.
[45] Vgl. Troels Engberg-Pedersen, „Paul in Mark 8:34–9:1" (in diesem Band).

50 n. Chr., aus der keine Briefe erhalten sind, muss Paulus Spuren hinterlassen haben: Er missionierte im Auftrag der antiochenischen Gemeinde, vertrat sie auf dem Apostelkonzil und trennte sich im Konflikt von ihr. Am intensivsten wird Paulus Spuren bei denen hinterlassen haben, mit denen er zusammen gearbeitet hat: bei Barnabas und anderen antiochenischen Christen. Barnabas stand im antiochenischen Konflikt am Anfang auf seiner Seite, bildete dann aber zusammen mit Petrus eine zwischen Paulus und Jakobus vermittelnde Gruppe (Gal 2,11– 14). Meine Vermutung ist: Traditionen aus dem Kreis dieser vermittelnden Gruppe um Petrus und Barnabas sind ins MkEv eingegangen.[46] Denn das MkEv verbindet die durch Petrus repräsentierte synoptische Tradition mit Elementen einer paulinischen Theologie. Für diese Annahme kann man folgende Beobachtungen und Überlegungen anführen.

1) Nach dem Apostelkonzil war Paulus das Evangelium an die Völker, Petrus das Evangelium an Israel anvertraut. Die Wendungen *„Evangelium der Unbeschnittenheit"* und das *„der Beschneidung"* in Gal 2,7 weisen auf einen von Paulus unabhängigen Sprachgebrauch. Das MkEv führt das Evangelium aber weder auf Petrus noch auf Paulus zurück, sondern auf Jesus selbst (Mk 1,15). Da Petrus aber zusammen mit seinem Bruder Andreas die ersten sind, die zu „Menschenfischern" bestimmt werden (Mk 1,17) – zweifellos, um das Evangelium zu verbreiten –, ist das Evangelium im MkEv noch immer indirekt mit Petrus verbunden. Jedoch bahnt Jesus selbst, und d. h. weder Petrus noch Paulus, den Weg zur Heidenmission: Jesus beauftragt den Gerasener mit der Verkündigung in seinem Haus: ἀπάγγειλον in Mk 5,19 erinnert im Wortstamm an εὐαγγέλιον. Der Gerasener verkündigt dann in der ganzen Dekapolis. Jesus selbst bestätigt in Mk 13 den Auftrag an alle Jünger, das Evangelium allen Völkern zu verkündigen (Mk 13,10). Paulus ist diese Verbindung des Evangeliums mit dem irdischen Jesus und allen Aposteln vertraut, was oft übersehen wird.[47] Denn er schreibt in 1 Kor 9,14:[48] „So hat auch der Herr befohlen,

---

[46] Ich habe diese Hypothese schon einmal in: Gerd Theißen, *Die Religion der ersten Christen. Eine Theorie des Urchristentums* (Gütersloh: Gütersloher Verlagshaus 2000), 346–348, kurz skizziert.

[47] Oft wird übersehen, dass der Begriff „Evangelium" auch bei Paulus mit dem irdischen Leben Jesu verbunden wird: (1) mit seiner Geburt aus Davids Stamm (Röm 1,3), (2) mit der Aussendung der Apostel (1Kor 9,14) und (3) mit seinem Tod (1 Kor 15,3). Alle Stellen sind bei Paulus Tradition. An solch eine Tradition kann der Mk-Evangelist anknüpfen, wenn er das Evangelium vor Ostern „anfangen" lässt. Für Paulus beginnt das Evangelium erst mit Ostern.

[48] Sie klingt auch sonst in 1 Kor 9 an. Vgl. Björn Fjärstedt, *Synoptic Traditions in 1 Corinthians. Themes and Clusters of Theme Words in 1 Corinthians 1–4 and 9* (Uppsala: Teologiska Institutionen 1974). Wahrscheinlich führt Paulus diese Ausrüstungsregeln auf den irdischen Jesus

dass, die das *Evangelium* verkündigen, sich vom *Evangelium* ernähren sollen." Vorher spricht Paulus von Petrus und den „übrigen Aposteln" (1 Kor 9,5f). Das „Evangelium" ist hier nicht erst wie sonst bei Paulus die nachösterliche Verkündigung. Das MkEv knüpft an diesen weiteren Evangeliumsbegriff an, wie er hier gegen den sonstigen Sprachgebrauch des Paulus in 1 Kor 9,13 sichtbar wird, und korrigiert die einseitige Zuordnungen des „Evangeliums" zu Petrus und Paulus. Es macht Jesus zum Ursprung des Evangeliums. Im MkEv finden insofern die Auseinandersetzungen des Apostelkonzils ein Echo und ein Ende.

2) Der Evangeliumsbegriff des Apostelkonzils könnte sich auch in einem zweiten Punkt im MkEv widerspiegeln: Petrus hat dort die Heidenmission bejaht. Sie wurde durch Offenbarung an Paulus legitimiert, so wie die Israelmission durch Offenbarung an Petrus begründet wurde (Gal 2,8f). Die Offenbarung an Petrus ging der an Paulus voraus. Auch Paulus erkennt an, dass das Evangelium zuerst (πρῶτον) den Juden, dann den Heiden gilt (Röm 1,16; 2,9,10). Aber er nivelliert diesen Unterschied immer wieder: Alle, Juden und Heiden, sind Sünder (Röm 3,9; 11,32). Alle sind in der Gemeinde gleich (Gal 3,28). Es gibt keinen Unterschied zwischen ihnen (Röm 10,12). Das MkEv aber hält am Vorrang der Juden fest. Jesus sagt zur Syrophönikerin: „Lass zuerst (πρῶτον) die Kinder satt werden ..." (Mk 7,27). Sie überzeugt Jesus, weil sie die Vorrangstellung der Juden anerkennt. Eine solche Öffnung für Heiden ohne radikale Gleichstellung von Juden und Heiden ist im Kreis um Petrus und Barnabas gut vorstellbar. Eine gemäßigte Öffnung wird ja auch sonst mit Petrus und der Bekehrung des heidnischen Centurio Cornelius in Caesarea verbunden (Apg 10,1–11,18). Könnten solche Petrusüberlieferungen vorausgesetzt sein, wenn sich im MkEv ein anonymer römischer Centurio als erster Heide zu Jesus bekennt (Mk 15,39) und sein Bekenntnis neben das Bekenntnis des Juden Petrus (Mk 8,29) zu stehen kommt?

3) Paulus und Barnabas, die auf dem Apostelkonzil gemeinsam auftreten, unterschieden sich von Petrus und den anderen Aposteln dadurch, dass sie ihren Lebensunterhalt selbst verdienten. Ihnen war bewusst, dass Jesus eigentlich befohlen hatte, dass Apostel vom Evangelium leben (1 Kor 9,14). Diese Position wird im MkEv an einer redaktionell gestalteten Stelle auch ausdrücklich mit dem „Evangelium" verbunden, wenn den Jüngern verheißen wird, dass sie hundertfachen Ersatz für ihre verlassenen Familien finden werden (Mk 10,28f; vgl. auch Mk 6,8). Das MkEv steht hier also der Position des Petrus nahe, der in

---

zurück, nicht auf den Erhöhten. Wenn er die Einsetzungsworte zum Abendmahl in 1 Kor 11,23ff als Worte des „Herrn" zitiert, denkt er eindeutig an den irdischen Jesus.

Mk 10,28 f ja auch der Gesprächspartner Jesu ist, und es weicht von der Position des Paulus ab. Eben deshalb könnte es im Dialog mit ihm und Barnabas stehen. Nach dem MkEv haben die Jünger nämlich alles verlassen, um Jesus nachzufolgen. Neben vielen Personen, die die Jünger verlassen, werden auch Äcker genannt. Von Barnabas war bekannt, dass er einen Acker verkauft und den Erlös der Gemeinde gespendet hatte (Apg 4,37). Das geschah so selten, dass sich dieser eine Fall ausnahmsweise der Erinnerung eingeprägt hat. Ist an Christen wie Barnabas gedacht, wenn von denen die Rede ist, die Äcker verlassen haben? Natürlich ist ein „Verlassen" von Äckern (Mk 10,28) kein „Verkauf". Aber im Kontext des MkEv umschließt „Verlassen" auch ein „Verkaufen". Denn der reiche junge Mann war aufgefordert worden, seine Habe zu *verkaufen* (Mk 10,21). Die Jünger aber sollen so dargestellt werden, dass sie die Nachfolgebedingungen erfüllen, an denen er gescheitert ist.

4) Aufschlussreich ist ferner die Einstellung zu Speisefragen im MkEv: Mk 7,15 – 19 erinnert an die Position von Petrus und Barnabas im antiochenischen Streit (Gal 2,11–14). An und für sich ist die Unterscheidung von rein und unrein willkürlich (Mk 7,15). Jesus sagt aber nicht, welche praktischen Konsequenzen daraus zu ziehen sind. Er trifft nur eine prinzipielle Feststellung über den Ursprung von rein und unrein.[49] Dass daraus praktisch folgt: „Alle Speisen sind rein", ist eine zusätzliche Geheimlehre Jesu, in der ein Lasterkatalog verarbeitet wird, wie wir ihn als Form oft in den paulinischen Briefen finden. Solche Geheimlehren signalisieren: Es ist besser, wenn man mit diesen Themen nicht in die „Öffentlichkeit" geht, um kein Ärgernis zu verursachen.[50] Bei erfolglosen Exorzismen (Mk 9,28 f)[51] und Rangstreit in der Gemeinde (9,33 – 37) ist das plausibel, beim Verbot der Ehescheidung (10,10 – 12) dort nahe liegend, wo Ehescheidungen (wie in einer heidnischen Umwelt) selbstverständlich waren. Bei Rein und Unrein ist es ganz evident (Mk 7,17 – 23). Denn hier hatten die Gemeinden schon früh erfahren, dass diese Fragen ein Konfliktpotential enthalten (Gal 2,11 – 15). Die Position der vermittelnden Partei von Petrus und Barnabas im antiochenischen Konflikt kommt der des MkEv nahe: An und für

---

49 Vgl. G. Theißen, „Das Reinheitslogion Mk 7,15 und die Trennung von Juden und Christen", in: G. Theißen, *Jesus als historische Gestalt* (FRLANT 202; Göttingen: Vandenhoeck 2003), 73 – 89.
50 Vgl. die Geheimlehre Jesu in Mt 17,24 – 27 über die Tempeldrachme. Sie hat den Zweck, Ärgernis in der Öffentlichkeit zu vermeiden. Ein vergleichbares Motiv könnte hinter den vier Geheimlehren im MkEv stehen.
51 Vormoderne Heiler übernehmen oft nur Kranke bei Heilungsaussicht. Die anderen sortieren sie aus. Als Albert Schweitzer in Lambarene anfing, riet ihm ein einheimischer Mitarbeiter, die unheilbar Kranken nach Hause zu schicken, das würde seinen Ruf als Arzt festigen. A. Schweitzer hat sich nicht an diesen Rat gehalten. Vgl. Nils Ole Oermann, *Albert Schweitzer 1875 – 1965. Eine Biographie* (München: Beck 2009), 140.

sich ist alles rein, deshalb konnten Petrus und Barnabas am Anfang mit Paulus die Speisegebote missachten. Aber um Streit zu vermeiden, können sie ihre eigenen Überzeugungen auch „geheim" halten. Daher hielten sie die Speisegebote anderen Judenchristen zuliebe ein, obwohl sie deren Prämissen nicht teilen.⁵²

5) Auch in der *theologia crucis* der Engelbotschaft (Mk 16,7) und in der Dialektik von Tod und Leben in der Leidensnachfolge (Mk 8,34 f) klingt möglicherweise der antiochenische Konflikt nach. Nach Gal 2,12 ff betont Paulus nämlich in ihm den Bruch mit der Vorzeit: „Ich bin mit Christus *gekreuzigt*" (Gal 2,19 f). Wie in Mk 16,7 begegnen das Stichwort „Kreuzigen" und die Dialektik von Tod und Leben. Wieder finden wir im MkEv einen „Dialog" mit Paulus, der nicht literarisch vermittelt sein muss. Dass seine *theologia crucis* nicht nur durch seine Briefe bekannt wurde, zeigt der Satiriker Lukian von Samosata, der anonym von Paulus als dem ersten Gesetzgeber der Christen spricht: Er habe die Christen gelehrt, „jenen gekreuzigten Sophisten anzubeten" (τὸν δὲ ἀνεσκολοπισμένον ἐκεῖνον σοφιστήν, Per.Prot. 13).⁵³ Die Aussage von Jesus „dem Gekreuzigten" (ἐσταυρωμένος) findet sich im Martyrium des Polykarp im Munde von Heiden (Eus KG IV, 15,41). Erst recht können Christen die *theologia crucis* kennen, ohne die Briefe des Paulus gelesen zu haben. Interessant ist dabei, dass im MkEv indirekt Petrus für die *theologia crucis* der Engelbotschaft in Mk 16,7 beansprucht wird: Die Frauen sollen die Botschaft des Engels den Jüngern und Petrus mitteilen, sagen aber aus Furcht niemandem etwas. Möglicherweise soll der Leser schließen: Niemand konnte diese Botschaft kennen – außer Petrus und die anderen Jünger, wobei vorausgesetzt wäre, dass die Frauen ihnen später doch noch die Botschaft ausgerichtet hätten. Möglicherweise soll der Leser aber auch denken: Petrus und die anderen Jünger sind unabhängig von den Frauen dem Auferstandenen begegnet, was ihre (auf unabhängigen Zeugen basierende) Botschaft glaubwürdig macht. Auf jeden Fall wird hier eine an Paulus erinnernde *theologia crucis* mit Petrus verbunden.

Diese Zuordnungen der Berührungen zwischen Paulus und MkEv zu einem Milieu um Petrus und Barnabas passt ausgezeichnet zur altkirchlichen Tradition über die Entstehung des MkEv. Nach Papias hat „Markus" das MkEv aufgrund mündlicher Traditionen des Petrus verfasst (Euseb KG III, 39,14 f). Markus galt als Neffe des

---

52 Eine andere Deutung vertritt E.K.Ch. Wong, *Evangelien*, 89–98: Das Mk-Evangelium will gegen Paulus zur ursprünglichen Lehre Jesu zurückkehren.
53 Vgl. dazu Peter Pilhofer in: P. Pilhofer u. a. (Hg.), *Lukian. Der Tod des Peregrinos. Ein Scharlatan auf dem Scheiterhaufen* (SAPERE IX, Darmstadt: Wiss. Buchgesellschaft 2005), 64.

Barnabas (Kol 4,10). Er war mit Paulus und Barnabas verbunden (Apg 12,25; 15,37.39) und begegnet später in der Umgebung des Petrus (1 Petr 5,13). Es ist zwar m. E. unwahrscheinlich, dass im MkEv Erinnerungen des Petrus niedergeschrieben sind.[54] Die altkirchliche Zuschreibung des Evangeliums an einen Markus in der Umgebung des Petrus ist dennoch traditionsgeschichtlich aufschlussreich: Die Namen Markus, Barnabas und Petrus stehen für eine vermittelnde Strömung im Urchristentum, in der sich synoptische Überlieferungen mit dem Einfluss des Paulus (unabhängig von seinen Briefen) verbunden haben. In diesem traditionsgeschichtlichen Milieu könnte das älteste Evangelium entstanden sein. Das MkEv ist ja in der Tat so geschrieben, dass der Verfasser am ehesten an Petrus als Garanten der (synoptischen) Tradition denkt. Er teilt mit Paulus einige Traditionen, grenzt sich jedoch von ihm ab: Das Evangelium für die Heiden ist Aufgabe aller Apostel, der Vorrang der Israelmission gilt ohne Vorbehalt, mit dem Evangelium ist ein Unterhaltsanspruch verbunden, in Speisefragen denkt er pragmatischer als Paulus. Dabei hat das MkEv eher den Paulus der antiochenischen Zeit als den Paulus der späteren Europamission im Blick. Später konnte Paulus nämlich Unterstützung von seinen Gemeinden annehmen (Phil 4,10–20), konnte im Streit zwischen Starken und Schwachen über Speisefragen pragmatisch denken (1Kor 8,1–11,1; Röm 14,1–15,6) und den grundsätzlichen Vorrang Israels betonen (Röm 9–11).[55] Der Mk-Evangelist dürfte sein Evangelium in der festen Überzeugung geschrieben haben, er gebe Jesustraditionen wieder, die Petrus und andere Jünger vermittelt haben. Petrus ist Zeuge von Anfang an (Mk 1,16ff) und wird am Ende als Zeuge der Auferstehungsbotschaft genannt (Mk 16,7). Aber der Mk-Evangelist teilt nicht immer die Sichtweise des Petrus: Er macht wiederholt deutlich, dass Petrus Jesu Würde missverstanden hat (Mk 8,27–33; 9,2–10). Ich

---

[54] Die Argumente sind: Der Mk-Evangelist gibt in seinen Erzähltexten geprägte Traditionen wieder, die durch mehrere Erzähler und wiederholtes Erzählen geformt sind. Er schweigt von der grundlegenden Ostererscheinung vor Petrus und kennt neben der Grabesüberlieferung nur eine Gruppenerscheinung vor den Jüngern (einschließlich des Petrus) in Mk 16,7. Sofern er in Mk 9,2–10 Reminiszenzen einer Ostererscheinung vor Petrus verarbeitet hat, wertet er die in ihr begründete Christuserkenntnis des Petrus als unzureichend. Nach dem Apostelkonzil galt Petrus als Ursprung des „Evangeliums" für die Juden, das MkEv aber führt den Ursprung und Anfang des „Evangeliums" auf Jesus selbst zurück. Das MkEv weiß, dass Petrus eine Schwiegermutter hatte, sagt aber nichts von der Frau des Petrus, die ihn später begleitete (1 Kor 9,5). Weiß er vielleicht doch etwas von ihr? In der Antwort an *Petrus* in Mk 10,28 spricht Jesus nicht davon, dass die Jünger ihre Frauen verlassen haben.

[55] Wenn Paulus Juden einen Vorrang als Weinstock gibt, so ist das der Vorrang einer radikalisierten Gnade – weil Juden nach Entfernung aus dem Weinstock wieder eingepfropft werden. Ihre Rettung ist vom Erfolg seiner Heidenmission abhängig. Dieser Vorrang Israels ist nicht mit Mk 7,27 vergleichbar.

vermute daher: Der Verfasser des MkEv kennt synoptische Jesustraditionen, die er mit Petrus assoziiert, darüber hinaus aber kennt er auch Paulus, will beide Traditionen verbinden und ist im Milieu des syrischen Christentums zu Hause.[56]

Diese Berührung mit Paulus – wenn auch nicht mit dem Paulus der Europamission und der dort entstandenen Briefe – passt zu den wenigen Jesustraditionen bei Paulus. Wenig beachtet wurde dabei bisher, dass *alle* Aussagen des Paulus über den historischen Jesus durch das MkEv bestätigt werden: Jesus gilt als Davidssohn.[57] Einer seiner Brüder heißt Jakobus;. daneben hat er weitere Brüder.[58] Er erlaubt keine Ehescheidung, hält alles für rein,[59] sendet seine Jünger ohne Vorrat in die Welt.[60] Unter den Jüngern ist Petrus verheiratet.[61] Jesus deutet bei seinem letzten Mahl seinen Tod.[62] Er wird verraten, misshandelt, gekreuzigt und begraben.[63] Juden und Römer sind beteiligt.[64] Nach seinem Tod erscheint er dem Petrus und den Zwölfen.[65] Sie wurden überzeugt: Er lebt.[66] Darüber hinaus klingen

---

56 Wir wissen nicht, wer das älteste Evangelium geschrieben hat. Johannes Markus könnte trotz aller Schwierigkeiten (trotz der geographischen Fehler in Mk 5,1ff und 7,31) sein Verfasser sein. Es basiert aber wohl kaum auf Petruserinnerungen. Die Verbindung zu Petrus wird bei Papias wahrscheinlich betont, um dem ältesten Evangelium Legitimation zu verschaffen. Möglicherweise wurde das MkEv aber erst sekundär „Markus" zugeschrieben: Im Vergleich zum beeindruckenden MtEv mit einem Apostel als Verfasser war die Zuschreibung des weniger imponierenden MkEv an einen Apostelschüler plausibel. Darin äußert sich ein Werturteil, wie es auch Papias bezeugt, wenn er das MkEv gegen Kritik verteidigt. Aus dem Lk-Prolog geht zudem hervor, dass Evangelienautoren keine Augenzeugen sein mussten. Das Argument, bei einem fingierten Verfassernamen hätte man einen Apostelnamen gewählt und nicht den eines Apostelschülers, ist nicht so stark, wie man meinen könnte. Ferner wurde das MkEv m. E. wahrscheinlich in Syrien geprägt, weil sich die im MkEv nachweisbaren Traditionen hier begegnet sind. Sein traditionsgeschichtlicher Ort muss aber nicht sein Entstehungs- und Publikationsort sein. Seine älteste Bezeugung führt mit Papias in den Osten. Oft wird vergessen, dass Papias von einer Entstehung des MkEv in Rom nichts sagt, das erschließt erst Irenäus aus dem Zeugnis des Papias (adv.haer. III,1,1,2). Zum Bild des Markus im frühen Christentum vgl. C. Clinton Black, *Mark, Images of an Apostolic Interpreter* (Minneapolis: Fortress 1994).
57 Röm 1,3; Mk 10,47f.
58 Zu Jakobus vgl. Mk 6,3 / Gal 1,19; 1Kor 15,7; zu den weiteren Brüdern 1 Kor 9, 5; Mk 6,3.
59 Zum Scheidungsverbot vgl. 1 Kor 7,10 / Mk 10,10 – 12; zur Reinheit: Röm 14,14 / Mk 7,15.
60 Zur Aussendung ohne Vorräte vgl. 1 Kor 9,14 / Mk 6,8f.
61 Zum verheirateten Petrus vgl. 1 Kor 9,5 / Mk 1,29 – 21.
62 Vgl. die Einsetzungsworte 1 Kor 11, 21– 26 / Mk 14,22 – 25.
63 Vgl. zur Misshandlung Röm 15,3 / Mk 15,15.19, zur Kreuzigung: Gal 3,1/ Mk 15,24, zum Begräbnis 1 Kor 15,3 / Mk 15,42 – 47.
64 Verantwortlich für den Tod Jesu sind Juden in1 Thess 2,15 / Mk 14,53 – 65 und Römer: 1 Kor 2, 8 / Mk 15,1ff.
65 1 Kor 15,3; Mk 16,7.
66 1 Kor 15,3ff; Mk 16,6.

bei Paulus Jesusworte aus der Logienüberlieferung an, ohne dass sie explizit auf Jesus zurückgeführt werden. Wenn die expliziten Aussagen des Paulus über Jesus aber ausnahmslos mit dem Jesusbild des MkEv übereinstimmen, dann spricht das dafür, dass Paulus sein Wissen aus einem Überlieferungsstrom bezog, der später auch im MkEv schriftlich fixiert wurde.

Unser Ergebnis ist: Das MkEv steht in einer synoptischen Tradition, die mit den Jüngern Jesu (mit Petrus an ihrer Spitze) verbunden ist, es führt aber zugleich einen Dialog mit Paulus, der durch mündliche Traditionen vermittelt ist. Paulus wiederum zeigt in seinen Briefen eine gewisse Nähe zu dem Traditionsstrom, der später im MkEv niedergeschrieben wurde. Diese gegenseitigen indirekten Einwirkungen lassen sich am ehesten in Syrien vorstellen – unabhängig davon, wo das Mk-Evangelium letztlich niedergeschrieben und publiziert wurde. J. Marcus ist daher zuzustimmen: „Mark writes in the Pauline sphere of activity and shows some sort of Pauline influence in his thought, although he is not a member of a Pauline ‚school' ... he has not studied, internalized, and imitated Paul's letters."[67] Der traditionsgeschichtliche Ort des MkEv könnte das syrische Christentum sein, in dem sich Paulus und Petrus, Barnabas und Markus begegnet sind. Das MkEv ist Ausdruck einer vermittelnden Richtung. Es hat seinen traditionsgeschichtlichen Ort im großen Strom der synoptischen Jesusüberlieferungen, deren Träger im syrischen Urchristentum mit Paulus in Verbindung gekommen waren.

---

67 J. Marcus, *Mark 1–8*, 75.

Eve-Marie Becker
Earliest Christian *literary activity*: Investigating Authors, Genres and Audiences in Paul and Mark

1 The quest for *literary activity*

The production and reception of literary texts is embedded in a larger environment, which we call "Literaturszene" or *'literary activity'*.[1] By this, we mean the social and cultural infrastructure viz. the 'literary life'[2] that has been established at various prominent political and cultural centers, such as Athens, Alexandria or Rome, since Classical antiquity. The founding and upkeep of libraries or the formation of rhetorical schools (cf. Suetonius, *De grammaticis et rhetoribus* 3.4)[3] are the most visible signs of this *literary activity*. However, as well as prominent places, we might also assume an important and widespread literary environment from Hellenistic times onwards.[4]

In part, *literary activity* mirrors the overall structure in which all factors of producing, receiving and preserving literature interact (albeit in different times, cultures and languages). However, we also have to consider the existence of various literary sub-systems, which we could call 'clusters' or 'claims' of *liter-*

---

[1] Cf. in general: T. Paulsen and P. L. Schmidt, "Literary activity." *BNP* 7 (2005): 638–650; eidem, "Literaturbetrieb." *DNP* 7 (1999): 317–329, 317: "L(iteraturbetrieb) wird definiert als jede Form der Interaktion zw(ischen) Autoren oder den Interpreten ihrer Werke... und anderen an deren Produktions- oder Rezeptionsprozeß Beteiligten (zum Beispiel Auftraggeber, Publikum, Leser) ...". Recently, D. N. Sánchez Vedramini, *Eliten und Kultur. Eine Geschichte der römischen Literaturszene* (240 v.Chr.–117 n.Chr.), Tübinger althistorische Studien 7 (Bonn: Habelt, 2010), has tried to reconstruct the Roman "Literaturszene" from 240 BCE to 117 CE. Such a reconstruction is very much under dispute, as C. W. Hedrick shows in his review of the book: Idem, "Rezension: Dario N. Sánchez Vedramini: Eliten und Kultur. Eine Geschichte der römischen Literaturszene (240 v.Chr.–117 n.Chr.), Bonn: Habelt, 2010." *Sehepunkte* 12 (february 2012), Nr. 2, http://www.sehepunkte.de/2012/02/19707.html.
[2] See the translation of E. Fantham's book into German, below.
[3] C. Suetonius Tranquillus, *De Grammaticis et Rhetoribus*. Edited with a translation, introduction, and commentary by R. A. Kaster (Oxford: Clarendon Press, 1995). – In general see: T. Morgan, *Literate Education in the Hellenistic and Roman Worlds*, Cambridge Classical Studies (Cambridge: Cambridge University Press, 1998).
[4] Cf. H. Flashar, *Aristoteles. Lehrer des Abendlandes* (München: C. H. Beck, 2013), 15: "Es gab längst einen über die ganze griechische Welt sich erstreckenden regelrechten Buchhandel...".

ary activity, in which diverse cultural or religious groups organize their literary life specifically.

My contribution aims to provide a survey on how we could imagine a commencing 'literary activity' in earliest Christianity. For this, we need to look at the earliest literary sources respectively – the Pauline epistolography and the Markan gospel narrative – and we have to discuss the following questions: Do we have any evidence for how the production and reception of literature was organized in earliest Christian times? Is it even possible to identify differences between a 'Pauline' and a 'Markan' cluster of *literary activity*? Or, to phrase it in more general terms, how can we best envisage the earliest processes of literary production among Christ believers between ca. 50 and 70 CE, and which role do Paul and Mark play in this respect?

In order to approach this set of questions, we need to acknowledge that there is very little valid information on how earliest Christian clusters organized their literary life. Even Luke in his comprehensive account of the earliest missionary activities and community life does not shed any light on how Paul may have organized his letter-writing, when and how and under which conditions he wrote his letters, or who precisely was in charge of delivering and transmitting them. It is only in Acts 15 that we learn about the writing and transmitting of an 'official letter', which, for Luke, may have even served a primarily documentary function (Acts 15:23–29). Neither does Luke provide clear information about how his gospel-writing was managed, besides some hints on patronage in earliest Christian times ("Theophilus").[5] Instead, the preface in Luke's gospel reveals its author's literary ambitions, techniques, and intentions. The literary milieu as such, however, remains more or less a mystery.

With this in mind, how can we gain an insight into the earliest Christian 'literary scene(s)'? In the field of Classics, it has recently been suggested that the process of *recitatio* – the public reciting of literature – can be seen as a key element of *literary activity*, especially in the 1st and 2nd centuries CE. In general, *recitatio* implies the processes of performing, i.e. publishing, promoting and per-

---

5 Cf. in general: B. K. Gold, *Literary Patronage in Greece and Rome* (Chapel Hill/London: University of North Carolina Press, 1987), especially 1–10: Patronage based on "wealth, occupation, and/or status... (and) a particular attitude toward art and literature", ibid., 1. – J. Marshall, *Jesus, Patrons, and Benefactors. Roman Palestine and the Gospel of Luke*, WUNT 259 (Tübingen: Mohr Siebeck, 2009), limits himself to a socio-historical analysis of patronage (*patrocinium*) in Jesus' time without considering literary strategies, as found e.g. in Lk 1:1–4. For information on the literary motifs of patronage in the sense of dedication, their function within literary culture, and their impact on textual readings, cf.: S. Culpepper Stroup, *Catullus, Cicero, and a Society of Patrons. The Generation of the Text* (Cambridge: Cambridge University Press, 2010). – To the impact of patrons on *recitatio*, e.g.: Pliny, Ep. 8.12.1–2.

ceiving ancient literature. Accordingly, by investigating processes of *recitatio*, i.e. oral performance and the interaction of *audience* and author, it might be possible to gain a valuable insight into the primary setting in which earliest Christian writings – letters as well as gospel narratives – came into being.

2 *Recitatio:* The interaction of author, *audience* and *genre*

In Hellenistic-Roman literary culture, the *recitatio* is a key element of *literary activity*. It seems to be of specific importance for the publication, perception and critique of literature as well as for its production and promotion: it is itself no less than a "social practice".[6] Florence Dupont (1999) even goes as far as to claim that a literary text is only considered as literature *because* of its (public) reading: "the invention of literature... consists in exactly that: the writing of texts that not only demands to be read... but also place the reader in the position of being the subject of the speech act, rather than an instrument for the oral expression of a text".[7]

Recitatio is first and foremost built upon a strong interrelation between author, performer and *audience*. This interaction is not one-sided (producer – performer – recipient), and it cannot be investigated on a synchronic level only, as is often the case in the exegetical field of *performance criticism*.[8] Rather, *recitatio* takes place in a certain historical context and, as such, it also 'retroacts' the process of producing literature. In other words, the *audience* also becomes involved in the historical process of producing literature. We can find examples of this in Virgil's case – at least as it is presented to us by Suetonius – and,

---

[6] F. Dupont, "*Recitatio* and the reorganization of the space of public discourse." In *The Roman Cultural Revolution,* eds. T. Habinek and A. Schiesaro (Cambridge: Cambridge University Press, 1997), 44–59, 56.
[7] F. Dupont, *The Invention of Literature. From Greek Intoxication to the Latin Book,* trans. J. Lloyd (Baltimore/London: John Hopkins University Press, 1999), 9. "Given that the reader becomes the father of the writing that is read, he becomes capable of defending it and commenting on it; since he can master the language that produced it, he can also master its meaning", ibid. Dupont refers (8f.) e.g. to M. Charles, *La rhétorique de la lecture* (Paris: Éditions du Seuil, 1977).
[8] Cf., e.g.: R. Horsley et al., eds., *Performing the Gospel. Orality, Memory, and Mark* (Minneapolis: Fortress, 2006); K. M. Hartvigsen, *Prepare the Way of the Lord. Towards a Cognitive Poetic Analysis of Audience Involvement and Events in the Markan World,* BZNW 180 (Berlin/Boston: Walter de Gruyter, 2012); T. E. Boomershine, "Audience Address and Purpose in the Performance of Mark." In *Mark as Story. Retrospect and Prospect,* Resources for Biblical Studies 65, eds. K. R. Iverson and C. W. Skinner (Atlanta: Society of Biblical Literature, 2011), 115–142.

on a theoretical level, in Cicero, who pays attention to the fact that oratory is dependent on the historical *audience* in quite a similar way (Orat. 8.24).[9]

More generally speaking, we could say that *recitationes* took place in an interactive manner that also had huge implications for the production of literature. Recently, David Konstan (2009) has highlighted how *recitatio* can therefore be seen as an (if not *the*) elementary aspect of *literary activity*. In particular, Konstan analyzes how oral performance also retroacts the production of literature. According to Konstan, the public reading happens by involving the *audience* actively in the process of text-reception.[10] Plutarch's treatise *De audiendis poetis* is of particular interest in this respect. Here, Plutarch discusses explicitly how the youth should react to the reception of poetry. Since Plutarch discussed these questions and similar questions that related to literacy, it implies that ancient authors appreciated the extent to which such an involvement of *audience* in the process of *recitatio* also retroacted their own work as producers of literature. Konstan concludes: "An expectation of active participation on the part of the public – coming up with answers…, accounting for apparent inconsistencies in a text – conditioned the way authors and orators composed their works".[11] We could generalize to an even greater extent here and say: "audience matters for interpretation".[12]

However, we need to go one step further; indeed, we need to progress beyond issues of performance and audience involvement only. As soon as we investigate the interrelation of author and *audience*, we in fact discover that the literary *genre* appears to be the basic link of literary communication. Since a literary *genre* functions as an element of convention, it steers the process by which an author addresses his *audience* and, vice versa, the *audience* itself retroacts the author's literary production. In other words, a literary *genre* stimulates reading expectations. We thus need to widen our preliminary description of the interaction of author and *audience*, by stating: author, *audience* and *genre* are interrelated in the process of literary communication.

---

9 "Semper oratorum eloquentiae moderatrix fuit auditorum prudentia…".
10 Cf. D. Konstan, "The Birth of the Reader. Plutarch as Literary Critic." *Scholia* 13 (2004): 3–27; idem, "The Active Reader and the Ancient Novel." In *Readers and Writers in the Ancient Novel*, Ancient Narrative Supplementum 12, eds. M. Paschalis et al. (Groningen: Barkhuis, 2009), 1–17, especially 8f. – To the text: I,28/14d-36f. Cf. also: Plutarch, *De Audiendo*, I,75/37a-48d.
11 D. Konstan, *Reader*, 13.
12 S. Mason, "Of Audience and Meaning. Reading Josephus' *Bellum Judaicum* in the Context of a Flavian Audience." In *Josephus and Jewish History in Flavian Rome and Beyond*, JSJS 104, eds. J. Sievers and G. Lembi (Leiden/Boston: Brill, 2005), 71–100, 73.

But what role does the *audience* play in regard to the production of literature, and how does the literary *genre* in particular appear as such a communicative tool between author and *audience?* On the one hand, we could speak about the *audience's* expectations of specific *genres* ('gattungsbezogene Erwartungen'): the *audience* retroacts the production of literature according to what its generic expectations are. But, on the other hand, we can also locate certain expectations among the *audience* towards various authors as such ('autorenbezogene Erwartungen')[13] – of course, this only applies once an author is well established. The author-related expectations of the Roman *audience* played an eminent role. This appears to be the case with Virgil, especially when composing his later work (*The Aeneid*, for instance), as Werner Suerbaum (1999) has identified.[14] However, if an author was still unknown to his readers, the *audience's* expectations were directed more towards the literary *genre* than towards the composer of the text himself. Having said this, in both instances, we are dealing in general with socio-cultural conventions. Suerbaum, thus, has defined a literary *genre* as a 'group of texts which can be assigned to certain conventions'.[15]

Therefore, the investigation of ancient *audience* in its interaction with author and *genre* plays a pivotal role in recent studies in the history of ancient literature, such as Graeco-Roman history-writing. If we wish to obtain a glimpse into *literary activity*, we therefore need to look at the interaction of author, *audience* and literary *genre*. Today, these and similar questions are mostly approached from a *comparative* perspective. Simon Hornblower (2004), for instance, suggests how we can use Thucydides' *genre*-oriented reflections on history-writing (1.22.4) to draw further conclusions for reconstructing the *audience* that was addressed in his work. Let us look at the prominent passage in Thucydides' writing in more detail. After unfolding his methodological principles for research and composing the story of events, the historian says:

> "... It may be that the lack of a romantic element in my history will make it less of a pleasure to the ear: but I shall be content if it is judged useful by those who will want to have a clear understanding of what happened – and, such is the human condition, will happen again at

---

13 Cf. e.g. W. Suerbaum, *Vergils "Aeneis". Epos zwischen Geschichte und Gegenwart*, RUB 17618 (Stuttgart: Philipp Reclam jun., 1999), 121 ff.
14 W. Suerbaum, *Vergils "Aeneis"*, ibid.
15 W. Suerbaum, *Vergils "Aeneis"*, 123: "Eine *literarische Gattung*... könnte man als eine Gruppe von Texten bezeichnen, die sich bestimmten Konventionen zuordnen lassen".

some time in the same or a similar pattern. *It was composed as a permanent legacy, not a showpiece for a single hearing...*".[16]

According to Hornblower, Thucydides "writes ostensibly for posterity", but the continuing formulation "does not quite deny the possibility of local, oral performance, perhaps of certain highly-finished episodes".[17] In order to elaborate in more detail on how Thucydides addresses his historical *audience*, Hornblower suggests a contrastive comparison between the literary setting in which the Greek historian was active, and that of the poet Pindar, who was writing approximately two generations earlier:

> "Pindar and Bacchylides were surely equally well travelled and similarly cater for a dual audience... At the same time Pindar undoubtedly writes for local performance, and that is specially true of some of the fragmentary poems... Sometimes Pindar seems clearly to be writing for civic festivals. Sometimes again we can detect the atmosphere of a symposium: of the epinikians, *Nemean 9* for Chromios of Aitna is the most explicit evidence here... But 'sympotic' does not automatically mean 'aristocratic' or 'anti-democratic'... Sometimes epinikian poetry ostensibly written for individuals, and the great families they belong to, can be shown to contain strong signs of civic involvement and to reflect topical civic initiatives and politics... Some odes, the shorter ones, were apparently written for immediate performance by improvised choruses at the athletic festival itself, whereas the longer ones were sung at the victor's home city. Some of the odes, not just the longer ones, were also danced, and choral dancing is not just a collective but a community activity".[18]

Here we can see how diversely and intricately the profile of literary authors and their works can be described. Such a 'profiling' has to be conducted according to a distinctive look at ancient *audiences*, which requires a variety of literary concepts that apply to specific kinds of social events and literary performances. Once again, author, *audience* and *genre* are interrelated. Since the production and reception of literature might be seen as a comprehensive communicative process, we also have to look for the author and the *genre* when investigating the *audience*, and so forth.

---

16 Translation according to: Thucydides, *The Peloponnesian War*, trans. M. Hammond. With an Introduction and Notes by P. J. Rhodes (Oxford: Oxford University Press, 2009), 12 (italics by Eve-Marie Becker).
17 S. Hornblower, *Thucydides and Pindar. Historical Narrative and the World of Epinikian Poetry* (Oxford: Oxford University Press, 2004), 33. – Cf. also e.g.: C. W. Marshall, "Literary Awareness in Euripides and His Audience." In *Voice Into Text. Orality and Literacy in Ancient Greece*, Mnemosyne Supplement 157, ed. I. Worthington (Leiden/New York/Köln: Brill, 1996), 81–98.
18 S. Hornblower, *Thucydides*, 34–36.

In her book *Roman Literary Culture*, Elaine Fantham (1996/98) generalizes this perspective. She demonstrates how *literary activity* has to be analyzed distinctively according to the different types of literature (= *genres*), such as historiography and poetry.[19] In other words, a *literary genre* is part of a specific literary milieu in which author and *audience* interact. We can also apply this insight to the field of early Christian literature. By investigating the *literary activity* in early Christianity, we can get in touch with the literary characteristics of various types or *genres* of texts, such as letters (epistolography) and gospel literature. If we then presume that authors, *audiences* and literary *genres* are indispensably interconnected, we claim the communicative function of literature and do not simply believe in 'literature as such'; a paradigm that refuses any idea of a communicative setting.[20]

At this point, we could make a preliminarily conclusion that the investigation of *literary activity* and the cognition of how authors, *audiences* and literary *genres* interact tell us something about the diverse *literary concepts* that are represented either in the form of letter-writing or in the *genre* of gospel-writing. Viewed in this light, literary *genres* are nothing less than a communicative link between author and *audience*, in that they define the literary interaction between both groups and, thus, contribute to the development of *literary activity*. Therefore, to a large extent, literary *genres* even reflect the literary milieu. In his well-received book *Genres and Readers*, Gian Biagio Conte (1994) highlights the role of literary *genres* in the ancient culture of literacy in a similar fashion: "genres are to be conceived [of] not as recipes but as strategies; they act in texts not *ante rem* or *post rem* but *in re*".[21]

I would now like to examine to what extent these observations can be applied to the two most prominent areas of Christian *Anfangsliteratur*, which were composed between ca. 50 and 70 CE: the Pauline letter-writing and the Markan gospel-concept respectively. By looking at both types of literature compara-

---

19 Cf. E. Fantham, *Roman Literary Culture. From Cicero to Apuleius*, (Baltimore: John Hopkins University Press, 1996); eadem, *Literarisches Leben im antiken Rom. Sozialgeschichte der römischen Literatur von Cicero bis Apuleius*, trans. T. Heinze (Stuttgart/Weimar: Metzler, 1998).
20 E. Hemingway, *A Moveable Feast. The Restored Edition.* Foreword by P. Hemingway. Edited with an Introduction by S. Hemingway (London: Arrow Books, 2011), 112: "... The completely unambituous writer and the really good unpublished poem are the things we lack most at this time". – German translation: Idem, *Paris, Ein Fest Fürs Leben. A Moveable Feast*, trans. W. Schmitz (Reinbek bei Hamburg: Rowohlt Verlag, 2011), 129: "... Was uns in diesen Zeiten am meisten fehlt, sind Dichter, die keinerlei Ehrgeiz haben, und gute Gedichte, die unveröffentlicht bleiben".
21 G. B. Conte, *Genres and Readers. Lucretius, Love Elegy, Pliny's Encyclopedia*, trans. G. W. Most. With a Foreword by C. Segal (Baltimore: John Hopkins University Press, 1994), 112.

tively, we might immediately re-consider what the implications are for investigating authors and *audiences* in earliest Christianity. We may also consider further perspectives and ask whether such a comparative view will ultimately lead us to more specific distinctions regarding the process of literary communication. Will we – ultimately – have to assume different 'literary scenes' behind Pauline epistolography and the Markan gospel-narrative?

3 Author, *audience* and *genre* in 1 and 2 Corinthians

Studying *literary activity* in regard to the *Pauline letters* is a comparatively straightforward task. Let me take the Corinthian Correspondence as an example. Thanks to certain references in the Pauline letters, we have a general idea of how the processes of transporting, delivering, reciting and copying the letters took place: Paul's letters were sent to the Corinthians *via tabellarii* – private messengers who worked as Paul's co-workers and who, at the same time, acted as transmitters of information[22] (e.g. 1 Cor 1). So, first and foremost, there is a social function inherent in the delivery of letters.[23] After the letters were received in church, it is likely that they were read publically in the community (e.g. 1 Thess 5:27; Rom 16:16). This comes *de facto* close to what Harry Gamble (1995) describes as the 'publication' of letters.[24] In other words, we could also call this reading a form of *recitatio*.

Since the process of receiving and interpreting the Pauline letters is primarily based on the factor of *orality*, it also resembles the process of producing letters, because orality is as much a significant factor for the letter-writing act. This corresponds to Paul's own idea of letter-writing as a *communicative* process: the Pauline letters facilitate the communication between Paul viz. his co-workers as senders and the recipients in Corinth during periods of personal absence (*parousia*-motif). Such a communicative function of letter-writing is reflected in three aspects of ancient epistolary theory itself:

---

[22] Cf. e.g. Rom 16:1; 1 Cor 16:10; 2 Cor 8,16f.; Eph 6:21; Col 4:7. – See in general: E.-M. Becker, *Schreiben und Verstehen. Paulinische Briefhermeneutik im Zweiten Korintherbrief*, NET 4 (Tübingen/Basel: Francke Verlag, 2002), 44–102.
[23] Cf. R. Jewett, *Romans. A Commentary*, Hermeneia (Minneapolis: Fortress, 2007), 941–948.
[24] "Publication... occurred when Paul's letter was read aloud to the gathered community, presumably in the context of the service of worship", H. Gamble, *Books and Readers in the Early Church. A History of Early Christian Texts* (New Haven/London: Yale University Press, 1995), 96.

(1) Here the idea of letter-*writing* is to continue a conversation between emitter and recipient, so that the recipient is mentally present while the author is writing the letter and, vice versa, the emitter becomes present in the recipient's house. Paul himself reflects this *parousia-motif* explicitly on several occasions (e.g. 2 Cor 10:10; Phil 1:27; 2:12). The *parousia-motif* reaches so far that it even includes the sharing of and participation in emotionality.[25]

(2) Letter-*reading* is also dependent on the personal interaction between author and reader/*audience*; an insight which is very much emphasized by modern authors. The English writer Vita Sackville-West (1926) writes:

> "The art of reading letters, too, is at least as great as the art of writing them, and possessed by as few. The reader's cooperation is essential. There is always more to be extracted from a letter that at first sight appears, as indeed is true of all good literature, and letters certainly deserve to be approached as good literature, for they share this with good literature: that they are made out of the intimate experience of the writer, begotten of something personally endured".[26]

However, these insights into the letter-reading act also apply to antiquity. Accordingly, Paul's letter-writing is dependent on his *audience's* expectations and their willingness to read and understand him correctly. As was the case with Virgil and the relation he had to his readers, i.e. the Roman *audience*, the Corinthians might have developed certain 'author-oriented expectations': throughout the correspondence process (cf., e.g., 1 Cor 5:9; 7:1), during which Paul soon became a well-established letter-writer, the Corinthians' expectations of the *genre* of letter-writing soon shifted towards *Paul* as the letter-writer (e.g. 2 Cor 10:10). In some parts of 1 Cor and 2 Cor, Paul himself reflects (on) this interdependency, and it does indeed appear that he was increasingly convinced that it was his *person* – not least for reasons of apologetics – that gradually moved into the centre of communication. And for the Corinthians themselves, these '*autorenbezogene Erwartungen*' meant that they were increasingly eager to read not simply *what* Paul said, but what *Paul* said, since the literary medium of letter-writing was known to the communities and, for the first time, was well approved.

Paul, in fact, cares about his *audience:* he demonstrates an increasing awareness of the letter-writing act and the letter-reading act (e.g. 2 Cor 1:12–

---

25 Cf. E.-M. Becker, "Paulus als weinender Briefeschreiber (2 Kor 2,4). Epistolare *parousia* im Zeichen visualisierter Emotionalität." In *Der zweite Korintherbrief. Literarische Gestalt – historische Situation – theologische Argumentation. FS zum 70. Geburtstag von D.-A. Koch*, FRLANT 250, ed. D. Sänger (Göttingen: Vandenhoeck & Ruprecht, 2012), 11–26.
26 V. Sackville-West, *Passenger to Teheran* (London/New York: Tauris Parke Paperbacks, 2008), 26.

14; 10:9–11) and, in this frame, reflects the form and function of the letter-*genre* as well as its sub-types (cf. 2 Cor 3:1ff.; Rom 16:1f.). By doing so, he finally develops various ideas on a 'letter-hermeneutics' that reach far beyond the pure oral preaching of the gospel (cf. 1 Thess 1:9). But, even so, his interest in *literary activity* should not be overstated; it remains rather limited, since Paul maintains the idea that his letter-writing has a primarily concrete and situational communicative purpose, aiming to continue his oral proclamation and teaching of the gospel in Corinth as well as his personal administrative work during his personal absence.

(3) Such a strong interdependency between letter-writing and letter-reading influences as well as reflects the *literary characteristics* of the letter-*genre:* in 'real letters', author and *audience* are bound to the same 'level of reference'.[27] Heinrich Dörrie (1974) claims that everything written in a contemporaneous mode in antiquity is in no need of explanation, "denn alle Begleit-Umstände sind allen Hörern und Lesern bekannt"[28]. This statement is certainly true for the Pauline letters; for example, it is consistent with the time when Paul merely pointed to his opponents in Corinth (2 Cor 10–13), offering no further explanation as to their identity, but expecting his readers to know perfectly well about them.[29] In this respect, the Pauline usage of the pronoun τὶς (e.g., 1 Cor 6:1; 2 Cor 2:5; cf. also: 2 Cor 10:10f.), instead of specifying a certain person,[30] is paradigmatic for Paul's letter-writing strategy. Conversely, it can be said that all types of explanatory comments within ancient literature identify an author who does not have a distinct and contemporary group of readers in mind, but who produces a text for a broader and later, possibly posterior, *audience*; or, in any case, for an *audience* that is not defined or limited in advance. Since Paul in his letter to the Romans does not address a sharply defined *audience* but writes for a part-

---

27 For a recent general discussion of the philological dimensions of Roman epistolography, see H. Halla-aho, *The non-literary Latin letters. A study of their syntax and pragmatics*, Commentationes Humanarum Litterarum 124/2009 (Helsinki: Societas Scientiarum Fennica/The Finnish Society of Sciences and Letters, 2009). – Review: G. Galdi, *Gnomon* 83 (2011): 317–322.
28 H. Dörrie, "Zur Methodik antiker Exegese." *ZNW* 65 (1974): 121–138, 122f.
29 Thus, we do not necessarily need to assume that a lack of concrete information would point to a 'hidden transcript': Cf. A. Standhartinger, "Aus der Welt eines Gefangenen. Die Kommunikationsstruktur des Philipperbriefs im Spiegel seiner Abfassungssituation." *NT* 55 (2013): 140–167, 166 – with reference to: E. Heen, "Phil 2:6–11 and Resistance to Local Timocratic Rule: Isa theo and the Cult of the Emperor in the East." In *Paul and the Roman Imperial Order*, ed. R. A. Horsley (New York: Trinity Press, 2004), 125–153. – Cf. also: R. A. Horsley, ed., *Hidden Transcripts and the Art of Resistance*, Semeia Studies 48 (Atlanta: Society of Biblical Literature, 2004).
30 Cf. M. E. Thrall, *The Second Epistle to the Corinthians*, vol. 1, *Introduction and Commentary on II Corinthians I-VII*, ICC (London/New York: T & T Clark, 1994/2004), 171f.

ly unknown or broader group of readers, we can detect that Paul himself might have already had a writing to posterity in mind.

Thus far, we have been able to observe an interdependency between the processes of letter-writing and letter-reading that ultimately points to the fact that the latter significantly influences the process as well as the *genre* of letter-writing. In other words, Paul's concept of letter-writing is embedded in a specific literary environment or milieu, or rather a *literary activity*, where author and *audience* are interconnected by means of a specific literary *genre:* the *genre* of a Pauline 'community-letter'.[31]

4 Author, *audience* and *genre* in Mark

Studying *literary activity* behind the Markan gospel is a rather complicated task[32] since, on the textual level, we lack clear remarks on authorship as well as the intended *audience:*[33] We have no superscriptions nor adscriptions, which – in the case of the Pauline letters – would at least lead us to the primary addressees. So, how can we progress further and shed light on the 'literary scene' behind the Markan gospel?

In recent Markan scholarship, focus has been placed on either the investigation of *audience*[34] – partly in a historic[35] but mostly in a synchronic sense[36] – or

---

[31] For the *genre* of Pauline letters, see: Cf. C. Hoegen-Rohls, *Zwischen Augenblickskorrespondenz und Ewigkeitstexten. Eine Einführung in die paulinische Epistolographie*, BThSt 135 (Neukirchen-Vluyn: Neukirchener, 2013).
[32] Cf. recently: E. W. Klink III, "Gospel Audience and Origin: The Current Debate." In *The Audience of the Gospels. The Origin and the Function of the Gospels in Early Christianity*, LNTS 353, ed. idem (London/New York: T&T Clark, 2010), 1–26.
[33] The lack of superscriptions and adscription in the case of the Markan gospel, however, has some interesting implications (see below).
[34] The discussion concerning the Gospel's audience(s) still suffers from an overly narrow approach to genre-matters ('biography'). See also various contributions, in: E. W. Klink III, ed., *The Audience of the Gospels. The Origin and the Function of the Gospels in Early Christianity*, LNTS 353 (London/New York: T&T Clark, 2010); E. W. Klink III, "Conclusion: The Origin and Function of the Gospels in early Christianity." In *ibid.*, 153–166, 165 also points to these kinds of presuppositions.
[35] On the quest for primary addresses: Cf. R. Bauckham, "For Whom Were Gospels Written?" In *The Gospels for All Christians. Rethinking the Gospels' Audiences*, ed. idem (Edinburgh/Grand Rapids: W. B. Eerdmans, 1998), 9–48. Bauckham's suggestions have not satisfied Markan scholars so far, for instance when read against patristic evidence: Cf. M. M. Mitchell, "Patristic Counter-Evidence to the Claim that "The Gospels Were Written for All Christians"." *NTS* 51 (2005): 36–79; cf. the response to this: R. Bauckham, "Is there Patristic Counter-Evidence? A

the discourse on literary *genre*.³⁷ So far, it has not been claimed that a literary scene must have existed in which author, *audience* and *genre* interact. With this in mind, it could be suggested that the investigation of author and *audience* would illuminate the literary *genre* and, vice versa, that the *genre*-discourse would reveal important insights into the profiling of author and *audience*. However, Markan scholars have thus far failed to reach a comprehensive appraisal of *literary activity*³⁸ as well as a discourse on how it – in the case of the Markan gospel – might have been placed in the literary history of the early Principate.³⁹

Response to Margaret Mitchell." In *The Audience of the Gospels. The Origin and the Function of the Gospels in Early Christianity*, LNTS 353, ed. E. W. Klink III (London/New York: T&T Clark, 2010), 60–110. However, one can doubt if the Markan community as such can be identified: " I do not think that there are convincing arguments for connecting the author of Mark to a particular community, neither Rome nor Antioch. But, in my opinion, this does no harm. It is more important to draw a cultural, rather than a regional, portrait of the author, i.e. to understand Mark's author as a cultural person", O. Wischmeyer, "Forming Identity Through Literature: The Impact of Mark for the Building of Christ-Believing Communities in the Second Half of the First Century C. E." In *Mark and Matthew, Comparative Readings I: Understanding the Earliest Gospels in their First-Century Settings*, WUNT 271, eds. E.-M. Becker and A. Runesson (Tübingen: Mohr Siebeck, 2011), 355–378, 364. – Cf. on the socio-historical profile of the Markan gospel: H. N. Roskam, *The Purpose of the Gospel of Mark and its Historical and Social Context*, NT.S 114 (Leiden/Boston: Brill, 2004); I. H. Henderson, "Reconstructing Mark's Double Audience." In *Between Author & Audience in Mark. Narration, Characterization, Interpretation*, New Testament Monographs 23, ed. E. Struthers Malbon (Sheffield: Sheffield Phoenix Press, 2009), 6–28. – Cf. also: A. Winn, *The Purpose of Mark's Gospel. An early Christian Response to Roman Imperial Propaganda*, WUNT 2.245 (Tübingen: Mohr Siebeck, 2008).

36 Cf. on *oral/aural criticism*, e.g.: C. W. Hedrick, "The Role of 'Summary Statements' in the Composition of the Gospel of Mark. A Dialogue with Karl Schmidt and Norman Perrin." *NT* 4 (1984): 289–311; J. Dewey, "Oral Methods of Structuring Narrative in Mark." *Int.* 43 (1989): 32–44, especially 36: "When one hears the Gospel, the passages (Summarien, E-MB) do not seem set off in kind; they too are 'visible'".

37 Cf., for instance: A. Yarbro Collins, *Mark. A Commentary*, Hermeneia (Minneapolis: Fortress, 2007), 15–44. Cf. also, more generally: J. A. Diehl, "What is a 'Gospel'? Recent Studies in the Gospel Genre." *CBR* 9 (2011): 171–199.

38 Mark's '*Sitz im Leben*' is too soon contextualized especially in the frame of 'service': Cf. e.g. L. Hartmann, "Das Markusevangelium, für die lectio solemnis im Gottesdienst abgefasst?." In *Geschichte – Tradition – Reflexion. Festschrift Martin Hengel*, vol. 1, eds. H. Cancik et al. (Tübingen: Mohr Siebeck, 1996), 147–171; cf. lately: M. Müller, "The Place of Mark and Matthew in Canonical Theology: A Historical Perspective." In *Mark and Matthew II, Comparative Readings: Reception History, Cultural Hermeneutics, and Theology*, WUNT 304, eds. E.-M. Becker and A. Runesson (Tübingen: Mohr Siebeck, 2013), 259–269, 260–261. However, we do not have any evidence for a liturgical reading of early Christian literature in Christ-believing communities up to the second half of the 2nd century CE, cf. O. Wischmeyer, "Forming Identity", especially 367f.; eadem, "Kanon und Hermeneutik in Zeiten der Dekonstruktion. Was die neutestamentliche

In order to survey such a 'literary milieu' comprehensively, we need to consider the interacting of author and *audience* via the production *and* reception of a certain literary *genre*, i.e. the gospel literature. But how can we shed light on the *literary activity* behind the Markan gospel? My suggestion is to learn from recent work in the field of Classics and, from here, we may once again adopt a comparative analysis through which we can examine *literary activity* in Hellenistic-Roman prose literary fields contemporary to the Markan gospel, such as history-writing. In order to illuminate the literary scene behind the gospel writings in the last third of the 1st century CE, we can apply relevant insights to the Markan gospel and its *audience*.

John Marincola (2009)[40] has recently identified that – in contrast to Greek historiography[41] – we do not find many explicit references to the groups of *audience* that are addressed in Roman historiography. Furthermore, in this respect, Roman historiography is quite similar to what we find in the gospel writings. So, what does Marincola do in order to shed light on the interrelation between author and *audience* in Roman historiography? How can this approach possibly help us to analyze and better understand the *audience* of the Markan gospel[42] as well as its effect on the production of the gospel-*genre*?

4.1 *Reconstructing* audience

As a first step, Marincola tries to reconstruct the *audience* of Roman historiography according to what can be said about the implications of the literary *genre*

Wissenschaft gegenwärtig hermeneutisch leisten kann." In *Kanon in Konstruktion und Dekonstruktion. Kanonisierungsprozesse religiöser Texte von der Antike bis zur Gegenwart. Ein Handbuch*, eds. E.-M. Becker and S. Scholz, (Berlin/Boston: Walter de Gruyter, 2012), 623–678, here with reference to: C. Buchanan, "Questions Liturgists Would Like to Ask Justin Martyr." In *Justin Martyr and His Worlds*, eds. S. Parvis and P. Foster (Minneapolis: Fortress, 2007), 152–159.
39 Cf. in general: M. Lowrie, *Writing, Performance, and Authority in Augustan Rome* (Oxford: Oxford University Press, 2009). However, there is an increasing interest among scholars studying early Christianity to consider the intellectual milieu in which early Christianity came into being, cf., for instance, lately: K. Eshleman, *The Social World of Intellectuals in the Roman Empire. Sophists, Philosophers, and Christians* (Cambridge: Cambridge University Press, 2012).
40 Cf. J. Marincola, "Ancient Audiences and expectations." In *The Cambridge Companion to the Roman Historians*, ed. A. Feldherr (Cambridge: Cambridge University Press, 2009), 11–23. – Cf. also: C. Pelling, *Literary Texts and the Greek Historian*, Approaching the Ancient World (London/New York: Routledge, 2000), 1–5.
41 Cf. e. g.: Thucydides, 1.22.4; Polybius, 9.1.2ff. – Cf. in general: A. Momigliano, "The historians of the ancient world and their audiences. Some suggestions." *ASNP* 8 (1978): 59–75.
42 Cf. A. Yarbro Collins, *Mark*, 96ff.

("history's audience").⁴³ This step is possible, since we assume that certain literary *genres* address certain *audiences* specifically:

(a) The subject of literature will correspond to the audience as its social location. Thus, in the case of gospel literature, the *audience* would mainly be 'Christ believers' (Mk 1:14 f.; Lk 1:1–4), who could either be Jesus followers or leading figures of the Jesus movement⁴⁴. Since subject and genre are interrelated, we might also assume that the social milieu and, thus, the *audience* varies according to different styles of writing,⁴⁵ which we can observe from Mark to Luke.⁴⁶

(b) *Conceptual variations* between different texts which belong to the same literary *genre* point to a different or modified *audience*. Such variations are already visible between Mark and Matthew or Luke, but even more so between the gospel writings of the 1st and the 2nd or 3rd century CE.

(c) Historiographical authors tend to write for *posterity* (see already Thucydides). This implies the broadening and enlargement of the group of *audience*, which forms part of the author's literary *strategy*. Such a strategy is already visible on the textual level, even in Mark; by providing factual explanation (e.g. Mark 15:5, 22) or by interlacing narrative comments (e.g. Mark 7:19; 13:14), Mark obviously has a certain *audience* in mind that is neither locally nor temporally connected (directly) to the story told in the gospel narrative. But what could be the literary *intention* behind such a strategy? Thucydides intends to write for posterity since he is convinced that the 'story of events' also provides general insights into the "human condition" (cf. above) and is, thus, of meta-historical significance and importance. Accordingly, the gospel writer Mark will consider his gospel account to be either a founding story or to deliver exceptional insights

---

43 J. Marincola, "Audiences", 11 ff.
44 This is the idea by I. H. Henderson, "Reconstructing", 6, 22 – with reference to e.g. Mark 9:42–50 and to M. Korenjak, *Publikum und Redner. Ihre Interaktion in der sophistischen Rhetorik der Kaiserzeit*, Zet. 104 (München: Verlag C. H. Beck, 2000), 42–46. "Both sophistic audiences and gospel audiences were presumed to include hearers at quite clearly distinguished levels of social status and intertextual competency", I. H. Henderson, "Reconstructing", 22.
45 Dennis Pausch (2004) identifies the fact that, in the 2nd century CE, different groups of readers of biographical literature also depend on different authors/styles of writing (e.g. Pliny; Gellius; Suetonius). Therefore, we need to discuss the social and intellectual coinage of audiences and readers according to specific individual texts: Cf. D. Pausch, *Biographie und Bildungskultur. Personendarstellungen bei Plinius dem Jüngeren, Gellius und Sueton*, Millennium-Studien 4 (Berlin/New York: Walter de Gruyter, 2004), 22–24.
46 Here we have to take into account the meaning of patronage in Lk 1 and in antiquity in general – see above.

into Jesus' mission; in any case, he will view it as a story that keeps its relevance beyond contemporary readers and *audiences*. Mark 14:9 points in this direction.

(d) The Markan gospel is written in Koine and, thus, uses the language of the "dominant power", as Fergus Millar has identified.[47] The gospel literature seems to address a wide and open *audience*. The vast number of text manuscripts documenting the spreading of Matthew's gospel (among others) points to the gospels' general literary success and high dissemination rate of gospel narratives from the very outset.[48]

4.2 "Generic expectations"

As a second step, Marincola works out certain aspects of what he calls "generic expectations".[49] The question raised here is: what does the *audience* expect of the *genre* of history-writing, and how do these expectations influence the historian when composing his work? Such a question leads us closely to the interaction of *audience* and author so that not only processes of receiving, but also processes of producing literature, are considered in their reciprocity. However, in the case of the Markan gospel, our evidence for 'generic expectations' is weak: Mark's gospel writing is the first of a new *genre* and cannot relate to readers' existing expectations. It is worth considering what conclusions can be drawn from this.

(e) We can hardly assume that the *audience* had already developed 'autorenbezogene Erwartungen' (in Suerbaum's terms),[50] since it is unlikely that Mark was already a well-known author. However, against this background, we can view the anonymity under which 'Mark' composes his book in a different light. It could be that Mark – in contrast to Paul – was not able to reveal his

---

[47] F. Millar, "Latin in the Epigraphy of the Roman Near East." In *Rome, the Greek World, and the East*, vol. 3, *The Greek World, the Jews, and the East*, Studies in the History of Greece and Rome, eds. H. M. Cotton and G. M. Rogers (Chapel Hill: The University of North Carolina Press, 2006), 223–242, 226.
[48] D. G. Martinez, "The Papyri and Early Christianity." In *The Oxford Handbook of Papyrology*, ed. R. S. Bagnall (Oxford: Oxford University Press, 2009), 590–622, 595f. However, regarding Mark, the history of textual transmission seems to be less successful: Cf. E.-M. Becker, "The Reception of "Mark" in the 1st and 2nd centuries C. E. and its Significance for Genre Studies." In *Mark and Matthew II, Comparative Readings: Reception History, Cultural Hermeneutics, and Theology*, WUNT 304, eds. eadem and A. Runesson (Tübingen: Mohr Siebeck, 2013), 15–36.
[49] "... orientation, truth, praise and blaime, the 'movement' of history'", J. Marincola, "Audiences", 16–22.
[50] See above.

name, since he was not established nor legitimized as a literary author. Otherwise, the anonymity of the gospel literature would be a matter of literary transmission rather than literary conceptualization; a headline or *titulus* has been inserted later.⁵¹

(f) Since the author of the Markan gospel cannot refer to 'generic expectations', he needs to affiliate his book to the history of literature in a different way. He does this from the outset and, thus, meets general expectations in ancient literature⁵². He offers two options to his readers: by referring to Isaiah (Mk 1:2), he places his writing in the tradition of Israelite prophecy⁵³ and, secondly, by making use of the term εὐαγγέλιον (Mk 1:1; 14 f.), the author of the Markan gospel recalls a keyword of Pauline mission and teaching (e. g. 1 Thess 1–2; Cor 15:1; Rom 1:1) and, in doing so, connects his narrative to the tradition of gospel proclamation.

So, does Mark address an *audience* that is specifically acquainted with Pauline teaching and terminology? And would his gospel account – approximately ten years after Paul's death – accordingly offer a deeper understanding of what εὐαγγέλιον means or how the pre-history of Paul's 'gospel' proclamation might be conceived? Or is the Markan gospel-concept to be read *against* a contemporary 'Pauline' writing, i.e. Colossians (cf. Col 1:5 f., 23)? And does this have a supportive or a competitive literary feature regarding contemporary Pauline pseudepigraphy?

We can make a preliminary conclusion that, for those affiliated with the Christian ἐκκλησία, the term 'gospel' in Mark 1 will sound polyvalent.⁵⁴ Firstly, it defines the early Christian, at least the Pauline, missionary preaching (cf. 1 Cor 15:1; Mark 13:10). Secondly, in the Markan gospel narrative, it is transferred

---

51 Cf. S. Petersen, "Titel II. Neutestamentlich." *LBH* (2009/2013): 601–602.
52 Gian Biagio Conte has emphasized how, in poetic literature, the opening of a work is particularly important: "The opening situates the poetic act and by situating it justifies it", cf.: Idem, *The Rhetoric of Imitation. Genre and Poetic Memory in Virgil and Other Latin Poets.* Edited and with a foreword by C. Segal (Ithaca/London: Cornell University Press, 1986), 69–95 (quotation: 70).
53 It is important to read this quotation formula also in a *literary* sense – for analogies regarding the contents of tradition that is preserved here, cf.: B. Chilton et al., eds., *A Comparative Handbook to the Gospel of Mark. Comparisons with Pseudepigrapha, the Qumran Scrolls, and Rabbinic Literature,* The New Testament Gospels in their Judaic Contexts 1 (Leiden/Boston: Brill, 2010), 63–68.
54 Cf., e.g.: M. Burrows, "The Origin of the Term 'Gospel'." *JBL* 1/2 (1925): 21–33; H. Koester, *Ancient Christian Gospels: Their history and development* (London: SCM Press, 1990), 1–23; P. Pokorný, *From the Gospel to the Gospels. History, Theology and Impact of the Biblical Term 'Euangelion',* BZNW 195 (Berlin/Boston: Walter de Gruyter, 2013).

to Jesus' Galilean ministry (Mk 1:14f). Thirdly, within the act of composing a narrative gospel account, the term is finally assigned to the present gospel narrative itself (Mk 1:1). Thus, the Markan *audience* might expect the following from the gospel narrative: the information, interpretation and narrative conceptualization (= *narratio*) about/of the gospel story, which even includes special knowledge and thus puts the *audience* in a privileged position,[55] and the proclamation and/or missionary propaganda of the gospel as *kerygma*. Regarding the latter, the Markan *audience* would understand itself in continuity with Pauline tradition.

5 Investigating Paul and Mark in the light of *literary activity*

So, what can we learn about the *literary activity* behind the Pauline and the Markan texts respectively? Is it possible to specify diverse literary milieus in early Christian times? By comparing Paul and Mark in order to illuminate the literary milieu in which both *genres* of literature are embedded, we can make several observations:

(a) The Pauline letters and the Markan gospel share a topic: the engagement in the εὐαγγέλιον. This is not exceptional in ancient literature; history, for example, is a topic that is also dealt with in historiography as well as in other kinds of prose-writings and/or treatises (s. e. g. Cicero, e. g. fin 5:51). The *polysemy* of εὐαγγέλιον implies that the subject is already a popular and a prevalent one.

(b) The polyvalent usage of the term εὐαγγέλιον within letter and gospel writings points to a diverse need in dealing with the gospel, either by interpreting it in regard to contemporary questions or by narrating it to the youth and/or later generations. In part, there seems to be a common *literary activity* visible behind the debate on the εὐαγγέλιον in early Christian literature. Even so, we should distinguish between the *audiences* to which the Pauline letters and the gospel narrative are addressed.

(c) The Pauline letters are first and foremost authoritative-written contributions to Paul's ongoing interaction with certain communities. The Markan gospel, however, is primarily a literary narration on the gospel story with an informative

---

[55] Cf. S. P. Ahearne-Kroll, "Mysterious Explanations. Mark 4 and the Reversal of Audience Expectation." In *Between Author & Audience in Mark. Narration, Characterization, Interpretation*, New Testament Monographs 23, ed. E. Struthers Malbon (Sheffield: Sheffield Phoenix Press, 2009), 64–81, 65.

purpose and a proclamatory message. These differences in literary style and strategy can be specified even further:

Firstly, the missing *superscriptio* in the gospel literature does not only mark a significant difference from the letter literature. It also indicates that the gospel writings neither intend to be authoritative literary texts nor to have an apostolically based kerygmatic and/or paraenetic intention (s. differently: parts of later apocryphal gospels). Instead, Jesus himself proclaims the proximity of God's βασιλεία (Mk 1:14f.).[56]

Secondly, the missing *adscriptio* in the gospel literature does not only mark a significant difference from the letter literature. It also indicates that the gospels neither intend to reach a concise *audience* nor a specific community. This does not exclude the possibility, however, that certain communities as communities might have looked for copies of the gospel texts. Besides, individual readers such as 'Luke' had literary access to the Markan gospel.

Thirdly, even if we assume that Paul and Mark share certain Synoptic traditions, we can see a difference in how the authors present these traditions, not only in literary conceptualization but also in the mode of explication: while Paul, for example, refers to the tradition of the Lord's Supper as a *paradosis* (1 Cor 11:23–25; Mark 14:22–24) and points to sayings material in a didactic context (1 Cor 7:10; Mark 10:11), Mark embeds both types of traditions in a pre-historiographical, i.e. a narrative, account and, from here, prepares the Lukan approach to history-writing.[57]

Interestingly, both authors – Paul and Mark – also vary in how they provide possible 'insider information'. In other work, I have argued that 2 Cor 3:4–18 alludes to a Synoptic tradition of a transfiguration scene that is also used in Mark 9:2–8.[58] While Mark narrates an explicit story based on pre-Markan traditions, Paul only alludes to it, and, thus, he presupposes that his readers know what

---

56 For a discussion of this, cf.: E.-M. Becker, "Die Konstruktion von ‚Geschichte'. Paulus und Markus im Vergleich." In *Paul and Mark*, BZNW 198, eds. O. Wischmeyer et al. (Berlin/Boston: Walter de Gruyter, 2014) (forthcoming), see also: G. Theißen, *Die Entstehung des Neuen Testaments als literaturgeschichtliches Problem. Vorgetragen am 27.11.2004*, Schriften der Philosophisch-historischen Klasse der Heidelberger Akademie der Wissenschaften 40 (Heidelberg: Universitätsverlag Winter, 2007), 135.
57 In general: E.-M. Becker, "Patterns of Early Christian Thinking and Writing of History: Paul – Mark – Acts." In *Thinking, Recording, and Writing History in the Ancient World*, ed. K. A. Raaflaub (Hoboken: Wiley-Blackwell, 2014), 276–296.
58 Cf. E.-M. Becker, "2 Corinthians 3:14, 18 as Pauline Allusions to a Narrative Jesus Tradition." In *"What Does the Scripture Say?": Studies in the Function of Scripture in Early Judaism and Christianity*, LNTS 470, eds. C. A. Evans and H. D. Zacharias (London/New York: T & T Clark International, 2012), 121–133.

this story actually is about and which protagonists he has in mind. While Paul's readers seem to be familiar with all circumstances related to the delivery and possibly also to divergent interpretations of this story (cf. H. Dörrie, above), Mark obviously addresses an *audience* which he intends to sustain with solid narrative material.

(d) In terms of characterizing the *literary genre*, we could attempt to invert the perspective. In other words, we could raise the question of how the 'gospel', as a concept of remembering and preaching the substrate of Christian *kerygma*, shifts when it is transformed from an epistolographical to a 'historiographical' writing. To put it differently: how does the literary *genre* as such transform basic patterns of early Christian theology, ethics, social interaction and literary culture (= 'identity')? This question seems to be most important regarding the understanding of Mark's gospel-concept, since Paul's letter-writing is primarily affiliated to the structures of immediate communication while Mark also addresses posterior readers.

Paul and Mark, both authors, use argumentative as well as narrative forms. Therefore, we can hardly claim that from Paul to Mark there was a transfer from the argumentative to the narrative (in an autobiographical context in particular, Paul himself already acts as a narrator).[59] So the question remains: why has Mark, only ca. ten years later than Paul, developed a new literary *genre*[60] that has an overall narrative frame and structure and that deals comprehensively with the narrative on the past as with the 'beginnings of the gospel' (Mk 1:1)? It seems as though it is mainly the divergence of *literary activity* behind Paul and Mark – implying different kinds of literary authority as well as the shift in *audience* and *genre* expectation – that stimulates conceptual differences; either epistolary or pre-historiographical literature points to a diversification of literary milieu(s), already in earliest Christian times. Comparing Paul and Mark thus provides various insights into how early Christian literature came into being and how it forms an essential part of Christian literary communication and *literary activity* in the second half of the 1st century CE. Author, genre and audience cooperate in the processes of the identity-making – indeed in divergence and variety.

---

[59] Cf. to this debate, for instance: R. B. Hays, "Is Paul's Gospel Narratable?." *JSNT* 27 (2004): 217–239.

[60] To the classification of this *genre* see lately: C. Markschies, "Spruchevangelien." In *Antike christliche Apokryphen in deutscher Übersetzung*, vol. 1, *Evangelien und Verwandtes*, eds. C. Markschies and J. Schröter (Tübingen: Mohr Siebeck, 2012), 480–482. – I would like to thank Sarah Jennings (external copyeditor at Aarhus University) for her help with language revision.

Mogens Müller
In the Beginning was the Congregation
In Search of a *Tertium Comparationis* between Paul and Mark[1]

1 Introduction

"In the beginning was the sermon." These often quoted words by Martin Dibelius could be complemented with the equally fundamental statement: "In the beginning was the congregation." Sermon and congregation belong together as inseparable entities and as presuppositions for the emergence of a special Christian literature which is secondary not only to the sermon but likewise to the congregation. This truth was spelled out by the famous Danish clergyman, theologian and hymn writer Nikolaj Severin Grundtvig (1783–1872) in 1825 in his so-called "unparalleled discovery", whereby he overcame the challenge of Rationalism.[2] The Church should not be subjected to any "exegetical papacy", but realise that it was in existence before the New Testament. It is the Church which has created Scripture, not Scripture which has created the Church.[3] Of course it has to be added that with the appearance of the New Testament books and the process of their canonization they became highly influential in the continuing development of the church.

---

[1] For generous help in improving the English of this article I warmly thank Revd. Jim West, ThD. I also want to thank Elizabeth Struthers Malbon for her written comments on the original paper which have contributed to some corrections and clarifications.

[2] Cf. Mogens Müller, "The Hidden Context. Some Observations to the Concept of the New Covenant in the New Testament." In *Texts and Contexts. Biblical Texts in Their Textual and Situational Contexts. Essays in Honor of Lars Hartman*, eds. Tord Fornberg and David Hellholm (Oslo: Scandinavian University Press, 1995), 649–58. In his recent textbook, *Det Nye Testamente – en lærebog* (Copenhagen: ANIS, 2010), 15, Geert Hallbäck coins the sentence: "In the beginning was the service" ("I begyndelsen var gudstjenesten"), pointing to the manifestation of the congregation.

[3] Although not with the same intended consequence, a similar observation was made half a hundred years before by Gotthold Ephraim Lessing in "Zusätze des Herausgebers zu den Fragmenten des Ungenannten." In Lessing (ed.), *Fragmente des Wolffenbüttelschen Ungenannten* (5. Auflage, Berlin, 1895), 299: "Der Buchstabe ist nicht der Geist, und die Bibel ist nicht die Religion. ... Auch war die Religion, ehe eine Bibel war. Das Christentum war, ehe Evangelisten und Apostel geschrieben hatten." – See the recent thorough analysis of Lessing's contribution in Francis Watson, *Gospel Writing. A Canonical Perspective* (Grand Rapids, Michigan: Eerdmans, 2013), 62–103.

From this it naturally follows that the New Testament literature has come into existence to fulfil the needs of the Christian congregations. Thus these writings were primarily meant for internal use. If this is obvious enough in the case of Paul's letters, it has been more difficult to realise with respect to the Gospel of Mark – and the later gospels. It has taken some pain to reach the view that also the gospels were primarily written to answer the needs of the congregations. And to be more precise: to function in the Christian service alongside with readings from the first Bible of the Church, the Jewish holy books which eventually – with the coming into being of Christian holy writings – became the Old Testament.

2 Paul – the first known Christian author

But let us – also for chronological reasons – begin with Paul. It is obvious that the Pauline letters belong to another genre than the gospels. Written in concrete situations and addressing special problems their aim was to support and strengthen the new life which was established through the apostle's preaching of the gospel. Thus – as it has been argued in later years – the *paraenesis* at the end of most of Paul's letters is not only a convention, a fading out after the more important theological argument, but its very conclusion. To be a Christian – according to the mind of Paul – was to live not only in the belief in Jesus Christ as the crucified and resurrected Lord, but also in obedience to the will of God.[4]

The authority and power exercised by the resurrected and glorified in the theological universe of Paul corresponds to a new life according to the will of God. Thus obedience is the turning point in the sequence which the hymn in Philippians 2:6–11 draws of the life of Jesus. In the beginning he renounces his divinity, that is, he leaves his so-called pre-existence to assume humanity. And the only thing we learn about his human life is that he is obedient, even to death on a cross. This obedience is then rewarded with an exaltation which results in the bowing of every knee in heaven and on earth and under the earth and the confession of every tongue "that Jesus Christ is Lord, to the glory of God the Father".[5] In its context this mythical image follows as the justi-

---

[4] The following paragraphs on Paul reproduce parts of my article, "Paul – The oldest Witness to the Historical Jesus." In *Is This Not the Carpenter? Examinations on the Historicity of the Figure of Jesus*, eds. Thomas L. Thompson & Thomas Verenna, Copenhagen International Seminar (London: Equinox Publishing Ltd, 2012), 117–30.

[5] The Bible is quoted according to *The Holy Bible. Revised Standard Version* (London: Thomas Nelson and Sons Ltd, 1952).

fication of an ethical admonition to the Philippians: "Let each of you look not to his own interests, but to the interests of others. Have this mind among yourselves, which you have in Christ Jesus" (Phil 2:4–5).[6] And the conclusion is that the Philippians should show the same obedience "and work out [their] own salvation with fear and trembling; for God is at work in [them], both to will and to work for his good pleasure" (Phil 2:12–13). Similarly, in 2 Corinthians 8:9 Jesus Christ is included as an example, this time for the Corinthians. They are admonished to offer an abundant gift of money for the collection for Jerusalem, and this because "you know the grace of our Lord Jesus Christ, that though he was rich, yet for your sake he became poor, so that by his poverty you might become rich".

The few times Paul adduces words of Jesus – in his terminology they are labelled "words of the Lord" – it is always in the context of admonition. In 1 Corinthians 7:10 Paul thus quotes the Lord for a prohibition aimed at married women against divorce, and later in the same epistle he mentions another commandment of the Lord (1 Cor 14:37), although it is not quite clear which is meant. Only once in his letters does Paul tell about an event from the life of Jesus, namely the institution of the Lord's Supper on the night he was delivered (1 Cor 11:23–25), and characteristically it happens in connection with yet another admonition to the Corinthians to show consideration for each other when coming together for the Supper.

Accordingly, when Paul relates what is basic in Christianity, it is the new conduct of life which is emphasized as what counts. Thus, in Galatians 5:6 it is said: "For in Christ Jesus neither circumcision nor uncircumcision is of any avail, but faith working through love." Later in the same letter (Gal 6:15) we find a similar formula: "For neither circumcision counts for anything, nor uncircumcision, but a new creation" (cf. 2 Cor 5:17). And a third saying in the same vein occurs in 1 Corinthians 7:19: "For neither circumcision counts for anything nor uncircumcision, but keeping the commandments of the Lord." The interpretation of the law, which according to Paul is included in faith in Christ, thus concentrates on the commandments that address the relations to fellow men, while the whole legislation concerning ritual things and what makes one a Jew is abandoned as not constituting any foundation for the proper relationship with God. Accordingly, in Romans 13:8–10, Paul is able to conclude his admonition in the following way:

---

[6] With regard to Phil 2:4 I follow the interpretation of Troels Engberg-Pedersen, "Radical Altruism in Philippians 2:4." In *Early Christianity and Classical Culture. FS Abraham J. Malherbe*, eds. John T. Fitzgerald, Thomas H. Olbricht and L. Michael White. NT.S 110 (Leiden: Brill, 2003), 197–214, understanding the saying as exclusive and not as mostly – and in RSV – in the meaning "not only, but also".

> Owe no one anything, except to love one another; for he who loves his neighbour has fulfilled the law. The commandments: "You shall not commit adultery, You shall not kill, You shall not steal, You shall not covet," and any other commandment, are summed up in this sentence, "You shall love your neighbour as yourself." Love does no wrong to a neighbour; therefore love is the fulfilling of the law (πλήρωμα οὖν νόμου ἡ ἀγάπη; cf. Gal 6:14–15).

However, it is not a new ethic Paul is preaching. It mostly consists of quotations from the law of Moses, namely the ten commandments and the commandment to love one's neighbour as oneself. When, for instance in Galatians 6:15, a new creation is mentioned, it is with regard to the recreation of the mind and will of man which happens in an encounter with the gospel. It is about the indicative behind the imperative. The proclamation of God's love for man aims at creating a new obedience, the reason for which is no longer fear of punishment or the attempt to make oneself in God's eyes deserving of salvation. But belief in God's love, so to speak, brings about the obedience which shows itself in love for fellow man. The transition in the understanding of the law is expressed in Romans 8:2: "For the law of the Spirit of life in Christ Jesus has set you free from the law of sin and death" (cf. Gal 6:3; 1 Cor 9:21).

If one asks for a complex of concepts which connects gift and duty, the answer is to be found in the concept which not without reason gave birth to the name of the Christian part of the Bible, the New Covenant, the New Testament. The letters of Paul also contain the oldest indications of the fact that the earliest Christian communities regarded themselves as the fulfilment of not least the prophecy of the Book of Jeremiah (38:31–34^{LXX})[7] containing this concept, namely the prophecy that God will make a *new* covenant with his people:

> Behold, days are coming, quoth the Lord, and I will make a new covenant with the house of Israel and the house of Jouda. It will not be like the covenant that I made with their fathers in the day I took them by the hand to bring them out of the land of Egypt, because they did not abide in my covenant, and I was unconcerned with them, quoth the Lord, because this is the covenant which I will make with the house of Israel after those days, quoth the Lord. Giving I will my laws in their mind, and I will write them on their hearts, and I will become a god to them, and they shall become a people to me. And they shall not teach, each his fellow citizen and each his brother, saying, 'Know the Lord,' because they shall all know

---

[7] I quote the Septuagint version according to *A New English Translation of the Septuagint and Other Greek Translations Traditionally Included under That Title*, ed. Albert Pietersma (Oxford: Oxford University Press, 2007, ²2009), because the Greek translation, among other things, in v. 33 brings the plural form "laws", allowing for a new legislation, where MT has the singular "law", clearly pointing back to the law from Sinai. The only direct quotation of the passage from Jeremiah in the New Testament, Hebrews 8:8–12, is according to the Septuagint.

me, from their small even to their great, because I will be gracious regarding their injustices, and remember their sins no more.

In the Book of Ezekiel 36:26–27 (cf. 11:19–20) the concept of the new covenant, although in this book it is not called new, is expanded with the feature that God at that time will also offer his people a new heart and a new spirit:

> And I will give you a new heart, and a new spirit I will give in you, and I will remove the stone heart from your flesh and give you a heart of flesh. And I will give my spirit in you, and will act so that you to walk in my statutes and keep my judgments and perform them.

This covenant theology is probably the presupposition of Paul's whole thinking about the new life.[8] In 2 Corinthians 3 it becomes explicit. In this chapter Paul speaks of the Corinthians as a letter from Christ, delivered by the apostle, "written not with ink but with the Spirit of the living God, not on tablets of stone but on tablets of human hearts" (2 Cor 3:3). Clearly then it is the imagery around the institution of a new covenant, not least from the Book of Ezekiel, which here shows its influence. If Paul does not quote Jeremiah 31:31 explicitly – he only speaks of the new covenant here and in 1 Corinthians 11:25, in connection with the institution of the Supper – it is because the aspect of the Spirit is fundamental in his employment of the concept.[9] Thus Paul in what follows speaks of himself – in *pluralis maiestatis* – as the one whose "sufficiency is from God, who has qualified us to be ministers of a new covenant, not in a written code but in the Spirit; for the written code kills, but the Spirit gives life" (2 Cor 3:5–6). I think the 'we' of his self-designation as a "minister of a new covenant (ὁ διάκονος καινῆς διαθήκης)" stands at the very heart of Paul's self-understanding.

Admission into the new covenant took place in baptism, the origin of which it is difficult to map but which all the same occurs as a matter of fact in the letters of Paul (cf. 1 Cor 1:13–17, the "baptism theology" in Romans 6, further Col 2:11–15 where baptism is said to replace circumcision being itself a circumcision

---

8 While previously the concept of the new covenant did not play any substantial role in the understanding of New Testament theology, the picture has changed in the last decades. Pioneering in this regard was Lars Hartman in his article "Bundesideologie in und hinter einigen paulinischen Texten." In *Die paulinische Literatur und Theologie. The Pauline Literature and Theology*, ed. Sigfred Pedersen. Teologiske Studier 7 (Århus: Aros & Göttingen: Vandenhoeck & Ruprecht, 1980), 103–18. Cf. also M. Müller, 'The Hidden Context' (see note 1).
9 This has been shown by Carol K. Stockhausen, *Moses' Veil and the Glory of the New Covenant* (AnBib 116; Rome 1989). Cf. *idem*, "2 Corinthians 3 and the Principles of Pauline Exegesis." In *Paul and the Scriptures of Israel*, eds. Craig A. Evans & James A. Sanders, JSNTSup 83 (Sheffield: Sheffield Academic Press, 1993), 143–164, esp. 154–8.

made without hands). In baptism the baptized partake of the Spirit which makes new life possible and unfolds it. Proclamation and Spirit are bound together by unbreakable ties (cf. 1 Cor 2:4–5) and 1 Corinthians bears witness to the manifestation of the Spirit in the congregational life and shows that it could be hard to control. Thus Paul a couple of times in this letter has to "supersede" what sounds like a Corinthian slogan, namely "all things are lawful", adding: "but not all things are helpful", one time claiming that nothing should enslave anybody (1 Cor 6:12), the second that not everything builds up (1 Cor 10:23). To Paul, being a Christian obviously is to live in the manifestation of the Spirit performing a life in accordance with the will of God with regard to how everyone should behave towards his fellow man.

3 The Gospel of Mark – an attempt to write *Scripture*

To what extent Paul's letters have been read in service also after their first intended use is difficult if not impossible to determine. But 2 Peter 3:15–16 leaves us with an – albeit late – indication that relatively early on they existed as a *corpus*. At the time of 2 Peter, however, a new sort of Scripture had for long entered the Christian service. Probably no more than fifteen to twenty years after Paul wrote his letters, an *anonymus* created a narrative account of the life and accomplishment of Jesus. Of course this author widely collected and included existing stories. But he was the first to put them together in a sequence running from Jesus' baptism and ending with the story about the empty tomb. Thereby this author entered into the genre well known from the Jewish holy books of making theology through telling a story.[10]

Understood in this way, the first gospel was not only later received as *Scripture:* it had also been intended to be so. This seems confirmed from the oldest reference to written gospels in Justin Martyr's *Apology* where he tells about the "the memoirs of the apostles (τὰ ἀπομνημονεύματα τῶν ἀποστόλων)" as being read alongside with the "writings of the prophets" on Christian gatherings on the day called Sunday (I 67), the same memoirs having just been identified as those called "gospels" (αὐτῶν ἀπομνημονεύμασιν, ἃ καλεῖται εὐαγγέλια, I 66).

---

[10] The following paragraphs reproduce parts of an article, "The Place of Mark and Matthew in Canonical Theology: A Historical Perspective." In *Mark and Matthew II. Comparative Readings: Reception History, Cultural Hermeneutics and Theology,* eds. Eve-Marie Becker & Anders Runesson. WUNT 304 (Tübingen: Mohr Siebeck, 2013), 259–69.

Later, in the *Dialogue with Trypho*, Justin even seems to know of four such "gospels" (*Dial* 103:8). Their very use in worship anticipates their later establishment as canonical.

This special aspect in the genesis of the Gospel of Mark has been seen not only by Michael Goulder and others subscribing to a lectionary hypothesis,[11] but also by Lars Hartman. In an article dedicated to Martin Hengel he reaches a positive conclusion to the question whether the Gospel of Mark was written "für die lectio sollemnis im Gottesdienst".[12] In this context, Hartman introduces some important considerations, even assuming that Colossians 3:16 describes the sociolinguistic situation in which the gospels – when first written – found their natural place.

If it was primarily created to be read in worship, the very special character of this text may be explained. As is common in the world of religions, Christian worship constitutes a meeting between God and man. Here – among other things – divine deeds in the past are made present in the cult and relevant to the cult participants. Accordingly, the Jewish Sabbath worship consisted of Scriptural readings, which were followed by an exposition. "Thus the past also was made present and fruitful for the actual life of the believer through the reading of the Gospel and through the teaching and admonition attached to it, as well as in hymns (Col 3:16). In this way the Gospel played an essential role for the identity of the listeners; its content laid the foundation and they were strengthened and confirmed through its being made present."[13]

I think that Lars Hartman has seen a very important aspect in the genesis of the Gospel of Mark – and of the gospel genre as such as represented by the four gospels which later became canonized. They were primarily meant to be read to Christian audiences, maybe even for use in worship alongside or instead of texts from the Jewish "Bible".[14] Thus it is also natural to look for the obvious pattern

---

11 See Goulder, *Midrash and Lection in Matthew* (London: SPCK, 1974, ²1977) and *The Evangelists' Calendar* (London: SPCK, 1978). On Mark, see especially *The Evangelists' Calendar*, 241–306. Marc Goodacre, *Goulder and the Gospels. An Examination of a New Paradigm* (JSNTSup 133; Sheffield: Sheffield Academic Press, 1996) admits the difficulties in evidencing the lectionary hypothesis but refers to its obvious "explanatory power" (360–2).
12 See "Das Markusevangelium, 'für die lectio sollemnis im Gottesdienst abgefasst'?" In *Geschichte – Tradition – Reflexion*. FS Martin Hengel, eds. H. Cancik, H. Lichtenberger & P. Schäfer, vol. 1 (Tübingen: Mohr (Siebeck), 1996), 147–171; quoted according to the reprint in Hartman, *Text-Centered New Testament Studies*, ed. David Hellholm. WUNT 102 (Tübingen: Mohr Siebeck, 1997), 25–51.
13 Hartman, "Das Markusevangelium", 45 (my translation from the German).
14 I am well aware of the selective character of my presentation of the "genre" of the Gospel of Mark. Eve-Marie Becker, *Das Markus-Evangelium im Rahmen antiker Historiographie*. WUNT 194

for the gospels precisely in biblical narratives, and here not least the stories about Elijah and Elisha in 1 and 2 Kings. In this way, the Gospel of Mark fulfils the same function as the Pauline gospel.[15] That is, Paul's gospel facilitated the new life which he expected the members of his congregations to realize. However, where Paul did not of course intend to produce "Scripture", but addressed concrete congregations in concrete situations, the author of Mark took the further step of writing anonymously and now, in principle, for all congregations.

In Markan usage, "gospel" is still the sum of the series of events which he describes, not his book. It has the same content as it has for Paul.[16] This pertains also to the inclusion of the term at its beginning. The step to identify these two entities as one is only a small one.[17] It is also natural to take the genitive Ἰησοῦ Χριστοῦ in Mark 1:1 as primarily an objective genitive and not a subjective one: Jesus Christ is the gospel. On the other hand, the Gospel of Mark indicates a substantial transformation of the different Jesus traditions which had until then existed separately or in small collections. It is to the abiding credit of the *Formgeschichte* approach to point out that the different traditions about Jesus' sayings and actions, his suffering and death, have been formed by their use in preaching and teaching prior to their inclusion in the gospel story. The internal consistency and the final form of many of the single pericopes confirm this conclusion. It also informs us of their authoritative status in preaching and teaching.

By the transformation of a Pauline vertical Christology concerned with the heavenly authority of Christ into a horizontal story, the author behind the Gospel

---

(Tübingen: Mohr Siebeck, 2006), 6–36 ('Geschichte und Probleme der jüngeren Markus-Forschung') offers an instructive overview over other aspects of the discussion of the character and goal of Mark, without, however, mentioning Hartman's contribution.

15 Cf. the old misunderstanding of Paul's expression "my gospel" as referring to a special written gospel. Thus Marcion thought it was the gospel behind the distorting reworking of it in the Gospel of Luke, which, accordingly, he "cleansed", while Eusebius, in his *historia ecclesiatica* III 4:7 refers to a tradition telling that Paul used to think of the Gospel of Luke when he wrote "according to my gospel".

16 Julius Wellhausen expressed it clearly in *Einleitung in die drei ersten Evangelien* (Berlin: Georg Reimer, ²1911), 99: "Es ist nicht Lehre, sondern Botschaft, und zwar naturgemäß von einem bereits geschehenen, nicht von einem erst zu erwartenden freudigen Ereignis. Also nicht die Lehre Jesu oder die Verheißung Jesu, sondern die Botschaft von Jesus Christus. Er ist das Objekt, und das Evangelium handelt über ihn als den Christus. Diese allein dem Wortlaut entsprechende Bedeutung hat τὸ εὐαγγέλιον bei Paulus. Mit Paulus stimmt Markus überein."

17 Cf. the observation in Martin Dibelius, *Die Formgeschichte des Evangeliums* (Tübingen: Mohr (Siebeck), 1919), 81 n. 1; (³1959 = ²1933), 264 n. 1, that where Mark 13:10, 14:9 have τὸ εὐαγγέλιον, the author behind the Gospel of Matthew changes it to τοῦτο τὸ εὐαγγέλιον. "Für Markus ist das Evangelium eine ausserhalb des Buches stehende Grösse; Matthäus kann mit Recht sagen: "dies Evangelium, das ich in meinem Buche darbiete"."

of Mark seemingly wanted to "narrativise" this very authority. However, by moving away in this manner from the more charismatic sort of authority, he opened the door for a more traditional authority that insisted upon offering the true and therefore correct 'Jesus tradition'. This shift, described by means of the authority model of Max Weber, has been emphasized by my colleague Geert Hallbäck in a series of contributions.[18] And another colleague of mine, Troels Engberg-Pedersen, in a brief article, has even argued for the thesis that there exist extensive similarities between Paul in his letters and the Gospel of Mark.[19] Thus Troels Engberg-Pedersen is inclined to understand the Gospel of Mark as a narrativisation of concepts which in one way or the other are central in the letters of Paul as well. This demands a reading of the Gospel of Mark as a narrative construction. Once this is done, it is quite remarkable to notice the amount of meaning which is indisputably present in the text, but which is only seen once one allows oneself to read it in this way. Thus Troels Engberg-Pedersen finds that the reader of Mark would very likely see what we also find in the paraenetic sections of Paul's letters; this leads him to speak of the "indirect paraenesis of the Gospel of Mark" (186).

4 The *tertium comparationis* between the letters of Paul and the Gospel of Mark

The shift from the letter form of Paul to the narrative gospel form of Mark thus had its *tertium comparationis* in the consciousness they aimed at creating, summarized under the heading of "new creation (καινὴ κτίσις)". This aspect would be substantially strengthened if the thesis of my former colleague Henrik Tronier were accepted that the Gospel of Mark was composed as an allegory. Thus Tronier claims "that Mark was *written* the way Philo *interpreted* the biblical narratives

---

18 "The Earthly Jesus. The Gospel genre and the types of authority." In *The New Testament in Its Hellenistic Context*, eds. Gunnlaugur A. Jónsson, Einar Sigurbjörnsson & Pétur Pétursson, Proceedings of a Nordic Conference of New Testamente Scholars, held in Skálholt; Studia theologica islandica 10 (Reykjavík, 1996), 135–45. Later also, for instance, in "Den himmelske og den jordiske Jesus. Om forskellen mellem hymnernes og evangeliernes Jesus-billede." In *Frelsens biografisering*, eds. Thomas L. Thompson & Henrik Tronier. Forum for Bibelsk Eksegese 13 (Copenhagen: Museum Tusculanum, 2004), 190–213. It should be observed that Hallbäck does not draw the same conclusions as I do with regard to the relation between Paul and the Gospel of Mark.
19 "Biografisering. Teologi og narration i Markusevangeliet kap. 8–10." In *Frelsens biografisering* (see the preceding note), 177–89.

about the lives and journeys of Abraham and Moses, the founders of the Jewish people" and that "by means of allegorical *composition* Mark continued the aim and strategy of Paul's allegorical *interpretation* of scripture, the law and the Jewish ethnic identity markers in the construction of a Christ-believing identity vis-à-vis non-Christ-believing, law-abiding Jews".[20] That, however, needs further work to be made probable.[21]

Even without this argument, however, it is possible to argue that the Gospel of Mark consists of a text more or less written as Scripture: it is a story meant for devotional reading to reveal the divine to hearers/readers who constitute a "community of interpretation" by participating in the new covenant and possessing the spirit. Martin Dibelius' definition of the Gospel of Mark "as a book of secret epiphanies (als ein Buch der geheimen Epiphanien)",[22] is still valid. It is, however, only the believing reader/hearer living after Easter who is able to decode the revelation.

Maybe the use of the Gospel of Mark for devotional reading in Christian congregations also offers the clue to the writing of the later gospels. Since it was primarily a *theological* narrativisation of the the gospel of Jesus Christ, representatives of other theological positions found it necessary to rewrite the story of the

---

20 See Tronier, "Markusevangeliets Jesus som biografiseret erkendelsesfigur. 'Ny skabelse' fra Paulus til Markus." In *Frelsens biografisering* (see note 8), 237–71. Quoted according to the "rewritten" English edition in "Philonic Allegory in Mark." In *Philosophy at the Roots of Christianity*, eds. Troels Engberg-Pedersen & H. Tronier. Working Papers 2 (Copenhagen: The Faculty of Theology Biblical Studies Section, 2006), 9 and 10.
21 Interestingly, William R. Telford, *The Theology of the Gospel of Mark* (New Testament Theology; Cambridge: Cambridge University Press, 1999), 67, closes the paragraph on Mark and Paul as follows: "With the development ... of the narrative-critical tools and the increasing sensitivity on the part of scholars to the nuances of narrative theology, Volkmar's original suggestion that Mark's Gospel is an allegorical presentation of Pauline teaching in the form of a narrative may be due ... for a comeback." A recent attempt in this direction, Bartosz Adamczewski, *Q or not Q. The So-Called Triple, Double, and Single Traditions in the Synoptic Gospels* (Frankfurt am Main: Peter Lang, 2010), takes this approach to its extreme. Thus in a chapter with the heading 'Mark's use of his sources', 227–74, Adamczewski concludes that "the critical-intertextual analysis of Mark reveals, [that] the Markan work has been composed as a systematic, sequential, hypertextual reworking of the letters of Paul the Apostle and, to some extent, of Homer's *Iliad*." The thesis of Adamczewski needs a thorough critical assessment, also his dating the Gospel of Mark as late as 100–110 (see 396–7).
22 *Die Formgeschichte des Evangeliums* (Tübingen: Mohr (Siebeck), 1919), 64; (^{3}1959 = ^{2}1933), 232. Cf. 279: "Also ist das Markus-Evangelium seinem letzten Gepräge nach gewiß ein mythisches Buch – aber was von der Prägung gilt, gilt nicht vom Material: die in dem Evangelium gesammelte Tradition ist nur zum kleinsten Teil, in den Epiphanie-Geschichten und in einigen Novellen, mythischen Charakters, in der Mehrzahl ihrer Stücke erscheint Jesus nicht als mythische Person."

earthly Jesus as they received it from their predecessor or predecessors. A comparison of the four New Testament gospels reveal an astonishing freedom to construct and reconstruct the Jesus tradition in order to promote the authors' special understanding of the gospel. In turn, such freedom must be attributed to the author of the first gospel.[23]

---

[23] A key to understand this "freedom" could be the genre or interpretation strategy labelled "rewritten Bible" or "rewritten Scripture". Cf. Mogens Müller, "The New Testament Gospels as Biblical Rewritings: On the Question of Referentiality" (forthcoming in *Studia Theologica*).

II. Texts and Interpretations

Oda Wischmeyer
Romans 1:1–7 and Mark 1:1–3 in Comparison

Two Opening Texts at the Beginning of Early Christian Literature[*]

Romans 1 and Mark 1 are the opening sections of two of our earliest Christian texts and therefore can be regarded not only as historical records or sources but also as important theological statements at the outset of early Christian literature.[1] This general insight leads to the following foci in my comparison: (1) the textual dimension; (2) the literary dimension related to the issue of genre; (3) the literary dimension concerning the question of authorship and audience, the social setting of both texts, as well as the issue of textual pragmatics; (4) the literary dimension of quotations and references; and (5) the literary function of the key term εὐαγγέλιον.

Though a comprehensive comparison would necessitate the inclusion of historical and theological issues,[2] in this essay I am focussing especially on the beginnings of Christian *literature*. Of particular interest is its function as an instrument for the written communication of the central message of those newly-formed groups of Jews and Gentiles who confessed Jesus of Nazareth as Χριστός. My point of departure is the observation that both of these opening sections refer to this central message as εὐαγγέλιον, and give this theme a dominant place at the very beginning of their deliberations or narrative, respectively. This means that in a *literary* comparison of both texts special attention should be paid to the term εὐαγγέλιον and its meaning and function regarding the *writtenness* of the gospel.

---

[*] I am particularly grateful for the helpful references and critical comments of Elizabeth Struthern Malbon and Margaret M. Mitchell made during the Copenhagen conference and to Dieter T. Roth, University of Mainz, for his assistance with the English version of this paper.
[1] In the following I shall use the term 'early Christian literature' in the precanonical sense of: 'literature of Christ-confessing authors and communities'.
[2] One of the most important contributions to the question of the theology of Rom 1 is to be found in G. Agamben's interpretation of Rom 1:1 (G. Agamben, *Il tempo che resta. Un commentato alla Lettera ai Romani* (Torino: Bollati Boringhieri, 2000). See also O. Wischmeyer, "Die Zeitkonzepte von Paulus und Markus im Vergleich." In *Paul and Mark. Two Authors at the Beginnings of Christianity*, vol. 1. BZNW 198 (Berlin/Boston: Walter de Gruyter, 2014) (forthcoming).

1 The texts

1.1 The beginning of the Gospel of Mark has often attracted significant scholarly attention, largely due to the fact that the opening verses of the first Gospel permit an initial and crucial consideration of the *intentio auctoris*, irrespective of the fact that the author remains anonymous.[3] Most scholars agree that the quotation from Isaiah functions as the key statement for interpreting Jesus as Χριστός (1:1) and υἱὸς θεοῦ (1:1)[4] throughout the entire narrative. The function of verse 1, along with the extent and the syntactic structure of verses 1–3 or 1–4, is, however, disputed.

If one regards the indication of time, places, and *personae* as the main components in constructing a narrative, it is evident that the first narrative unit begins with ἐγένετο in verse 4 and includes verses 4–13.[5] The *persona* is John the

---

[3] For the interpretative consequences of the term '*intentio auctoris*' see: "Autorenintention." In *Lexikon der Bibelhermeneutik* (Berlin: de Gruyter, 2009), 63–66. For traces of the *intentio auctoris* in the Gospel of Mark see O. Wischmeyer, "Identity Formation by Literature. The Impact of Mark for the Building of Christ-Believing Communities in the Second Half of the First Century A.D." In *Mark and Matthew*, vol. 1, WUNT 271, eds. E.-M. Becker and A. Runesson (Tübingen: Mohr Siebeck, 2011), 355–378. I prefer referring to the text as having a 'hidden author' instead of considering it an 'anonymous writing' (see footnote 118).

[4] For the discussion of the textual variants involving υἱὸς θεοῦ see the commentaries of J. Gnilka, *Das Evangelium nach Markus*, EKK II/1,2 (Zürich/Neukirchen-Vluyn: Neukirchener Verlag, ³1989); J. Marcus, *Mark 1–8*, AB 27 (New York: Doubleday, 2000); M.E. Boring, *Mark. A Commentary*, The New Testament Library (Louisville/London: Westminster John Knox Press, 2006); A. Yarbro Collins, *Mark*, Hermeneia (Minneapolis: Fortress Press, 2007). M. Peppard, *The Son of God in the Roman World* (Oxford: Oxford University Press, 2011), focusses on the political dimension of the Roman title 'Son of God', and argues that the early Christian title for Jesus must be read in this hermeneutical context. Unfortunately, however, he does not consider the quotation of Isaiah and the whole Jewish tradition.

[5] On the theme of a Markan "prologue" see E.-M. Becker, "Mark 1:1 and the Debate on a 'Markan Prologue'." *Filologia Neotestamentaria* 22 (2009): 91–106. Becker gives a thorough overview of the discussion since the 19th century, and on that basis argues convincingly against H.-J. Klauck, *Vorspiel im Himmel? Erzähltechnik und Theologie im Markusevangelium*, BThSt 32 (Neukirchen-Vluyn: Neukirchener Verlag, 1997). She states "that already Mark 1:4 opens up the Gospel narration and that only Mark 1:1–3 has to be regarded as a literary unity: Mark 1:1–3, however, is in no case part of a 'Markan prologue' or a 'prologue' in itself. These verses are rather more to be understood as a *prooemium* to the overall prose-text of the Gospel narrative, consisting of a 'Buchüberschrift'/title (1:1) and an opening introductory close (1:2–3)", Becker, "Mark 1:1", 91. – A different division is preferred by J. Gnilka, J. Marcus, M.E. Boring, and A. Yarbro Collins who read verses 2–15 as the first narrative unit. See the careful discussion in Marcus, 137f. Lit.: Gnilka, 39, footnote 1. For my own reading see: O. Wischmeyer, "Zitat und Allusion als literarische Eröffnung des Markusevangeliums." In *Im Namen des Anderen. Die Ethik des Zitierens*, eds. J. Jacob and M. Mayer (München: Wilhelm Fink Verlag, 2010), 175–186. For a highly detailed

Baptist, whose agency, place, and time seem to be known by the intended audience; therefore, the author feels that he does not need to provide a biographical, historical, or topographical introduction of John nor of the place of his baptizing ministry. The author does not comment on any of these in detail. This means that the intended audience is expected to have at least some knowledge of the historical and geographical conditions in which John's and Jesus' ministry took place. In other words, the author writes from an internal perspective[6] and expects a Christ-believing readership that already has a certain prior understanding of what will follow in the narrative.[7] In contrast to the beginning of Mark's narrative, Matthew and Luke chose a neutral or external perspective for the *initium* of their narratives by introducing their protagonists through genealogies, nativity stories, and precise dating.

The second narrative unit in Mark begins with the temporal phrase μετὰ δέ (verse 14) that indicates a change of time and at the same time leads the reader to a new place, namely, to the region of Galilee.[8] The structure of verses 4–13 is shaped by the copulative conjunction καί. The textual unit is composed of small narrative sub-units that are connected by καί+verb (Verses 5a.b.6.7.9a. b.10.11.12.13a.b.c). Regarding the *personae,* the appearance of Jesus in verse 9, as a second person after John, causes a slight break within the first unit that carries the narrative forward. In short, Mark 1:4–13 functions as the prehistory of the Jesus narrative in that the verses combine the mission of John the Baptist and the first public appearance of Jesus.

This structure means that 1:1–3 must be read in syntactical contrast to 1:4–13. These first three verses constitute a textual unit of their own, functioning as

---

discussion of the various types of divisions see M.E. Boring, "Mark 1:1–15 and the Beginning of the Gospel." *Semeia* 52 (1990): 43–82. In his commentary, Boring understands verse 1 as a title: "Mark 1:1 is best understood as the author's title to the whole Gospel, rather than as an element in the first sentence of the narrative", Boring, *Mark. A Commentary,* 29. – Recently Morna Hooker has argued that the Gospel of Mark should be read in the context of the movement of the ancient Greek tragedy and that in this perspective Mark 1:1–13 works as prologue: M. Hooker, "Good News about Jesus Christ, the Son of God." In *Mark as Story: Retrospect and Prospect*, SBL Resources for Biblical Study 65, eds. Kelly R. Iverson and Christopher W. Skinner (Atlanta: Society of Biblical Literature, 2011), 165–180, 166.

6 See D.E. Aune, "Genre Theory and the Genre-Function of Mark and Matthew." In *Mark and Matthew*, vol. 1, 145–175, 164: "Mark was produced by a member of a particular discourse community and was intended for intramural consumption". I basically share this perspective; however, in my contribution on "Identity Formation by Literature" I have pointed out (as did A. Yarbro Collins) that a narrative is in any case written for a broader audience.
7 See point 3 of this essay.
8 The same division is found in Nestle-Aland. Collins divides the units between verse 15 and 16, Marcus reads verses 14.15 as sub-unit of what he calls the "Markan Prologue (1:1–15)", 137.

an opening clause for both the gospel as a whole and the first narrative unit.⁹ Since, however, the grammatical structure and the function of verse 1 in relation to verses 2–3/4 remain disputed, despite the many discussions of the interpretation of verses 1–3/4, I shall briefly outline the syntactic proposals:

(1) Verse 1 is an independent sentence without predicate (cf. Mt 1:1) and functions as a heading or title, either of the first narrative unit or of the whole Gospel. Verses 2–4 constitute one compound sentence that compares a quotation from Isaiah with John the Baptist: "According to what is written in Isaiah, ... [so] was John in the desert". In this reading, however, the expected οὕτως would be lacking in verse 4.¹⁰ The Old Testament quotation would – at least initially – be heard or read as an interpretation of John's message.

(2) A different reading integrates verse 1 syntactically into verses 1–3. Verses 1–3 constitute one compound sentence and work as the thematic and narrative opening of the Gospel.¹¹ The καθώς of verse 2 corresponds to the opening phrase ἀρχὴ τοῦ εὐαγγελίου in verse 1. The story of John the Baptist begins in verse 4 and leads the reader into the narrative. The reading of verse 4 as a new and independent sentence makes grammatical sense because the phrase ἐγένετο Ἰωάννης without καί marks the beginning of an independent narrative unit (cf. 14:1 as opening clause of the passion narrative as a whole unit). Furthermore, this reading avoids the problems that are caused in the first proposal by the lack of the particle οὕτως. The problem with this proposal, however, is the lack of a verb in verse 1; nevertheless, in my opinion this proposal remains the most probable one.

(3) A third view divides verses 1–4 into three sub-units: verse 1 is a title without predicate (as in the first proposal). Verses 2–3 are one compound sentence. Verse 4 is a new opening clause for the narrative of John the Baptist.¹² In this reading verse 1 functions as a title for the whole Gospel.

(4) A forth approach is based on the tradition-historical (*traditionsgeschichtliche*) method. Joachim Gnilka understands verses 2–15 as the *initium* of the Gospel of Mark that was composed by Mark, who brought together different tradi-

---

9 With J. Marcus against Becker, Mark 1:1 (see above footnote 5).
10 This is the proposal of Nestle-Aland. A. Yarbro Collins chooses this reading and in her translation inserts the missing ὡς in brackets, 133.
11 This is the proposal of J. Marcus, 141, with which I agree (Wischmeyer, "Zitat", 179). This view was proposed as far back as H.A.W. Meyer, *Die Evangelien des Markus und Lukas*, KEK 1,2 (Göttingen: Vandenhoeck&Ruprecht, ²1846), 12–14.
12 This is the reading of E.-M. Becker, *Das Markus-Evangelium im Rahmen antiker Historiographie*, WUNT 194 (Tübingen: Mohr Siebeck, 2006), 102–111, 238–252 (cf. also her contribution on the Markan prologue, above footnote 5). Becker reads verse 1 as a heading. Her interpretation of verses 1–4 is similar to that of J. Marcus (proposal 2).

tions.[13] According to this perspective, Gnilka translates verses 1.2.3 as separate and independent sentences without verbs and continues by identifying verse 4 as a new and the first complete sentence.

Although I prefer the second proposal, the text offers no definitive indication in one or the other syntactical direction. In other words, it is impossible to achieve certainty concerning the precise syntactical structure of Mark 1:1–3. Eve-Marie Becker has pointed out correctly that the verses 1–3 have a "unique...structure"[14] with regard to the combination of verse 1 (without predicate) and verses 2–3 with its complicated mixed quotation. She prefers the idea that verse 1 functions as a "Buchüberschrift",[15] but that ἀρχή "remains polyvalent",[16] so that we cannot precisely state whether the author refers to the biography of Jesus, to the prophetic roots of the *Heilsgeschichte,* or to the book *initium.* In any case, it is, first of all, clear that the Greek of the author, and especially his syntactical skill, is rather unpolished. At the very least, he wrestles stylistically with the quotation.[17] Secondly, the opening unit's use of the scriptures (καθὼς γέγραπται) reveals not only the author's interest in Isaiah 40 (ἐν τῷ Ἠσαΐᾳ τῷ προφήτῃ) but also its hermeneutical significance for the Jesus narrative as a whole and the story of John the Baptist in particular. Thirdly, the term of ἀρχή indeed remains polyvalent, as E.-M. Becker argues.[18] It is obvious that the author intends to allude to Old Testament opening formulae such as Gen 1:1 or – more specifically – Hos 1:2b.[19] In this sense he writes in the tradition of the *Scriptures.* In addition, however, M.E. Boring points to Phil 4:15, where Paul uses the *syntagma* of 'the beginning of the gospel' in the sense of his missionary proclamation of Jesus Christ.[20] It is possible that Mark 1:1–3 draws together these two areas of religious and literary knowledge shared by both the author and his audience.

1.2 Rom 1:1–7 is the expanded greeting of a letter addressing a variety of themes that was written by Paul to the members of the early Christian communities (κλητοὶ Ἰησοῦ Χριστοῦ) in Rome. These verses constitute a complex, but grammatically correct, syntactic unit whose basic structure is that of the particular Pauline

---

13 Gnilka, *Das Evangelium nach Markus,* 40.
14 Becker, "Mark 1:1", 103.
15 Becker, "Mark 1:1", 100. See the four different options on page 101.
16 L.c.
17 See the considerations concerning the quotation below.
18 See also Boring, *Mark. A Commentary,* 32.
19 See Collins, *Mark,* 131.
20 Boring, *Mark. A Commentary,* 32. Mark 1:1 is close to Paul in more than one point, and the later authors choose very different introductory phrases (see below).

letter opening. This address differs from the Greek form in that instead of employing the usual form: "Paul, to all who are in Rome χαίρειν" he writes: "Paul [...], to all [...] who are in Rome χάρις [...] ὑμῖν". Scholars do not agree on the explanation for the origin of the structure of the Pauline letter opening,[21] but it is a common observation that the expanded address of Rom 1:1–7 requires special attention, both because of its historical context and because of its theological significance.

The text begins in the conventional manner with the name of the letter writer. It is undisputed that Romans is an orthonymous document and that we are reading an authentic Pauline letter. Paul writes under his usual Greek name but without referring to any co-writers, or at least other addressors, as he does elsewhere. The same applies to the addressees, the members of the house churches in Rome, in that Paul does not here mention anybody by name. However, we have some knowledge about a considerable number of named individuals on account of the list of greetings that is added in chapter 16. Since Paul is not known personally by most of the Roman Christians, he introduces himself in an official way, using a tripartite title that includes not only his name,[22] but also the titles δοῦλος Ἰησοῦ Χριστοῦ[23] and κλητὸς ἀπόστολος.[24] Paul adds a further explanation to the second title: ἀφωρισμένος εἰς εὐαγγέλιον θεοῦ.[25] This last phrase provides Paul with the opportunity to explain the main content and fundamental meaning of εὐαγγέλιον θεοῦ, which he accomplishes by inserting a comment with four primary emphases: (1) the *previous history* of the εὐαγγέλιον θεοῦ in verse 2, (2) the *subject* of the εὐαγγέλιον θεοῦ in verses 3–4,[26] (3) his own *authority* and charge regarding the εὐαγγέλιον θεοῦ in verse 5, and (4) the role of the *addressees* in the process of announcing the εὐαγγέλιον θεοῦ in verse 6. Analogous to his threefold introduction, Paul addresses the Romans with care and respect by applying three titles to them as well: 'Romans',[27] ἀγαπητοί, and κλητοί—the same characterization that he applied to himself.[28] In this

---

21 This question is of no importance in the context of this investigation.
22 See R. Jewett, *Romans*, Hermeneia (Minneapolis: Fortress Press, 2007), 99 f.: "Paul" is a *signum*.
23 Also Phil 1:1 (along with Timotheus). Also Tit 1:1: δοῦλος θεοῦ.
24 Also 1 Cor 1:1.
25 See Gal 1:15 in an autobiographical summary. The phrase is not found in any other letter opening.
26 This passage is twofold: verse 3 is concerned with the origin of Jesus, verse 4 is more elaborate and deals with his divine function.
27 See Gal and 1 Cor. Different from Galatians, Paul does not use the address of 'Romans', but 'all Christians in Rome'.
28 See the use of κλητοί in verse 6.

way, he intends to construct and express an equal religious and social status for himself and his addressees. In verses 5 and 6 Paul includes himself and the Roman communities into the process of communicating the εὐαγγέλιον to 'all nations'. Paul closes his address with his usual[29] greeting, which by combining greeting and blessing thereby gives more weight, authority, and religious power to the addressor. The opening as a whole is the expression of Paul's high self-assessment as well as of his attempt to attribute equal honour to the Roman Christians. Furthermore, the elevated language of his address is part of his literary strategy of introducing himself (not his co-workers or other communities) to the Romans (not only to those he knows personally) by means of a tightly constructed and argued document that functions as a kind of official, theological manifesto. In Rom 1:1–7 Paul opens a line of communication with the Roman Christian communities, combining personal communication with a more formal approach. The opening section is so carefully written that we can speak of a literary text in the proper sense of the word.

1.3 By comparing the short texts found at the outset of Mark and Romans in terms of their textual structure we can observe a pattern of vocabulary, ideas, and arguments that have much in common. Both texts very closely connect (1) the authority of the prophets with (2) a ground breaking message (εὐαγγέλιον) and with (3) the person of Jesus as Messiah (Χριστός) and son of God (υἱὸς θεοῦ). At the same time, the lack of a personal introduction by the author of the Gospel of Mark contrasts sharply with the number of titles through which Paul emphasizes his authorship, his person, his mission, and his authority. The Gospel of Mark directs the focus of its audience exclusively to the narrative of Jesus Christ, son of God. The opening of Paul's letter to the Romans, by contrast, claims the author's apostolic authority to proclaim and comment on the εὐαγγέλιον θεοῦ. Roughly the same holds true for the addressees or the audiences: Paul, in his respectful and detailed address to the Christ-believing communities in Rome, combines a personal concern in a current situation with the expression of appreciation and high regard; whereas, the author of the Gospel of Mark gives no indication of the nature of his audience. To put it briefly: both texts deal with the same message (εὐαγγέλιον θεοῦ), but whereas Paul employs an elaborate strategy of pursuing personal communication on equal terms with the Christian communities in Rome, the author of the Gospel of Mark avoids an explicit connection with his audience and instead, by quoting Isaiah, establishes a type of general literary-religious communication with his audience.

---

29 See 1 Cor 1:3; 2 Cor 1:2; Gal 1:3; 1 Thess 1:1; Phil 1:2; Phlm 3.

2 Literature: the question of genre

This first observation leads us to a consideration of the different genres of both texts, as their respective genres have important implications for the different communicative situations discussed above. The Letter to the Romans belongs to the epistolographic genre; the Gospel of Mark is a narrative. Since scholars have not been able to agree on the specific definition of either the genre of Paul's letter or of the Gospel of Mark, I shall briefly consider the present state of the discussion.[30]

2.1 For the Letter to the Romans, Robert Jewett[31] has summarized the main positions advocated in scholarly work since the publication of Karl Paul Donfried's "The Romans Debate" in 1977.[32] Jewett points out that before Wilhelm Wuellner's new approach[33] two major paradigms of interpreting the genre and the purpose of the letter were advanced. On the one hand, Romans was interpreted as "a theological treatise or a circular letter", and on the other hand, as "a situational letter". Jewett observes: "The conclusion one is inclined to draw from these valuable essays…is that the conflict is irresolvable".[34] This statement sheds light on the important scholarly impact made by Wuellner's approach. Jewett argues that Wuellner took a first and decisive step forward by introducing rhetorical theory into the issue and by pleading for the interpretation of Romans as part of the epideictic genre instead of the deliberative or apologetic or forensic genre. Jewett himself offers new and promising perspectives for interpreting the genre of Romans by considering the theory of rhetoric and the theory of epistolography in more detail. He aims to modify Wuellner's hypothesis and present it in a concrete form by applying Theodore C. Burgess' categories of epideictic literature.[35] He pays special attention to Burgess' 19th category of "ambassador's speech".[36]

---

[30] The following remarks may demonstrate that despite the ingenious critique of D.E. Aune, "Genre Theory and the Genre-Function of Mark and Matthew." In *Mark and Matthew*, vol. 1, 145–175, concerning the concept of literary genres as a whole, genre questions still remain important and indispensable interpretative instruments for reading the New Testament texts. Only a careful discussion of the genre issues will provide a reliable basis for fresh interpretative approaches.
[31] R. Jewett, *Romans*, Hermeneia (Minneapolis: Fortress Press, 2007), see also idem, "Romans as an Ambassadorial Letter." *CBQ* 36 (1982): 5–20.
[32] K.P. Donfried, ed., *The Romans Debate* (Minneapolis: Fortress Press, 1977).
[33] W. Wuellner, "Paul's Rhetoric of Argumentation in Romans." *CBQ* 38 (1976): 330–351 (= K.P. Donfried ed., *The Romans Debate*. Rev. ed. [Edinburgh: Clark, 1991], 128–146).
[34] Jewett, *Romans*, 42.
[35] Th. C. Burgess, *Studies in Classical Philology* 3 (1902) 110–113.
[36] Jewett, *Romans*, 43.

On this basis he interprets Romans as "a unique fusion of the 'ambassadorial letter' with several of the other subtypes in the genre: the parenetic letter, the hortatory letter, and the philosophical diatribe".[37] Both scholars, Wuellner and Jewett, combine and mix characteristic features from different fields including epistolography, rhetoric, rhetorical theory, theory of literary genres, and philosophical genres, without, however, discussing the connection between these items. Jewett, moreover, fails to name any literary examples of ambassadorial letters.[38] Nevertheless, Jewett's labelling of the Letter of Romans is extraordinarily helpful because he widens the interpretative horizon of the genre-discussion by pointing out that Paul claimed a "diplomatic role"[39] for himself and that "Paul's self-identity"[40] was strongly shaped by his self-understanding as an ambassador (πρεσβευτής)[41] of God.[42] These observations create the opportunity for a particular political reading of Romans in the sense that Paul understood his apostolic mission within the framework of the *imperium Romanum* (1:5).[43]

If one agrees with Jewett's analysis,[44] the leading role of the term εὐαγγέλιον in the address will become more evident. The ἀπόστολος[45] or πρεσβευτής writes an official letter to a city or a province (in the case of Romans to the Christian communities in Rome) announcing his arrival and promoting and interpreting his broader mission (in the case of Romans the εὐαγγέλιον). He presents the values which he wants to get the people (in the case of Romans the Christian communities in Rome) to embrace and expresses the desire for them to help him with his further mission (in the case of the Christians in Rome with his mission in Spain). Interpreted through the lens of Jewett, the letter is the instrument of a

---

37 Jewett, *Romans*, 44.
38 But see Philo's *Legatio ad Gaium*. The Legatio is not an ambassadorial letter, but the *legatio* is the reason for Philo's report.
39 Jewett, *Romans*, 45.
40 Jewett, *Romans*, 46.
41 See 2 Cor 5:20.
42 See Jewett, *Romans*, 44–46. The term *ambassador* fits Paul better than the more general label of *agent* that is often used in recent scholarship on Paul.
43 See G. Theissen, *Die Entstehung des Neuen Testaments als literaturgeschichtliches Problem*, SHAW phil.-hist. Kl. 40 (Heidelberg: Winter, 2007), on the diplomatic letters, 105 f.; O. Wischmeyer, "Die paulinische Mission als religiöse und literarische Kommunikation." In *Die Anfänge des Christentums*, eds. F.W. Graf and K. Wiegandt (Frankfurt: Fischer, 2009), 90–121.
44 For details see O. Wischmeyer, ed., *Paul. Life, Setting, Work, Letters* (London-New York: Clark, 2012), 256. In my analysis I point out that 1:18–3:20 should be read as τύπος κατηγορικός and 3:21–8:29 as τύπος αἰτιολογικός. Romans has a rich internal structure, a factor that is implicitly conceded by Jewett when he adds – not very clearly however – the aspects of *parenesis* and *diatribe* to his main characteristic of Romans as an ambassadorial letter.
45 See Jewett, *Romans*, 44.

first communication of the εὐαγγέλιον, which can be interpreted as the basic concern of the ambassador's mission. If we read Romans from this perspective, the letter appears as what it is: an instrument of communication within a particular *literary* strategy of the apostle or ambassador Paul that, at the same time, retains its evident theological, i.e. propositional, character.

2.2 The debate over the gospel genre is perhaps even more complicated and intriguing than the debate concerning the genre of Romans. Collins gives an outline of the current state of research in her commentary,[46] sketching the development of the most prevalent view since Charles H. Talbert,[47] namely, the biography-hypothesis. I will not discuss the earlier history of research and the works of, e.g., Johannes Weiß and Friedrich Leo nor the studies of Richard A. Burridge,[48] Klaus Baltzer,[49] and Detlev Dormeyer.[50] Collins herself contributes to the further development of the biography-hypothesis by proposing "a new classification, according to function",[51] listing six types of biography (encomiastic, scholarly, didactic, ethical, entertaining, historical biography). She tends towards the view that the "historical type of biography is the one that is most similar to the Gospels",[52] but also notes their "important affinity with...the didactic type".[53] Further, for Collins the gospels are "close to the historical monograph, which focuses on a single person".[54] Collins argues: "Whether one defines Mark as a historical biography or a historical monograph depends on one's perception of where the emphasis in Mark lies: on the activity and fate of Jesus or on God's plan for the fulfilment of history in which he played a decisive role."[55] In this scholarly context Collins herself enriches the category of 'historical biogra-

---

46 Yarbro Collins, *Mark*, 19–43.
47 Ch.H. Talbert, *What is a Gospel? The Genre of the Canonical Gospels* (Philadelphia: Fortress Press, 1977); idem, "Biographies of Philosophers and Rulers as Instruments of Religious Propaganda in Mediterranean Antiquity." *ANRW* 2.16.2 (Berlin: de Gruyter, 1978): 1619–1651.
48 R.A. Burridge, *What are the Gospels? A Comparison with Graeco-Roman Biography* SNTSMS 70 (Cambridge: University Press, 1992) (2nd rev. ed. Grand Rapids/Cambridge: Eerdmans; Dearborn, MI: Dove Booksellers, 2004).
49 K. Baltzer, *Die Biographie der Propheten* (Neukirchen-Vluyn: Neukirchener Verlag, 1975).
50 D. Dormeyer, *Das Markusevangelium als Idealbiographie von Jesus Christus, dem Nazarener*, SBB 43 (Stuttgart: Katholisches Bibelwerk, ²2002).
51 Collins, *Mark*, 30.
52 Collins, *Mark*, 33.
53 Collins, *Mark*, 33.
54 Collins, *Mark*, 33. See also E.-M. Becker's definition of Mark as "personenzentrierte Geschichtsschreibung", *Das Markus-Evangelium*, 191–194.264f.411.
55 Collins, *Mark*, 33.

phy' or 'historical monograph' through the inclusion of the eschatological dimension in the light of Mark 13. Accordingly, she defines Mark as an "eschatological historical monograph".[56] It is clear that Collins is not particularly interested in a definitive decision on the question of genre in terms of either biography or historiography, but in the particular Jewish category of eschatology. Though Collins thereby – like Jewett for Romans – introduces non-literary, that is theological or religious, categories into the discourse on the genre of the Gospel of Mark, her definition makes sense in that one cannot speak about history and historiography in Mark without acknowledging the eschatological or, more precisely, the apocalyptic character of the idea of history in the first Gospel. To some degree this eschatological aspect distinguishes the Gospel of Mark from Greek and Roman historiographical monographs.[57] Whereas Collins leaves the question of the biography-hypothesis open, and finds the eschatological dimension of Mark more significant, Eve-Marie Becker has modified the discussion concerning the biography-hypothesis, which recently has been advanced once again by Gerd Theissen.[58] She argues in the other direction by painstakingly connecting Mark to Hellenistic historiography and interpreting Mark's narrative as a new subgenre – 'gospel' – in the broader flexible and innovative literary framework or *laboratorium* according to which Hellenistic historiography is defined by contemporary classical scholars. Her definition has three clear advantages compared to the biography-hypothesis. (1) She argues strictly within the field of Hellenistic genre-theory without including additional elements from the fields of history of religions or theological interpretation. (2) The definition enables us to understand the author's *literary* task as shaping a historical narrative on the basis of various traditions and thereby to take seriously the history of traditions behind the coherent narrative. This means that we cannot read Mark simply on the synchronic level like a novel, but must always consider the prior tradition and the author's interest in passing down this tradition to his audience by embedding it in the context of his narrative. (3) Interpreting Mark as at least partly belonging

---

56 Collins, *Mark*, 42.
57 There is, however, a certain eschatological perspective in some Hellenistic-Roman historiographical writings, especially in Josephus. See also the future dimension of Pliny's *panegyricus* on Traian 17 and 18 (R.A.B. Mynors, *XII Panegyrici Latini* (Oxford: Oxford University Press, 1964). See: *Plinius der Jüngere. Panegyrikus. Lobrede auf den Kaiser Trajan*. Edited, translated and with an introduction by W. Kühn, Texte zur Forschung 51, (Darmstadt: Wissenschaftliche Buchgesellschaft, [2]2008). Kühn comments on paragraph 17 as follows: "Eine Vision des Triumphs, den Trajan nach siegreicher Beendigung des 1. Dakerkrieges i.J. 103 feierte. Wenn die Überarbeitung des Panegyrikus nicht später als 101 anzusetzen ist, dann war dies eine echte Prophezeiung", 187.
58 See Theissen's support of the biography-hypothesis: *Entstehung*, 84–92.

to the genre of historiography leads to the recognition of the general historical dimension of the first Gospel. While Paul and the author of Mark share an apocalyptic view of history as God's activity in regard to humanity, the historical dimension of the Gospel of Mark and the historiographical approach to Jesus are not in focus in Romans or in Paul's letters in general.[59]

David E. Aune has recently written a remarkable article on "Genre Theory and the Genre-Function of Mark and Matthew"[60] that gives a valuable critical update of the broader genre-discussion, in particular from the perspective of contemporary literary criticism. Aune once more takes Richard A. Burridge's monograph on the genre of the gospels as his point of departure.[61] He argues along the lines of the biography-hypothesis, but modifies the hypothesis by introducing the aspect of parody: "...the Gospel of Mark..., represents both an imitative and transformative reaction to existing literary genres, i.e., Mark in particular is a type of Greco-Roman biography in the special sense that it is a parody of that genre."[62] Aune arrives at his definition through a comparison of Mark with Hellenistic-Roman biographies. He notices the differences between the literary-cultural milieu and the values that are predominant in the Hellenistic-Roman literature and those that are passed on in the Gospel of Mark.[63] Aune's new attempt to read Mark as a critical contribution to Greco-Roman biographical literature, however, is not as far removed from the historiography hypothesis as one might assume. He stresses the affinity of his genre hypothesis with historical truth: "Mark's narrative is designed to convey truth and meaning as well as authority, plausibility, and realism".[64] I would like to place even more emphasis on the historical impact of the Gospel of Mark for the shaping of the overall Jesus

---

[59] This statement does not deny that Paul had an idea of history in general and of the historical dimension of Jesus in particular. But in his letters he does not elaborate on the history and mission of Jesus between Galilee and Jerusalem, but focuses rather on the present and future impact of the death and resurrection of Christ for 'Jews and Greeks'. See the contribution on "History" by E.-M. Becker in vol. 1 of *Paul and Mark*.

[60] D.E. Aune, "Genre Theory", 145–175.

[61] R.A. Burridge, *What are the Gosples?*. Though Aune argues convincingly along the lines of contemporary genre theory, I would like to have seen discussion on the historiography hypothesis and the genre discussion in the field of classics. See the article on "Gattungen." In *Lexikon der Bibelhermeneutik* (Berlin: de Gruyter, 2009), 189–193. W. Kofler refers to a 'Kreuzung der Gattungen' for Hellenistic-Roman literature, idem, "Gattungen", 192.

[62] Aune, "Genre Theory", 147. Aune understands 'literary parody' as defined by S. Dentith, *Parody* (London and New York: Routledge, 2000). It is a "cultural practice which provides a relatively polemical allusive imitation of another cultural production or practice" (Dentith, *Parody*, 9, quoted by Aune on page 169).

[63] Aune, "Genre Theory", 167f.

[64] Aune, "Genre Theory", 165.

narrative. But what Aune certainly ignores in his contribution is the question of whether Mark only *de facto* works as a parody of the Greco-Roman biography or whether this effect is intended. The latter would result in a substantial difference of scholarly constructions of the author because it would take for granted that at least in some way the author not only knew biographies, but beyond that had the intention of giving a literary answer to them in the form of a parody. In other words, in this case the author would have interacted in a sophisticated way with the Hellenistic-Roman literary scene. It seems to me as though it may be a bit bold to make such a claim.

2.3 Defining the genre of Mark has two consequences for a comparative interpretation. In the first place, it means that the Gospel was written as a coherent narrative and should be interpreted using the methods of narrative criticism.[65] Because neither the author nor the audience of the first Gospel is known to us, all questions concerning the literary purpose and the pragmatics of the text necessarily remain controversial. The modern reader and interpreter can only refer to and is thus entirely dependent on the narrative itself. Secondly, the narrative itself is neither a novel nor a romance – that would make it a literary fiction – nor is it an apocalyptic outline of God's meta-history – this would make it an apocalypse in the proper literary sense. Rather, it contains numerous elements of a historical narrative: real topographical, chronological, prosopographical, and political data.[66] But these criteria also apply to the genre of biography and, as Collins has pointed out, chapter 13, at least, adds the aspect of apocalyptic expectation to the narrative.

The Letter to the Romans on the contrary is a document contemporary with its time and with references to the current situation, including Paul's own situation (chapters 15 and 16). Paul, however, does not offer historical data or allusions to contemporary history in his address to the Romans,[67] whereas Mark begins his narrative with the well-known historical figure of John the Baptist. It would be too simple to claim the contrast between past and present as the main difference between Mark 1 and Romans 1, but it is important that a compar-

---

[65] See especially E. Struthers Malbon, ed., *Between Author and Audience in Mark: Narration, Characterization, Interpretation* (Sheffield UK: Sheffield Phoenix Press, 2009); E. Struthers Malbon, *Mark's Jesus: Characterization as Narrative Christology* (Waco, Texas: Baylor University Press, 2009).
[66] This is confirmed bei Aune, "Genre Theory", 165 f.
[67] One could argue that Paul mentions the historical David, but in his argument David is first and foremost a theological figure.

ison of the genres considers the different concepts of time of both authors.⁶⁸ Furthermore, though, both texts share an apocalyptic view of the future (Romans 13) – a view that must be part of the comparison too.

In sum, the discussion concerning the genre of *Mark* or the attempt to attach a particular genre label to the gospel is open. Proposals that combine characteristics from different fields (as Collins does) seem to be reasonable, since the Gospel of Mark is a hybrid piece of religious literature. At any rate, it is an example of *narrative literature* in the Early Christian communities. To some degree it corresponds to Hellenistic-Roman narrative genres, but at the same time it is also something new and immediately successful in that creates its own successors already within one generation. Concerning the genre of *Romans*, the proposal of Robert Jewett is particularly promising and it has certain elements in common with the composite proposals for Mark. The category of an ambassadorial letter is also a hybrid, a synthesis of form and content, but nevertheless seems to fit the letter quite well. Like the Gospel of Mark, the Letter to the Romans was successful in terms of genre-building: texts like Ephesians or Hebrews make use of the expanded letter form and its elevated style.

3 Literature: authors, audiences, and textual pragmatics

Comparing both texts in respect to their *literary* character beyond simply the question of genre requires, first of all, discussion of their different literary settings and conditions, in particular discussion of authorship and the role of the authors, to the extent that they can be reconstructed from the introductory passages of both texts. According to the recent shift from *Redaktionsgeschichte* to *Rezeptionsgeschichte* and the interest in interpreting New Testament texts, and especially the gospels, from the perspective of orality⁶⁹ rather than of writtenness,

---

68 See O. Wischmeyer, "Die Zeitkonzepte".
69 In this contribution I cannot discuss the concept of orality that is promoted by a group of scholars in connection with the Gospel of Mark (see the introduction to oral tradition in the gospels in the well-balanced article by W.H. Kelber, "Oral tradition (NT)." *ABD* 5 (1992), 30–34). Kelber is right in stating: "Whatever the genetic history of the Gospels, their narrative design appeals to the ear more than to the eye...There is no suggestion that the Gospels are oral traditional literature, e.g., direct transcriptions of the same oral story...The marks of textuality are unmistakably present in the Gospels. But textual constructions and dependencies notwithstanding, the gospel narratives still operate in the interest of an aesthetics of hearing", 32. I share Kelber's evaluation, but it applies to almost every kind of Greco-Roman literature and

New Testament scholarship has focussed extensively on the issue of the *audience* of the gospel narrative. Many scholars underscore the oral performance of the early Christian texts in community gatherings[70] and attempt to interpret the Gospel of Mark along the lines of its supposed function in the services. I have commented elsewhere on this approach,[71] pointing out that our knowledge of the earliest history of community-services is far too limited for precise statements concerning the role of the gospels in these services. In addition, the Gospel of Mark clearly is a coherent and well-composed narrative of considerable length that has been passed down to us as a written document. It is, therefore, best interpreted as written by an author and to be understood as intended to be read or recited as a whole.[72] At the same time, of course, the Gospel of Mark was recited in Early Christian communities. Public and private oral performances were part of the literary life of the Greco-Roman culture, and it is vital to consider the communicative factor of the recital of literary texts both in the Greco-Roman and in the Jewish culture to which the emerging Christian communities of the first century A.D. still belonged. Public recitals of narrative and poetic literature, as well as of rhetorical texts or other prose texts (*Sachprosa*), do not negate the significance or the conception of the literary author in Greek and Roman literature. To the contrary, the *author* remains one of the vital components of literary criticism (*Literaturwissenschaft*), especially after the renowned and protracted debate on the 'death of the author',[73] the outcome of which was not only the rehabilitation

---

therefore does not work well for defining the particular literary attributes of the gospels. In my view the Gospel of Mark is a first attempt of a member of an Early Christian community to author a book on τὸ εὐαγγέλιον Ἰησοῦ Χριστοῦ in the shape of a written narrative. Therefore I utilize the term *author* instead of narrator or even storyteller. E. Struthers Malbon avoids the fallacy of mere orality by applying the method of narrative criticism to the Gospel of Mark. She argues that narrative criticism analyses the text itself and outlines its narrative quality: E. Struthers Malbon, "Narrative Criticism: How Does the Story Mean?." In *Mark and Method*, 2nd ed., New Approaches in Biblical Studies, eds. J. Capel Anderson and St. D. Moore (Minneapolis: Fortress Press, 2008), 23–49.
70 See e.g. Collins, *Mark*, 598. More detailed: M. Müller, "The Place of Mark and Matthew in Canonical Theology." In *Mark and Matthew*, vol. 2, WUNT 304, eds. E.-M. Becker and A. Runesson (Tübingen: 2013), 259–269, 260f. (with reference to Lars Hartman).
71 O. Wischmeyer, "Identity Formation by Literature", 367.
72 This is not meant to imply that Mark must or should always be read or recited all at once but that it was meant to be received as a whole and not in separate textual units.
73 See: F. Jannidis, G. Lauer, M. Martinez and S. Winko, eds., *Texte zur Theorie der Autorschaft* (Stuttgart: Reclam, 2000); see the article on author. In *Lexikon der Bibelhermeneutik* (Berlin: de Gruyter, 2009), 60–63.

of the category,⁷⁴ but also a fresh awareness of the interpretative implications of the concept. In any case, the comparison of the literary role of the author of Romans and the Gospel of Mark sheds light on the importance of the concept for our enterprise.

3.1.1 The ambassadorial epistle to the Romans – if we label Romans in this way – has been shown to be a text that functions as a tool for establishing successful communication between Paul and the Christ-confessing communities in Rome. The Letter to the Romans is not an epistle in the philosophical or literary sense; nevertheless, its meticulous rhetorical structure, stylistic quality, vitally significant subject matters, and underlying pragmatics reveal that Romans has also meta-communicative virtue⁷⁵ that certainly allows the letter to be viewed as high-quality religious literature.⁷⁶ As I have already pointed out, Paul, in taking advantage of the opportunity presented in the form of the letter opening, presents himself as a religious leader and shapes his official position extremely conspicuously, autonomously, and independently as God's direct minister (δοῦλος) and agent (ἀπόστολος) or ambassador. He continues and strengthens this personal presentation in verses 8–15.⁷⁷ In this way, though the stress on Paul's authorship in Rom 1 is partly due to the letter genre, verse 1 also expresses Paul's particular and excessive self-conceptualizing and Rom 1:1–7 works as the *literary* self-presentation or self-fashioning of Paul's person at the beginning of the letter.⁷⁸ He claims the title of an apostle for himself⁷⁹ and thereby attributes to himself the utmost honour in the religious and social communities of the earliest Christians. Moreover, he connects his person so tightly with God's salvific plans that he appears to play a particularly vital role in God's salvation history. We have no evidence for any other person in the first generation of Christians claiming a comparable position for their own person.⁸⁰ Quite the contrary: the texts that aim to honour and dignify the person and the religious role of Peter

---

74 See: F. Jannidis, ed., *Rückkehr des Autors. Zur Erneuerung eines umstrittenen Begriffs*, (Tübingen: Niemeyer, 1999).
75 E.-M. Becker, *Schreiben und Verstehen. Paulinische Briefhermeneutik im Zweiten Korintherbrief*, NET 4 (Tübingen: Francke Verlag, 2002), 133–140.
76 For this term see Theissen, *Entstehung*.
77 See also 15:14ff. and Gal 1:1.11f.15.
78 Compare the cultural gesture of 'self-fashioning' by the English renaissance authors (Stephen Greenblatt). However, Paul does not conceptualize himself as author, but as apostel!
79 Compare the different manner in which Luke constructs his depiction of Paul in Acts.
80 R. Jewett reads Paul's self-presentation and his estimation of the Roman Christians as an expression of the honour-shame concept, *Romans*, 46ff. This reading makes sense particularly for Rom 1:1–7.

(Mt 16:17–19; John 21:15–19) are part of the authors' narrative, not instruments of the personal self-presentation of Peter.

3.1.2 The author of the Gospel of Mark uses a different *literary* strategy. He begins his communication with his literary audience with the phrase Ἀρχὴ τοῦ εὐαγγελίου Ἰησοῦ Χριστοῦ υἱοῦ θεοῦ, a phrase that must be read first of all in continuity with the Hebrew prophets, and especially as analogous to Hos 1:2: Ἀρχὴ λόγου κυρίου πρὸς Ὡσηε. Comparing Hosea with Mark, however, is important not merely to become aware of the same introductory terms in ἀρχὴ λόγου κυρίου and ἀρχὴ τοῦ εὐαγγελίου Ἰησοῦ Χριστοῦ,[81] which establish a clear connection between the two texts, but also in order to notice a major difference regarding the literary setting. The opening of Hosea names a person from the Jewish past, the prophet Hosea. Though Hosea is not directly introduced as the author of the biblical 'Book of Hosea' or as the author of the λόγοι, nevertheless, the name 'Hosea' marks a historical person with whom the Book of Hosea is connected and from whom it has taken its point of departure and its distinct authority. But who is the person with whom the Gospel of Mark is affiliated? Or, in other words, who is the person who 'authorises' the following narrative? It is not the prophet Hosea because even though the wording of verse 1 can be heard or read as an allusion to the Book of Hosea, it avoids alluding to the prophet as author. John the Baptist (v. 4) is the person through whom the author dates the beginning of his narrative; yet, he is part of the narrative and not its author. The prophet Isaiah is quoted in verse 2, but he is not part of the history of the ἀρχή in that he only predicts the history of the ἀρχὴ τοῦ εὐαγγελίου Ἰησοῦ Χριστοῦ. John's mission is interpreted by the quotation from Isaiah, and in this way, both the prophet and John function as the theological and historical point of departure for the Gospel narrative, but not as the authority behind the following texts. Actually, Jesus himself is the individual in focus at the very beginning of the Book of Mark. It is Jesus about whom the book is written. Jesus is the subject of the author's narrative, but even Jesus is not introduced or thought of as the author of the Gospel.[82] The second double genitive, Ἰησοῦ Χριστοῦ, can be interpreted as either an objective or as a subjective genitive (in the sense of Mark 1:14); however, it does not name the author in the sense of 'the εὐαγγελίον, *written* by Jesus'. The author's name or person simply is not made known to the audience. Instead, the author creates a literary setting that leads the auditor to ex-

---

[81] See Collins, *Mark*, 131.
[82] Against G. Theissen, *Entstehung*, who speaks somewhat vaguely or metaphorically of Jesus as the charismatic figure at the beginning of the Gospel.

pect a prophetic narrative.[83] An audience educated in the Jewish tradition would remember the beginning of the Book of Hosea and its prophetic message and at the same time recognize the prophetic quotation from Isaiah. In this scenario, no self-introduction by the author is needed.

In sum, the opening to the Gospel uses the term εὐαγγέλιον in an ambiguous way, disguising both whether εὐαγγέλιον Ἰησοῦ Χριστοῦ should be read either as a subjective or an objective genitive and the exact nature of the relationship between the εὐαγγέλιον and Isaiah. There is no author – neither God nor Jesus Christ nor a prophet nor a person like Μᾶρκος – and there is no address to an audience. The authority that underlies the narrative is the authority of Jesus Christ in continuity with the prophets, that is to say of the εὐαγγέλιον itself. The authority of the Gospel of Mark is not that of an author but rather the foundation upon which the narrative is constructed. The questions of whether or to what extent the author reflected upon his own role in writing the narrative of the ἀρχὴ τοῦ εὐαγγελίου Ἰησοῦ Χριστοῦ cannot be answered. But it is obvious that the author was not interested in the role of an author, whether in regard to his own person, to his authority, to the apostolic dignity of his sources, or to his literary competence. In this respect what the author writes comes to the audience as a direct narrative report without an author.[84] The narrative obtains its authority by its *brevitas*, its evidence, and first and foremost by its content: the message of the εὐαγγέλιον Ἰησοῦ Χριστοῦ.

3.1.3 The self-understanding and self-presentation of the authors turns out to be one of the primary issues in the comparison of Romans and Mark. On the one hand we find one of the leading persons of early Christianity interpreting himself as ἀπόστολος Ἰησοῦ Χριστοῦ without any substantial personal connection to or even knowledge of Jesus of Nazareth, and on the other hand we read the oldest report on what Jesus of Nazareth did and said as recorded by an author who does not give any reference either to his own person and authority or to his sources.[85] As a result, the author does not provide his literary audience with insight into his commission. There is no reference to a commission mediated either by Jesus himself, a community, or the apostle Peter. This literary attitude may lead New Testament scholarship to a fresh discussion of the different concepts of authorship,

---

83 This observation is close to A. Yarbro Collins' definition of the genre of Mark.
84 This is very different from the Gospel of Luke and the Gospel of John. It is only in the Gospel of Matthew that the author hides himself in the same way.
85 Notice the different way in which a person like Papias of Hierapolis authors his collection of λόγια κυρίου.

authority,⁸⁶ self-presentation, and reference – questions that need to be considered not only in some type of labelling such as 'apostolic' or 'deutero-apostolic' or 'orthonymous', 'pseudonymous', or 'anonymous' writing, but which need to be located within the broader context of contemporary Greek, Roman, and Jewish literature and their concepts of authoring their books.⁸⁷

3.2.1 The analysis of the audience leads to results corresponding to those concerning the authorship. By drawing from the Letter to the Romans scholarship has achieved significant insights into the particular character of the early Roman Christian communities. The first audience of the Letter to the Romans has been reconstructed in the ground-breaking study on the early Roman Christianity by Peter Lampe.⁸⁸ Lampe reconstructs about seven Christian groups in Rome that were founded by returning refugees after the edict of Claudius. Only the house of Aquila and Prisca seems to have named their assembly ἐκκλησία. Jewett argues that the majority of Roman Christians belonged to what he labels "tenement churches". He calls into question the hypothesis of house-churches by stating: "If the evidence of agapic communalism were taken seriously, it would be clear that at least in Rome and Thessalonica the numerical preponderance of groups fell in the category of tenement churches."⁸⁹ For my purposes in this essay it is unnecessary to refer to the historical details of Lampe's and Jewett's reconstructions; however, it is important to stress that Romans 16,⁹⁰ with its rich and unparalleled data concerning the Roman Christians, documents not only Paul's interest in Christian persons – male and female – and his personal approach to his mission of preaching the εὐαγγέλιον, but highlights his ability to establish personal connections even with communities to whom he was un-

---

86 The theme of the authority of Paul's letters is also discussed in G. Theissen, *Entstehung*, 105, 134.
87 Possible concepts are: eyewitness, informants, historiographical studies, reference to documents and sources, old tradition, inspiration, and other kinds of authorizing. Particularly interesting is the way of authorizing public declarations like laws or *edicta* by beginning with a political self-presentation. Quite another way of authorizing is the concept of pseudepigraphy as writing under the name of one of the leading figures of Israel that is an essential part of Jewish literary culture.
88 P. Lampe, *Die stadtrömischen Christen in den ersten beiden Jahrhunderten*, WUNT II/18 (Tübingen: Mohr Siebeck, ²1989).
89 Jewett, *Romans*, 69.
90 See Jewett for the purpose of chapter 16, *Romans*, 949–984. Jewett's excellent analysis shows that the deliberations concerning the original place and role of chapter 16 in Paul's correspondence (see, O. Wischmeyer, ed., *Paulus*, 282–284) often overlook the communicative situation of the letter. Chapter 16 is best read as an original part of Romans.

known. We come to realize that Paul would not write a letter without commenting on his own person, creating a communicative situation, and addressing a particular audience.

3.2.2 Adela Collins provides a detailed and balanced introduction to the issue of the "Audience and Purpose" of Mark's Gospel.[91] She, to a certain degree, rejects the Galilee-hypothesis (W. Marxsen), the Rome-hypothesis (B. Incignieri), and Hendrika Roskam's monograph on the purpose of Mark as a an apology for the Galilean Christians after 70 A.D. in a situation of persecution,[92] but Collins also finds Richard Bauckham's idea of "The Gospels for all Christians"[93] rather speculative. Her conclusion is modest and fair: "The evidence is not strong enough to point definitively to either Rome or Antioch, but it is compatible with both locations (and others). With regard to the purpose of Mark it is likely that the author had more than one aim."[94] If we follow Collins,[95] we can conclude that the audience of Mark was not restricted to a certain city or region, as Joel Marcus or Henrika Roskam contend, but that it can be reconstructed as an ordinary early Christian community in one of the urban centres of the *imperium Romanum* – such as Antioch, Smyrna, Ephesus, or Rome[96] – where communities of reasonable size had already been formed. These communities were not as homogeneous as some scholars assume. Robert Jewett has convincingly demonstrated the plurality of factions among the communities in Rome,[97] and we need not comment on the obvious factions in Corinth and in Antioch. It can therefore be concluded that there is neither a need to reconstruct the social milieu of the audience of the Gospel of Mark in a particular regional sense nor a

---

[91] Collins, *Mark*, 96–102.
[92] H. Roskam, *The Purpose of the Gospel of Mark in Its Historical and Social Context*, NTSuppl 114 (Leiden: Brill, 2004). See also A. Winn, *The Purpose of Mark's Gospel. An early Christian Response to Roman Imperial Propaganda*, WUNT 2.245 (Tübingen: Mohr Siebeck, 2008).
[93] R. Bauckham, "For Whom Were Gospels Written?." In *The Gospels for All Christians: Rethinking the Gospel Audiences*, ed. idem (Grand Rapids: Eerdmans, 1998), 9–48. See J. Marcus' discussion against Bauckham, *Mark 1–8*, 26–28. I. H. Henderson, "Reconstructing Mark's Double Audience." In *Between Author and Audience in Mark: Narration, Characterization, Interpretation*, New Testament Monographs 23, ed. E. Struthers Malbon, (Sheffield: Sheffield Academic Press, 2009), 6–28, argues in favour of Bauckham's proposal.
[94] Collins, *Mark*, 101 f. J. Marcus pleads for Antioch and for a historical context of persecution, 33–37.
[95] See the detailed analysis in O. Wischmeyer, "Identity Formation by Literature" (see above footnote number 3).
[96] There is no evidence pointing to Alexandria in either the papyri or early Christian tradition.
[97] Jewett, *Romans*, 70–72.

need to outline the author's (or the book's) distinct purpose. The only issues concerning which there is relative certainty are, on the one hand, the close affinity of the audience to the Septuagint – at least in the author's mind and in his literary strategy – and, on the other hand, the interest of the audience in a 'Jesus-narrative'. The audience wants to hear or to read a detailed account of Jesus's life, his teaching, and in particular of his death. It is through the manner in which the author of the Gospel structures and presents the εὐαγγέλιον that we find the main difference between the audience of Romans and the audience of the communities of the Gospel of Mark.

3.3 The issue of pragmatics can be addressed rather briefly. As I have already contended, the pragmatics of the Letter to the Romans has been outlined convincingly by Robert Jewett. The letter serves a primary purpose,[98] namely the mission to Spain, and thereby contains concrete textual pragmatics. Paul writes as part of his preparation for the mission to Spain, and the members of the Roman Christ-believing communities are asked to support his mission. As for comparable textual pragmatics of Mark, I agree with the statement of Adela Collins that Mark functions as a narrative. Unlike the Letter to the Romans, Mark serves several different purposes and need not be reduced to concrete practical purposes. Even if one concedes that 13:14 includes a dramatic address to the readers with a concrete demand, one need not reduce the whole narrative with its broad narrative and parenetic materials to a call to leave Jerusalem. If the advice to flee had been what the author had in mind, he would have presented it in another way and in a manner that the audience could follow. After all, is it really reasonable to state that the rather long and detailed narrative of Mark served the purpose of warning the Christ-believing communities to leave Jerusalem?

It is obvious that both texts are operating, from the outset, with different pragmatics. This difference arises out of the different communicative situations and corresponds to the different genres and different concepts of authorship and authority. In other words, the difference is due to the differing *literature* involved. We need not restrict ourselves to the genre difference, however, and can advance the discussion by raising the specific issue of the *literary* function of both texts. I would like to suggest that the author of the Gospel of Mark wrote the first Christian book,[99] and thereby, for the first time, introduced early Chris-

---

[98] Jewett, *Romans*, 80–941. In my view Jewett's analysis is an important step forward concerning the topic of "The reason for Romans", see A.J.M. Wedderburn, *The Reason for Romans* (Edinburgh: Clark, 1988).
[99] This statement does not intend to interpret the εὐαγγέλιον in verse 1 in the sense of the 'book of the Gospel'; see Boring, *Mark. A Commentary*, 31: "Here, however, 'the gospel of Jesus Christ'

tianity into the different fields and contexts of contemporary literary activity, i.e., the Greco-Roman and the Jewish literature of the 1st century A.D.[100] Additionally, I would contend that only Mark, and not Romans, functions as a book and is thereby to be regarded as a genuinely new attempt to create religious literature.

4 Quotations and references

The topic of the book[101] can be explored further by discussing the function of references and quotations in both opening texts. Whereas Mark begins with a long mixed quotation attributed to Isaiah, in Romans 1 Paul refers to the prophets and their holy scriptures in general.

4.1 The Letter to the Romans was probably written by Paul in the spring of 56 A.D. during his stay in Corinth in the house of Gaius. The letter was dictated to Tertius, who also was a member of the Christian community in Corinth. Paul seems to have had suitable circumstances for the composition of a very long and complicated letter, namely, being hosted by Gaius and being equipped with a secretary. At that moment he seems to have been enjoying a good relationship with the members of the Corinthian community, a community that he not only established, but that also was one of his most important and successful.[102] For my argument here, the presence of prosperous former members of the Jewish community in Corinth, who had been converted[103] to the Christian confession,[104] is

---

refers not to a book but to the good news of God's saving act in Jesus Christ, the message proclaimed by the church of Mark's day".

100 In my view it is one of the most remarkable characteristics of the culture of the first century A.D. that three cultural spheres existed side by side: the highly developed and most prestigious Greek literature, a rather young, but already extremely advanced Latin literature, and the Greek literature of the Jews who lived within the Roman Empire. The Jewish literature of the 1st century is quite varied in terms of genre, topics, and style and includes authors such as Philo, Josephus, the author of 4 Macc etc. New Testament scholarship should realize that 1st century Greek speaking Jewish culture had a manifold and high ranking literary activity that achieved, at least to some degree, the level of the contemporary Hellenistic-Roman literature.

101 See the new approach to the issue of the codex in: R.S. Bagnell, *Early Christian Books in Egypt* (Princeton, N.J.: Princeton University Press, 2009).

102 See D. Zeller, *Der erste Brief an die Korinther*, KEK 5 (Göttingen: Vandenhoeck & Ruprecht, 2010), 29–45. See also the contributions in: Ch. Karakolis, K. Bezelos and S. Despotis, eds., *Saint Paul and Corinth*, vol. 2 (Athens: 2009).

103 For the term 'conversion' see D. Stoekl Ben Ezra, "Confession, Judaism: Second Temple and Rabbinic Period." In *Encyclopedia of the Bible and Its Reception* (in press).

104 1 Cor 8:6; 12:3 and Rom 10:10. The term is ὁμολογεῖν.

of special interest. Perhaps they were able to provide Paul with Greek manuscripts of at least Isaiah and the Psalms. Be that as it may, he was in a location where 'Scripture' was well known and also, in some way or other, available. The notable stylistic and aesthetic quality of Romans in general, along with the meticulously outlined prescript that serves as its rhetorical *exordium*,[105] fit this scenario. As we have already seen, in Romans Paul is not far from some kind of literary activity in the narrow sense of the word. It is within this framework that Rom 1:2 must be interpreted. The wording of ὃ προεπηγγείλατο διὰ τῶν προφητῶν αὐτοῦ ἐν γραφαῖς ἁγίαις has no parallel in the New Testament writings and attracts the attention of the audience by its elevated style.[106]

4.2 Some similar, or at least related, aspects can be found in the complicated introductory passage of Mark.[107] The author combines different quotes from the prophets ascribing them to Isaiah.[108] Though the passage of Mark 1:1–4 is somewhat opaque in its syntax, as I have already demonstrated, the brief and tightly structured text is striking and attracts the attention of the audience in the same way as Romans 1. The passage is the beginning of a *book* and addresses the author's purpose in connecting his book with 'scripture'. Thus, the introductory passage is the expression of both the author's consistent approach to his own way of writing some kind of narrative, only later designated a 'gospel', and his connection to 'scripture', i.e., the normative library of early Christianity that was also the normative library of Judaism.[109] It is the same kind of combining old and new that we find in the prescript of Romans. As I have pointed out, we know almost nothing about the author of the Gospel of Mark and about his audience, but there is at least some evidence for positing that both author and audience are to be located within a Jewish and early Christian literary environment similar to that which Paul benefitted from at Corinth.[110]

---

105 See Jewett, *Romans*, 95–126.
106 See Jewett, *Romans*, 103 for details and for relevant literature.
107 For the grammar, the vocabulary, the style, and the composition of the Gospel, see the article by D. Stökl Ben Ezra, "Markus-Evangelium." In *RAC Lfg. 187* (Stuttgart: Hirzel, 2010), 173–207 (Lit.). Stökl points to the Semitic, Aramaic, Greek, and Latin linguistic aspects of Mark as well as to the *sermo humilis*: M. Reiser, *Syntax und Stil des Markusevangeliums im Licht der hellenistischen Volksliteratur*, WUNT 2.11 (Tübingen: Mohr Siebeck, 1984); J.K. Elliott, ed., *The Language and Style of the Gospel of Mark. An Edition of C.H. Turner's 'Notes on Markan Usage'. Together with Other Comparable Studies*, NTSuppl 71 (Leiden: Brill, 1993).
108 For an analysis, see O. Wischmeyer, "Zitat".
109 Whether this refers to the Septuagint or to other Greek versions of the Jewish scriptures cannot be discussed here.
110 See my considerations in "Identity Formation by Literature", (see above footnote 3).

4.3 The collection of the Jewish texts which we label the 'Septuagint' undoubtedly served as the one and only basic library for Paul and for the author of the Gospel of Mark. For both authors 'scripture' is the constant interlocutor.[111] It is not necessary to demonstrate this point anew; however, to mention it helps round off my argument. All the scholarly work that has been done on the issues of quotations, intertextuality, and audience in Mark has pointed to the same conclusion: the Markan world of ideas and its basic point of reference is the world of 'Scripture', i.e., the Jewish literature and literary activity. Daniel Stökl Ben Ezra's important observation concerning Mark: "Wichtiger ist für das Verständnis vom Verhältnis des Autors zur nichtjüd[ischen] Welt die Beobachtung, dass keine nichtjüd[ischen] Quellen zitiert werden",[112] also applies to Paul. But at the same time, Paul was able to win non-Jews for the Christian communities, and the Gospel of Mark, at least to a certain extent, was written for a non-Jewish audience. We have to realize that the cultural boundaries between Jewish and non-Jewish literature were not as rigid as they often seem to be in scholarly discussions. Both authors, Paul and 'Mark', were deeply rooted in the Jewish culture and nevertheless created something at least partly *new* – the gospel genre and the community-letter – that was soon accepted by a certain number of non-Jews and further developed by members of the growing Christian communities. When Paul refers to the prophets at the very beginning of his most important letter, a letter that we have seen is close to epistolographic literature, he demonstrates not only the general connection between his message and the Jewish scriptures, but also affiliates himself with the sacred *library* of Judaism.

Moreover, the practice of quoting from normative, formative, or classical literature that we find at the beginning of Mark is part of the common, traditional literary culture of Greco-Roman literature that is shared not only by Jewish authors like Philo and Josephus, but that is also used in the Qumran pesharim,[113] which make their own contribution to Jewish literature.

---

111 See Stökl, "Markus-Evangelium", 186: "Wie Sprache, Vorstellungswelt u[nd] Theologie erkennen lassen, ist das M. ein jüd[isches] Ev[angelium], das für Leser geschrieben wurde, die mit jüd[ischen] Traditionen u[nd] Institutionen vertraut waren". I agree with the use of the term 'jüdisches Evangelium', insofar as the term mainly identifies a cultural and literary milieu. Stöckl is also right in stating: "Ein der nichtjüd[ischen] Literatur u[nd] Religionen Unkundiger kann das M. problemlos verstehen. Andersherum war u[nd] ist dies nicht möglich", 192f. But on the other hand it is also true that not only Paul's preaching, but also the Gospel of Mark must have been read and understood by non-Jews.
112 See Stökl, "Markus-Evangelium", 192. Stökl also discusses very carefully possible allusions.
113 See 1QS 8:13ff in comparison with Mark 1:2. See the magisterial article by H. Hübner, "New Testament, OT quotations." In *ABD* 4 (1992), 1096–1104. Concerning the citation praxis in the pesharim see the article by D. Dimant, "Pesharim, Qumran." In *ABD* 5 (1992), 244–251; C.

5 εὐαγγέλιον

My analysis of the introductory passages of the Letter to the Romans and the Gospel of Mark intends first and foremost to reshape the reconstruction of the very beginnings of early Christian *literature*. Early Christian literature, recently reconsidered by Gerd Theissen as a matter of 'Literaturgeschichte'[114] in order to reconstruct the development of early Christianity, is a phenomenon that has hitherto neither been sufficiently considered or portrayed as contributing to ancient 'religious literature' nor adequately discussed in terms of its theoretical relevance. In my view, the emergence of a distinct literature as early as the first generation of Christ-confessing Jews and non-Jews deserves more scholarly attention. The communities did not have an automatical need for their own literature because they were rooted in the Septuagint and additionally may have used several non-Septuagint texts including sapiential, apocalyptic, and narrative works of Jewish origin. To a certain degree they were also familiar with Jewish exegetical literature. Therefore it is rather astonishing that a 'literature of their own' developed as early as in the first or second generation of Christ-confessing communities. Paul, an individual without a permanent residence, not to mention a residence of his own, became the first Christian author,[115] and the author of the Gospel of Mark wrote the first Christian book. Both authors introduced a literature of their own for the early Christian communities. The overall purpose was not yet to establish a 'Christian' literary culture, but to better communicate the εὐαγγέλιον. The εὐαγγέλιον[116] was primarily oral proclamation, that is, preaching (Rom 1:15; Mark 1:14f.); however, Paul, ever since his Letter to Thessalonica (about 50 A.D.),[117] communicated with his communities not only face to face, but also in written form, not only for the purpose of transmitting information, but also in order to shape his message of the εὐαγγέλιον by developing and explaining it in detail through a letter. This is precisely what he did in the first eleven chapters of Romans.

McCarthy, "Pesharim." In *EDEJ* (2010), 1050–1059. A. Lange and M. Weigel, *Biblical Quotations and Allusions in Second Temple Jewish Literature*, JAJS 5 (Göttingen: Vandenhoeck&Ruprecht, 2011).
114 G. Theissen, *Entstehung*.
115 See O. Wischmeyer, "Paulus als Autor." In O. Wischmeyer, *Von Ben Sira zu Paulus. Gesammelte Aufsätze zu Texten, Theologie und Hermeneutik des Frühjudentums und des Neuen Testaments*, WUNT 173, ed. E.-M. Becker (Tübingen: Mohr Siebeck, 2004), 289–307.
116 See A. Lindemann's contribution on the gospel in *Paul and Mark*, vol. 1.
117 See E. Ebel, "1 Thessalonians." In *Paul. Life, Setting, Work, Letters*, ed. O. Wischmeyer (London/New York: T&T Clark, 2012), 139–148, 144.

My contribution on "Paul and Mark" focused on this issue: the comparison of the communication of the εὐαγγέλιον in Paul's letters and the communication of the εὐαγγέλιον by a Jesus-book, written by a 'hidden author'.[118] If we understand this configuration as the twofold 'origin' of Christian literature and theological culture, we will also be able to make important contributions to the question of early Christian *identity*. 'Christology' in its twofold appearance as literary narrative and as written argumentative communication shapes the beginnings of early Christian social, institutional, individual, and intellectual identity. Comparison in this sense works neither '*motivgeschichtlich*' nor '*traditionsgeschichtlich*', but attempts to understand the intellectual and cultural dynamic of Christian origins to the extent that we are able to reconstruct it from its literary heritage.

---

118 For the concept of the hidden author see G.B. Conte, *The Hidden Author: An Interpretation of Petronius's Satyricon* (Berkeley/Califonia: University of California Press, 1996).

Jan Dochhorn
Man and the Son of Man in Mark 2:27–28

An Exegesis of Mark 2:23–28 Focussing on the Christological Discourse in Mark 2:27–28 with an Epilogue Concerning Pauline Parallels

I Introduction

The last two verses of the Markan pericope about plucking ears of corn on the Sabbath proclaim the superiority of both man and the Son of Man over the Sabbath (Mark 2:27–28). Why do man and the Son of Man appear here side by side? And what concept is presupposed when both of them are claimed to be superior to the Sabbath? These are the questions with which this article primarily deals. It will lead to the reconstruction of an anthropological and Christological concept underlying Mark 2:27–28 which finds parallels elsewhere in the New Testament and was apparently important for the Messianology of Early Christianity. This program implies that the question of the Sabbath does not lie in the focus of this analysis. It likewise implies a concentration on Mark rather than Paul; this is an exegesis of Mark 2:23–28 and especially Mark 2:27.28. However, Pauline parallels will often turn out to be important for the exegetical work to be done here, and therefore I hope this article can also contribute to the Pauline aspect of this volume. In order to ensure this, the present article concludes with an epilogue evaluating the most important Pauline parallels discussed in this exegesis on Mark 2:23–28 (esp. 27–28). In the following sections, first a relatively detailed analysis of Mark 2:23–28 with special regard to Mark 2:27–28 will be presented (II). After that, the Pauline parallels will be discussed briefly (III).

II The Pericope about plucking ears of corn on the Sabbath (Mark 2:23–28) and the meaning of Mark 2:27–28

We will start with a discussion about the position of this pericope in its context which will demonstrate that it originally belonged to a Pre-Markan collection of apophthegmata (1). After that, the pericope will be analyzed (2). The third paragraph (3) will focus on the statements about the Sabbath and man and Son of Man in Mark 2:27–28.

1 The context of Mark 2:23–28: A collection of polemical apophthegmata

The pericope about plucking ears of corn on the Sabbath in Mark 2:23–28 belongs to a series of apophthegmata[1] that describe how in a special situation Jesus defended his own and his disciples' religious practice against objections of certain opponents, especially the scribes and the Pharisees. This series begins with a narration about Jesus healing a lame person which turns into a debate about the authority of the Son of Man to forgive sins (Mark 2:1–12). It ends with a healing on the Sabbath in a synagogue and a discussion about healing on the Sabbath (3:1–5). Mark 3:6 relates that the Pharisees and Herodians decided to find out how they could kill Jesus. This verse thereby connects the series of apophthegmata in Mark 2:1–3:5 with the broader context of the Gospel, which culminates in the passion and resurrection of Jesus (Mark 14–16).

It has been assumed for some time that in Mark 2:1–3:6 a Pre-Markan collection of apophthegmata has been preserved, which had existed separately as a – probably – written source. The original content of this collection has been disputed; especially the question of whether it ended with our pericope or with the following one is relevant.[2] For the purpose of this article it is important to comment on this source-critical assumption, because for a study devoted to Mark and Paul it should be relevant to know whether we are dealing with something from Mark himself or with a tradition that he has taken up (and that has influenced him). I consider the theory that Mark 2:1–3:6 has roots in an older written collection of polemical apophthegmata to be plausible, and I assume that this collection originally included the four pericopae written down in Mark 2. This view can be justified by the following arguments:

---

[1] For the term "apophthegma" cf. Georg Strecker, *Literaturgeschichte des Neuen Testaments*, Uni-Taschenbücher 1682 (Göttingen: Vandenhoeck 1992), 201–205.
[2] Concerning an older collection underlying Mark 2:1–3:6, cf. Heinz-Wolfgang Kuhn, *Ältere Sammlungen im Markusevangelium*, Studien zur Umwelt des Neuen Testaments 8 (Göttingen: Vandenhoeck 1971), 53–98 (whom I follow in some ways); Darrell J. Doughty, "The Authority of the Son of Man", *ZNW* 74 (1983): 161–181 and Eve-Marie Becker, *Das Markus-Evangelium im Rahmen antiker Historiographie*, WUNT 194 (Tübingen: J.C.B. Mohr 2006), 283–296; for background on the research debate cf. Dieter Lührmann, *Das Markusevangelium*, HNT 3 (Tübingen: J.C.B. Mohr 1987), 56.

1. The four pericopae written down in Mark 2 are related to each other by strong links that make them a composition of specific cohesion. The first and the last pericope both culminate in statements concerning the authority of the Son of Man, cf. Mark 2:10 and Mark 2:28. Thereby Mark 2:10 and the last verse of Mark 2, the saying about the Son of Man as Lord of the Sabbath in Mark 2:28, form a complete circle, which leads to the assumption that the collection of apophthegmata originally ended here.

This circular composition dealing with the authority of the Son of Man harmonizes with another compositional device in Mark 2: each apophthegma is marked by statements made by Jesus concerning his role. According to these, Jesus functions as the Son of Man who can forgive sins (Mark 2:10), as a doctor who heals the sick (Mark 2:16), as somebody who has come in order to call sinners (Mark 2:17), as the bridegroom whose wedding guests cannot fast (Mark 2:19–20), and as the Son of Man who is also the Lord of the Sabbath (Mark 2:28). The title dominating this series of self-designations is the term "Son of Man" as it appears at the beginning and the end of this series.

Mark 2:1–28 is obviously a collection characterized by a strong Christological focus, if we are allowed to take the terms "Christology" or "Christological" not in the narrow sense of Messianology, but in the sense of general considerations concerning Jesus' functions and the titles that are related to these functions.

2. The context of Mark 2:1–28 is dominated by devices of composition that do not disharmonize with those characterizing Mark 2:1–28, but point in another direction: the context of Mark 2 is mainly given structure by the remark in Mark 3:6 that, in co-operation with the Herodians, the Pharisees decided to put Jesus to death. This remark gives the context of Mark 2 the character of a prelude that points to the passion of Jesus in Mark 14–16. The unit concluded by this remark is Mark 1:21–3:6. This unit is framed by narrations dealing with how Jesus put together his inner circle, cf. the vocation of Simon, Andreas and the Zebedaids in Mark 1:16–20 and the foundation of the group of the Twelve in Mark 3:7–19. The unit in Mark 1:21–3:6 begins with a miracle in a synagogue (Mark 1:21–28) and ends with a miracle in a synagogue (Mark 3:1–5). However, the first miracle makes Jesus popular (Mark 1:28), whereas the last one provokes a conflict which leads to the decision of the Pharisees and the Herodians to do Jesus to death (Mark 3:6). The whole composition is thereby given a dramatic structure. The context of the first and the last pericope fits this dramatic structure: The pericopae following Mark 1:21–28 deal with the popularity of Jesus and his – hesitant – interaction with a euphoric crowd (cf. 1:32–34.35–37.44.45), whereas the pericopae preceding Mark 3:1–6 prepare the final conflict constellation by polemic discourses dealing with the religious conduct of Jesus and his disciples (2:1–3:5).

For the macrostructure of Mark 1:21–3:6 the pericope about healing on the Sabbath in Mark 3:1–5 is of crucial importance: it points back to the first pericope, Mark 1:21–28, which also takes place in a synagogue, and it directly prepares the zenith of the whole unit in Mark 3:6. Its importance for Mark 1:21–3:6 is a good reason to assume that it was composed or taken up from tradition for this context and did not belong to Mark 2:1–28.

Mark 2:1–28 does, as already stated, not disharmonize with the focus on the passion which gives Mark 1:21–3:6 its special character. However, Mark 2 is marked by a strong internal agenda, which does not exclude the notion of Jesus' death (cf. Mark 2:19b-20), but has another predominant focus: Jesus' authority, first as the Son of Man and then as somebody who is described by a lot of titles dealing with the salvific role he played on earth.

3. Some traits of Mark 2:1–28 differ from the Gospel of Mark as a whole. At least one theme is encountered in this collection alone: the importance of fasting is only relativized in Mark 2:18–20. If the hint at fasting as an exorcistic technique in Mark 9:29 *varia lectio* belongs to the original text of Mark 9:29, then we could even detect a tension between a text belonging to Mark 2 and another passage in the Gospel.[3] Some of the Christological titles used in Mark 2 never appear again in Mark: Only in Mark 2:16 is Jesus a doctor, only in Mark 2:19–20 is he a bridegroom. Also the Christological concepts associated with the title "Son of Man" are unique in the larger context of the Gospel: only here does the Son of Man forgive sins (2:10) and only here is he labelled as the Lord of the Sabbath (2:28); in other passages of the Gospel of Mark the dialectics of suffering and triumphant parousia are dominant features connected with the Son of Man.[4]

The image of the Son of Man developed in Mark 2 principally fits into this constellation: by describing the authority of the Son of Man, this chapter enables the reader to understand why the fact that the Son of Man would suffer is aston-

---

3 In Mark 9:29 ℵ* B 0274 k and in a citation of Mark 9:29 by Clemens Alexandrinus, Eclogae Propheticae 15:1 Jesus says about a special kind of demons: τοῦτο τὸ γένος ἐν οὐδενὶ δύναται ἐξελθεῖν εἰ μὴ ἐν προσευχῇ ("only by prayer can this kind go out"). The majority of the witnesses read ... ἐν προσευχῇ καὶ νηστείᾳ ("by prayer *and fasting*"). Here fasting – along with prayer – is an exorcistic technique. The short text is preferred by NA[27], whereas the long text is regarded as original by Erich Klostermann, *Das Markusevangelium*, HNT 3 (Tübingen: J.C.B. Mohr ³1936), 92.
4 Passages mentioning the Son of Man dealing with his suffering are encountered in Mark 8:31; 9:12; 9:31; 10:33; 14:21.41. Passages dealing with his triumphant parousia include Mark 8:38; 13:26; 14:62 (the last word on the Son of Man!). Other passages are to be found in Mark 9:9 (resurrection) and 10:45 (the Son of Man has come in order to be servant).

ishing (cf. Mark 8:31–33). However, Mark 2 does not need this context, whereas obviously this context needs Mark 2.

There are two further conspicuous tensions between Mark 2 and its Markan context, which also both deal with Christology. The first is the total lack of Christology in the pericope immediately following this collection: Mark 3:1–5 debates a halakhic problem associated with the observance of the Sabbath. But in contrast to Mark 2:23–28, which also thematizes the Sabbath, in Mark 3:1–5 Jesus does not justify his nonconformist practice by a Christological claim; Mark 3:1–5 remains within the area of an exclusively halakhic debate. Here we can detect an important incongruity, which again shows that Mark 3:1–5 and Mark 2 belong to different layers.

The second tension involves the implicit Christology of Mark 2:23–28. As we will demonstrate, the hint at David in Mark 2:25–26 should evoke Christological connotations. However, in Mark 12:35–37 a central Christological connotation connected with David is proved to be insufficient by the Markan Jesus: Christ should not be regarded as Son of David, because David himself calls him κύριος in Ps 109:1 LXX. It seems that Mark in Mark 2:25–26 has taken up Christological material which points to a Davidic Messianology although he explicitly rejects this kind of Messianology in Mark 12:35–37. The same phenomenon can be observed in Mark 10:47.48 where the title "Son of David" is used by the blind Bartimaios. In the Pre-Markan tradition, this could well have been a positive statement establishing Christ as Son of David, in the Markan context it is perhaps important that Bartimaios calls Jesus "Son of David" *before* he follows him (cf. Mark 10:52).

We can conclude that Mark has adopted the pericope about plucking ears of corn on the Sabbath from a written source which included the four polemical apophthegmata in Mark 2. The original wording of this source need not be reconstructed here. Important for the present purpose is simply the fact that probably both the references to the Son of Man and the Christological motives in the sayings concluding the apophthegmata already belonged to the Pre-Markan source, because they are, as this section has shown, specific to the composition of Mark 2.

2 The Pericopae on plucking ears of corn on the Sabbath (Mark 2:23–28). A Short Exegesis

Mark 2:23–28 is, as already stated, a polemical apophthegma: it tells how Jesus in a special situation reacted to objections by short sayings connected with that situation.

The situation is described in Mark 2:23: Jesus was walking through the fields on the Sabbath, and his disciples, who accompanied him, were plucking ears of corn. They thereby provoked the objections of the Pharisees who claimed that plucking ears of corn is not allowed on the Sabbath (2:24). It is obviously not a problem as such that the disciples are plucking ears of corn; this is permitted (cf. Dtn 23:26; Josephus, Ant IV:234).[5] Nor is the fact that Jesus and his disciples are walking around in the fields a matter of contention although this could contravene rules forbidding walking around on the Sabbath.[6] The narration seems to imply that the Pharisees *see* the disciples plucking ears of corn. Perhaps the narrator even presupposes that the Pharisees are in the field. This would, if it were the case, indicate that the narrative introduction of this apophthegma has been composed by someone who was not really well informed about the rules pertaining to walking around on the Sabbath.

Important for the narrative economy of this section, however, is the opinion voiced by the Pharisees that plucking ears of corn does not conform to the rules of the Sabbath: we can only guess about the background to the objection proposed by the Pharisees;[7] the narrator does not display any inclination to delve into this. Important are merely the answers given by Jesus.

---

[5] Concerning the discussions about this rule in Rabbinic literature cf. Boaz Cohen, "The Rabbinic Law Presupposed by Matthew XII,1 and Luke VI,1", *HTR* 23 (1930): 91–92. Cf. also the rabbinic sources mentioned in Gustaf Dalman, *Arbeit und Sitte in Palästina*, Band II: *Der Akkerbau*, Schriften des deutschen Palästina-Instituts 5 (Gütersloh: Bertelsmann 1932) (reprint: Hildesheim: Olms 1987), 339, note 6.

[6] Lib Jub 50:12 forbids taking a path on the Sabbath. CD 10:21 restricts the distance that one can go on the Sabbath to 1000 cubits; those pasturing cattle are permitted 2000 cubits according to CD 11:5–6. Widespread is the prohibition of more than 2000, cf. Jerome, Epistula 121:10,20 (CSEL 56/1:49 – cited by Klostermann (1936 [n. 3], 29) and the hint at the σαββάτου ... ὁδός in Acts 1:12, which fits the 2000 cubits because the distance between Jerusalem and the Mount of Olives mentioned there amounts to ca. 2000 cubits, cf. Josephus, Antiquitates XX:169 and Hans Conzelmann, *Die Apostelgeschichte*, HNT 7 (Tübingen: J.C.B. Mohr ²1972), 27. The whole tractate mErubîn presupposes this rule, cf. also mShabbat 23:3–4. The biblical background was in the view of the Rabbis Ex 16:29, cf. Hermann Leberecht Strack / Paul Billerbeck, *Kommentar zum Neuen Testament aus Talmud und Midrasch*, zweiter Teil: *Das Evangelium nach Markus, Lukas und Johannes und die Apostelgeschichte* (Munich: C.H. Beck 1924), 590–594 (many rabbinic texts concerning this rule). Cf. Lutz Doering, *Schabbat. Sabbathalacha und -praxis im antiken Judentum und Urchristentum*, Texte und Studien zum Antiken Judentum 78 (Tübingen: J.C.B. Mohr 1999), 87–94 (Lib Jub 50:12); 145–151 (CD); 151–154 (Acts 1:12 and other sources recording a premishnaic rule restricting the way of the Sabbath to 2000 cubits).

[7] Probably the narrator presupposes the rule that harvesting is forbidden on the Sabbath. This rule is formulated in Ex 34:21 and mShabbat 7:2. mShabbat 12:2 states more precisely that even very small quantities may not be harvested. However, plucking ears of corn is not mentioned in mShabbat. A passage in Jewish literature that explicitly forbids plucking ears of corn on the

These answers consist of three sayings (2:25–26.27.28). Over the course of the history of research, the multiplicity of sayings concluding this apophthegma has led to different attempts at decomposition.[8] These were mainly the result of a typical assumption of traditional *Formgeschichte*, namely that ideally and originally only one saying would conclude an apophthegma.[9] The degree to which such methods of decomposition can help to identify the oldest state of a tradition (perhaps also an original situation in the life of Jesus) does not need to be debated here, because here it is more important to explore what was nearest to Mark, i.e. the Pre-Markan collection in Mark 2. And concerning Mark 2, we can state that especially apophthegmata preserved in this chapter are concluded by more than one saying, cf. Mark 2:16.17 and 2:19a.19b.20. Probably this feature already belonged to the Pre-Markan collection.

This is all the more plausible since the sayings concluding the apophthegmata also share something that has already been mentioned, namely their focus on Christology. On that theme, we can observe a tendency which will also turn out to be of central importance for the series of sayings in Mark 2:23–28: the sayings usually proceed from an implicit Christology to an explicit Christology. In Mark 2:16 Jesus mentions the fact that not the healthy but rather the ill requires a doctor, thus defending his solidarity with sinners. This saying

---

Sabbath can be found in Maimonides, Hilkhot Shabbat 8:3 (cited by Klostermann [1936 [n. 3], 29]). Maimonides considers plucking ears of corn as a kind of harvesting. However, this is a very late source. Klostermann l.c. mentions also Philo, De Vita Mosis II:22 (Cohn / Wendland IV:205), where even plucking one leaf from a tree is forbidden on the Sabbath. According to Doering (1999 [n. 6], 428–429), a rule transmitted in CD X:22–23 indicates that the halakha formulated by the Pharisees in Mark 2:24 fits contemporary positions in the development of halakha. CD X:22–23 decides that on the Sabbath one is not permitted to eat anything except meals already prepared, or fruits rotting in the fields. Ears that are still growing do not rot.

8 Cf. the reviews presented by Rudolf Bultmann, *Die Geschichte der synoptischen Tradition*. Ergänzungsheft, bearbeitet von Gerd Theißen und Philipp Vielhauer (Göttingen: Vandenhoeck ⁵1979), 18–19 and Becker (2006 [n. 2], 283–285); cf. moreover the analyses of Doughty (1983 [n. 2], 169–170) and Doering (1999 [n. 6], 409–432).

9 Becker (2006 [n. 2]) classes the fact that Mark 2:23–28 is concluded by many sayings as a *Spannung* (p. 170). Very typical of traditional *Formgeschichte* is the decomposition proposed by Doughty (1983 [n. 2]), who identifies 2:25–26 as a Markan composition and writes: "The original controversy story concluded with the decisive pronouncement in V. 27" (ibid. 170). The original conclusion is for him a "decisive" short sentence – not a long exegetical discussion. Cf. also Martin Dibelius, *Die Formgeschichte des Evangeliums* (Tübingen: J.C.B. Mohr ⁶1976), 60–63 about the practice caused by the needs of preaching to add explanatory sayings to originally shorter paradigms. Also Rudolf Bultmann, *Geschichte der synoptischen Tradition*, FRLANT 29 (Göttingen: Vandenhoeck ⁹1979), 64–65 states that often sayings were added to apophthegmata (he demonstrates that this happened not least in the redactional activity of Matthew and Luke).

implies that Jesus is the doctor. Mark 2:17 then explicitly states something about Jesus' identity: he has come in order to call sinners. Something similar can be observed in Mark 2:19–20: In Mark 2:19a Jesus explains the non-ascetic behaviour of his disciples by the fact that the (then) present was the time of the wedding and that the bridegroom was accompanying them. The reader may guess that Jesus is the bridegroom and that this term points to a Messianic function of Jesus, since a Messianic connotation of the bridegroom metaphor is not unknown in Early Christianity (cf. Rev 19:7.9; 21:9). As a consequence, we can detect an implicit Christology in Mark 2:19a. The following words take up the bridegroom motif and transform it in order to present an explicit Christology: Mark 2:19b mentions an absence of the bridegroom and thereby evokes Christological associations that are specific to Jesus, who is also – after his presence on earth – in a special sense absent (cf. perhaps Mark 13:33–37). Mark 2:20 makes these notions explicit and offers the reader the clear knowledge that Jesus is the bridegroom, whose death constitutes a new ecclesiastical practice of fasting. The introductory pericope of Mark 2 likewise fits into this same pattern: Jesus first talks about the power of the Son of Man to forgive sins (Mark 2:10). The reader may conclude from Mark 2:5 – where Jesus has forgiven the lame person his sins – that Jesus is that Son of Man. This conclusion is corroborated by the following healing that works as an *a fortiori* argument. It is left to the reader to apply with certainty to Jesus the title "Son of Man".

A similar structure can be found in Mark 2:25–26.27.28. These three sayings may be interpreted as follows:

Mark 2:25–26: Jesus begins with a biblical story based on 1 Sam 21:2–7. He says: when Abjathar was High priest, David together with his companions entered the house of God. David ate the loaves presented to the Lord which only the priests may eat. He also gave these loaves to his companions. The reason for this unusual action was hunger. It is not stated that it took place on the Sabbath. Obviously the focal point of the narrative is not that David did something on the Sabbath but that he ignored a law reserving the loaves of presence for the priests (cf. Lev 24:9).

The relationship between this story and its biblical reference text is complicated in many respects: **1.** By mentioning Abjathar, Mark or his source is wrong. According to 1 Sam 21:2, the actual priest was Achimelekh, the father of Abjathar.[10] **2.** The "house of God" was actually a temple in Nob (cf. 1 Sam 21:2);

---

[10] Jerome has observed this error, cf. Epistula 57:9,4–5 (CSEL 54:519). Becker (cf. note 2) comments that Mark has adopted the error from his source (ibid. p. 296). I support this view

the story in Mark does not explicitly mention the non-Jerusalemitic identity of that temple. **3.** The Markan story adds a motive for David and his companions to eat the loaves: David was hungry. This is not explicitly stated in 1 Sam 21:2–7, but undoubtedly fits the story line.[11] **4.** Like Mark 2:25–26, the biblical text does not explicitly state that it was a Sabbath when David ate the holy bread. That the story took place on a Sabbath, however, could be concluded from the information given in 1 Sam 21:7 that the bread handed out to David was bread which was taken away from the presence of the Lord and had to be replaced by fresh bread (cf. Lev 24:8, where the replacement of these loaves is supposed to take place on the Sabbath).[12] However, there is no hint in Mark 2:25–26 that the narrator understands the biblical text in that way, although this would suit the context in his story (which deals with the Sabbath). **5.** Unlike Mark 2:25–26, the biblical text does not relate that David gave these loaves also to his companions. According to 1 Sam 21:2–3, David visits the priest in Nob alone; 1 Sam 21:3 explicitly states that David's companions are elsewhere. They are, however, in an obscure manner mentioned in 1 Sam 21:5–6 (they could have had sexual intercourse, which obviously would have prevented the priest from giving David the holy bread). For the Markan (or Pre-Markan) Jesus, they were apparently present in the temple. The companions of David are mentioned twice in Jesus' story – and do not have a solid biblical foundation. To conclude, they are obviously important. The reason can be found in the fact that they correspond to the disciples of Jesus, and these, not Jesus, were accused by the Pharisees (cf. Mark 2:24).

The function of the story told by Jesus results from the parallel constellation formed by Jesus and his disciples on the one hand and David and his companions on the other. In this constellation, the companions and the disciples are beneficiaries, whereas David and Jesus take the initiative enabling them to benefit. However, Jesus' initiative can only be concluded by analogy from the biblical story he tells and could be described as follows: His disciples pluck ears of corn on the Sabbath because Jesus allows them to do so. And his permission is

---

since there are good reasons to assume that Mark was not that deeply interested in the story about David and Abjathar in Mark 2:25–26 and in this case took over elements that he did not verify (or elaborate on) in order to integrate it into his overall conception. This assumption is based upon the fact that Mark obviously overlooked the Davidic Christology underlying this story, cf. § II,1 of this article.

11 That David was hungry is also told in Jalquṭ to 1 Sam 21:5 (§ 130), see Billerbeck (1924 [n. 6], I:619).

12 Billerbeck (1924, [n. 6]) cites in Vol I, p. 618–619 rabbinic sources, bMenaḥot 95b and Jalquṭ to 1 Sam 21:5 (§ 130), where it is stated that the incident told in 1 Sam 21:2–7 happened on a Sabbath.

analogous to the fact that David ate from the holy loaves – thus reclaiming his right to dispose of them – before he gave them to his companions. The question of which *ratio* underlies the halakhic practice performed by David and Jesus is left open.

Research on this pericope sometimes prefers a non-Christological interpretation of the David analogy in Mark 2:25–26.[13] This might be the reading of Mark himself, who apparently was not keen on a Davidic Christology (see Mark 12:35–37). However, Davidic connotations are already associated with Jesus in Rom 1:3–4 which probably is based upon Pre-Pauline tradition.[14] In addition to that, Mark 2:25–26 is the first saying concluding the apophthegma in Mark 2:25–26 and may therefore be regarded as a parallel to the first sayings of Jesus in Mark 2:16 and 2:19a, which both show traces of an implicit Christology. It seems, therefore, plausible to find a Pre-Markan Davidic Christology in Mark 2:25–26, which to a certain degree is a parallel to the Pre-Pauline Christology in Rom 1:3–4 (see § III).

Mark 2:27–28: The sayings following the story about David are introduced by καὶ ἔλεγεν αὐτοῖς. This introduction makes Mark 2:27–28 a new interlocutory unit. This is important for the interpretation of Mark 2:28: by making Mark 2:27–28 a new interlocutory unit, the introductory formula καὶ ἔλεγεν αὐτοῖς binds 2:27 and 2:28 together. However, this does not mean that it separates Mark 2:27–28 from the preceding verses because there is strong thematic continuity between these two units. It rather stresses the importance of Mark 2:27–28. This is necessary since – after the comparatively long story told in 2:25–26 – these two short sayings would tend to be underemphasized were they not set a bit apart by a new introduction. A comparable phenomenon is encountered in Mark 7:9: here the phrase καὶ ἔλεγεν αὐτοῖς follows a long midrashic speech given by Jesus and criticizing pharisaic traditions (Mark 7:6–8), and it introduces a second midrash (Mark 7:9–13) dealing with the same theme.

Mark 2:27: Jesus' answer in Mark 2:25–26 has left open the question of just why David – and by analogy just why Jesus – can perform and establish a practice which (according to our text) overtly contradicts the view of the Pharisees. At this point, the underlying *ratio* is formulated: the Sabbath came into being for the sake of man and not man for the sake of the Sabbath. The specific meaning

---

13 Klostermann (1936 [n. 3]) for example writes: "Er [sc. Jesus] erinnert an das vorbildliche Verhalten Davids des Frommen (nicht etwa des Ahnherren des Messias)" (ibid. p. 30).
14 For the Pre-Pauline character of Rom 1:3–4 cf. E. Lohse, *Der Brief an die Römer*, KEK 4 (Göttingen: Vandenhoeck [15]2003), 64–67.

of this maxim may be concluded from the preceding story, which deals with human needs: David was hungry. As a consequence, in case of doubt, human needs are more important than Sabbath needs.

This view finds parallels in Jewish sources: In bJoma 84b-85b we encounter a long list of examples demonstrating that life-threatening danger supersedes the Sabbath. This rule is already formulated in mJoma 8:6b. In Jalqut to 1 Sam 21:5 (§ 130), David's behaviour in Nob is excused by the argument that his hunger threatened his life and that therefore the rules of the Sabbath were suspended (see Billerbeck [cf. note 6] I:619). In Mekhilta de Rabbi Jishmael, Kî tiśśa' 1 (to Ex 31:13) and bJoma 85b we find a saying that formally resembles Mark 2:27: לכם שבת מסורה ואין אתם לשבת ("The Sabbath is given to you, not you to the Sabbath").

However, Mark 2:27 not only formulates a halakhic principle. In order to argue for his controversial Sabbath halakha, Jesus refers more generally to the order of creation (for ἐγένετο as a term for "to be created" cf. John 1:3: πάντα δι' αὐτοῦ ἐγένετο). He defines the position of mankind in comparison with that of the Sabbath, and states that the Sabbath is subordinated to man in the sense that man is the *causa finalis* of the Sabbath. This view is in accordance with Jewish traditions which ascribe to mankind a pivotal position in the order of creation, particularly by maintaining that the world was created for the sake of man. Important for the interpretation of Mark 2:27 is mainly 2 Bar 14:8 because it resembles Mark 2:27 formally. There Baruch states that God has created man as the ruler of the world and that he was not created for the world but the world for him (ܡܛܠܬܗ ܥܠܡܐ ܐܠܐ ܥܠܡܐ ܠܗܢܐ ܐܬܒܪܝ ܗܘܐ ܗܘ ܠܐ).[15] Also Apc Sedr 3:2–4 is a parallel. There God states in a dispute with Sedrach that he has created earth, the sea and the goods of the earth for the sake of man (διὰ τὸν ἄνθρωπον).[16]

A reference to the order of creation is not untypical of the early Jesus tradition. This kind of argument can also be found in Mark 10:2–9, where Jesus points to Gen 1:27 and 2:24 in order to refute a possibility of divorce left open by Moses (cf. Mark 10:3 // Dtn 24:1.3). In Mark 10:2–9 the reference to the order of creation obviously aims at neutralizing a rule that derives from the Torah itself. This is not

---

15 Cf. Michael Kmosko (Ed.), *Liber Apocalypseos Baruchi Filii Neriae Translatus de Graeco in Syriacum*, Patrologia Syriaca I,2, (Paris: Firmin-Didot 1907), 1056–1300, especially p. 1093.
16 Cf. Otto Wahl (Ed.), *Apocalypsis Esdrae, Apocalypsis Sedrach, Visio Beati Esdrae*, Pseudepigrapha Veteris Testamenti Graece 4 (Leiden: Brill 1977), 37–48, especially 39. The Apc Sedr has been neglected in research so far. It is transmitted by only one codex from the 15th century (preserved in Oxford, Bodleian Library), cf. Wahl 13. Many passages in Apc Sedr find parallels in old Jewish tradition. At least parts of the narrative material presented in Apc Sedr are ancient.

necessarily the case in Mark 2:27 since the preceding verses do not openly state that the halakha defended by the Pharisees is Mosaic.

Mark 2:28: The verse concluding Mark 2:23–28 states that the Son of Man is Lord of the Sabbath. The title "Son of Man" has already been used in Mark 2:1–12. There the reader should have noticed that "Son of Man" is a title for Jesus. As a result, "Son of Man" here is a well-known Christological title; there should be no doubt in the reader that Jesus talks about himself in the third person singular. We can therefore maintain that like other apophthegmata found in Mark 2 this apophthegma is concluded by a word which formulates an explicit Christology.

The "Son of Man" is denoted "Lord of the Sabbath" (κύριος ... τοῦ Σαββάτου). The meaning of this designation may be deduced from the particle "also" (καί). This particle indicates that the Son of Man is already known as a Lord of something else. This can only point back to Mark 2:1–12, which deals with the power of the Son of Man to forgive sins. Apparently, Mark 2:28 implicitly states that the power to forgive sins gives Jesus the position of lordship with regard to the administration of sins. From Mark 2:7 we can infer the sense in which this lordship should be understood. There, the power to forgive sins is claimed to be the exclusive right of God himself. As a result, the Son of Man is, when he forgives sins, in the position of God. We may, therefore, assume that κύριος in Mark 2:28 is to be read in the maximalist sense of the word: The Son of Man is Lord with a capital "L"; he has (and not only with regard to the Sabbath) the position of the one who owns the secret name. Thereby Mark 2:23–28 is concluded by a word formulating the strongest claim concerning Christology that may be conceived; again we see a tendency to a climax concerning Christology in the concluding words of an apophthegma. But Mark 2:28 is not only important for Mark 2:23–28. It points back to and confirms the Son of Man Christology of Mark 2:1–12 thereby establishing a circular construction that includes the other Christological claims of Mark 2.

The importance of Mark 2:28 for the composition of the collection in Mark 2 makes it probable that the high Christology expressed by this verse derives from the Pre-Markan source. A Christology ascribing to Jesus the position of God is already plausible for Pre-Markan theology, since it is also known to Paul: the so-called *Philippians Hymn* of Phil 2:5–11 maintains that God gave Jesus Christ "the name above all names" (Phil 2:9) which according to Phil 2:11 may be identified as κύριος. The designation κύριος in the *Philippians Hymn* probably recalls the Hebrew word <ʾ*adōnāj*> which – according to Ps 110:1 MT // 109:1 LXX – represents both the Tetragrammaton and the royal (viz. Messianic or Christological) title אדני thus enabling a Christology ascribing to the Messiah the name (and thereby the position) of God. In 1 Cor 8:6 the phrase "one Lord Jesus Christ" (εἷς κύριος Ἰησοῦς Χριστός) runs parallel to the phrase "one God, the Father" (εἷς θεὸς ὁ πατήρ), which derives from the *Shma Jisrael*. Apparently, the monotheism of the *Shma Jisrael* is applied to Jesus Christ. The same tendency may be detected when in the salutations of the Pauline letters "Lord Jesus Christ" (κύριος Ἰησοῦς Χριστός) stands in parallel with "God, our Father" (θεὸς πατὴρ ἡμῶν).[17]

The use of the title κύριος in Mark 2:28 is generally consistent with the Gospel of Mark; Mark 12:35–37 also uses it in that sense. In that section, the Markan Jesus maintains that according to Ps 109:1 LXX the designation "Son of David" is not appropriate for the Christ, but rather κύριος. As already stated, in Ps 109:1 LXX this title designates both the name of God (יהוה) and the king (= Christ). This is probably the very fact to be observed by the reader of Mark 12:35–37, because Ps 109:1 LXX is explicitly cited in Mark 12:36 and the designation κύριος for Christ is marked as the important part of the citation in Mark 12:37. We may, therefore, conclude that Mark 12:35–37 formulates a Christology claiming the position of God for Christ viz. Jesus.[18] A narrative parallel to this "God Christology" may be found in Mark 6:45–52. When Jesus walks over the water he does something typical of God, cf. Job 9:8.[19]

The only element in Mark 2:28 which does not totally fit the Gospel of Mark is the syntactical position of the word κύριος: It is connected with a genitive attribute; the Son of Man is Lord *of* the Sabbath. Mark normally uses this title absolutely, cf. ὁ κύριος αὐτοῦ χρείαν ἔχει in Mark 11:3 (where αὐτοῦ designates an object); Mark 12:35–37 likewise points in this direction. Perhaps the unusual construction κύριος ... τοῦ Σαββάτου is a trait which derives from the Pre-Markan source.

---

17 Concerning God Christology in Paul cf. Jan Dochhorn, "Zu den religionsgeschichtlichen Voraussetzungen trinitarischer Gottesvorstellungen im frühen Christentum und in der Religion Israels", in *Trinität*, ed. Volker Henning Drecoll, Themen der Theologie 2 (Tübingen: J.C.B. Mohr 2011), 11–79, especially 15–24.
18 Concerning God Christology in Mark 12:35–37 see Dochhorn (2011 [n. 17], 29). A different exegesis of this text is proposed by Becker (2006 [n. 2], 271–283).
19 For a thorough analysis of Mark 6:45–52 and its parallels in the Gospels of Matthew and John, cf. John P. Meier, *A Marginal Jew*, Vol II: *Mentor, Message, and Miracles*, The Anchor Bible Reference Library (New York: Doubleday 1991), 905–924; 993–1003. See also Dochhorn (2011 [n. 17], 29–30).

3 Anthropology and Christology in Mark 2:27–28

One specific trait of Mark 2:27–28 has not been discussed so far: both verses are connected by the particle ὥστε ("so that"). This particle denotes a logical juncture between these two verses that should not be underestimated.[20] I propose to understand ὥστε as this word is usually understood: as a consecutive conjunction. As such it establishes a *nexus causalis* between Mark 2:27 and 2:28 which runs as follows: "The Son of Man is Lord of the Sabbath *because* man is according to the order of creation superior to the Sabbath". However, there remains the question of which specific kind of causal link may be detected between these two sentences. An *a fortiori* argument would indicate that "if Man is superior to the Sabbath, the Son of Man must *all the more* be the Lord of the Sabbath because he is more powerful (or something like that) than a normal man". An *a generali ad speciale* argument would conclude that the Son of Man is Lord of the Sabbath like other human beings because he is *also* a human being. Both of these causal connections suffer from the fact that particles representing "the more" or "also" are not connected to the Son of Man in the Greek text (καί = "also" in 2:28 is connected with the Sabbath and does not refer back to 2:27, but to 2:1–12). I suggest another causal connection which does not need any further logical particles: "The Son of Man is the Lord of the Sabbath because 'Son of Man' and 'Man' is in a special sense the same: the Son of Man is *the one* who represents the superiority of man to the Sabbath". Presupposed here is the notion that the Son of Man is the one who realizes the pivotal position man generally enjoys in the order of creation. The Son of Man is "the man", the exemplary man who realizes what mankind generally has or is. We can also use a more biblical term: the Son of Man is the New Adam or Adam in the better sense of the word. We should, however, not forget that (Jesus as) the New Adam is only the subject of the sentence in Mark 2:28. The predication attributed to him in Mark 2:28 is "Lord" and thereby the position of God (see § II,2).

Tradition-critical evidence corroborates an Adamic interpretation of Mark 2:27–28. Indeed, in many texts – especially in Pauline literature or literature associated with Paul – one may detect elements that seem better understandable if read with the notion that Christ is the exemplary man, who realizes the principal (original) cosmic superiority of man. I suggest that these texts are based upon a Son of Man Christology without actually mentioning the title Son of Man.

---

[20] Concerning the discussions caused by this juncture between Mark 2:27 and 2:28 see Doering (1993 [n. 6], 420–421).

– The first text to be adduced here is Hebr 1:1–2:9 which as a part of the letter to the Hebrews probably belongs to a milieu that has a certain affinity to Paul (cf. Hebr 13:23).[21] Hebr 1:1–2:9 primarily expounds the thesis that, by his post mortem enthronement, Jesus has become superior to the angels.[22] It is inter alia stated that the angels prostrate themselves before him (Hebr 1:6). This resembles Vita Adae et Evae 13 where it is related that the angels prostrated themselves before Adam immediately after he had been created. In accordance with that, the designation κληρονόμος ... πάντων, which is applied to the enthroned Son of God in Hebr 1:2, echoes what God says about man in Apocalypsis Sedrach 6:2 (Wahl [cf. note 16], 40): ἐποίησα αὐτὸν φρόνιμον καὶ κληρονόμον οὐρανοῦ καὶ γῆς καὶ πάντα αὐτῷ ὑπέταξα ("I have made him wise and the heir of heaven and earth, and I have subordinated everything to him"). We have good reason to assume that there are in fact intended Adamic connotations in Hebr 1:1–2:9 because these would fit well the verses concluding the whole section: Hebr 2:5–9 applies to the one who has acquired this extraordinary position the designation "man" (ἄνθρωπος) and cites as biblical reference Ps 8:5–7, a *locus classicus* of biblical anthropology proclaiming the cosmic superiority of man (alluded to in Apc Sedr 6:2, cf. πάντα αὐτῷ ὑπέταξα at the end of that verse and Ps 8:7). It seems probable that Hebr 1:1–2:9 depicts Jesus as the one who has – after his enthronement – become the man *par excellence* and is therefore superior to the angels as was Adam at the time of his creation. Son of Man Christology probably lies in the background of this conception: the enthronement theology presented in Hebr 1:1–2:9 harmonizes with the well-established concept that the Son of Man is an eschatological figure endowed with power (cf. Dan 7:14; Mark 14:62). Beyond that, we should not overlook the biblical reference cited in Hebr 2:6–8, namely Ps 8:5–7: it begins with a sentence in which "man" and "Son of Man" stand in parallel to one another, cf. Hebr 2:6 // Ps 8:5: τί ἐστιν ἄνθρωπος, ὅτι μιμνῄσκῃ αὐτοῦ, ἢ υἱὸς ἀνθρώπου[23], ὅτι ἐπισκέπτῃ

---

21 Hebr 12:23 mentions Timothy as someone who is known to those addressed. The New Testament does not know any Timothy except for the one who was a disciple and assistant of Paul. Concerning a sociological affinity between Hebrews and Paulinism cf. Knut Backhaus, "Der Hebräerbrief und die Paulus-Schule", *BZ* 37 (1993): 183–208.
22 Cf. Jan Dochhorn, "Die Christologie in Hebr 1:1–2:9 und die Weltherrschaft Adams in Vit Ad 11–17". In *Biblical Figures in Deuterocanonical and Cognate Literature*, eds. Hermann Lichtenberger / Ulrike Mittmann-Richert, Deuterocanonical and Cognate Literature. Yearbook 2008 (Berlin: De Gruyter 2008), 281–302.
23 Ps 8,5 and the quotation in Hebr 2,6 use the anarthrous form υἱὸς ἀνθρώπου, whereas the Gospels have the arthrous form ὁ υἱὸς τοῦ ἀνθρώπου, cf. Joseph Fitzmyer, "The New Testament Title 'Son of Man' Philologically Considered". In Joseph A. Fitzmyer, *A Wandering Aramean. Collected Aramaic Essays*, SBL.MS 25 (Missoula: Scholars Press 1979), 143–160, especially 144–

αὐτόν; ("What is man, that you remind him, and the Son of Man, that you take care of him?"). After that this verse is applied to Jesus (cf. Hebr 2:9). Indirectly Jesus is identified both as man and as Son of Man.

– Features pointing to an Adamic Christology may also be found in a text written by Paul himself: 1 Cor 15:23–28. This passage depicts how God after Christ's resurrection subordinates everything to Christ (excluding himself). This scenario is mainly built upon two biblical texts, namely Ps 109:1–2 and – again – Ps 8. Especially the notion that everything will be put under Christ's feet (1 Cor 15:27) points to Ps 8 (cf. Ps 8:7). Once more we encounter Ps 8, which describes the cosmic superiority of Man, and its anthropological concepts are applied to Jesus Christ. Paul was probably aware of the anthropological implications of this Psalm. This is indicated by the fact that the whole unit is preceded by an Adam-Christ typology (1 Cor 15:22). Apparently for him Christ was the new Adam who after his resurrection realized the position which Adam, and that is to say man generally, should possess. Beyond that, there is good reason to assume that in 1 Cor 15:22.23–28, too, a Son of Man Christology functions as the traditional background: In 1 Cor 15:47 Christ is presented as the eschatological "man from heaven" (ἄνθρωπος ἐξ οὐρανοῦ). This verse is part of a passage (1 Cor 15:44b-49) that compares the first man (Adam) and the last man (the man from heaven = Christ) and is thereby strongly related to the Adam-Christ typology in 1 Cor 15:22. Important is now the fact that the "man from heaven" (= Christ / the last Adam) with high probability recalls the Son of Man: Early Christianity generally imagines the Son of Man as coming from heaven in the last days, cf. Mark 13:26 par; Rev 14:14–26. In addition to that, the allusions to Ps 8 in 1 Cor 15:23–28 may likewise indicate that Son of Man Christology lies in the background since Ps 8:5 includes the term "Son of Man" (see above).

– A third text to be mentioned in this series is the notice about the temptation of Jesus by Satan in Mark 1:13. Three motifs in this short text point to contemporary concepts about Adam as they are developed in the Vita Adae et Evae. **1.** In Vit Ad 44 (15–21), it is primarily the Devil who misleads (first Eve and then) Adam to eat from the forbidden tree (he does it by inspiring the serpent). The temptation motif in Mark 1:13 probably recalls a Satanological interpretation of Gen 3, which is attested here and elsewhere in Early Judaism (cf. Sap Sal 2:23–25; 2 En 31:3–6;

---

145. There is not necessarily a strong conceptual difference between these two phrases, at least not in the New Testament, cf. John 5,27, which uses the anarthrous phrase in parallel to ὁ υἱός (cf. John 5,26), thus evoking a Christological meaning of the anarthrous phrase that in my view has the same value as the one of ὁ υἱὸς τοῦ ἀνθρώπου in John 1:51.

3. Bar 4:8; 9:7; Targum Ps-Jon ad Gen 3:4; PRE 13:2). **2.** The animals accompanying Jesus in the desert fit the harmony between Adam and the animals as it is described in Vit Ad 44 (15), a scene which is built upon the *dominium bestiarum* motif in Gen 1:26 ff. and perhaps Ps 8.[24] **3.** The angels serving Jesus possibly remind the reader of Adam's superiority to the angels as it is known especially from Vita Adae 13 (cf. also the late tradition in Abôth de Rabbi Nathan 1:11 about the angels roasting and chilling wine for Adam in the Gan Eden).[25] We have, as a consequence, good reason to assume that Mark 1:13 presents Jesus as the New Adam. With a certain degree of probability we can also assume that this New Adam Christology is connected to the Son of Man Christology as attested in other parts of the Gospel of Mark: As I have demonstrated elsewhere, the temptation of Jesus, the New Adam, by Satan in Mark 1:13 is strongly linked to the temptation of Jesus, the Son of Man, by the Satan Peter in Mark 8:31–33.[26] As a consequence, Mark 1:13 presents Jesus implicitly as both the New Adam and as Son of Man.

We have suggested that the logical juncture between man and Son of Man in Mark 2:27–28 may be explained by a Christological and anthropological concept that links Son of Man and Adam Christology. This thesis may be corroborated by the observation that the parallel texts pointing to this concept contain other features which also help to elucidate Mark 2:27–28. **1.** In all three texts, Christ's superiority is related to the cosmic order. This is clearly true for 1 Cor 15:23–28, where the ἀρχαί, δυνάμεις and ἐξουσίαι and Death that will be subordinated to Christ are cosmic powers. Elsewhere Paul is aware of the concept of Christ's cosmic superiority, cf. 1 Cor 3:22–23: εἴτε Παῦλος εἴτε Ἀπόλλως εἴτε Κηφᾶς, εἴτε κόσμος εἴτε ζωὴ εἴτε θάνατος, εἴτε ἐνεστῶτα εἴτε μέλλοντα – πάντα ὑμῶν, 23 ὑμεῖς δὲ Χριστοῦ, Χριστὸς δὲ θεοῦ ("Paul as well as Apollos and Kephas, world as well as life and death, things present as well as things to come – everything belongs to you, 23 and you belong to Christ, and Christ to God"). The cosmology and Christology of this text link it strongly with 1 Cor 15:23–28, not least by its theocentric perspective, cf. 1 Cor 15:28. We may therefore assume that it belongs to the same thematic complex. To conclude: For Paul, Christ's superiority has cosmic dimensions. This fits Mark 2:27–28 well, where

---

24 Cf. Dochhorn, "Christologie" (2008 [n. 22]).
25 Cf. Samuel Schechter (Ed.), *Aboth de Rabbi Nathan* (Wien: Knöpflmacher 1887) (reprint: Hildesheim: Olms 1979), 3, lines 19–20 and Kaim Pollak, *Rabbi Nathans System der Ethik und Moral. Zum erstenmale übersetzt und mit Anmerkungen versehen* (Budapest: Adolf Alkalay & Sohn 1905), 15.
26 Cf. Jan Dochhorn, "The Devil in Mark" (forthcoming, in an anthology edited by Erkki Koskenniemi), § 3.

Christ is superior to the Sabbath, which in 2:27 is presented as a part of the order of creation. Christ's position of power is also related to the cosmic order in Hebr 1:1–2:9: The whole world is subordinated to the man mentioned in Ps 8:5–7, cf. Hebr 1:2; 2:5. Motifs recalling a cosmic dominion of man also appear in Mark 1:13: The animals accompanying Jesus probably recall Adam's power over the animals as this is described in Vit Ad 44 (16), and the angels serving him probably recall Adams superiority to the angels, cf. Vita Adae 13. **2.** In all three texts an Adamic Christology is accompanied by Christological motifs suggesting a Messianology which – in the strict sense of the term Messianology – denotes Jesus as the eschatological king of Israel. In Hebr 1:1–2:9 the enthroned "man" occupies the position at the right hand of God (Hebr 1:3b). He is thereby the king of Israel described by Ps 110:1; cf. the citation of this verse in Hebr 1:13. The same is true for 1 Cor 15:23–28, which links Ps 8 and Ps 110:1 together. A cross reading of Ps 8 and Ps 110:1 is well attested in other texts, too, cf. Mark 14:62, where the Son of Man sits at the right hand of the Power, and probably also Mark 12:36, where Ps 109:1 LXX is cited in a wording that seems to be influenced by Ps 8:7 LXX (Mark has ὑποκάτω instead of ὑποπόδιον, probably because he has been influenced by Ps 8:7 LXX; see BECKER [cf. note 2], 274). A combination of Son of Man Christology and Messianology is probably also intended in Mark 1:13 and its context. Mark 1:13 presents Christ implicitly as the Son of Man, and the preceding verses, which deal with the baptism of Jesus, depict him as the Son of God. Especially the voice from heaven proclaims him as the son of God, and the words spoken by this voice recall Ps 2:7. There the king of Israel is denoted by this title. The baptism of Jesus has thereby a Messianic connotation. A combination of Messianology and Son of Man Christology can also be detected in Mark 2:27–28 and its context: Mark 2:28 deals with the Son of Man, whereas Mark 2:25–26 evokes Davidic Christology, which in the source underlying Mark 2 may have hinted at the notion that Jesus is the eschatological king of Israel. **3.** In 1 Corinthians and Hebrews the power position of Christ has consequences for others, namely Christians. 1 Cor 15:23–28 is primarily meant to illustrate that the resurrection of Christ also implies the resurrection of Christians, and 1 Cor 3:22–23, which mentions Christ's power position, ascribes just this position to the Christians in Corinth. According to Hebr 1:1–2:9, Christ's superiority to the angels has consequences for Christians as well: they no longer belong to the Torah which is promulgated by angels (Hebr 2:2), but to Christ (Hebr 2:3). Here, being associated with the "New Adam" obviously constitutes a distance from the Torah. This may be important for the interpretation of Mark 2:23–28, where rules of the Torah are discussed.

Finally, one crucial moment needs to be mentioned: common to all three parallels to Mark 2:27–28 is the fact that Ps 8 plays an important role. This is especially true for 1 Cor 15:23–28 and Hebr 1:1–2:9. Obviously this Psalm was needed in order to establish a Son of Man Christology which interpreted the Son of Man as the New Adam, viz. the man *par excellence*. I suppose that the reason for this special role of Ps 8 may be found in Ps 8:5. This verse introduces the anthropological unit of Ps 8, and here the terms "man" (ἄνθρωπος) and "Son of Man" (υἱὸς ἀνθρώπου) appear side by side. This has probably led to the idea that what is true for man is true for the Son of Man. Nothing else is said in Mark 3:27–28: man has the primary position in the order of creation, and therefore this is the position of the Son of Man (who realizes the power position of man). I can easily imagine that Ps 8:5 is the exegetical background to Mark 2:27–28: in both texts, man and Son of Man appear side by side, and they appear in the same order.

If this is true, the result of this exegesis of Mark 2:27–28 would be comparably simple: Mark *2:27–28 is based upon Ps 8:5. Both verses belong together as Ps 8:5a and Ps 8:5b belong together.* By identifying this exegetical foundation of Mark 2:27–28 we may have found a biblical source text which aided early Christians significantly in establishing their Christology. We could identify a Son of Man, viz. New Adam, Christology associated with Ps 8 that probably had its exegetical point of departure in Ps 8:5. It is attested in a Pauline text, in the Letter to the Hebrews (which has certain affinities to Paul), and in a tradition taken up by Mark.

III Mark and Paul: An epilogue

On two occasions Pauline parallels were important for the interpretation of Mark 2:23–28, especially the concluding words in Mark 2:27–28. In both cases, the parallels concern Christological claims expressed in the Markan text or his traditional source.

1. The first Christological claim echoed in the Pauline material is the Davidic Christology underlying the story Jesus tells about David and Abjathar in Mark 2:25–26. The parallel is to be found in Rom 1:3–4, the only hint at a Davidic Christology in a Proto-Pauline Text. It is therefore with a high degree of certainty based upon tradition taken up by Paul. Thereby, we can conclude that within Early Christianity, the Davidic Christology is quite old, even prior to Paul. However, far more important is what happens with this Davidic Christology in Rom 1:3–4, because this can shed light on similar processes in the Markan text: in Rom 1:3–4, Davidic Christology is overlaid by another type of Christology. The claim that Jesus is the son of David is associated with his "flesh" (σάρξ) and appears to be subordinated to another claim, namely the Christological title "Son of God" which is associated with "spirit" (πνεῦμα) in Rom 1:4 and – in Paul's intended sense – probably points to a God Christology (cf. Rom 9:5). The God Christology might be the Pauline reading, but a juxtaposition of "Son of David according to the flesh" *versus* "Son of God according to the Spirit" is probably already traditional.[27] Similar structures may be observed in Mark 2:23–28: An implicit hint at a Davidic Christology may be identified in the story about David and Abjathar (Mark 2:25–26), but the pericope concludes with explicit Christological claims identifying Jesus as the Son of Man and ascribing to this Son of Man the power of the Lord (Mark 2:28). Here a Davidic Christology is apparently overlaid by a Christology that culminates in predications attributing to Jesus the position of God.

We have, however, already stated that the Christological construction identified in Mark 2:23–28 is not of Markan origin, but derives from the written source taken up by Mark in Mark 2 (see § II,1). We may thereby state: a God Christology can obviously not only be ascribed to the latest layers of Synoptic tradition, it is – as the Pauline parallels also show – an older phenomenon. Apparently, we cannot easily reconstruct a history of Christology that would classify a "high Christology" as a later development within Early Christianity. In this context another caveat must also be formulated. When I say that a Davidic Christology appears to be subordinated in Mark 2:23–28, this should not be understood in diachronic categories. The Davidic Christology is not necessarily the older concept that was later integrated into the frame of a Son of Man Christology identifying this Son of Man with God. The frame is not necessarily younger than the concept integrated by the frame. Concerning the Pre-Markan tradition in Mark 2,23–28 this means: the story about David and Abjathar is not necessarily older than the saying in Mark 2,28 which ascribes to the Son of Man the position of God. A quick glance at later layers of Early Christian literature will corroborate this caveat: the heyday of a Davidic Christology would come after Mark's source in Mark 2 was written; most of the attestations of Christ as the Son of David belong to writings that probably are to be dated later than Mark, cf. Luke 1:32; Matt 1:1; 12:23; 21:9.15; 2. Tim 2:8; Barn 12:10 Ign Eph 18:2; Smyrn 1:1 (and other passages in Ignatius' authentic letters that all depend on Rom 1:3). This is, however, not true for Mark himself: he not only subordinates the Davidic Christology (like Paul and his source [?] and also the collection taken up in Mark 2); he even abrogates

---

[27] More about the Pre-Pauline tradition in Rom 1:3–4 and its Pauline reading may be found in Dochhorn, "Voraussetzungen" (2011 [n. 17], 23; 45; 47). For the Pre-Pauline character of Rom 1:3–4 cf. Lohse (2003 [note 14], 64–67).

it, as we may conclude from Mark 12:35–37 (see § II,2), thereby radicalizing the God Christology he has already found in the source underlying Mark 2. We may assume that Mark was not aware of the Davidic Christology that was implied by the story about David and Abjathar in Mark 2:25–26.

2. The second Christological concept that is to be debated here is the Son of Man Christology in Mark 2:27–28 that identifies the Son of Man as the Man *par excellence* or as the New Adam. As we have stated in § II,3, this concept finds a Pauline parallel in 1 Cor 15 and a parallel akin to Pauline theology in Hebr 1:1–2:9. The structure underlying this concept is exegetical work on Ps 8:5 that enabled Christian theologians to identify Man *in genere* and the Son of Man and may thereby explain why both in 1 Cor 15 and in Hebr 1:1–2:9 statements normally associated with the Son of Man are associated with Christ as "the Man" or the New Adam. What we have found is nothing less than an exegetical substructure that was important for an early Christian cohabitation of Adamic motifs and a Son of Man Christology.[28] And Mark 2:27–28 is probably a very important witness to this substructure: We have already stated in § II,3 that the sequence "Man" / "Son of Man", as it is found in Ps 8:5, also appears in Mark 2:27–28 because there a word pertaining to Man is followed by a word pertaining to the Son of Man. Thus Mark 2:27–28 implicitly takes up Ps 8:5; we are not presented with an explicit exegesis or citation but with new words created upon implicit exegetical suppositions. We may often observe that haggadic inventions which implicitly work with scriptural reference texts are older than parallels that make these references explicit.[29] This might indicate that we should not underestimate the *ancienneté* of Mark 2:27–28, but more than a possibility cannot be formulated here. How old it is depends not least on the question of how old Adamic moments in the Messianology of Early Christianity are. Did Jesus describe himself

---

28 Cf. Michael Goulder, "Psalm 8 and the Son of Man", *NTS* 48 (2002): 18–29 who also stresses the importance of Ps 8:5 as an exegetical source text for early Christology. He supposes that the whole Son of Man Christology derives from Pauline Christianity (especially Mark and the author of Hebrews) and that the exegesis of Ps 8:5 in Hebr 2:6–9 is the starting point for this development.

29 An example of this observation are the parallels between haggadic narrations about Adam and Eve in the Vita Adae et Evae and the exegetical comments leading to what are in principle the same stories in parallels preserved by the rabbinic Midrash Bereshit Rabbah, cf. Gary A. Anderson, "The Penitence Narrative in the Life of Adam and Eve", *Hebrew Union College Annual* 63 (1992): 1–38.

in these categories? Did he use the term "Son of Man" in order to explain his self-image, and if he did, did this title have any Adamic connotations?[30]

We are far from Mark and Paul, and that means: we are probably dealing with earlier layers of Early Christian religion, perhaps with Jesus himself. This does not happen by chance: when we are discussing Christological concepts attested by early Christian authors, we must be aware of the possibility that we are confronted with concepts which primarily belong to the traditional presuppositions upon which our authors depend. The redaction criticism established in New Testament research after the Second World War and modern synchronism has in some respects been helpful for refining our view on Early Christianity, but it could also lead to overlooking the fact that the Christian authors have their predecessors. In other words: something happened in Early Christianity before the texts known to us were formulated; something happened before Mark and Paul. This is especially true for Christological concepts: we have good reason to assume that a lot of them were generated quite early, and this pertains to Christological claims ascribing to Jesus the position of God as well.[31] Many special elements may be found that Mark and Paul have in common. This article points to something more general: Mark and Paul share Christological ideas because they are witnesses to Early Christian theology. Their common material may simply be very old.

---

[30] Concerning the debate about the Son of Man cf. Mogens Müller, *The Expression "Son of Man" and the Development of Christology* (London: Copenhagen International Seminar 2008).
[31] Cf. Dochhorn, "Voraussetzungen" (2011 [n. 17], 14–31).

Kasper Bro Larsen
Mark 7:1–23: A Pauline Halakah?

1 Introduction: Mark in the Pauline Sphere?[1]

Was the Gospel of Mark a Pauline Gospel, written under the influence of the Apostle Paul? The question is of great importance for any attempt at reconstructing the ideological and sociological trajectories of the Christ movement in the first century CE. In 1923, Martin Werner formulated a negative answer to the question, which became the standard solution to the problem in New Testament scholarship of the twentieth century: The apparent similarities between Paul and Mark, Werner claimed, are not exclusively Pauline features but general and widespread ideas and concepts that flourished in Early Christianity.[2] During the 1990s, the consensus was increasingly challenged, and Joel Marcus' article "Mark—Interpreter of Paul" (2000) became the pinnacle of that trend.[3] Marcus

---

[1] This article was first presented at the "Mark and Paul Beyond the Gospel/Letter Divide" research seminar in Copenhagen (August 24–27, 2011). I wish to thank the participants for valuable comments and suggestions, especially Prof. Elizabeth Struthers Malbon, my official respondent, and Prof. Troels Engberg-Pedersen, who made remarks in the editing process. Stacey Cozart and Nick Marshall took time to improve the English language of the article, for which I am most grateful.

[2] The view-point rendered above represents the statements in the conclusion of Werner's book: "Wo Markus mit Paulus übereinstimmt, handelt es sich immer um allgemein-urchristliche Anschauungen." See Martin Werner, *Der Einfluss paulinischer Theologie im Markusevangelium: Eine Studie zur neutestamentlichen Theologie*, BZNW 1 (Giessen: Alfred Töpelmann, 1923), 209. Occasionally, Werner describes the parallels between Paul and Mark more narrowly as belonging to Gentile Christianity (1923, 202). Werner's monograph was intended as a refutation of Gustav Volkmar's speculative assertion that the Gospel of Mark was a Pauline allegory. See Volkmar, *Die Religion Jesu* (Leipzig: Brockhaus, 1857) and *Die Evangelien oder Marcus und Die Synopsis der kanonischen und ausserkanonischen Evangelien nach dem ältesten Text mit historisch-exegetischem Commentar* (Leipzig: Fues's Verlag [R. Reisland], 1870).

[3] Joel Marcus, "Mark—Interpreter of Paul." *NTS* 46 (2000): 473–87. See also Michael D. Goulder, "Those Outside (Mk. 4.10–12)." *NT* (1991): 289–302; John R. Donahue, "The Quest for the Community of Mark's Gospel." In *The Four Gospels 1992: Festschrift Frans Neirynck*, eds. Frans van Segbroeck et al., BEThL 100 (Leuven: Leuven University, 1992), 2:817–38; Wolfgang Schenk, "Sekundäre Jesuanisierungen von primären Paulus-Aussagen bei Markus." In Segbroeck et al. 1992, 2:877–904; John R. Donahue, "Windows and Mirrors: The Setting of Mark's Gospel." *CBQ* 57 (1995): 1–26; and William R. Telford, *The Theology of the Gospel of Mark*, New Testament Theology (Cambridge: Cambridge University, 1999), 164–69 with a more comprehensive list of references.

called for a reconsideration of the many similarities between Paul and Mark, and mentioned, for example, the use of εὐαγγέλιον ('gospel') as a key term, Jesus' victory over demonic powers and his summoning of a new era, the portrayal of Jesus as the new Adam, emphasis on faith, criticism of Peter, the missionary transition from Jews to Gentiles, and the eschatological change in Torah practice (Marcus 2000, 475–76). In the article, Marcus' test case was the 'theology of the cross', which he saw as a Pauline hallmark and an indicator of Pauline influence in later writings. Marcus asserted that this exact hallmark is present in Mark's narrative of the crucified Messiah, whereas it fades down in the other gospels. Thus, contrary to Werner, Marcus described Mark as an interpreter of Paul, well situated within the apostle's sphere of influence.

In recent years, Marcus' article has yielded renewed discussion of the question concerning possible Paulinism in Mark.[4] The present article contributes to this discussion by suggesting a *via media* between Werner and Marcus on the basis of another test case: the halakic controversy and school dialogues on purity and impurity in Mark 7:1–23, where Jesus renounces standard Jewish dietary practice by stating that "... there is nothing outside a person that by going in can defile" (7:15; NRSV).[5] Such a test case may be more or less well-chosen. The reason to consider this particular pericope is not only that it represents a stance on Jewish dietary practice comparable to Paul's (Rom 14; 1 Cor 8; 10; Gal 2), but also that this particular stance was an essential issue in his epistles, and even a controversial one that, according to his own epistles, separated him from other, competing forms of early Christ belief. The practice of abandoning Jewish dietary norms in order to establish trans-ethnical communities of Christ believers characterizes both Paul's theology and his missionary practice, possibly even more than does his Christology or so-called 'theology of the cross'—the main phenom-

---

4 Michael F. Bird, "Mark: Interpreter of Peter and Disciple of Paul." In *Paul and the Gospels: Christologies, Conflicts and Convergences*, eds. Michael F. Bird and Joel Willitts, LNTS 411 (London: T&T Clark, 2011), 30–61; James G. Crossley, "Mark, Paul and the Question of Influences." In Bird and Willits 2011, 10–29; David C. Sim, "Matthew's Use of Mark: Did Matthew Intend to Supplement or Replace His Primary Source?" *NTS* 57 (2011): 176–92.

5 In the present article, 'halakic' and 'halakah' are used in a broad sense referring to Jewish regulations concerning the adequate interpretation of ritual and ethical commandments in the Torah. In early Judaism, halakic debates dealt with practices in which Jews would display their group identity, both internally between different forms of Judaism and externally vis-à-vis the dominant Greco-Roman culture. See Peter J. Tomson, "Halakhah in the New Testament: A Research Overview." In *The New Testament and Rabbinic Literature*, eds. Raimund Bieringer et al., JSJSup 136 (Leiden: Brill, 2010), 137–40.

ena of interest in Werner and Marcus. On that basis, Mark 7:1–23 appears to be a crucial text in the discussion of possible Pauline influence on Mark.⁶

But is it at all methodologically possible to identify Pauline influence on other writings of the Christ movement when the texts contain no direct quotations? The road to exegetical results is paved with methodological difficulties, the most substantial ones relating to the nature of the sources available to us and to the disputed questions concerning cultural and religious context. Of course, the only way to determine Pauline influence is to isolate elements that are *exclusively* Pauline and then to search for them in Mark. But how can we know the *differentiae specificae* of Pauline thought when Paul's own letters are the only surviving sources from the pre-Markan Christ movement? We are left with virtually nothing to compare Paul with.⁷ The lack of necessary sources and the fact that those available to us have been selected in order to suit later theological agendas leaves us with a wide range of unknown quantities in the equation. Scholars may be able to identify main agendas in the Pauline epistles available to us ('theology of the cross', life 'in Christ', abandonment of Jewish purity practice, etc.), but we cannot demonstrate that these agendas were *exclusively* Pauline. Our map of mid-first century Christ belief is a fragmented one with plenty of blank spaces. Other groups independent of Paul may very well have developed similar views—and handed them over to Mark without leaving clear traces in the surviving sources. I am therefore quite hesitant about the entire endeavour.

If, however, we are content that of historical reconstruction is not about proof, but about greater and lesser degrees of probability on the basis of available sources, the question becomes how much we can in fact make probable. Here, Marcus' ambition is too high, Werner's too modest. On the one hand, it is very difficult to make plausible that the parallels between Paul's epistles and Mark's Gospel are necessary indications of Pauline influence (Marcus); on the other hand, it is not sufficient to say that the parallels are only representative of shared, undisputed elements of first-century Christ belief (Werner). Rather,

---

6 Unfortunately, Werner was very brief in his discussion of Mark 7:1–23 (Werner 1923, 79–81). Concerning Paul's radical understanding of halakah, scholars generally understand Paul's addressees as either Jews and Gentiles in conjunction (James D.G. Dunn, *Romans*, Word Biblical Commentary 38a-b [Dallas: Word Books, 1988]) or as exclusively Gentile (Stanley Stowers, *A Rereading of Romans: Justice, Jews, and Gentiles* [New Haven, Yale University Press, 1994]). According to the latter option, Paul's halakic practice was conventional in regard to Jewish Christ believers like himself. The discussion is important for understanding the historical Paul, but has little impact on the reception-historical question discussed in the present article.
7 The hypothetical Q source is not relevant in the present context since it does not address purity halakah.

some of the shared notions in Paul and Mark situate both authorships on the same side in the controversies of the Christ movement, thus implying that these shared notions represent the Christ belief of Gentile-dominated, Diaspora communities in opposition to the Christ belief in Jewish populations, most notably among the 'pillars' in Jerusalem. Paul's letters, in other words, may provide an outline of the halakic controversy landscape on which we may place Paul and Mark rather close to each other. The purity halakah in Mark 7 is a halakah for Gentile communities, but not necessarily Pauline. In order to make that case, however, we must examine and evaluate the possible Pauline parallels in the pericope. As we shall see, they are quite numerous but point in different directions.

2 Mark 7:1–23: Jesuanic Halakah or the Halakah of Gentile Christ Believers?

Before searching for possible Pauline connections, it is necessary to discuss the *Traditionsgeschichte* of the pericope in Mark 7:1–23. If the traditions concerning the rejection of Jewish dietary practices go back to the historical Jesus, the question of Pauline influence becomes even more complex, since we will be dealing with applied Jesuanic halakah in both Paul and Mark. The question comes down to whether or not the abandonment of the Jewish dietary code in vv. 14–19 is likely to have been expressed in an early first-century Jewish-Palestinian setting in the environment of the historical Jesus. It is obvious that the pericope as it appears in the present Markan context is very much redactional. For example, Jewish hand-washing and purity practices, whether real, retrojected, or fictional, are explained to a Gentile audience (vv. 3–4, 11), and in v. 19b the redactor brings in an explanatory clause that reinforces the radicality of the preceding Jesus saying: "Thus he declared all foods clean [καθαρίζων πάντα τὰ βρώματα]."[8] Moreover, in terms of Mark's narrative of the development of Jesus' ministry, the peri-

---

[8] Hand-washing before meals is not a biblical requirement and was according to E. P. Sanders not practised in Second Temple Judaism, let alone by the Pharisees. The rabbinic material, which probably describes later practices, discusses hand-washing for different purposes of ritual purity but not as a general obligation at meals (see E. P. Sanders, *Judaism: Practice and Belief, 63 BCE-66 CE* (London: SCM, 1992, 437–38). For recent discussions, however, see Eyal Regev, "Pure Individualism: The Idea of Non-Priestly Purity in Ancient Judaism." *JSJ* 31 (2000): 176–202 and Yair Furstenberg, "Defilement Penetrating the Body: A New Understanding of Contamination in Mark 7.15." *NTS* 54 (2008): 176–200. If hand-washing practices appear for the first time in sources from the Diaspora (*Arist*. 305–6; *Sib. Or*. 3.591–3; cf. Sanders 1992, 223–4; 437), it may be an indication of a Diaspora setting for Mark 7:1–4a.

cope appears as the point of opening toward the Gentile world by preparing the way for the subsequent exorcism where Jesus heals the Syrophoenician woman's daughter (7:24–30).[9] In the Markan context, Mark 7:1–23 clearly appears as an explanation and legitimization of Gentile Christ believers' interpretation of the Jewish dietary code, as the pericope is connected with the mission to the Gentiles. Nevertheless, most exegetes, having noticed the redactional elements in the text, continue to trace the Jesus sayings in vv. 14–19 (fully or partially) back to Palestinian, Aramaic sources or even to the historical Jesus himself. This has been done both on the basis of the criterion of dissimilarity[10] and the criterion of contextual plausibility.[11] But the radical rejection of the dietary code is not a very plausible option within the halakic spectrum of pre-70 Palestine.[12] It may only apply to the context of the historical Jesus if, as James D. G. Dunn has argued, the Jesus saying in v. 15 is originally to be heard not as a radical *not-this-but-that* statement ("not unclean food, but unclean heart defiles"), but as a relative *less-this-than-that* statement ("unclean food defiles less than unclean heart") (Dunn 1990, 47; cf. Sanders 1990, 28). It would then be in accordance with the prophetic tradition and the majority of ancient Jewish voices, whose criticism of sheer outward piety did not call into question the basic interdependence between outward and inward purity (see Isa 29:13, cf. Mark 7:6–7; Isa 1:10; 58:1–14; Hos 6:6; Amos 5:21–24; Philo, *De migr. Abr.* 89–93; Pseudo-Phocylides 228; *m. Sotah* 9:15).[13] A similar, relative meaning of the saying seems to be preserved in the Matthean version of the pericope, which famously omits the inference of the redactor in Mark 7:19b (Matt 15:1–20). Moreover, Matt 15:20 concludes that "... to eat with unwashed hands does not defile", which in a

---

9 Elizabeth Struthers Malbon, "Echoes and Foreshadowings in Mark 4–8: Reading and Rereading." *JBL* 112 (1993): 213–32.
10 Rudolf Bultmann, *Die Geschichte der synoptischen Tradition*, FRLANT 12/29, 7th ed. (Göttingen: Vandenhoeck & Ruprecht, 1967 [1921]), 110, 158.
11 See, e.g., James D. G. Dunn, "Jesus and Ritual Purity: A Study of the Tradition-History of Mark 7.15." In *Jesus, Paul and the Law: Studies in Mark and Galatians* (London: SPCK, 1990 [1985]) 37–60; Roger P. Booth, *Jesus and the Laws of Purity: Tradition History and Legal History in Mark 7*, JSNTSup 13 (Sheffield: JSOT Press, 1986); 96–114; Thomas Kazen, *Jesus and Purity Halakhah: Was Jesus Indifferent to Impurity?* CBNTS 38 (Stockholm: Almqvist & Wiksell International, 2002), 60–88, 345 and *Issues of Impurity in Early Judaism*, CBNTS 45 (Winona Lake: Eisenbrauns, 2010), 113–35. For a more skeptical approach, see Heikki Räisänen. "Jesus and the Food Laws: Reflections on Mark 7:15." *JSNT* 16 (1982): 79–100.
12 E.P. Sanders, *Jewish Law from Jesus to the Mishnah: Five Studies* (London: SCM, 1990), 23–28.
13 See Menahem Kister, "Law, Morality, and Rhetoric in Some Sayings of Jesus." In *Studies in Ancient Midrash*, ed. J. L. Kugel, Harvard Center for Jewish Studies (Cambridge: Harvard University Press, 2001), 145–54.

very explicit manner directs criticism away from the dietary code in general toward hand-washing only.

Despite the possibility that the logion in v. 15 may have appeared in the relative sense at an earlier moment in its history of transmission, its meaning in Mark is radical (*not this, but that*).[14] Such radical neglect of Jewish dietary practice, expressed from within a Jewish world-view, probably does not go back to the historical Jesus, but has parallels in a Jewish Diaspora context. The radical or pure allegorists in Philo (*De migr. Abr.* 89–93), who abandoned circumcision and Sabbath on the basis of their recognition of the spiritual meaning of the Torah, is a parallel example.[15] In the Christ movement, similar halakah appeared where the movement crossed ethnic boundaries, such as in Antioch (Acts 11:20; Gal 2). It thus appeared in Gentile or ethnically mixed circles of Christ believers (Acts 10–11; *Gos. Thom.* 14; see Räisänen 1982). In other spheres of the Christ movement, however, radical purity halakah was met with opposition. As mentioned, Matthew played down the radicalism of Mark 7:1–23 on the basis of his view of the Torah (Matt 5:17–20). 'Judaizers' sought to promote circumcision and maybe also Jewish dietary practice among Gentile Christ believers in Galatia (Gal 2:12–14; 4:10; 6:12). Revelation criticizes Nicolaitans (possibly identical with the false apostles in 2:2 and the Jezebel followers in 2:20), who eat food sacrificed to idols (Rev 2:12–21). Luke mentions Christ-believing Pharisees who argue for full Torah fulfilment for Gentile Christ believers (Acts 15:5), whereas the Lukan version of the so-called apostolic council ends up representing a compromise between conventional and radical halakah in the Christ movement (Acts 15; 21:25). Paul and Mark, however, in terms of halakah both belong to the radical side of the spectrum. Here, Paul was an important voice, but that does not in itself establish a necessary line of influence from him to the first evangelist.

---

14 Recent scholarship presents various attempts at understanding the halakah of Mark 7:1–23 in a relative, 'Matthean' sense, yet not always—and this is my main concern—with a clear differentiation between tradition (the historical Jesus) and redaction (Markan ideology). See, e. g., Kister 2001, 151; James Crossley, "Mark 7.1–23: Revisiting the Question of 'All Foods Clean'." In *Torah in the New Testament: Papers delivered at the Manchester-Lausanne Seminar of June 2008*, eds. Peter Oakes and Michael Tait, Library of New Testament Studies 401 (London: T&T Clark, 2009); Thomas Kazen, "Jesus, Scripture and *Paradosis*: Response to Friedrich Avemarie." In Bieringer et al. (eds.) 2010, 281–88.

15 John M. G. Barclay, *Jews in the Mediterranean Diaspora: From Alexander to Trajan (323 BCE–117 BCE)* (Edinburgh: T&T Clark, 1996), 109–10.

3 Possible Pauline Parallels in Mark 7:1–23

Having situated the radical halakah of Mark 7:1–23 in the context of Gentile Christ belief, I shall now present the possible terminological, ideological, and formal overlaps with Paul's letters in the text. Some overlaps are more significant than others, and in the following sections they are dealt with in their order of appearance in Mark's Gospel.

3.1 Pharisaic Antagonists from Jerusalem (Mark 7:1)

Is Mark casting the Pharisees according to a Pauline dramaturgy? The pericope takes place by the Sea of Galilee (6:53) and begins with an exposition of its main characters: the Pharisees and scribes on the one hand, Jesus and his disciples on the other.[16] The Pharisees and scribes gather around Jesus. From an early point in the gospel narrative, Mark defines the Pharisees and scribes as the main antagonists to Jesus in terms of halakic questions such as table fellowship (2:16), fasting (2:18), and Sabbath observance (2:24; see also 10:12 on marriage and 12:13–14 on tax payment). In 3:6, where Mark states that the Pharisees (together with the Herodians) decided to have Jesus killed, they leave the stage for a while and do not reappear until the present scene. Now, are Marks Pharisees Pauline Pharisees? A couple of features in the text could be taken as hinting in that direction. First, the very identification of the main antagonists as Pharisees might be Pauline in the sense that Paul describes his own past opposition to the Christ movement as one of Pharisaic opposition partly based on mutually divergent halakah (Phil 3:5–6; cf. Acts 26:5). That being said, however, Paul does not describe his opponents in, for example, Galatia and Philippi as Pharisees, so the concept of Pharisaic antagonism to the Christ movement does not appear as a crucial Pauline construct. Rather, it seems more likely that the casting of the antagonist in Mark 7, possibly with early roots in the ministry of the historical Jesus, reflects a more general, mutual animosity and competition between the Christ movement and the Pharisaic party in the post-Easter decades of the first century (e.g., Matt 23; John 12:42).[17] The second possible hint at a Pauline colouring of the antagonist in Mark 7 is the fact that they are described as coming "from Jerusalem" (ἀπὸ Ἱεροσολύμων, v. 1). Paul also has opponents in Jerusalem (Gal 2:1–

---

[16] The crowd is introduced and addressed subsequently in v. 14.
[17] Matthew articulates this conflict more strongly than Mark (e.g., Matt 5:20; 23:1–36), whereas the mention of "believers who belonged to the sect of the Pharisees" in Acts 15:5 modifies the picture.

4, 12 [ἀπὸ Ἰακώβου]; 4:25; Rom 15:31), but since opposition is often linked to Jerusalem in the first-century texts of the Christ movement, this parallel also seems quite accidental (see, e.g., Luke 13:33–35 par. (Q); John 5:1, introducing the phase of antagonism in the Johannine narrative; Acts 4:5). Mark's use of Jerusalem in 7:1 is first and foremost a narrative feature by which he constructs the holy city as negative space and portends the passion events taking place at that destination (3:22; 10:33; 11:15–18).[18] To conclude on this point, the portrait of the antagonists in Mark 7 (Pharisees, Jerusalemites) is a general and not particularly Pauline feature in texts from the Christ movement in the first century.

3.2 *Koinos* (κοινός) Language (Mark 7:2, 5, 15, 18, 20, 23)

The Pharisees and scribes notice that Jesus' disciples eat with defiled hands (κοιναῖς χερσίν, v. 2), i.e., without washing them before the meal. By using the adjective κοινός ("common") to describe cultic pollution, Mark applies the term in a way unfamiliar to Greco-Roman readers, of which he is conscious, apparently, since he explains the term to his audience (ἀνίπτοις, "unwashed"). More conventional Greek adjectives would be μιαρός (cognate with *miasma*) or ἀκάθαρτος, the latter of which Mark frequently employs in other pericopes (1:23, 26–27; 3:11, 30; 5:2, 8, 13; 6:7; 7:25; 9:25). In fact, κοινός and the equivalent verb κοινοῦν do not appear at all with this particular meaning ('[to make/to regard] unclean, profane') in contemporary texts by non-Jewish Greco-Roman authors.[19] In Paul, however, it appears once: "I know and am persuaded in the Lord Jesus that nothing is unclean [κοινὸν] in itself" (Rom 14:14). Paul and Mark share this use of language with other writers in the Christ movement (Acts 10:14–15, 28; 11:8–9; 21:28; Heb 9:13; 10:29; Rev 21:27), and it is no Pauline invention. Though the cultic use of κοινός is rare in the Septuagint and absent in Philo, it seems to reflect the language of Hellenistic (predominantly Diaspora) Judaism and it appears in texts both earlier and later than Paul's letters and Mark's Gospel (1 Macc 1:47, 62; *Let. Aris.* 315; Josephus, *Ant.* 3.181; 11.346; 12.320; 13.4; *4 Macc* 7:6).

---

18 Elizabeth Struthers Malbon, *Narrative Space and Mythic Meaning in Mark*, The Biblical Seminar 13 (Sheffield: JSOT Press, 1991 [1986]), 30–49, 160.
19 Friedrich Hauck, "κοινός." In *ThWNT*, eds. Gerhard Kittel and Gerhard Friedrich (Stuttgart: Kohlhammer, 1932–79), 3:789–810.

3.3 Leaving the Tradition of the Elders (Mark 7:3–5, 8–9, 13)

Having witnessed the purity practice of Jesus' disciples, the Pharisees and the scribes confront Jesus by asking why he and his disciples desert "the tradition of the elders [ἡ παράδοσις τῶν πρεσβυτέρων]" (7:5). Once again, the vocabulary is of interest when looking for Pauline parallels. In Gal 1:14, Paul recalls his previous zeal for the traditions of his ancestors (τῶν πατρικῶν μου παραδόσεων) and refers to *paradosis* in a way that is comparable to Mark in spite of the differences in context. Both Paul and Mark understand the term as referring to Jewish, traditional supplements to the Torah, more or less explicitly associating *paradosis* with Pharisaic halakah, which is also the case in Josephus (*Ant.* 13.408: κατὰ τὴν πατρῴαν παράδοσιν; cf. 13.297; *m. Avot* 1:1). Since Josephus, undoubtedly in a social location far beyond the Pauline sphere, describes Pharisaic teachings in language similar to that of Paul and Mark, the concept was probably widespread in Greek-speaking Jewish circles of the Diaspora. However, the use of the concept in both Paul and Mark deviates from Josephus in two remarkable ways: They speak of *paradosis* as something which is left behind by Christ followers (Mark 7:5; Gal 1:13–17; 2:15–16; cf., Col 2:20–22), and, as we shall see in the following section, they both claim that *paradosis* is a merely human construct (Mark 7:8; Gal 1:10–12, 15–16; cf. Col 2:20–22). Whether this was a common, negative understanding of *paradosis* among Gentile Christ believers or a specifically Pauline idea can hardly be decided from the sources.

3.4 God's Revelation versus Human Tradition (Mark 7:6–13)

In Mark 7:8, Jesus describes the "tradition of the elders" as "human tradition" (τὴν παράδοσιν τῶν ἀνθρώπων). This change in terminology is occasioned by a quotation from Isa 29:13, which introduces Jesus' answer to the Pharisees and scribes. The quotation reduces the doctrines of Israel to merely "human precepts" (ἐντάλματα ἀνθρώπων), thus turning the social distinction in the text (Pharisees and scribes vs. Jesus and his disciples) into an ontological distinction between the human and the divine. Pharisaic *paradosis* is not an expression of the will of God, but of the will of human beings who, by means of their *paradosis*, in fact do annul the word of Moses and of God (7:8–9, 11, 13). In contrast, the reader understands that the halakah of the Markan Jesus, by not being a *paradosis*, is the true expression of the will of God. In Paul, the argument for abandoning Jewish dietary practice is also based on the ontological distinction between God and humans, between higher divine revelation and earthly, relative authorities, the argument running through Gal 1–2 (e.g., Gal 1:1, 10–12, 16;

2:2, 20). The significance of this parallel, however, is relativized by the fact that the distinction is foundational in Jewish thought, not least in apocalyptic forms of Judaism, and thus represents a general feature in Jewish, halakic argumentation and polemics. Yet, in the Deutero-Pauline tradition, the Epistle to the Colossians contains a number of more specific and thus striking parallels to the Markan text in terms of how the argument is fabricated. First, the author speaks disapprovingly of *paradosis* by not only evoking the ontological distinction between the human and the divine, but also using the same terminology as in Mark 7:8, which is different from that of Josephus. The author thus warns against "… philosophy and empty deceit, according to human tradition [κατὰ τὴν παράδοσιν τῶν ἀνθρώπων]" (Col 2:8). Second, the text criticizes the Jewish dietary code and ritual system by alluding to the same Isaianic text as the one being quoted in Mark 7:6 (Isa 29:13). Conventional Jewish practices comply with ordinary, human precepts and doctrines (κατὰ τὰ ἐντάλματα καὶ διδασκαλίας τῶν ἀνθρώπων; Col 2:22; see also Tit 1:14; Heb 9:10). This allusion to Isa 29:13 in Colossians is obvious when we consult the Septuagint, taking notice of the phraseology. Here Isaiah complains that Israel worships the Lord in vain, "… teaching human precepts as doctrines [διδάσκοντες διδασκαλίας ἐντάλματα ἀνθρώπων]." The fact that Isaian phraseology is reproduced in Col 2:22 renders probable that even the expression in Col 2:8 (κατὰ τὴν παράδοσιν τῶν ἀνθρώπων) owes the latter part of its phrasing to Isa 29:13.[20] What can be concluded from this? Both Mark and the author of the Epistle to the Colossians criticize Jewish dietary practices as ungodly, human *paradosis* with reference to Isa 29:13. When focusing on Mark 7:1–23, this may be one of the most specific links that can be established between Mark and the Pauline tradition, albeit in this case not to Paul himself, assuming that Colossians is pseudepigraphal. This observation may indicate that the question of 'Deutero-Paulinism in Mark' (or, in the reverse, Markan elements in Deutero-Pauline literature) is worth raising to the same extent as the traditional question. If there is any Pauline influence in Mark, was it mediated through the followers of Paul?

---

[20] The same may apply to the Deutero-Pauline admonition in Tit 1:14. The texts warns against Jewish *muthoi* and "… commandments of humans [ἐντολαῖς ἀνθρώπων; in mss. F and G: ἐντάλμασιν ἀνθρώπων] who reject the truth" (my translation). Once again, a Deutero-Pauline text relates Isa 29:13 with criticism of Jewish purity halakah, yet in this case without using the term *paradosis*.

3.5 Satire of Divergent Halakah (Mark 7:6, 9, 16, 19a)

As Jesus introduces the above-mentioned quotation from Isaiah, he claims that the Pharisees and the scribes are the real objects of Isaiah's criticism, comparing them to actors (ὑποκριταί; v. 6). Later, in v. 19a, he ridicules the Pharisaic concern for pure foods since food eventually "... goes out into the sewer [εἰς τὸν ἀφεδρῶνα]."[21] Paul also speaks of his opponents in a satirical mode, not least when it comes to halakah (e.g., Gal 1:7; 3:1; 6:12, 17; Phil 3:2), and like Mark he describes adherence to Pharisaic/Jewish *paradosis* as hypocrisy (Gal 2:13; cf. Mark 7:6; 1 Tim 4:2). This language, describing religious and moral insincerity as hypocrisy and using the hypocrite as an object of scorn, however, belongs to the literature of the Jewish Diaspora in general, which diminishes its significance in terms of Pauline influence on Mark (see also Matt 23:13–15, 23, 25, 27, 29).[22] Likewise, the satirical tone is a general feature of halakic polemics. Some Qumran texts, for example, give the opponents a sobriquet corresponding to their erroneous halakah: "seekers of smooth things" (דורשי החלקות, i.e., those who prefer lenient interpretations. See, for example, 4Q169 3–4 II, 2).

3.6 Outward versus Inward Piety (Mark 7:14–23)

In Mark 7, the social and ontological dichotomies mentioned above in section 3.4 are complemented by an anthropological dichotomy concerning outward and inward obedience toward God's will. Once again the quotation from Isaiah in vv. 6–7 introduces the distinction by contrasting lips and hearts ("This people honours me with their lips, but their hearts are far from me"; Mark 7:6; Isa 29:13). The distinction, however, does not govern the text until the final section in vv. 14–23, when Jesus addresses the crowd, and ἔξωθεν ("from outside") and ἔσωθεν ("from within") become key words (7:15, 18, 21, 23). Also Paul's criticism of Jewish law observance is very much dependent on the anthropological distinction between the external and the internal. In Paul, the external has many designations, e.g., σάρξ ('flesh'; Rom 2:28; Gal 6:12–13; Phil 3:3–4), γράμμα ('letter'; Rom 2:29), πρόσωπον ('face, appearance'; 2 Cor 5:12) and τὸ φανερόν ('the visible'; Rom 2:28), whereas the internal is πνεῦμα ('spirit'; Rom 2:29), καρδία

---

[21] Verses 9 and 16 also seem to contain satirical or ironical statements. Verse 16 is not attested in the major codices (ℵ and B) and in a limited number of other witnesses. According to Nestle-Aland[28], the verse is secondary in spite of the fact that the majority of majuscule manuscripts include it.
[22] Ulrich Wilckens, "ὑποκρίνομαι." In Kittel and Friedrich 1932–79, 8:558–71.

('heart'; Rom 2:29; 2 Cor 5:12) and τὸ κρυπτὸν ('the hidden'; Rom 2:29). As already touched upon, outward piety without inner piety is called pretence or hypocrisy (ὑπόκρισις) in both Paul and Mark (Gal 2:13; Mark 7:6), whereas the seat of inward piety is the heart (καρδία; Mark 7:6, 19, 21; Rom 2:29; 2 Cor 5:12). Even though Paul and Mark thus share the anthropological dichotomy as a discursive strategy in relation to dietary halakah, this language is not at all exclusively theirs but relates, for example, to the idea of the new covenant of the heart present in the Septuagint and Early Judaism (see, e.g., Jer 31:33; Ezek 36:25–27; 1QS IV,9–11, 20–21; Philo, *De migr. Abr.* 89–93; *Yerushalmi Tractate Berakhot* 1:2).

3.7 Abandoning Jewish Dietary Customs is a Question of Higher Understanding (Mark 7:16, 18)

The halakah of the Markan Jesus is not for everyone to understand. A certain cognitive competence is required in order to turn (1) from Pharisaic halakah toward Jesus' teachings (the social distinction), (2) from human tradition toward God's will (the ontological distinction), and (3) from the outward to the inward (the anthropological distinction). Accordingly, Jesus concludes the public part of the pericope with the words: "Let anyone with ears to hear listen" (v. 16; see note 21). The explication is given to the disciples only, behind doors, and away from the crowd (v. 17). Jesus accuses the disciples of being ἀσύνετοί ('ignorant') in v. 18. In other words, radical halakah is comprehensible only to a limited group of insiders; and thus a fourth, cognitive distinction between knowledge and ignorance is established. Similarly, in Paul, only the grown-ups in faith with a higher understanding are able to see dietary practices as what they really are in Christ: indifferent *adiaphora*. Some have γνῶσις ('knowledge'; 1 Cor 8:10), while others do not (1 Cor 8:7, 9); and the members of the Christ movement embody different levels of συνείδησις ('conscience, awareness') concerning pagan sacrificial meat (1 Cor 10:25–30). The weak in faith or ignorant are those who abstain from eating allegedly impure food since they have not recognized its neutrality in terms of religious and moral identity and status (Rom 14:1–2; cf. Gal 3:1, 3). Once again, however, while Paul and Mark share a common notion concerning Jewish dietary practices by connecting practice and knowledge, the parallels do not offer clear evidence of Pauline influence on Mark. According to Philo, the 'radical allegorists' in Alexandria saw their radical halakah in a similar manner as exclusively available, not for the masses, but for those in the know (*De migr. Abr.* 90).

3.8 Everything is Clean (Mark 7:19b)

In v. 17, Jesus withdraws from the crowd in order to address his disciples in a private setting—a typically Markan narrative move (see 4:10; 10:10; 13:3).[23] In vv. 18–19a, Jesus explains the parable given in v. 15 concerning the relation between outward and inward purity and defilement, and a redactional comment follows. This comment—"Thus he declared all foods clean [καθαρίζων πάντα τὰ βρώματα]" (7:19b)—at first sight appears as a specific link between Paul and Mark in terms of the dietary code. It gives voice to the notion that all foods are in principle clean, which is certainly a claim found in Paul's letters (e.g., 1 Cor 8:8: "Food will not bring us close to God [βρῶμα δὲ ἡμᾶς οὐ παραστήσει τῷ θεῷ]" and Rom 14:14: "... nothing is unclean in itself [οὐδὲν κοινὸν δι' ἑαυτοῦ]"), but of course also appears in other texts from the Christ movement (e.g., Acts 10:15; Col 2:16–23; Tit 1:15; Hebr 13:9). The very wording of Mark 7:19b is particularly interesting in relation to Rom 14:20b. In Rom 14, Paul seems to be mediating between Christ believers who adhere to Jewish food customs and those who do not. Without going into detail, one may say that Paul's principal claim appears in 14:20b: "All [foods] are indeed clean, [πάντα (τὰ βρώματα, see 14:20a) μὲν καθαρά] ..." (my translation). The statement resembles Mark 7:19b, which thus may appear as an allusion to Paul. Yet, on the other hand, Paul may be quoting a motto of a certain party among Roman Christ believers, as is often claimed of other similar statements with πᾶς in his letters (e.g., 1 Cor 6:12; 8:1; 10:23).[24] If so, both Paul and Mark may be referring to a common slogan among Gentile Christ believers.[25] In some contexts, Paul adds a clause of modification by means of his characteristic affirmation-with-modification strategy: Food concerns are *adiaphora*, but only as long as they do not scandalize Christ-believing brothers (1 Cor 10:25–30; Rom 14:13–23). In Mark, we do not find this Pauline modification. The most obvious reason seems to be that food concerns have become less controversial in the Markan context. Mark writes for a second-generation audience with greater Gentile dominance and does not

---

[23] Adela Yarbro Collins, *Mark: A Commentary*, Hermeneia (Minneapolis: Fortress, 2007), 342n15.
[24] Dale B. Martin, *The Corinthian Body* (New Haven: Yale University Press, 1995), 70. The motto reappears in a different form in Tit 1:15 ("To the pure all things are pure [πάντα καθαρὰ τοῖς καθαροῖς]").
[25] It is probably not possible to identify them more narrowly. Heikki Räisänen, however, suggests that the 'Hellenists' in Acts 6:1–8:3 were the founders of early radical halakah in the Christ movement. See "The 'Hellenists'—A Bridge between Jesus and Paul?" In *The Torah and Christ: Essays in German and English on the Problem of the Law in Early Christianity*, Publications of the Finnish Exegetical Society 45 (Helsinki: Kirjapaino Raamattutalo, 1986), 242–306.

have to face the mixed-ethnicity issues of Paul's generation. Another important difference between Paul's and Mark's abandonment of the dietary code is the source of authority in the argument. Paul's argument is monotheistic. God is lord of all and thus everything is clean in principle (Rom 14:3–11; 1 Cor 8:6; 10:26; see also Acts 10:36).[26] This argument is absent in Mark 7:1–23. Belonging to the second generation of the Christ movement, Mark seeks the authority of halakah in the earthly Jesus (see also Werner 1923, 90).[27]

3.9 Purity and Defilement are Ethical Matters (Mark 7:21–23)

When the Markan Jesus abandons Jewish dietary practice, he does not reject the idea of purity and defilement as such. Rather, the purity system is reduced to covering only moral, interpersonal concerns. Likewise, what matters in Paul's epistles is neither food nor circumcision, but ethical conduct according to God's will (Rom 13:8–10; 1 Cor 7:19; Gal 5:6; 6:15). Such a separation of moral and cultic purity as well as the disregard of the latter is highly unusual in early Judaism. Philo's opponents, the 'radical allegorists', however, seem to have shared this approach to halakah with communities of Gentile Christ believers. In the New Testament, the focus on ethical purity and impurity is not least thematized in virtue and vice lists, an example of which is found in Mark 7:21–22.

---

[26] See Peter J. Tomson,. *Paul and the Jewish Law: Halakha in the Letters of the Apostle to the Gentiles*, CINT 3/1 (Assen: Van Gorcum, 1990), 254–58. One possible exception to the *theo*logical argument in Paul may be the passage in Rom 14:14. Paul states that nothing is unclean in itself, of which he is persuaded "… in the Lord Jesus [ἐν Κυρίῳ Ἰησοῦ]." With the latter phrase, the apostle is either speaking of participation "in Christ" or referring to a Jesus tradition of the sort transmitted in Mark 7.

[27] Gentile Christ believers in the first century CE based their understanding of purity halakah on three main authorities: the eschatological Christ event and its revelation of God as lord of all (Paul), the Jesus tradition (Mark) and the history of the early church (Luke). Luke, interestingly, omits Mark 7 as part of his 'great omission'. If this is not by chance, then Luke is uncomfortable with Mark 7, either because it does not correspond with the halakic compromise of the apostolic council (Acts 15) or because he wants to situate the new halakah and the mission to the Gentiles, not in the first, Jesuanic period, but in the second, ecclesial period of fulfilment in salvation history. Hence, Luke postpones the abandonment of the dietary laws to Peter's revelation in Acts 10–11.

3.10 The Vice List (Mark 7:21–22)

Pauline (and Deutero-Pauline) literature is a genuine greenhouse for ethical catalogues. Here we find most of the virtue and vice lists appearing in the New Testament, whereas the genre rarely appears beyond epistolary literature.[28] The most remarkable exception, however, is the vice list at the conclusion of the pericope in Mark 7:1–23 (see also Matt 15:19; Rev 9:21; 21:8; 22:15). This might hint at Pauline influence on Mark 7:1–23, but Paul certainly did not invent the genre. Virtue and vice lists are Greco-Roman literary forms that appeared in philosophical, primarily Stoic and Cynic, contexts where they functioned as devices of ethical instruction. We do not encounter virtue and vice lists in the Hebrew Bible, but they emerge in Jewish texts during the Greco-Roman period (e.g., in the Wisdom of Solomon, the *Testaments of the Twelve Patriarchs*, and in Philo). The vices mentioned in Jewish vice lists are influenced by the values of the Torah and of the Decalogue, in particular. This is also the case in Mark 7:21–22—and even more so in the shorter Matthean version, which seems to change the order of the vices for the purpose of creating a better alignment with the order of the ten commandments (Matt 15:19). The cardinal vice in Mark's list is "evil intentions [οἱ διαλογισμοὶ οἱ κακοί]" (v. 21), i.e., defilement originating from the human heart (Gen 6:5), the inner side of the above-mentioned anthropological dichotomy. The following vices are all elaborations of the cardinal vice of evil intentions. The twelve vices are presented asyndetically, and they appear in the plural in vv. 21–22a, in the singular in v. 22b. The chart below demonstrates that the vices in the Markan list have parallels in Pauline (and Deutero-Pauline) vice lists, but certainly also in other texts of Jewish origin as well as in non-Jewish Greco-Roman texts.

---

28 The following twenty-three vice lists are generally accepted as such by New Testament scholars: Matt 15:19; Mark 7:21–22; Rom 1:29–31; 13:13; 1 Cor 5:10–11; 6:9–10; 2 Cor 12:20–21; Gal 5:19–21; Eph 4:31; 5:3–5; Col 3:5–8; 1 Tim 1:9–10; 6:4–5; 2 Tim 3:2–5; Titus 1:7; 3:3; Jas 3:14–16; 1 Pet 2:1; 4:3, 15; Rev 9:21; 21:8; 22:15. See John T. Fitzgerald, "Virtue/Vice Lists." In *Anchor Bible Dictionary*, ed. David Noel Friedman (New York: Doubleday, 1992), 6:857–59.

Vices in Mark 7:21-22[29]	Identical vices in Pauline and Deutero-Pauline vice lists	Identical vices in vice lists in texts from the Christ movement and early Judaism	Identical vices in vice lists of Greco-Roman authors[30]
διαλογισμός κακός ('evil thought, evil intention')	Κακία ('evil, vice'): Rom 1:29-30; Eph 4:31; Col 3:5, 8; Tit 3:3	Κακία: 1 Pet 2:1; T. Ash. 2.5; T. Benj. 8.1; T. Gad 5.1; Philo, Cher. 93; Spec. Laws 1.281; Post. 93; 1 Pet 4:15 (κακοποιΐα, 'evil-doing')	κακία ('vice') appears as the main category to be expanded upon in the vice lists (see Vögtle 1936, 61)
πορνεία ('sexual immorality')	1 Cor 5:10-11; 6:9; Gal 5:19; Eph 5:3, 5; Col 3:5; 1 Tim 1:10	Rev 9:21; 21:8; 22:15; 1QS IV, 10 (רוח זנות)[31]; 3 Bar. 4;17; 8·5; 13ι'4ι 2 En. 10:4-6; Jub. 7:20; 23:14; T. Ash. 2.5; T. Iss. 7.2; T. Levi 14.5-6; T. Reu. 3.3	Diog. Laert. 6.85
κλοπή ('theft')	1 Cor 6:10 (κλεπτοσύνη, 'theft')	1 Pet 4:15 (κλεπτοσύνη); Rev 9:21 (κλέμμα, 'theft'); Wis 14:25; 3 Bar. 4:17; 8:5; 13:4; 2 En. 10:4-6; T. Ab. 10:5; T. Ash. 2.5; T. Levi 14.5; T. Reu. 3.6; Sib. Or. 2.257; Philo, Decal. 171; Her. 173; Conf. 117	Dio Chrysostom, Virt. (Or. 69) 9; Stobaeus, Ecl. 2.93.1
φόνος ('murder')	Rom 1:29; Gal 5:21 (according to, e. g.,	1 Pet 2:1 (according to ms. B); 4:15; Rev 9:21;	Corp. Herm. 1.23

---

29 For the sake of comparison, the schema only contains parallels of cognate words in Greek, while possible synonyms are generally disregarded. All vices in the schema are stated as nouns in the nominative singular, even if they appear otherwise in the original texts (for example, in the plural or in verbal form).

30 The literary material from non-Jewish Greco-Roman authors is enormous. As a consequence, the schema cannot be comprehensive. The following works have been consulted for identification of Greco-Roman vice catalogues: Anton Vögtle, *Die Tugend- und Lasterkataloge im Neuen Testament exegetisch, religions- und formgeschichtlich untersucht*, NTA 16 (Münster: Verlag der aschendorffschen Verlagsbuchhandlung, 1936); Siegfried Wibbing, *Die Tugend- und Lasterkataloge im Neuen Testament und ihre Traditionsgeschichte unter besonderer Berücksichtigung der Qumran-Texte*, BZNW 25 (Berlin: Alfred Töpelmann, 1959); Ehrhard Kamlah, *Die Form der katalogischen Paränese im Neuen Testament*, WUNT 7 (Tübingen: J.C.B. Mohr [Paul Siebeck], 1964); and Fitzgerald 1992.

31 1QS is, of course, not a Greek text but displays so many possible parallels to Mark that it cannot be disregarded.

Vices in Mark 7:21–22[29]	Identical vices in Pauline and Deutero-Pauline vice lists	Identical vices in vice lists in texts from the Christ movement and early Judaism	Identical vices in vice lists of Greco-Roman authors[30]
	mss. A, C, and D); 1 Tim 1:9 (ἀνδροφόνος, 'manslaughter')	21:8; 22:15; Wis 14:25; 3 Bar. 4:17; 8:5; T. Ab. 10:5; Sib. Or. 2.256; ἀνδροφόνος: Philo, Decal. 170; Her. 173; Spec. Laws 4.84; Conf. 117	
μοιχεία ('adultery')	1 Cor 6:9; Gal 5:19 (according to, e.g., mss. א² and D)	Wis 14:26; 3 Bar. 4:17; 8:5; 13:4; T. Ash. 2.5; T. Levi 14.6; 17.11; Philo, Decal. 168; Her. 173; Spec. Laws 4.84; Conf. 117	Dio Chrysostom, Virt. (Or. 69) 9; Stobaeus, Ecl. 2.93.1
πλεονεξία ('greed')	Rom 1:29; 1 Cor 5:10–11; 6:10; Eph 5:3, 5; Col 3:5	1QS IV, 9 (נפש רחוב); T. Ash. 2.5; T. Gad 5.1; T. Levi 14.6; Philo, Agr. 83; Sacr. 32	Plutarch, Sera 555E; 565C; Dio Chrysostom, Invid. (Or. 77/78) 39; Corp. Herm. 1.23; 13.7
πονηρία ('wickedness'; vv. 22, 23)	Rom 1:29; Col 3:8; 1 Tim 6:4	1QS IV, 9 (רשע); T. Ash. 2.5	Dio Chrysostom, Virt. (Or. 8) 8; Corp. Herm. 1.23
δόλος ('deceit')	Rom 1:29	1 Pet 2:1; 1QS IV, 9 (שקר, רמיה, כחש); Wis 14:25; T. Benj. 6.4; T. Iss. 7.4; Sib. Or. 2.257	Corp. Herm. 13.7
ἀσέλγεια ('licentiousness')	Rom 13:13; Gal 5:19;	1 Pet 4:3; Wis 14:26; T. Levi 17.11	(Pseudo-)Plutarch, Lib. ed. 13 A; Dio Chrysostom, Fel. Sap. (Or. 23) 7
ὀφθαλμὸς πονηρός ('evil eye')	—	m. Avot 4:9; 5:22 (רעה עין)[32]	—
βλασφημία ('abusive speech, blasphemy')	Eph 4:31; Col 3:8; 1 Tim 6:4; 2 Tim 3:2	1QS IV,11 (לשון גדופים)	Plutarch, Tranq. an. 468B
ὑπερηφανία ('arrogance')	Rom 1:30; 2 Tim 3:2;	1QS IV, 9 (גוה לבב ורום); T. Levi 17.11; T. Reu 3.5	—
ἀφροσύνη ('foolishness')	—	1QS IV, 10 (אולת); Philo, Post. 93; Cher. 71; Conf. 90	Dio Chrysostom, Fel. Sap. (Or. 23) 7; Virt. (Or. 8) 8

---

32 'Evil eye' is a semitic expression and does not appear in Greco-Roman catalogues.

The chart first of all shows that most vices in Mark 7:21–22 have their equivalents in Pauline and Deutero-Pauline catalogues. The following examples bear particular resemblance to Mark's list: Rom 1:29–31 (six parallels), Col 3:5–8 (five parallels), 1 Cor 6:9–10 (four parallels), and Gal 5:19–21 (from two to four parallels).[33] Yet, the same vices also appear in other contemporary vice lists, quite significantly more frequently in texts of Jewish provenance than in non-Jewish texts, and most remarkably in 1QS IV,9–11 (seven Hebrew parallels), *T. Ash.* 2.5 (six parallels), Wis 14:25–26 (five parallels), *T. Levi* 14.5–6 (four parallels) and *3 Bar.* 4:17; 8:5 (four parallels in both lists). Thus, the overlaps between the Markan list and Pauline lists are relatively numerous, but so are the parallels with other ancient vice lists. Moreover, a vice like εἰδωλολατρία ('idolatry'), which appears frequently in Pauline and Deutero-Pauline catalogues (1 Cor 5:11; 6:9; Gal 5:20; Eph 5:5; Col 3:5), is missing in Mark; and the sequence of the vices does not follow Paul's catalogues. It seems that Mark and Paul were simply using the same genre of popular moral philosophy and both infused it with Jewish norms and values as did other Jewish authors of the time. Moreover, in contrast to some of their Jewish contemporaries, they agreed upon disregarding cultic vices for ethical ones, as did other first-century writers from the Christ movement.

4 Conclusion

The present article was a test case study concerning possible Pauline influence on the Gospel of Mark. By examining the various points of possible contact between the halakah in Mark 7:1–23 and Paul's views of the Jewish dietary code, I have shown that the parallels are in fact quite numerous. As regards the question in the title of the article, however—"Mark 7:1–23: A Pauline Halakah?"—the results are ambiguous. Though parts of Mark 7:1–23 may have a Jesuanic origin, the pericope as it stands in Mark certainly does not represent Jesuanic halakah. Neither does it represent a code of conduct that any first-century Christ believer, whether Jew or Gentile, would agree upon, as was Werner's modest conclusion in 1923. But how much further can we go in terms of specificity? Is Mark 7:1–23 a Pauline halakah? In my opinion, the parallels, in spite of being relatively numerous, are not specific enough to warrant such a conclusion. Nevertheless, on the

---

33 See also the table in Vincent Taylor, *The Gospel according to St. Mark* (London: Macmillan, 1980 [1952]), 346. Taylor concludes that the terminology in Mark 7:21–22 is Pauline probably because he only includes New Testament material in the analysis.

basis of our general knowledge of first-century Christ belief, we may assert that Mark 7 is *closer to* Pauline dietary halakah *than to* other available types of halakah in the Christ movement (e.g., 'Judaizers', Peter, Matthew, and even to the Lukan compromise). As mentioned in the introduction, this study of Mark 7:1–23 points toward a *via media* between Werner and Marcus as the most reasonable path to tread. The pericope in Mark 7:1–23 is neither 'ecumenical' (Werner), nor necessarily Pauline (Marcus), but legitimizes the dietary practices of Gentile Christ believers (Pauline or not) by means of the Jesus tradition. In fact, the Gospel genre in which the pericope appears is very much about establishing traditional authority for the second and third generations in the Christ movement. In Paul, we notoriously encounter very little legitimization of this kind, and he does not argue for his radical halakah on the basis of the teachings of Jesus. However, the following generations of Gentile Christ believers apparently regarded this as a deficit and thus produced etiological texts that would refer the origin of these customs back either to divine revelation, as in Peter's vision in Joppa in Acts 10, or to a *Herrenwort*, as in Mark 7:15. It is sound to say that Mark 7:1–23 is a halakah that makes sense in a Gentile Christ believing context and that it derives its authority, first and foremost, from the Jesus tradition and, secondarily, from the scriptural condemnation of empty worship (Isa 29:13). This result may be disappointing as regards a search for Pauline-Markan connections, but on the basis of Mark 7:1–23 alone, this is as far as we can go. Yet, a test case cannot stand alone but must be compared with other test cases in order to form a full scenario, both in terms of quantity (the number of parallels) and quality (the specificity of any parallels). This article contributes to the overall discussion—while scholarship awaits that the next Werner will pick up his worn-out gauntlet and present scholarship with an up-to-date synthesis.

Troels Engberg-Pedersen
Paul in Mark 8:34–9:1: Mark on what it is to be a Christian

Aims and strategy

This essay has two overall aims. The most basic is to reach an adequate understanding of Mark 8:34–9:1. I shall show that there is no completely clear consensus on this among recent commentators – or to the extent that there is, that it is not quite accurate. We need a better understanding that will incorporate what has been well said about the text. The second aim is to show that in constructing his text Mark was drawing on Paul in specific, clearly identifiable ways. The two aims go closely together. The claim is that if one reads Mark in the light of certain specific, Pauline conceptions, one may reach a more adequate understanding of the Markan text than commentators have so far managed to achieve. In the context of the present book, there also is the third aim of contributing to the wider discussion of the relationship between Mark and Paul. I shall take up this issue towards the end of the essay by listing a number of corollaries that follow from its main claims. But focus will be on the chosen text itself: to understand it better, by the help of Paul.

It is obvious that this approach is methodologically risky. Will I not be reading Paul *into* Mark instead of finding the apostle *within* the evangelist? Here the task lies in showing that there is enough material in the Markan text itself that actually calls for the Pauline interpretation. There are certain elements in Mark 8:34–9:1 that need to be accounted for before one can say that one fully understands this text; and these elements require an interpretation similar to the one to be given of certain comparable ideas in Paul. If that is the case, then ideally one does not need to bring in Paul at all in order to grasp the meaning of the Markan text. In practice, however, it helps and makes the interpretative enterprise much easier. Another question is whether the Pauline link will prove to be sufficiently specific (as against reflecting a more general, Christian viewpoint) for it to be valid to postulate a link directly back from Mark to Paul. This is the issue that is raised by all essays in the present book, but one that pertains more to the wider claims about Mark and Paul than to understanding Mark 8:34–9:1 itself. In this second regard the task will be to develop the degree of specificity that is required to substantiate the Pauline link. Not just any similarity with Paul will suffice. It must, in some determinate sense, be characteristically Pauline to serve its wider purpose. Both methodological issues must be resolved for it to be possible to find *Paul*, in particular, *within* Mark 8:34–9:1.

I shall begin from presenting some recent positions on the overall meaning of the text. Next we shall look at the text itself, including its likely literary construction by Mark vis-à-vis the pre-Markan tradition (outside of Paul). Then we shall bring in Paul and work towards articulating the meaning that Mark apparently attempted to bring across. Since that meaning will come out as stating nothing less than *what it is to be a Christian*[1] according to Mark, there will be some gains from having paid careful attention to the vocabulary and line of thought of this particular text. Finally, we shall draw out those corollaries that I referred to: on the 'narrative philosophical' character of the Markan text, on the genre issue of narration versus letter-writing, on the position of Mark 8:34–9:1 within Mark as a whole and on Mark and 'theology'.

The main understanding since Haenchen: the trial-condemnation-crucifixion-interpretation

The basic verse for determining the meaning of 8:34–9:1 as a whole has been 8:34, which ends as follows: εἴ τις θέλει ὀπίσω μου ἀκολουθεῖν, ἀπαρνησάσθω ἑαυτὸν καὶ ἀράτω τὸν σταυρὸν αὐτοῦ καὶ ἀκολουθείτω μοι. In a famous article from the first period of redaction criticism, Ernst Haenchen placed the idea of taking up one's cross in direct connection with the historical situation of the readers for whom Mark had constructed or redacted his text:

> Das Leiden ist nicht nur Jesus auferlegt, sondern auch jedem, der sich zu ihm bekennt. Diese Einsicht bindet die beiden Teile dieses Abschnittes (viii 27–33 und viii 34 – ix 1) zusammen: hier wird die Einheit des Leidens bezeugt, die zwischen Jesus und seiner Gemeinde besteht. *Dem sein Kreuz tragenden Jesus kann man nur nachgehen, wenn man selbst das eigene Kreuz trägt.*[2]
>
> Der eigentliche ‚Sitz im Leben' für ein christliches Bekenntnis war für die Gemeinde des Mk. freilich das Bekenntnis angesichts der Verfolgung; das wird aus V. 34 ff. sehr deutlich (Haenchen 1963, 88).
>
> Man sollte dieses „er träge sein Kreuz" nicht abschwächen. ... Christ sein – das sagt Mk. hier mit einem Jesus-Logion – schliesst die Hingabe des Lebens in der Verfolgung ein, also

---

[1] Since I shall basically be arguing for a 'philosophical' reading of Mark (in a sense that will gradually become clear), I allow myself to put this tag in an Aristotelian form: τὸ τί ἦν Χριστιανῷ εἶναι.

[2] Ernst Haenchen, "Die Komposition von Mk vii 27-ix 1 und Par.", *NT* 6 (1963): 81–109, esp. 91 (my italics).

> das, was man später Martyrium genannt hat. ... von jedem Christen ist die Bereitschaft zur Lebenshingabe gefordert, wie sie Jesus vorgelebt hat (Haenchen 1963, 92, my italics).

One notes here the obviously correct point that one thing that binds 8:34–9:1 together with what comes before is the idea that Jesus is about to die (8:31) and that his followers must (in some sense) be prepared to do so too (8:34). One also notes the use of 'Sitz im Leben' and the redaction critical point that 'for Mark's community' the 'Sitz im Leben' was 'confession in a situation of persecution'.³ Finally, one notes the warning against 'weakening' Jesus' injunction that a true follower should 'take up his cross': "Man sollte dieses "er träge sein Kreuz" nicht abschwächen." Basically, what I find wrong about the half-consensus to be found among commentators and already articulated here by Haenchen is this idea that what Mark's Jesus has primarily in mind is his followers *literally* taking up 'their' cross and marching towards crucifixion and the concomitant claim that one should adopt this interpretation in order to avoid 'weakening' what it said.⁴ Instead, I shall argue that the phrase is to be understood metaphorically (but no less 'strongly') and that it concerns the kind of exclusive 'directedness' away from oneself and the world towards Christ that constitutes the essence of 'conversion'. Such directedness may also imply a willingness to die for the sake of Christ, but that is not the primary meaning of the phrase as it stands here.

According to Haenchen, however, the idea of confessing in a situation of persecution should in fact be taken quite literally. On 8:35 he states:

> Hier ist offensichtlich an eine Verfolgung gedacht, bei der man den einzelnen fragt: „Bist du Christ?", und ihn hinrichtet, wenn er das bejaht (Haenchen 1963, 93).

And on the idea in 8:38 that somebody might be "ashamed at me and my words", Haenchen first argues that being 'ashamed at' somebody equals 'denying' him and then states:

> Wenn man für dieses ‚sich schämen' einsetzt ‚verleugnen' (wie es die Q-Fassung bietet), so zeigt das Logion noch deutlicher seinen Sinn: Ein solches ‚verleugnen' oder ‚sich schämen' setzt voraus, dass man den Betreffenden nach seiner Zugehörigkeit zur Jesusgemeinde gefragt hat und dass er, um sein Leben zu retten, diese Zugehörigkeit bestritten hat. Ein solches Bekenntnis vor Gericht, welches das Leben preisgibt, darf man also nicht mit einem

---

3 As noted, Haenchen's article was one of the first that followed in the footsteps of the founding text for redaction criticism of Mark: Willy Marxsen, *Der Evangelist Markus, Studien zur Redaktionsgeschichte des Evangeliums*. FRLANT 49 (Göttingen: Vandenhoeck & Ruprecht, 1956).
4 Am I taking scholars too literally here? But see the quotations in the next few pages.

liturgischen Bekennen verwechseln; es meint vielmehr *jene Tat, die unmittelbar das Martyrium bringt* (Haenchen 1963, 94, my italics).

Haenchen is of course aware of the fact that there are no clear indications of any genuine persecution and martyrdom at the time of Mark's writing (Haenchen 1963, 92–93). But he suggests that the *fear* of it was real enough: *Angst* (Haenchen 1963, 93).

All of this goes together to suggest what I shall call the 'trial-condemnation-crucifixion' interpretation (TCC), which climaxes in the idea of martyrdom by crucifixion.

Later interpreters have adopted the same line. Bas van Iersel is a good example since he not only takes this interpretation to the extreme, but also explicitly states what kind of interpretation he is arguing against.[5] Here is first van Iersel going to the extreme (1998, 291, my additions in square brackets):

> [1] As the identity of the author of Mark is unknown, we do not know whether he himself experienced persecutions during which Christians were interrogated and threatened with torture or were actually tortured. [2] Things may be different, however, in the case of the first readers in Rome, for we know from Tacitus that the persecutions under Nero were not pogroms, ... but that those persecuted were arrested and interrogated by the authorities. [3] If the author had no knowledge of these Roman persecutions, he – and Jesus himself, if the words derive from him – could evoke a situation of oppression or persecution by employing elements from the stories about the Maccabaean martyrs, with which they could expect their audience to be familiar.

Note here how van Iersel is forced to speculate in order to convince himself and his reader about the postulated underlying historical situation. Note also the strongly rhetorical character of that speculation. (1) "[W]e do not know" ... whether Mark himself experienced persecutions nor whether the Markan Christians were interrogated and "threatened with torture *or were actually tortured*". No, indeed not: we do not know; so why ask? (2) We may also speculate about the first *readers* of Mark, but what does that tell us about Mark himself? (3) Finally, we may speculate that Mark (or Jesus himself!) "*could*" draw on the stories about the Maccabees: but why *should* we?

Here then is what van Iersel takes himself to be up against (the immediately following paragraph, my italics):

---

5 Bas M.F. van Iersel, *Mark. A Reader-Response Commentary*, JSNTSupp 164 (Sheffield: Sheffield Academic Press, 1998).

> Today's readers must be careful not to see this passage as being unrelated to a possible situation *of persecution*, and interpret it, for instance, as a call for an ascetic way of life that is characterized by self-renunciation or even self-contempt. Such an interpretation can only be thought reasonable when the Greek ψυχή is translated as 'soul', which is clearly incorrect in this context. The sayings are not about anything so vague as *general lifestyle*, but about a person's willingness to give his or her life for the sake of Jesus when this ultimate sacrifice is demanded.

'General lifestyle', an 'ascetic' way of life, 'self-renunciation', even 'self-contempt': that is how 'today's readers' might perhaps understand it. But No: the text is about *persecution* and willingness to *die* for the sake of Jesus.

Haenchen and van Iersel represent a clear-cut and extreme position. Other commentators lean in the same direction though without being quite so clearcut. For instance, Joachim Gnilka too insisted that one must not 'weaken' the idea of *Kreuzesaufnahme*.⁶ But he was also a little more cautious when he spelled out that the idea of *Kreuzesnachfolge* meant that 'readiness for martyrdom was *included*' in it.⁷ Similarly, he felt that the idea of taking up 'one's' cross implied a kind of broadening that would include all tribulations and temptations that might meet the Jesus follower.⁸ The lack of clarity here is suggestive. But it is also a tribute to Gnilka's perceptiveness. This text just is not fully captured if one reads it only from the perspective of TCC.

The other side of TCC: post-mortem vindication

There is another, complementary side to a reading along the lines of TCC, which comes out the moment commentators turn from 8:34 itself to the verses – in effect, the rest of 8:34–9:1 – that constitute the backing for Jesus' injunction in 8:34. Here the basic idea is that corresponding to the potential fate of condem-

---

6 Joachim Gnilka, *Das Evangelium nach Markus*, 2. Teilband. EKK II/2 (Zürich, Einsiedeln, Köln: Benziger / Neukirchen-Vluyn: Neukirchener, 1979), 23: "... eine abschwächende Interpretation der Kreuzesaufnahme ... [ist] abzulehnen." It is peculiar, however, that commentators in this line do not always remind us that they are thinking of martyrdom *by crucifixion*. Probably, their good sense prevented them from that.
7 "Es wird klar, dass Nachfolge Jesu Kreuzesnachfolge ist und Jüngerschaft die Bereitschaft zur Selbstpreisgabe und zum Martyrium miteinschliesst. Wer Jünger ist und dies noch nicht bedachte, von dem ist ein neuer Entschluss gefordert" (Gnilka 1979, 27).
8 "*Sein* Kreuz aufnehmen weitet die Forderung über die Todesbereitschaft um der Nachfolge willen aus und bezieht alle Drangsale und Anfechtungen, die dem Jünger widerfahren können, ein" (Gnilka 1979, 23, his italics). (It is not quite clear to me, though, why speaking of 'one's own' cross has those implications.)

nation and death for the confession of belonging to Jesus there is Jesus' promise of eschatological vindication and genuine life when 'the Son of Man' "arrives in the glory of his Father", as will happen soon. Most commentators emphasize – rightly to my mind – that this apocalyptic feature should in itself be understood quite literally and that there is a *Tun-Ergehen-Zusammenhang* here: corresponding to the claim made in 8:35 that "the one who wishes to save his soul (or life) will lose it" is the claim made in 8:38 that "the one who is ashamed of me and my words", namely, now here on earth, will experience that "the Son of Man will also [namely, then] be ashamed of him" (8:38). In fact, 8:38 may be said to spell out the full apocalyptic force implicitly contained in 8:35. (And similarly for the positive side stated later in 8:35 and implied in 9:1.)

Now this reading – which, I repeat, is no doubt correct in itself – complements the TCC interpretation in a quite straightforward sense. (Be ready to) *die now* (when you are brought to trial etc.); then you will gain *life then*. The reading is supported by the way it dissolves the apparent paradox in 8:35 of both losing and saving one's life, by referring 'losing' to *now* and 'saving' to *then*. Similarly, it gives point to the contrast between on the one hand losing one's life (now) "for my sake and for the sake of the gospel" (8:35) – and then saving it in the future; and on the other hand being ashamed (now) of "me and my words" (8:38) – and then, by implication, losing one's life in the future.

However, the fact that the idea of post-mortem vindication complements the TCC interpretation in such a straightforward manner does not, of course, determine the correctness of TCC itself. For there might well be other interpretations of 8:34 that might be similarly complemented by the idea of post-mortem vindication. That would also hold if the contrast to gaining life in the future was not the event of literally dying in the present, but for instance the state of being metaphorically 'dead to the world' in the present.

To see what is lacking in TCC we may consider three other recent and excellent commentaries, by Joel Marcus, Adela Yarbro Collins and Lars Hartman.

From TCC to something at once broader and more precise

Initially, at least, Joel Marcus is not a fervent advocate of TCC.[9] It is only gradually that this reading creeps in. Interestingly, this happens as it were in a back-

---

9 Joel Marcus, *Mark 8–16*. Anchor Yale Bible 27 A (New Haven, London: Yale University Press, 2009). All page references in this paragraph are to this commentary.

ward manner from Marcus' strong appreciation of the apocalyptic idea of postmortem vindication. Thus Marcus at one point writes as follows (Marcus 2009, 626, my italics and brackets):

> Mark's understanding of this self-sacrifice [as described in 8:35–37] is illuminated by comparison with 10:29–30, which is the other Markan passage that speaks of renunciation "for me and the good news." Here the primary sacrifices in view are separation from family and property, the things that are at the center of one's daily existence and therefore of one's "life." But there is also a reference to an existence "with persecutions," which presumably includes, in some cases, persecution unto death – a situation that the Markan community was apparently having to face (see 13:9–13). The meaning of "destroying one's life" in 8:35a, then, is probably *both literal and metaphorical*, and the case is probably the same with "saving one's life" in 8:35b. On the one hand [the metaphorical], it refers to outcroppings of the [blessed] age to come in the present evil one: the discovery of a new family in the Christian community, the communion of new "brothers and sisters and mothers and children" in shared houses and fields. On the other hand [the literal], it refers to a strictly eschatological hope, the certainty of eternal life "in the coming age" if and when the prop of mutual support is kicked away and the believer is called upon to make the ultimate sacrifice (cf. again 10:29–30) – an idea commonly found in Jewish martyrologies …

In the last sentence of this quotation we see how the idea of eschatological hope for eternal life is tied in with that of making "the ultimate sacrifice" here and now, in effect with TCC: "if *and when* the prop of mutual support is kicked away etc.". In a similar vein and marking the same direction of thought, Marcus has slightly earlier spoken of "… the apocalyptically realistic advice that, for *everyone*, life is *only* to be found by treading the pathway of death" (Marcus 2009, 624, his italics). Is this too to be taken literally? It is at least a sign that Marcus concludes back from a certain interpretation of the apocalyptic future to a martyriological present.

There is a second feature of Marcus' overall interpretation that he is more or less alone in emphasizing to this extent. Marcus senses a "military atmosphere" in the whole passage (615). For instance, in 8:34 the disciples are "summoned to join in the march" like "a soldier following a military leader into battle", indeed "to follow the Messiah Jesus into the eschatological battle" (624). Also, 8:35 "probably draws on pep talks from ancient generals … Our passage, then, is probably an eschatological overhaul of a common trope …" (626). 8:36–37 is about a "victory-through-renunciation" … that is "thoroughly apocalyptic" (627). And in 8:38–9:1 "… a militant royal figure … is coming into view. … Jesus' call to self-sacrifice is saved from becoming an invitation to masochism because it is coupled with the belief that the sacrifices demanded are part of a divine movement that is already secretly at work to transform the world …" (630).

What we see here, I think, is that what in 8:34–9:1 as a whole appears to be a justification (8:35–9:1) for the injunction given in 8:34 has instead become the main thing: victory in the eschatological battle. Indeed, the injunction to 'tread the pathway of death' has now become a means only to the superior goal of that victory. Otherwise, Marcus feels, it would just be "an invitation to masochism".[10] This, however, is where doubts should begin to creep in. One cannot criticize Marcus for not taking seriously the injunction to deny oneself and take up one's cross – after all, like van Iersel he speaks of "the ultimate sacrifice". But is that literal sense actually the one that is intended? What does it in fact mean to 'deny oneself'? And what is the point of doing it? Similarly, what *does* it mean here to 'take up one's cross'? And what is the point? The sense underlying these questions is that there is some central content to the two acts that gets lost once one sees only two alternatives here: either a means to an eschatological goal of apocalyptic victory – or masochism (or self-contempt). There is no doubt that the two acts are in fact seen in the former way and hence the risk of the latter is to some extent obviated. However, it does seem that self-denial and cross-carrying may also have some point in addition to being the literal means to a future apocalyptic end. In fact, it seems as if they may have such a point *before* they become the latter. What could that point be?

Here we come up directly against the question with regard to 'taking up one's cross' that I noted to begin with and that is also raised by Marcus himself in the long quotation about 'destroying (losing) one's life' and 'saving it': are these phrases to be taken metaphorically or literally?[11] It is when this question is then combined with the in itself quite correct perception that one should not 'weaken' the sense of 'taking up one's cross' (compare both Haenchen and Gnilka above and implicitly also van Iersel) that commentators end up deciding for the literal interpretation of the saying, which is certainly not a 'weak' one – Be prepared *literally* to carry your cross! And then we have TCC. However, this is a clear case of a *non sequitur*. We do not know that *only* the literal inter-

---

[10] Note how van Iersel warned against the note of 'self-contempt' and Marcus here against 'masochism'. Are we 'moderns' unable to understand an exclusive 'directedness' towards Christ in any other way? Is that an underlying reason why these commentators go for the wholly literal meaning of 'taking up one's cross'?

[11] Incidentally, it is not clear why Marcus prefers 'destroy' to 'lose' in his rendering of ἀπολέσαι. If the idea is that there is a higher degree of intentionality in 'destroy' than 'lose', then that idea does not seem to fit the first half of 8:35, where ἀπολέσει should clearly give expression to the *un*intended effect of '*wanting*' to save one's life/soul. But perhaps Marcus' choice is just for dramatic effect?

pretation qualifies for not being 'weak', just as we do not know that only the literal interpretation fits the idea of post-mortem vindication.

The same syndrome of settling for the literal interpretation presumably to avoid 'weakness' – though with some vacillation à la Gnilka – may be found in Adela Collins' commentary.[12] To begin with in her account of 8:34 she refers back to the calling of Peter, Andrew, James and John in Mark 1:17, 18, 20 and perceptively comments: "The commitment that is dramatized in those passages is articulated explicitly here" (Collins 2007, 408). This would not seem to call for a literal understanding of the cross-saying. Gradually, however, the literal interpretation takes over in a way that in effect gives us TCC (ibid., my italics and brackets):

> Literally, to take up one's cross meant to carry the crossbeam that would be used in one's crucifixion. [Then on Luke, who by adding καθ' ἡμέραν, "daily", in Luke 9:23 has adopted a wholly metaphorical sense.] In Mark, the phrase may have a metaphorical dimension, but *its force is primarily literal.*
>
> Verse 34 shocks by ... demanding that the follower of Jesus be prepared to meet the same fate [namely, as Jesus] (cf. 15:21 [! Simon of Cyrene carrying Jesus' cross], 30, 32). The literal impact of the language here would have been strong because execution by crucifixion was well known in the history of Judea and a method used by the Romans in the cultural context of Mark, broadly speaking. *The language reflects at least the expectation of persecution, if not its actuality* (cf. 13:9–11).[13]

Finally, Collins' comment on 9:1 provides the customary connection of TCC with the idea of post-mortem vindication. It has to be said, however, that here Collins also broadens TCC considerably in a manner for which she has not really given any argument (Collins 2007, 413, my brackets):

> The former [8:38] expresses a threat ... The latter [9:1] expresses a promise to those who deny themselves, take up their crosses, and follow Jesus loyally. The coming of the kingdom with power will vindicate them before those who persecuted them and will console them after their trials. This prophetic-apocalyptic conclusion provides a powerful incentive to faithful discipleship.

'Faithful discipleship' and 'loyal following': does Collins mean 'unto and into death', or does she have something broader in mind? And if so, what? The answer is at least not clearly spelled out.

Turning now to Lars Hartman, we may note that to begin with he appears to adopt a similar understanding, speaking, as he does, of "loyalty ... that may lead

---

12 Adela Yarbro Collins, *Mark. A Commentary.* Hermeneia (Minneapolis: Fortress, 2007).
13 And condemnation? And crucifixion?

to death"[14] and "particular circumstances, namely persecutions that are connected to one's loyalty to Jesus" (350). Towards the end, however (353), he also develops a line of thought that in effect changes the perspective completely. He first notes that "what the true followers of Jesus must be prepared to defend until death has to do with God's reign".[15] Next he reminds his reader that this reign has already manifested itself in powerrful ways during Jesus' stay in Galilee. In addition, however, God's "mysterious reign is ... also asserted in the enigmatic way of the Son of Man through sufferings and execution that lead to a new life – for many (8:31; 10:45; 14:24)". Here Hartman is clearly speaking of Jesus' sufferings and execution in particular since he alone died "for many". Then, however, comes the insight, when Hartman goes immediately on to speak of the followers (still 353, my italics):

> *To have turned round and received a share in that reign* means to let its powers work through oneself: thus the interpretation of the parable of the grain field takes for granted that the sowing would lead to rich fruit (4:20), and according to 3:36 Jesus' true family are those who do the will of God. Furthermore, in Jesus' subsequent teaching he tells the disciples that they must be servants of others (10:44) and must love God with all their heart and their neighbour as themselves (12:28–34).

Where did Hartman get this much broader – but no less forceful – reading? And what is he in fact talking about? I think he got it from his entirely correct, but also quite unacknowledged, sense of the actual meaning in the present context of 'denying oneself' and 'taking up one's cross'. And what he is talking about is precisely what he says: 'turning round' in the full, proper sense, that is, conversion. This of course implies a truly metaphorical meaning of 'cross-carrying' and I shall in fact argue against any interpretation that is either exclusively or primarily literal. But let it be stated with all the required emphasis: the claim is not that conversion of the kind called for in this text by Mark's Jesus *could* not lead to a preparedness for condemnation by crucifixion in which the Jesus follower would himself have to carry his cross to the place of crucifixion. Instead, the claim is that the *initial* act of converting to Jesus so as to 'follow' him is here conceived by Mark's Jesus as being metaphorically *similar* to, that is, *like*, literally 'taking up one's cross' on the road towards crucifixion – with all the concrete consequences (including a preparedness to be literally crucified if need be) that may *follow* from that initial act. And the claim is that it is the radical character

---

14 Lars Hartman, *Mark for the Nations. A Text- and Reader-Oriented Commentary* (Eugene, OR: Pickwick, 2010), 351. All page numbers in this paragraph are to this commentary.
15 Hartman builds this on ἕνεκεν ἐμοῦ καὶ τοῦ εὐαγγελίου in 8:35, rightly taking the latter to be the proclamation of God's reign.

of this initial act of conversion itself that Mark aims to identify by letting Jesus speak of 'denying oneself' and 'taking up one's cross'.

Mark's construction of 8:34–9:1

We have spent some time on critiquing a number of representative, recent readings of this text. The aim has been to lay bare the different elements in a syndrome of reading the text that has to be overcome before we can see what it is actually talking about. I now turn to the more constructive analysis of the text itself.

Commentators basically agree – rightly to my mind – that Mark 8:34–9:1 is a coherent whole that has been constructed by Mark himself on the basis of pre-existing material.[16] To commentators who accept the Q hypothesis this means that in 8:34–35 and 8:38 Mark builds upon Q material also to be found in Matthew and Luke in passages that are *not* the two parallel passages of Mark 8:34–9:1, viz. Mt 16:24–28 and Luke 9:23–27. For Mark 8:34–35 the 'Q parallels' on which Mark drew are Mt 10:38–39 and Luke 14:27 and 17:33. (See the helpful schema in Marcus 2009, 616.) For Mark 8:38 the 'Q parallels' are Mt 10:33 and Luke 12:9. This reconstruction evidently presupposes the two source hypothesis in the specific way that whereas Mark is taken to have constructed his own text on the basis of those bits and pieces – the 'Q parallels' – to be found in the '*non*-parallel' parts of Matthew and Luke, for the story as presented in Mark 8:34–9:1 itself Matthew and Luke, on their side, are taken to be drawing directly on Mark's account once he had constructed it. This is not the place to argue for this picture of Mark's text as standing between Q and the two later synoptic gospels.[17] Instead, I will take it for granted. What matters here is noting

---

16 E.g. Gnilka 1979, 22–23, Collins 2007, 407–408, who to a large extent follows Rudolf Bultmann, *Die Geschichte der synoptischen Tradition*. FRLANT 29 (Göttingen: Vandenhoeck & Ruprecht, 1921, and later editions, including 2nd ed., 1931), Marcus 2009, 622–623. Bultmann (1931, 86) saw Mark 8:34–37 as "eine sekundäre, durch leichte Assoziationen veranlasste Kombination" that was made up from "mindestens drei Worte", possibly even four. (Curiously, as far as I can see, Bultmann did not pay any real attention to the character and content of 8:34 in particular, in spite of the fact that in the text as we have it this is surely *the* most important verse.)

17 With regard to Mt 16:24–28 and Luke 9:23–27 vis-à-vis Mark 8:34–9:1, the usual procedure of argumentation is likely to provide interesting results. In fact, it seems quite persuasive for this text, at least, to see Matthew and Luke as trying to remove what they have found to be awkward in Mark. Compare, for instance, their different reactions to the somewhat awkward beginning of Mark 8:34 (Καὶ προσκαλεσάμενος τὸν ὄχλον σὺν τοῖς μαθηταῖς αὐτοῦ εἶπεν αὐτοῖς) at the be-

those places where Mark may have changed or added to the tradition known to him as evidenced by the supposed 'Q parallels'. The most important of these Markan changes are these:
- ἀπαρνησάσθω ἑαυτόν (8:34), which is apparently uniquely Markan,
- ἀράτω (τὸν σταυρὸν αὐτοῦ, 8:34) versus λαμβάνειν in Mt 10:38 and βαστάζειν in Luke 14:27,
- σῶσαι in Mark 8:35 versus εὑρίσκειν in Mt 10:39 and περιποιεῖσθαι and ζῳογονεῖν in Luke 17:33,
- the addition of καὶ τοῦ εὐαγγελίου to ἕνεκεν ἐμοῦ in Mark 8:35 in comparison with Mt 10:39 (nothing similar in Luke 17:33),
- the whole of 8:36–37,[18]
- ἐπαισχύνεσθαι in Mark 8:38 versus ἀρνεῖσθαι in Matthew and Luke,
- the whole of 9:1.

In addition to making these changes and additions, Mark has of course also constructed his text by tying all the various sayings together into a logical whole by means of four uses of γάρ.[19] Here the first γάρ, which introduces 8:35, explains why one will benefit from denying oneself and taking up one's cross: by being prepared to lose one's soul or life, one will in fact save it. Next, 8:36–37 specifically argue for the advantage of losing one's soul or life by denying oneself and taking up one's cross if, as 8:35 has claimed, one will in fact save it by being prepared to lose it in that way. The γάρ that introduces 8:36 presupposes the following thought, as it were between 8:35 and 8:36: '<And this (namely, losing one's soul or life "for my sake and for the sake of the gospel" so as to save it) is what one should do.> *For* what will it profit a human being to gain the whole world if he has also lost his soul or life?' In other words, if a person has lost his soul or life and so no longer actually exists, it does not benefit 'him' to have gained the whole world. What really matters is his 'soul or life': that there *is* a person who might benefit from this or the other thing. The γάρ that introduces 8:37 spells out

---

ginning of Mt 16:24 (Τότε ὁ Ἰησοῦς εἶπεν τοῖς μαθηταῖς αὐτοῦ) and Luke 9:23 (Ἔλεγεν δὲ πρὸς πάντας), respectively. Or compare their similar attempt at the beginning of Mt 16:26 (τί γὰρ ὠφεληθήσεται ἄνθρωπος, ἐὰν τὸν κόσμον ὅλον κερδήσῃ) and Luke 9:25 (τί γὰρ ὠφελεῖται ἄνθρωπος κερδήσας τὸν κόσμον ὅλον) to correct what may have been felt to be linguistically awkward about the beginning of Mark 8:36 (τί γὰρ ὠφελεῖ ἄνθρωπον κερδῆσαι τὸν κόσμον ὅλον).

18 Following Bultmann (1931, 101–102), Adela Collins (2007, 407–409) takes these verses to be "probably originally independent ... proverbial wisdom sayings" (409). However, though the idea itself may well be wisdom-like, we shall see that some of the more specific vocabulary points rather directly back to Paul.

19 See for this the fine sketch of the argument in Hartman 2010, 337–338.

and explains the thought of 8:36: a person cannot give anything in exchange for his soul or life. That is, if one has lost one's soul or life, no person is left who may either give or receive or benefit from anything. Finally, the γάρ that introduces 8:38 spells out how if one does not act on the injunction given in 8:34, one will lose one's soul or life for good when the Son of Man comes and sees that one has in this life "been ashamed of me and my words".[20] This statement also spells out, as we saw, how it is that the first half of 8:35 holds: that the one who wishes to save his life or soul will lose it. Conversely, 9:1 holds out a promise that if one does act on the injunction given in 8:34, one may in the end save one's soul or life when God's reign has arrived. Once again this statement therefore also spells out how it is that the second half of 8:35 holds: that the one who is prepared to lose his soul or life "for my sake and for the sake of the gospel" will in the end save it.[21] Understood in this way, one may well say that the passage runs quite smoothly from 8:34 via 8:35 directly to 8:38 – 9:1. The two intervening verses, 8:36 – 37, which we saw to be a Markan addition as a whole, deepen it considerably.

We cannot unfortunately discuss all the intricacies of meaning in the supposed Markan changes and additions. Here we must focus on those that are most relevant for determining the precise content of Jesus' injunction in 8:34.

The point of the Markan changes

At this point I will allow myself to introduce and draw on certain Pauline ideas and turns of phrase wherever they seem illuminating, well knowing the methodological dangers of this procedure.

Clearly, the Markan text is about life and death, or better in the reverse order: death and life. It is also about a contrast between 'oneself' (ἑαυτόν, whom one must deny, 8:34), which goes together with one's soul or life (8:35) as belonging to 'this world' (the whole cosmos, 8:36) – and on the other hand Jesus (8:34, 35), the gospel (8:35) and Jesus' words (8:38). However, on the Jesus side we should also place the soul or life that will be saved, and underneath everything we should place a 'self' that *underlies* the talk about losing and saving one's soul or life, the ὅς or person of 8:35 who may either lose or save his soul or life. Put-

---

20 Thus the γάρ that introduces 8:38 has this meaning: 'By contrast, the one who is ashamed etc.' (Scholars do not always pay sufficient attention to this contrastive use of γάρ.)
21 I therefore see much more of a reasoned argument in the text as a whole than Bultmann did when he spoke of it as being "eine ... durch leichte Assoziationen veranlasste Kombination" (see above n. 16).

ting these various contrasts together, we may say that the text is about the underlying 'self's 'dying to' the present world by denying the individual self ('himself', 'oneself'), which, by 8:36–37, is the ultimate entity that ties the underlying person or 'self' to the present world as a whole. Instead, the person or 'self' should be exclusively (and cognitively) 'directed' *away from* himself (and the earthly cosmos) *towards* Jesus, the gospel and his words.[22] What we have here is the expression of a reflection that turns on three or four things: (i) the individual self, (ii) this world and (iii) Jesus – and finally (iv) an underlying 'self' or person who *relates* to those other things. And the triangle is claimed to be of vital importance in relation to the ultimate question that the text is all about: death and life. The following figure will capture the logic of all this:

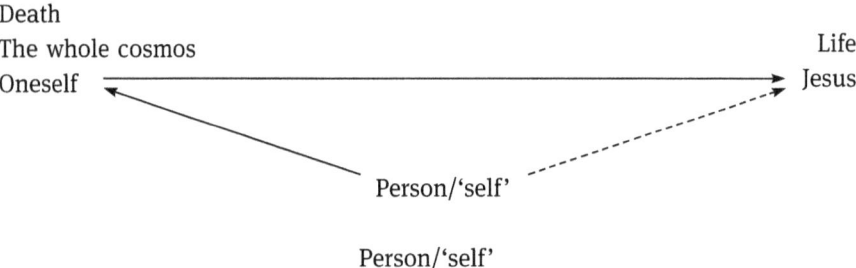

What the text is then saying is that by 'dying to' oneself *and* the present world to which the individual self is tied, and by being instead completely 'directed towards' Jesus, the person or underlying 'self' will gain life (and a new self – since the ψυχή of which the text speaks in 8:35–37 stands for both 'life' and 'soul'),[23] though a kind of life that is not of this world, but to be found in the kingdom of God.

This attempt to spell out the precise sense of the Markan Jesus' injunction in 8:34 ἀπαρνησάσθω ἑαυτόν καὶ ἀράτω τὸν σταυρὸν αὐτοῦ, with its further explanations in 8:35 and 8:36–37, is strictly derived from the text itself. It reflects the various, quite precise ideas articulated in those verses. It is also the case, however, that the proposed interpretation is made easier to arrive at in the light of certain closely similar ideas to be found in Paul. The most obviously relevant Pauline passages are Gal 2:19–20 and 6:14:

---

22 For the notion of being 'directed towards' cf. the Greek ἕνεκεν in ἕνεκεν ἐμοῦ καὶ τοῦ εὐαγγελίου.
23 Cf. the perceptive excursus on 'soul' and 'life' in Hartman 2010, 329–333.

Gal 2:19–20. 19 ἐγὼ γὰρ διὰ νόμου νόμῳ ἀπέθανον, ἵνα θεῷ ζήσω. Χριστῷ συνεσταύρωμαι· 20 ζῶ δὲ οὐκέτι ἐγώ, ζῇ δὲ ἐν ἐμοὶ Χριστός· ὃ δὲ νῦν ζῶ ἐν σαρκί, ἐν πίστει ζῶ τῇ τοῦ υἱοῦ τοῦ θεοῦ τοῦ ἀγαπήσαντός με καὶ παραδόντος ἑαυτόν ὑπὲρ ἐμοῦ.

Gal 6:14. Ἐμοὶ δὲ μὴ γένοιτο καυχᾶσθαι εἰ μὴ ἐν τῷ σταυρῷ τοῦ κυρίου ἡμῶν Ἰησοῦ Χριστοῦ, δι' οὗ ἐμοὶ κόσμος ἐσταύρωται κἀγὼ κόσμῳ.

What these passages do is to connect directly the individual's, that is, 'Paul's, experience of 'being crucified with Christ and to the cosmos' and instead being exclusively directed towards "the son of God, he who felt love for me and gave himself up for my sake". This is described in terms of the individual self's dying and the underlying self's dying to the whole world in order that this underlying self may then come to live by the fact that Christ lives in him. Furthermore, what these passages are describing is Paul's conception of conversion, a 'radical' conversion, in fact his own.[24] For our purposes, what is most striking is the fact that Paul employs the locution of being 'crucified with Christ' as the most adequate phrase for expressing what he wishes to bring out. And here there is absolutely no question that this might be understood in any other way than metaphorically. After all, Paul did not himself hang on a cross, neither together with Christ nor afterwards.

We should conclude that in 8:34–9:1 Mark is talking of a kind of radical conversion that is closely similar to the one described by Paul in his account of his own conversion. Converting in this way is a much broader phenomenon than being prepared to be literally crucified for the sake of Christ. But it certainly includes that idea when circumstances require it.

It is one thing, however, to see the similarity between Mark's account of what is required for being a 'follower' of Jesus and Paul's account of his own conversion. It is an entirely different thing to claim that Mark derived his account from Paul. Are there any indications that that might in fact be the case?

---

[24] It is customary to insist that Paul does not speak about his own 'conversion', but rather his 'call'. The point is a good one if it is meant to remind us that Paul did not move from one 'religion' called 'Judaism' to another called 'Christianity'. Still, the radical and distinctly one-sided character of the Pauline experience (as recounted by himself), namely, that it consisted in achieving a single focus (Christ) to the exclusion of everything else, is best captured by talking of a conversion.

Paul in Mark 8:34–9:1

There are several features of the Markan text that may be cited in support of finding Paul directly behind it.

There is first the phrase ἀπαρνησάσθω ἑαυτόν. According to Lars Hartman, this is "a particular Christian usage" (Hartman 2010, 326). In itself ἀπαρνεῖσθαι means "to say no to something or somebody" (ibid.). Thus in the present context the sense will be "to disown oneself, to let go of one's loyalty to oneself" (349–350). What makes this usage "specifically Christian" (349) is the fact that the act of disowning something or somebody is here turned towards oneself, as it so explicitly is in Mark through his marked use of the term ἑαυτόν. This is not just any old idea. Due to the implied notion of an awareness of 'oneself' – and thus of self-reflection – it seems to require the kind of explication that Paul had in fact given it in the quoted passages, where he speaks so strongly of an ἐγώ. Moreover, we do not have any other early Christian text (or any other texts at all before or contemporary with Paul) that speak in such a concentrated manner of an individual experience of existential change. It is a Pauline specialty.

Secondly, there is the fact that Mark apparently attempted to spell out the meaning of ἀπαρνησάσθω ἑαυτόν by adding the requirement of taking up one's cross. At least, it is possible to see the latter phrase as being intended to elucidate the former, which as we have just seen did require some elucidation. But that is of course exactly what Paul does too. Not only in the two quoted passages from Galatians, but also, for instance, in Phil 3:10 (in context) and Rom 6:1–14 does Paul employ the metaphor (as it clearly is) of 'dying with Christ' as the best way of spelling out the radical change of self-direction that he took to go with conversion. And in Paul too this particular choice was of course dictated by the fact that Jesus Christ had himself literally died "for the sake of" human beings (cf. Gal 2:20 and 1:4 – and of course Mark 10:45). As Christ had himself literally died for human beings, so they on their side should *metaphorically* 'die to themselves' and instead turn their directedness towards him.[25] Note, however (and the point is of crucial importance), that seeing Paul to be using a metaphor in this field does not in the least *weaken* his claim. Christians (like Paul himself) *are* dead to their former selves and to this world as a whole, only they will have to continue for a short while living in a somewhat reduced manner 'in the flesh' (cf. Gal 2:20).

---

[25] In fact, they should also – and in the very same movement – turn their directedness towards other human beings. That this is implied in Mark comes out very clearly in Mark 10:45 in its context (10:42–45). It is a central point also in Paul, see my *Paul and the Stoics* (Edinburgh/Louisville: T&T Clark/Westminster John Knox, 2000), passim.

From these two remarks on the specifically Pauline character of the central content of 8:34 we may move on to 8:35–37. Here one is immediately struck by a close similarity with Paul in 8:36, moreover a similarity for which there is apparently no counterpart in any pre-existing Q material on which Mark may have drawn. What I have in mind is Mark's use of the two terms κερδῆσαι and ζημιωθῆναι, which reminds one forcibly of Phil 3:7–8:

7 [Ἀλλὰ] ἅτινα ἦν μοι κέρδη, ταῦτα ἥγημαι διὰ τὸν Χριστὸν ζημίαν. 8 ἀλλὰ μενοῦνγε καὶ ἡγοῦμαι πάντα ζημίαν εἶναι διὰ τὸ ὑπερέχον τῆς γνώσεως Χριστοῦ Ἰησοῦ τοῦ κυρίου μου, δι' ὃν τὰ πάντα ἐζημιώθην, καὶ ἡγοῦμαι σκύβαλα, ἵνα Χριστὸν κερδήσω κτλ.

Here Mark is contrasting the values of this world with that of one's soul or life in terms of financial gain and loss in a manner that is closely similar to Paul's use of the same two terms to bring out the change from worldly gains to coming to see them all as so much loss "because of Christ" or rather "because of the overwhelming character of the knowledge of Christ Jesus". In other words, Mark is here transposing Paul's first person account of his own conversion (as Paul was articulating this experience to the Philippians), in which there is a change from a false κέρδος into a true one, into an a third person account of the person who does *not* undergo such a conversion but instead seeks to κερδῆσαι the whole world. It seems difficult to get rid of the feeling that Mark is here in fact drawing directly on Paul and hence that the topic of his whole account is precisely that of Paul's own account in that particular passage: conversion.

In the light of this reading of Mark 8:36 one may well reconsider what one would like to say about 8:35. As we saw, there is the possibility of Q material underlying this verse, which will account both for the paradoxical contrast that is made in it (of getting what one loses) and also for Mark's use of the term ψυχή. But we also noted that the precise contrast between ἀπολέσαι and σῶσαι was peculiar to Mark since both Matthew and Luke use other terms. Now it seems to me that if one is looking for the most precise contrast to ἀπολέσαι (which is found in the Q material too), one should choose precisely the term that Mark did choose: σῶσαι. Perhaps then Mark was inspired by the precise contrast between κερδῆσαι and ζημιωθῆναι that he had found in Paul to create a similarly precise contrast with regard to losing one's soul or life: saving it. If so, one could at least claim that he stayed squarely within a Pauline orbit since σῶσαι and σωτηρία are of course central Pauline terms. What I am suggesting here is that while the central vocabulary of 8:35 (ψυχή and ἀπολέσαι) is *not* found in Paul in this precise connection, the conceptual clarity of the Markan contrast does have a 'Pauline flavour'. In the light of the corresponding contrast in Phil 3:7–

8, which Mark seems to draw on directly in 8:36, it seems justified to claim that Paul *could* have written Mark 8:35![26]

However, once one has got so far, a striking and illuminating difference between Paul and Mark comes to light, one that we have already noted without quite giving it its due emphasis. Where Paul spoke in the first person of himself, Mark has his Jesus speak in the third person of his potential followers, cf. εἴ τις in 8:34, ὃς γὰρ ἐὰν and ὃς δ' ἂν in 8:35, ἄνθρωπον in 8:36, ἄνθρωπος in 8:37 and ὃς γὰρ ἐὰν in 8:38. The difference is huge and highly suggestive. *What Mark has done in 8:34–37 – on the proposed reading – is to generalize what Paul had said of himself so as to make it cover all Christ followers and then to put that generalization back into the mouth of Jesus.*

There is a fifth and final feature that supports linking Mark directly with Paul in this passage as a whole. This brings us to 8:38, where Mark is again likely to have drawn on Q material. However, to judge from Mt 10:33 and Luke 12:9 Mark appears to have changed an original ἀρνεῖσθαι into ἐπαισχύνεσθαι. Commentators rightly wonder about the reason for this.[27] Is ἐπαισχύνεσθαι weaker or broader than ἀρνεῖσθαι? Or is it not? And if it is, then what was Mark's reason for choosing it when using ἀρνεῖσθαι in 8:38 would seem to match so nicely with the injunction to ἀπαρνεῖσθαι ἑαυτόν in 8:34? Perhaps, then, the two terms are actually synonymous and so what we have in 8:38 is the concrete sense of denying Christ at a court hearing, in short TCC?

Well, *if* Mark did change an original ἀρνεῖσθαι to ἐπαισχύνεσθαι, it seems overwhelmingly likely that he did it for the precise purpose of broadening the perspective. As Adela Collins rightly comments, "the verb 'to be ashamed of' ... has the social sense of being ashamed about being associated with a dubious person or cause" (Collins 2007, 410–411), and this sense certainly does seem to broaden the perspective. Thus what we have is not just the situation underlying TCC, but *any* social situation where the act of denying oneself and taking up one's cross for the sake of Jesus and the gospel – that whole, exclusive directedness towards Christ – might be met with the kind of social disapproval that *might* generate a social sense of shame in the Jesus follower had he not actually and utterly renounced himself.

For this use of the term ἐπαισχύνεσθαι there is a Pauline precedent too, and in Paul's case in a missionary context. As commentators note, Paul uses the term in Rom 1:16.[28] Here is Rom 1:14–16:

---

26 I am of course fully aware of the oddity of this claim. The aim is to make the reader think of the very precise character of what is said in 8:35. It is 'Pauline'.
27 E.g. Marcus 2009, 629.
28 E.g. Collins 2007, 411 n. 134.

Ἕλλησίν τε καὶ βαρβάροις, σοφοῖς τε καὶ ἀνοήτοις ὀφειλέτης εἰμί, οὕτως τὸ κατ' ἐμὲ πρόθυμον καὶ ὑμῖν τοῖς ἐν Ῥώμῃ εὐαγγελίσασθαι. Οὐ γὰρ ἐπαισχύνομαι τὸ εὐαγγέλιον, δύναμις γὰρ θεοῦ ἐστιν εἰς σωτηρίαν κτλ.

Once again we see that what Paul had written about himself and his specific, missionary situation, Mark has his Jesus generalize into a comprehensive statement about how his followers should or should not behave. Understood in this way Mark's use of ἐπαισχύνεσθαι in 8:38 does match Jesus' injunction to ἀπαρνεῖσθαι ἑαυτόν in 8:34, only both verses are not about the concrete situation envisaged in TCC, but the much more fundamental decision to turn round and orient oneself and one's whole life towards Jesus Christ.

Concluding corollaries

We should conclude that Mark 8:34–9:1 is not primarily about confessing Christ in a trial situation and hence being prepared to take up one's cross quite literally on one's way towards being crucified – but instead about *the initial conversion*, to be understood metaphorically as a death to one's worldly self and the world at large in favour of a total directness towards Jesus. We should also conclude that this reading can be elicited from Mark's own text – but also that one is greatly helped in doing so by bringing in selected, but quite central ideas from Paul. Finally, we should conclude that these ideas are so special to Paul (since they were apparently invented by him to articulate his sense of his own conversion) that it is extremely unlikely that Mark either articulated them for himself or else found them somewhere else in early Christian tradition; instead he adopted them directly from Paul.

In the light of these claims we may draw out a few corollaries that concern the textual character of Mark 8:34–9:1.

The first point is that on this reading – even more than on any other – the text comes out as being exceedingly shrewdly constructed, where by calling it 'shrewd' I mean that it has real philosophical depth at the same time as it is both terse and immediately and strikingly impressive. Think of all that Mark has accomplished here by tying together those little bits and pieces derived from various traditions by means of an innocuous series of γάρs! In this respect I consider this text paradigmatic of Mark's Gospel as a whole, which – I would claim – repays the same kind of philosophical exegesis.

The second point has to do with the genre question that is being discussed in the present book. Mark wrote a gospel and so was fundamentally concerned with narratives and telling a story. No narrative is certainly contextless. Still, a narrative has its own intrinsic rules and telling a story requires that one focuses internally on the 'story world' as being different from the world in which the story is told. Hence the communicative aspect of telling a story is at most indirect. By contrast, Paul wrote letters, where the whole communicative point lies precisely in the direct address. This difference, which may of course be elaborated in several ways, is so great that one may well wonder to what extent and in what way one may find any kind of 'bridge' between two such different genres. However, in the present case we have found that what Mark did was first to generalize what Paul had said of himself (as part of his direct address of the Galatians, Philippians and Romans) so as to make it cover all Christ followers and next to put that generalization back into the mouth of Jesus as part of his narration. In this highly indirect way Mark did manage to address his listeners and readers, even from within the narrative.

A third point has to do with the position of Mark 8:34–9:1 within the larger narrative whole. As is generally recognized, 8:27 begins both the second half of the Gospel and also the section 8:27–10:52 in particular in which Jesus basically teaches his disciples before his arrival in Jerusalem. The teaching takes a number of forms and has a quite varied content. One kind of teaching focuses on who and what Jesus is. That is the topic not just of the three passion predictions taken on their own, but also – in the immediate environment of our passage – of 8:27–33 (which of course includes the first of those predictions), of 8:38–9:1 in our passage itself and of the transfiguration scene that immediately follows it (9:2–8/13). What, then, is the function of 8:34–9:1 within that wider setting? On the basis of the proposed reading, the answer seems clear. Mark is out to make the point that what happened to Jesus in the story has (or should have) *immediate and 'totalizing' consequences for Jesus' followers. They* should turn round completely by 'denying themselves' and 'taking up their cross' – or should we say, by 'dying to themselves'? – and in this way 'directing' themselves (in cognitive terms) completely towards the Jesus who had similarly died and – as we know not only from Paul but also from Mark himself (cf. 10:45) – died 'for them'. That is the most fundamental and ultimate 'teaching' that follows from Jesus' own fate. And that is the teaching that Jesus himself states *to* his followers in our passage. In this way, Mark 8:34–9:1 *together with* 8:27–33 constitutes a magnificent archway into everything that follows. Together, the two texts describe Jesus' fate and the consequences his followers should draw from that fate.

A fourth point has to do with theology, 'theologizing' and indeed 'philosophizing'. If everything that has been said so far is valid, it follows that in 8:34–9:1 and its immediate environment Mark is to an extreme degree 'doing theology' as part of his narration. Not only does he speak of who Jesus is ('Christology'): he also brings out in Jesus' own words in 8:34–9:1 the whole point for human beings of what happened to Jesus. This point may be captured – in a far more unsatisfactory way than in Mark's own text – in 'theological' or 'doctrinal' terms by such statements as that real life for human beings ('saving one's soul') lies in turning away from the natural world and the natural concern for one's self, soul and life and turning instead towards Jesus Christ (the resurrected 'Son of Man') with all that that implies. And what does it imply? The answer is probably given most clearly by Mark in 10:44–45, where Mark again connects directly what the 'Son of Man' has done (namely, come to διακονῆσαι καὶ δοῦναι τὴν ψυχὴν [!] αὐτοῦ λύτρον ἀντὶ πολλῶν) with what his followers should do (namely, be πάντων δοῦλος). This is 'theological anthropology' in the sense that it ties a picture of what it is to be a human being directly in with the divine. But it is also – though evidently not explicitly developed as such – *philosophical* 'anthropology' in the sense that it does speak of the 'self' and the 'soul' or 'life' of the human being and of how to lose or save that through a cognitive directedness. Truly, a lot of things are going on in this deceptively simple text.

So, do we have Paul in Mark 8:34–9:1? Yes. And he helped Mark to articulate 'what it is to be a Christian'.

III. Topics and Perspectives

Gitte Buch-Hansen
The Politics of Beginnings – Cosmology, Christology and Covenant: Gospel Openings Reconsidered in the Light of Paul's Pneumatology

During the last decades of the previous century, the so-called *New Perspective* on Paul managed to snatch Paul's letters from the grasp of Protestant exegesis. Paul was no longer seen as the great theologian of Christian *dogmata*, but became a pragmatic missionary negotiating his gospel among Jews and Gentiles. For a while that development brought Paul closer to Mark, whose gospel, too, had the inclusion of the Gentiles into God's kingdom on its prime agenda.[1] But

---

1 In *Jesus, Paul and the Law: Studies in Mark and Galatians* (London: SPCK, 1990), James D. G. Dunn draws attention to the parallels between the attitude to the law depicted in Mark's Gospel and in Paul's discussions of the law in Galatians and Romans. However, according to Dunn the similarities do not imply "a line of dependence between Mark and Paul, or Paul and Mark" (50), instead both "attest a line of theological reflection which (as Mark shows) grew out of Jesus' teaching on purity, particularly purity of foods" (50). Thus, the parallels "are perhaps most simply explained by the hypothesis that Paul knew not Jesus' teaching itself, but the interpretive line of theologizing which grew from it, which we see retained in Mark 7.17–19" (50). In Dunn's view, it is the Jesus traditions which constitute the common ground between Mark and Paul. Since Mark preserves these traditions, Dunn can speak about Mark as preceding Paul. For another scholar who finds parallels between Paul and Mark, see Henrik Tronier, "Markusevangeliets Jesus som biografiseret erkendelsesfigur: 'Ny skabelse' fra Paulus til Markus." In *Frelsens biografisering*, eds. Thomas L. Thompson and Henrik Tronier. Forum for Bibelsk Eksegese 13 (Copenhagen: Museum Tusculanums forlag, 2004), 237–271 and "Philonic Allegory in Mark." In *Philosophy at the Roots of Christianity*. Working Papers 2. Biblical Studies Section, the Faculty of Theology, University of Copenhagen (2006). Tronier argues that Mark has reinscribed Pauline theological concepts into his narrative account of Jesus. Gal 3:28 is biographized in Mark 5:1–8:21: "In Galatians 3–4 Paul had argued that Jewish and Gentile Christ-believers were in the same situation of slavery before the coming of Christ and the same situation of freedom after Christ. His aim was to introduce the idea of 'no difference' in Christ. A similar strategy of understanding is allegorically stamped into Mark's story about parallel historical events in Gentile and Jewish land after Jesus' first crossing of the ethnic borderline, the 'sea'" (2006, 40). According to Tronier, the value of this kind of comparative analysis does not depend on our ability to prove that Mark had read Paul's letters or even that he knew about their existence and content. In the present article, I do not take issue with the historical question whether Mark knew Paul and his letters. Instead, I am interested in the play between similarities and differences between New Testament texts and what these differences tell us about the changes in the

when the Pauline letters are read in the light of the more recent development within New Testament studies which takes the basically Stoic cosmology of Hellenistic philosophy into account, the distance between Paul and Mark is established again.[2] To a long tradition that has subscribed to Tertullian's questioning of Athens' relationship with Jerusalem, it may seem paradoxical that when the Pauline correspondence is read in the light of Stoic cosmology, Paul will – as we shall see – appear even more Jewish than most proponents of the 'old' *New Perspective* imagined.

In the Protestant paradigm on Paul, it was Galatians and Romans with their discussion of justification, faith and the Jewish Law that were seen as the inroad to Pauline theology. That did not change with the *New Perspective*. But with the recent, Stoically inspired, reframing of Paul's letters, the logical starting point for our study of Paul appears to be his cosmological reflections on the resurrection in 1 Cor 15.[3] When Gal 3 is read in this light, as we shall do in this article, Paul's statement that in Christ there is "neither Jew nor Gentile" (Gal 3:28) will refer to his conviction that ethnic *differences* no longer count, since – through the reception of Christ's spirit in their baptism – Gentiles have been physically incorporated into Abraham's line of descent and therefore literally become Jews. In other words, Paul's gospel invites the Gentiles into God's covenant with Judaism. In Romans, Paul explains how the Gentiles as "wild olive shoots" have been engrafted into the cultivated and pruned olive tree of Israel and now benefit from its roots (Rom 11:17). To Paul, *ethnicity* certainly mattered.

So Paul presupposes, confirms and upholds Israel's privileged relationship with God. But in the Gospel of Mark, Israel's advantages have apparently come to an end. Probably, it was the fall of the Jerusalem temple that provoked the author of Mark to redefine the relationship between Judaism and the Christ-

---

early Christian worldview and self-understanding. We will briefly return to Tronier's reading of Mark at the end of this article.

2 In spite of the fact that the Hellenistic discourse on cosmology was defined by Plato's *Timaeus*, Hellenistic cosmology remained Stoic. As Gretchen Reydams-Schils explains in *Demiurge and Providence: Stoic and Platonist Readings of Plato's Timaeus* (Turnhout: Brepols Publishers, 1999), "The task at hand, then, is to prove not only that Stoic and Platonist readings of Plato's *Timaeus* reveal such a discussion of assimilation, *but also that it displaced Plato's own work.* Later interpreters and readers did not focus on its content alone, *but included other interpretations as well,* often as though they belonged to the original text. Thus this tradition [...] is a prime example of the 'hermeneutical circle' in the strong sense: the *Timaeus* after the Stoics was significantly different from what it had been previously" (16, emphasis added).

3 The argument in Troels Engberg-Pedersen's book on *Cosmology and Self in the Apostle Paul: The Material Spirit* (Oxford: Oxford University Press, 2010) has "A Stoic Understanding of the *Pneuma* and Resurrection in 1 Corinthians 15" as starting point – and first chapter.

believing community. The rupture of the curtain in the temple occasioned by Jesus' powerful expiration is a telling symbol of Mark's negative conclusion with regard to Judaism's continuing status with God (Mark 15:38). In this situation, Paul's elaborate argument in favor of the Gentiles' inclusion into Israel's covenant and ancestry no longer made sense, and Mark had to find a new way to define the community of Christ-believing Jews and Gentiles. In Paul's congregations, the reception of the spirit in baptism had been the crucial and defining event, but in the Gospel of Mark this status is given to the meals which anticipate the Eucharist. While the Stoic reframing of Paul's letters makes the apostle to the Gentiles even less Protestant than the proponents of the *New Perspective* claimed, Mark's Gospel will now appear as the only canonical document on which a Lutheran theology of justification by faith may be grounded.

In this article, I intend to demonstrate how in Paul's letters and in the Synoptic Gospels an intimate relationship exists between the authors' Christology and their ethnic agenda – or, in other words, that in these texts the body of Christ has become the *site* on which Judaism's status *vis-à-vis* the increasingly Gentile church is negotiated.[4] The main part of the argument is devoted to a rereading of Paul's letters in the light of Stoic cosmology. As a test case, we shall see how Paul's cosmological Christology in 1 Cor 15 revises our understanding of the ethnic agenda of Paul's argument in Gal 3. We will then examine how this new reading of Gal 3 influences our understanding of Paul's Christology in his opening address in his letter to the Romans (1:1–4). Finally, we turn to the Synoptics in order to see how this revision of Paul's Christology affects the relationship between Paul and the Synoptics – and here special attention will be given to Mark. As we shall see, more is at stake in the opening narratives of the gospels than the high/low issue in theologians' dogmatic discussion about Christology.

A brief look at Rom 1:1–4 – the only passage in his letters in which Paul is directly engaged in Christology – will help us to define the objectives with which we are to take issue in the present article.

---

4 In my book, Gitte Buch-Hansen, *It Is the Spirit That Gives Life: A Stoic Understanding of Pneuma in John's Gospel*. BZNW 173 (Berlin: W. de Gruyter, 2010), I argue that also John's Gospel ought to be read in light of Stoic cosmology. But in contrast with Paul, the Jew-Gentile agenda plays no role in John. Probably because – as argued by Daniel Boyarin in "The Gospel of the Memra: Jewish Binitarianism and the Prologue to John." *HTR* 94.3 (2001): 243–284 – the Fourth Gospel belongs to a Jewish *koinê* around a Hellenized version of the Jewish wisdom tradition. Unfortunately, it will take us too far to include the Fourth Gospel in the present survey.

1 Introduction

Challenging the high-low distinction in New Testament Christology

It is generally recognized that the hymnal passages in Philippians and Colossians represent the earliest Christian traditions preserved in the New Testament. These passages are reminiscent of an early *high* Christology – that is, of Christ's heavenly preexistence – and they are often assumed to represent Paul's Christological stance. Nevertheless, Paul's opening address in his letter to the Romans is not as unambiguously high as many scholars would like it to be. On the one hand, the semantic flexibility of Rom 1:1–4 is acknowledged; on the other hand, it is explained away again by reference to a pre-Pauline formula of Jewish-Christian origin which Paul is assumed to have used in order to establish common ground with the congregations in Rome. After all, this "more primitive Christology" was just a piece of pleasing rhetoric.[5] Scholars discuss to what extent – if any – the adopted material in Rom 1:1–4 represents Paul's own view. Typically, the skeptical majority draws attention to the similar statement in Rom 8:3 which refers to God's "sending his own Son in the likeness of sinful flesh." Romans 8:3 is interpreted in light of the Philippian hymn (Phil 2:6–11) and this interpretation now serves as the matrix against which the adopted material in Rom 1:1–4 is sorted out. Byrne's explanation in his *Sacra Pagina* commentary on Romans is representative; Paul's introduction to the creedal formula "concerning his [God's] Son" (Rom 1:3):

> overwrites the more *primitive* Christology of the creedal formula. The latter associates Christ's divine sonship with the moment of his resurrection, whereas in Paul's eyes Jesus is uniquely God's Son (cf. 5:10; 8:3, 29, 32 [...]), not simply from the time of his resurrection but during his earthly obedience and possibly even as 'pre-existent' (Byrne 1996, 44, emphasis added).[6]

---

5 Brendan Byrne, *Romans*. Sacra Pagina 6 (Collegeville, Minnesota: a Michael Glazier Book, Liturgical Press, 1996), 44.

6 Joseph A. Fitzmyer's confirms Byrne's position in *Romans*. The Anchor Bible 33 (New York: Doubleday, 1993), "Although Paul never speaks of Jesus as an incarnate Son [...] his use of *huios* may imply some sort of preexistent filiation" (234). According to Leander E. Keck, Paul's Christology is even higher: "what matters for Christ's identity is his Sonship *before* he became 'Son of David' and his *present* Sonship with power because (or since) he was resurrected. Everything between these transitional events (Jesus' ministry) is bypassed; the crucifixion is assumed. This Christology lies at the heart of the good news of God in Romans". See Keck's *Romans*. Abingdon New Testament Commentaries. (Nashville: Abingdon Press, 2005), 45, Keck's emphasis.

Yet, other scholars see no tension in Rom 1:1–4. In his commentary on Romans, James D. G. Dunn states that "Paul would certainly see the earlier formula as congruent with his own Christology."[7] To Dunn, the creedal formula represents a "two-stage Christology":

> For those aware that the royal Messiah was also called God's Son [...] the phrase "in power" would be a natural qualification: Jesus did not first become God's Son at the resurrection; but he entered upon a still higher rank of sonship at resurrection. [...] That being said, it remains significant that these early formulations *and Paul* saw in the resurrection of Jesus a "becoming" of Jesus in status and role, not simply a ratification of a status and role already enjoyed on earth or from the beginning of time (Dunn 1988, 14, emphasis added).

As we shall see, the cosmological perspective on Paul will confirm Dunn's claim that Paul features a kind of two-stage Christology. Inevitably this invites a comparison between the opening address of Romans and Mark's beginning. After all, the messianic secret in Mark's Gospel can be seen as the evangelist's narrative version of the two-stage Christology: something happened in Jesus' baptism, but still more was lying in wait; the demons know and reveal that. Exegetes only rarely juxtapose Paul's opening address in Romans and Mark's introduction. Probably, the prevailing high-low distinction in New Testament Christology has prevented that.[8] But if Paul's Lord was neither the eternal Son from the beginning of time nor firstly recognized as such in the resurrection, but as the royal Messiah already received the title "Son" during his lifetime, the question begs to be asked: when and under which circumstances did that happen? Paul does not provide us with an answer; probably because it was the resurrected and pneumatically transformed Christ who constituted the focal point of his thinking. But Mark does. The author of Mark's Gospel, who endeavors to give us a biography of Jesus' earthly life, had to do that. So, according to Mark, it happened when God's spirit descended onto Jesus in his baptism (Mark 1:9–11). These con-

---

[7] James D. G. Dunn, *Romans*. Word Biblical Commentary 38 A (Dallas, Texas: Word Book, Publisher, 1988), 14.
[8] In this volume, Oda Wischmeyer compares Romans 1:1–7 and Mark 1:1–3. In her article "Romans 1:1–7 and Mark 1:1–3 in comparison. Two opening texts at the beginning of Early Christian literature," Wischmeyer focuses on Mark's and Paul's use of the term εὐαγγέλιον. See also R. Alan Culpepper, who draws attention to the parallels between Paul's opening address in Romans and Mark's Gospel in *Mark*. Smyth & Helwys Bible Commentary (Macon, Georgia: Smyth and Helwys Publishing, 2007), 43: "Within the New Testament, the reference in Romans 1:3 is especially important because it preserves a very early Christian confession. [...] The similarities with Mark are striking [...]". However, in the comparison I will undertake in my study, I will focus on Jesus' baptism in Mark 1:9–11.

siderations leave us with some questions: If Paul and Mark, as I am to argue, feature a kind of two-stage Christology in which the Jewish Messiah of David's seed only received his full divinity and power at the resurrection, why did these New Testament authors choose this *lower* Christology instead of the *higher* Christology of the earlier hymnal tradition, which was at their disposal? And why did Matthew and Luke change it again when they added their narratives of the virgin birth to the tradition they received from Mark?

Traditionally, the latter case has been explained by reference to the apologetic concerns which caused Matthew and Luke to replace Mark's adoption with the *high* Christology of the virgin birth; Jesus' *high* identity as Son of God superseded Mark's *low* Messianic pretentions.[9] When juxtaposed to Matthew's and Luke's theologically pregnant openings, the glory of Mark's Christology faded away. But the apologetic explanation presupposes that in the social world of early Christianity, adopted sons were of a lower esteem than biological children. But this seems not always to have been the case. In his 2010 article "The Eagle and the Dove: Roman Imperial Sonship and the Baptism of Jesus (Mark 1,9–11)," Michael Peppard challenges the prevailing understanding of Mark's Christology as *low*.[10]

Peppard reads Mark's story about Jesus' baptism in light of the practice of adoption in the imperial family. In the Augustan era, it was the chosen and adopted sons who qualified as heirs of the divinized Ceasar – and, consequently, as sons of god. Peppard also draws attention to the popular narratives about the elections of these royal heirs. Often bird omens guided and confirmed the choice and ritual installation of a young man as son and heir. According to the Roman historian Suetonius, Caesar's choice of Octavian as his son and successor was accompanied by the appearance of a dove which foreshadowed the peace to come (Peppard 2010, 445). Consequently, a Markan reader acquainted with imperial ideology and symbolism may have understood the baptism of Jesus as a divine adoption and a hint at Jesus' peaceful, but nevertheless imperial ambitions: "If readers of Mark consider the resonance of the concept of adoption in the Roman ideology of Mark's era, it does not appear to be a 'low' Christology at all" (441). Peppard concludes that when exegetes add the predicate *low* to adoption and *high* to the paternal seed, they apply modern – and foreign – standards to the ancient material; often political considerations carried greater weight than semen and blood (440). So, if we – also from the perspective of social history –

---

9 See e.g. Maurice Casey, *From Jewish Prophet to Gentile God: The Origins and Development of New Testament Christology* (Westminster: John Knox Press, 1991).
10 Michael Peppard, "The Eagle and the Dove: Roman Imperial Sonship and the Baptism of Jesus (Mark 1,9–11)." *NTS* 56 (2010): 431–451.

cannot uphold the high-low dichotomy in Christology, we must seek for another explanation of the introduction of the virgin birth in Matthew and Luke. As I have already suggested, the answer is to be found in the author's attitude with regard to Judaism's standing with God. But in order to understand *how*, we must first analyze the interaction between Christology and ethnicity in Paul's letters.

Whenever a new scholarly paradigm is introduced, our understanding and evaluation of earlier scholarship changes, and the history of research must be retold in light of the most recent developments. A brief look at the Pauline studies of the previous century will provides us with a historical framework for our dealing with the above outlined questions.

Stoic cosmology and the New Perspective on Paul

Within the last decade, New Testament studies on Paul focusing on Stoicism – and more recently, on Stoic cosmology – have brought the spirit into the centre of Paul's world.[11] This development is above all due to the work of Troels Engberg-Pedersen which was published in his 2010 book *Cosmology and the Self in the Apostle Paul: The Material Spirit*. The book is Engberg-Pedersen's sequel to his 2000 volume *Paul and the Stoics*.[12] Whereas the Stoic character of Paul's ethics was in focus in the first book, it is the Stoics' physics and pneumatic cosmology that constitutes the lens through which the letters are read in the most recent volume.[13] As already mentioned, the logical center around which Paul's theology evolves now appears to be his reflections in 1 Cor 15 on the physical and cosmological transformations involved in the resurrection. Paul himself expresses the importance of Christ's resurrection in the following way: "If Christ

---

[11] Troels Engberg-Pedersen, "The Material Spirit: Cosmology and Ethics in Paul." *NTS* 55 (2009): 179–197: "The importance of the *pneuma* in Paul's thought can hardly be overstated. In fact, once one has become attuned to it, one will find the *pneuma* everywhere in Paul, even where it is not actually mentioned" (179).

[12] Troels Engberg-Pedersen, *Paul and the Stoics* (Edinburgh: T & T Clark, 2000).

[13] In Stoic philosophy, the psychological description of the mental growth in wisdom and the physio-/cosmological description of the person's pneumatic constitution were two sides of the same coin. Thus, Stoicism parallels modern theories of cognition in which a material neurophysiological basis is recognized for mental processes at the same time as one has to renounce the possibility of simple reduction of cognition to chemistry. In Paul's world these two non-reductive discourses correspond to his discussion of 'faith' (cognition) and 'spirit' (chemistry), respectively. Whereas Engberg-Pedersen's *Paul and the Stoics* focuses on the first issue, *Cosmology and the Self in the Apostle Paul* is devoted to the latter.

has not been raised, then our proclamation has been in vain and your faith has been in vain" (1 Cor 15:14) and "of all people we are most to be pitied" (15:19).

After a lengthy – and basically Stoic – explanation about the specific relationship between a being's habitat and its bodily constitution (1 Cor 15:35–41), Paul finally reaches his point in verse 45 (Engberg-Pedersen 2009, 186; 2010, 26–38). In the resurrection, Christ has been transformed from his earthly mode of being – that is, as a body of flesh and blood – to a pneumatic body suitable for the life of a heavenly being: "The last Adam became a life-giving spirit (ὁ ἔσχατος Ἀδὰμ εἰς πνεῦμα ζῳοποιοῦν)." According to Paul, Jesus' resurrection and ascension took place in the same cosmic event. Subsequently, this transformation manifested itself when in baptism Christ's life-giving spirit was, so to speak, recycled to believers in order to initiate and assist the same process of transformation in them.[14] As Paul explains, Christ was the crucial first fruit and without his resurrection and ascent, the community's hope that soon they were to follow him would be "in vain" (Engberg-Pedersen 2010, 38; 51).

The new, cosmological perspective on Paul mediates between two major tendencies in modern scholarship on Paul: the *participation* paradigm having Ed P. Sanders as its main proponent, and the *justification* paradigm with James D. G. Dunn as prime advocate.[15] It is well known how in his seminal 1977 book *Paul and Palestinian Judaism: A Comparison of Patterns of Religion*, Sanders challenged centuries of Lutheran scholarship on Paul.[16] The contrast between law/deeds and faith/grace had led to a misrepresentation of Judaism and a misreading of Paul's letters. Instead, Palestinian Judaism should be characterized as *covenantal nomism*, and as such it was a religion based on God's grace, initiative and election. In his next book, *Paul, the Law, and the Jewish People* (1983), Sanders introduced the immensely helpful analytical categories: *getting-in* and *staying-in*.[17] In Judaism, the *getting-in* condition was given historically with God's promises to the patriarch Abraham, and the Law constituted God's guidance

---

14 Engberg-Pedersen explains: "The proposal is that Paul had the idea that the future transformation at the resurrection that would turn the mortal body of flesh and blood into an equally physical, but immortal body of *pneuma* was already solidly and quite concretely under way in the bodies of believers, who in connection with faith and baptism had received the *pneuma* from God" (2009, 188). See also Engberg-Pedersen 2010, 67–70.
15 For an overview of different tendencies within the *New Perspective*, see Magnus Zetterholm, *Approaches to Paul: A Student's Guide to Recent Scholarship* (Minneapolis: Fortress Press, 2009).
16 Ed P. Sanders, *Paul and Palestinian Judaism: A Comparison of Patterns of Religion* (London: SCM Press, 1977), 1–12.
17 Ed P. Sanders, *Paul, the Law, and the Jewish People* (Philadelphia: Fortress Press, 1983), 6–10. In my analysis, I make use of Sanders' categories. However, my application of his categories to the Pauline material differs from his.

of Abraham's progeny – his chosen people – *within* Israel's covenant. Sanders strongly emphasizes that Paul – wholly in accordance with Judaism's *covenantal nomism*, but in opposition to his Galatian opponents – did not understand law obedience as "an entrance requirement" (1983, 10; 17–29). Also Sanders' epigrammatic description of Paul's attitude to the Jewish Law is well known: the encounter with the risen Christ made Paul a retrospective critic of Judaism's institutions: the solution came before the plight. According to Sanders, it was Paul's idea of salvation through the spiritual participation in Christ which constituted the core of Pauline Christianity, and the whole argument about justification was secondary to that.[18]

Although Sanders' epigrammatic statement did not satisfy all New Testament scholars, the representation of Judaism as a religion of works-righteousness was from Sanders onwards a *no go*. Nevertheless, Sanders' work on Paul and Judaism stimulated a library of books that came up with ever new suggestions for the problems that the apostle to the Gentiles, after all, found with Judaism and the Law. James D. G. Dunn's 1983 article, "A New Perspective on Paul: Paul and the Law" inspired and named this tradition.[19] According to Dunn's reading of Paul, it was the *use* of the Law to produce boundaries between Jews and Gentile *within* the Christ-believing congregations which made the Law a problem. Whereas Sanders' Paul converted from Judaism to a new and different religion, the *New Perspective's* Paul remained a Jew who believed that the coming of the Jewish Messiah signaled the impending judgment when just Gentiles were to be incorporated into God's people.[20] Sanders' tradition and the proponents of the *New Perspective* came to represent two opposing tendencies with-

---

18 Sanders describes Paul's discussion of righteousness as belonging to his *transfer terminology:* "The righteousness terminology, especially the passive verb 'be righteoused,' is employed in his discussions of transferring from one status to another and does not often appear in discussions of maintaining the new status" (1983, 6). The discourse refers to the behavior expected of the person whose status has changed through faith and participation in Christ. Thus, according to Sanders, Paul's justification should not be identified with the Lutheran *simul justus et peccator.* Paul's *transfer terminology* belongs to the *staying-in* discourse. I agree. But when Sanders claims that Paul's argument in Gal 3 is about the getting-in of the Gentiles, I disagree.
19 James D. G. Dunn, "The New Perspective on Paul." *Bulletin of the John Rylands Library* 65 (1983): 95–122.
20 James D. G. Dunn, *The Epistle to the Galatians*. Black's New Testament Commentaries (London: A & C Black, 1993): "If we may speak of the event as a conversion it was not a conversion from the religion of Israel to a new religion, but a conversion from one viewpoint within Judaism, regarding the relation of Israel to the other nations (the Gentiles), to another viewpoint – conversion from suspicion of and antipathy to non-Jews, to concern for their conversion to the gospel of the Jewish Messiah" (3).

in Pauline scholarship: Was Pauline theology to be understood within the framework of a mysterious *participation* in Christ or was it the eschatological *justification* of the Gentiles which was at Paul's heart?

But when Paul's letters are read in the light of Stoic cosmology, it is no longer an either-or. Both traditions were partially right and both partially wrong. Sanders' approach to Paul was right with regard to the claim that participation in Christ constituted the core in Paul's gospel. But the claim that Paul's mysterious encounter with the risen Christ gave rise to a new religion was wrong.[21] Instead, Paul remained a Jew and his religion remained Judaism, as rightly claimed by the proponents of the *New Perspective*, and the participation in Christ was instrumental to that. The reception of Christ's spirit fulfilled, as I shall argue, the *getting-in* requirement with regard to the Gentiles' inclusion into Israel's covenant. However, advocates of the *New Perspective* were wrong in case they, like Dunn, stuck to a kind of forensic economy of justification in which faith in Christ was recognized by God as righteousness.[22] Paul's Jewishness warrants Dunn's interpretation: Paul's concept of righteousness and justice was Jewish and *relational* as opposed to Hellenistic ideas of virtue.[23] However, during the last decades, the Judaism-Hellenism dichotomy, which Dunn's argument presupposes, has been challenged within Pauline scholarship. Paul was a *Hellenistic* Jew who reinterpreted his Jewish heritage in terms of Hellenistic ideas (or the other way around).[24] Consequently, as also I am to argue, Paul's ideas about justification were both relational *and* virtuous, since participation in Christ (the relational)

---

[21] That development was first to take place some decades later when the synoptic gospels had to reinterpret the Pauline heritage in light of the changed perception of Judaism's status with God.

[22] The *content* of the Protestant doctrine of justification is not changed in Dunn's interpretation, but he *frames* Paul's doctrine differently. In Protestant Christianity, the doctrine concerns the relation between God and universal humanity, but according to the proponents of the New Perspective the doctrine is bound to a specific, historical situation. It was the means by the aid of which "the salvific playing field between Gentiles and Jews" was leveled. See Pamela Eisenbaum's critique in "A Remedy for Having Been Born of Woman: Jesus, Gentiles and Genealogy in Romans." *JBL* 123 (2004): 671–702 (673).

[23] "For whereas in Greek thought 'righteousness' or 'justice' was an ideal norm by which particular claims or duties could be measured, in Hebrew thought 'righteousness' was more a concept of relation. [...] to be righteous was to live within the covenant and within the terms it laid down (the law); to be acquitted, recognized as righteous, was to be counted as one of God's own people who had proved faithful to the covenant" (Dunn 1993, 133–34).

[24] Troels Engberg-Pedersen (ed.), *Paul Beyond the Judaism-Hellenism Divide* (Louisville, Kentucky: Westminster John Knox Press, 2001). Especially, "Introduction: Paul Beyond the Judaism/Hellenism Divide" by Engberg-Pedersen (1–16) and "Paul and the Judaism/Hellenism Dichotomy: Toward a Social History of the Question" by Dale B. Martin (29–62).

had a strong impact on the believers' behavior (the ethical) – as rightly claimed by Sanders (1983, 6). But all this we shall return to soon.[25] I shall argue – again in accordance with Sanders' description of Judaism – that for Paul, the debate on righteousness was a matter of *staying-in*, and the Law remained his ethical standard for the virtuous and just life expected of God's covenant people.

During the early centuries of Christianity, Paul's theology for a charismatic and ascetic Jewish community living at the edge of time was changed profoundly. First, the gospels adapted the Pauline heritage to the continuous reality of this world and also to the parting of the ways with Judaism. Later when subjected to Augustine's interpretation, Paul's letters offered a universal theology suited for a Gentile church which had become an alley of the Roman Empire. The new, Stoically inspired, cosmological perspective draws attention to a forgotten and foreign Paul who belongs to a period before these paradigmatic changes became standard Christian theology.

Getting-in, genealogy and the two-ways paradigm in Pauline studies

The above, briefly sketched interpretation of Paul and his theology leaves us with an apostle who to a large extent resembles the apostle to the Gentiles whom we encounter in the recent works of advocates of the so-called two-ways paradigm. Both Pamela Eisenbaum in "A Remedy for Having Been Born of Woman: Jesus, Gentiles and Genealogy in Romans" and Caroline Johnson Hodge in her *If Sons, then Heirs: A Study of Kinship and Ethnicity in the Letters of Paul* argue that it was the inclusion of the Gentiles into the Jewish covenant which was at the heart of Paul's thought.[26] Since the promise of the blessing was given explicitly to Abraham's progeny, the Gentiles' genealogy was the

---

25 For criticism of the Protestant bias in the *New Perspective*, see chapter 4: "Reading Paul as a Jew – Almost" in Pamela Eisenbaum, *Paul Was Not a Christian: The Original Message of a Misunderstood Apostle* (New York: HarperCollins Publishers, 2009), 55–66. This criticism has often come from Jewish interpreters of Paul, see Michael F. Bird & Preston M. Sprinkle, "Jewish Interpretations of Paul in the Last Thirty Years." *Currents in Biblical Research* 6 (2008), 355–376.
26 See Caroline Johnson Hodge, *If Sons, then Heirs: A Study of Kinship and Ethnicity in the Letters of Paul* (Oxford: Oxford University Press, 2007). Eisenbaum's and Hodge's readings of the Pauline letters are, according to themselves, indebted to work of Lloyd Gaston, *Paul and the Torah* (Vancouver: University of British Columbia Press, 1987); Stanley K. Stowers, *A Rereading of Romans: Justice, Jews, and Gentiles* (New Haven: Yale University Press, 1994); and John G. Gager, *Reinventing Paul* (Oxford/New York: Oxford University Press, 2002). However, Eisenbaum's and Hodge's works are original in the way they foreground the problem of the Gentiles' genealogy.

major obstacle to be overcome. Paul's elaborate discussions of righteousness must be subsumed into that agenda and concerned the Gentiles alone. In Paul's view, Israel was a righteous nation already; therefore the inclusion of the Gentiles into God's people demanded their righteousness, too.[27] But Christ's atoning sacrifice made up for that. Eisenbaum explains:

> I suggest that Paul understands the sacrificial death of Christ as both expiation for sin, particularly Gentile sin, and a reconciling sacrifice that enables Gentiles to be received into Abraham's lineage. [...] In this way, then, Jesus' blood sacrifice is efficacious for Jews, not because such sacrifice atones for sins committed by Jews but because it removes the pollution potentially brought into the community of Israel by Gentiles (Eisenbaum 2004, 698–699).

Apart from the new branch on the patriarch's pedigree, God's covenant with the Jews was in no way affected by the Christ event.

Eisenbaum's and Hodge's arguments are informed by antiquity's discourse on genealogy and patrilinearity; the Jewish identity as Abraham's progeny and heirs is an example of the latter.[28] The two scholars draw attention to the tension between the patrilinear ideology and the material fact that only the maternal parenthood could be confirmed. In order to maintain the social power administered through the patrilinear system, this ideological deficit had to be covered up. To achieve that, everything which was associated with the female reproduction was categorized as impure; above all, the woman's blood was seen as unclean. Since the mother's impurities were transferred to the child through pregnancy and birth, both had to be cleansed before they could return to ordinary social life (Jay 1992, 39–40; Eisenbaum 2004, 677–680). Yet, more was needed

---

[27] Eisenbaum explains: "Death may be a reality for everyone in the first age, Jews and Gentiles alike, but Jews, being children of God and in possession of Torah, have the means of cultic purity and are poised to receive their divine inheritance, whenever the time comes. Gentiles, on the other hand, are slaves to sin and flesh – this is the predicament captured in abbreviated form by the familiar Pauline phrase 'under the Law.' [...] Following cultural stereotypes, Paul regards Jews as 'naturally' obedient, not because they possess Torah but because they have already been incorporated into the patrilineage of Abraham and have a kind of 'genetic edge,' while Gentiles are morally and spiritually disadvantaged because they did not have the benefit of participation in this blessed lineage" (2004, 699–700).

[28] Both Eisenbaum and Hodge build on the work of Nancy Jay, *Throughout Your Generations Forever: Sacrifice, Religion, and Paternity* (Chicago and London: The University of Chicago Press, 1992) and "Sacrifice, Descent and the Patriarchs", *VT* 38 (1988): 52–70, (53; 56; 63) and of Stanley K. Stowers: "Greeks Who Sacrifice and Those Who Do Not: Toward an Anthropology of Greek Religion." In *The Social World of the First Christians: Essays in Honor of Wayne A. Meeks* eds. L. Michael White & O. Larry Yarbrough (Minneapolis: Augsburg Fortress, 1995), 293–333.

if the ideological exigency was to be overcome; the ties between the mother and *her* child had to be severed. In Greco-Roman culture, the transfer of the child from the mother to the father's lineage took place in a ritual which was performed at the family's hearth. Here the father gave a blood sacrifice which cleansed the child from maternal impurities. When, as a sign of acceptance, the father named the child, the offspring was incorporated into his family (Jay 1992, 30–40; 43–45; Stowers 1995, 315; Eisenbaum 2004, 679–80; Hodge 2007, 27).

Somewhat paradoxically, the patrilinear ideology implied a cultural degradation of biological fatherhood in favor of the social parent. Roman law distinguished between biological and social fatherhood which were called *genus* and *pater*, respectively. Only the offspring who was officially and ritually recognized by the social *pater* would count as a legitimate heir and was given access to the political influence inherent in his patrilinear heritage (Hodge 2007, 29–30). The distinction between *genus* and *pater* provided space for pragmatic solutions in case there was no – or no rightly qualified – heir. Adoption was a legitimate possibility and, as we saw in Peppard's article, the imperial family benefitted from that.

Eisenbaum reinterprets the traditional doctrine of Christ's atoning sacrifice in this context and understands the early Christian baptism in light of the ritual involved in paternal adoption. In the baptismal ritual, the Gentiles were cleansed, recognized by the (divine) father and renamed. Whereas Jews were *born* into God's people and Abraham's lineage, Christ-believing Gentiles became sons through *adoption* (Eisenbaum 2004, 700–02).[29] Appealing to the same contextual material, Hodge suggests another solution to the same genealogical problem. After all, Paul saw baptism as more than a cleansing and naming ritual; the reception of Christ's spirit made all the difference (Hodge 2007, 72–75). As argued in Aristotle's *On the Generation of Animals*, the male seed or semen was seen as a watery solution of the paternal soul/spirit. Therefore, the paternal lineage would live on throughout the generations as an extension of the ancestor's body.[30] It was in accordance with this idea that early Christians perceived the elemental mix of Christ's *spirit* and the baptismal *water* as God's seed.[31] But since

---

[29] Eisenbaum (2004), 701: "Gentiles receive the same 'adoption' (υἱοθεσία, 8:15) that Jews already possess (9:4)."
[30] Aristotle, *Generation of Animals (De generatione animalium)* LCL (Cambridge: Harvard University Press, 1942), xv; 735b10–36a30. See also Anthony Preuss, "Science and Philosophy in Aristotle's Generation of Animals." *Journal of the History of Biology* 3 (1970): 1–52 (3).
[31] This understanding is explicit in 1 John 3:9[NAS] "No one who is born of God practices sin, because His seed abides in him (ὅτι σπέρμα αὐτοῦ ἐν αὐτῷ μένει); and he cannot sin, because

Christ as a Jew was of Abraham's progeny, the reception of Christ's spirit also made up for the Gentiles' relation to the founding ancestor. The Christian baptism was a ritual of ethnic reconfiguration; the believer was transferred from his Gentile breed into Judaism. Whereas Eisenbaum focused on the meaning of Christ's sacrificial death, Hodge's interpretation hinges on the generative powers of the resurrected Christ. However, in both interpretations Christ provides for the *getting-in* requirements of the Jewish covenant.[32]

I follow Hodge in her understanding of Paul's argument for the inclusion of the Gentiles into God's people. But I miss a discussion of *how* Christ's spirit becomes available to believers in her analysis. The answer to that question is – as already suggested – to be found in 1 Cor 15:45. But, as my analysis will make clear, when Gal 3 is read against the backdrop of a Stoic understanding of 1 Cor 15:45, it is no longer possible to uphold the two-ways paradigm. Paul's – indeed, very complicated – argument in Gal 3 concerns both aspects of Sanders' covenantal life: with regard to the Gentiles, the focus is on the *getting-in* requirements; with regard to the Jews, the focus is on the righteousness expected of those who wish to *stay within* the covenant. Since the Jews were Abraham's sons *by birth*, the *getting-in* discourse did not concern them. But since – through their reception of Christ's spirit in baptism – the Gentiles had become Jews *by faith*, the *staying-in* discourse certainly concerned them, too. Whereas within the traditional Lutheran paradigm – but also within the *New Perspective* on

---

he is born of God (ὅτι ἐκ τοῦ θεοῦ γεγέννηται)." 'Generated' would have been a better translation, because the term 'born' signals that we speak in metaphors, which is not the case.

32 Although from a logical point of view there is a contradiction between the 'flexible' and 'constructed' adoption and the 'fixed' and 'essential' biological model of generation, this did not imply that the two models were mutually exclusive. On the contrary, in her book *Why This New Race: Ethnic Reasoning in Early Christianity* (New York: Columbia University Press, 2005), Denise Kimber Buell draws attention to the dynamic between the 'fixity' and 'fluidity' involved in most ethnic constructions. The tension between the 'essential' and the 'constructed' elements in discourses of race and ethnicity provides a flexibility which allows manoeuvring in situations where the essential dimensions appear problematic; the tension enables adaption to new situations. The problem with which Buell takes issue in her book is the historical mistake characteristic of much biblical scholarship, namely, of attributing the essentialist and racial thinking to Judaism, while Christianity is claimed to be an open identity which transcends racial/ethnic thinking. But this is a too simple version of history: Early Christians also identified themselves as a "new race." In her analyses, Hodge refers to Buell's work – and Buell to Hodge's. According to Buell, no such thing as *the* early Christian identity exists; consequently, it is the dynamic between the flexible and the fixed elements in that identity which ought to be studied. Whereas, in Hodge's and my own interpretation, Paul accedes to Judaism's 'fixity' and biological genealogy, Mark – as we shall see – accedes to the 'fluidity' and even does away with the fixed and essentialist aspects of the Jewish genealogy.

Paul (at least as it is represented by Dunn) – exegetes have completely ignored the genealogical *getting-in* requirements, proponents of the two-ways paradigm tend to absorb Paul's discussion of righteousness into the discourse of *getting-in* and, consequently, to see it as an exclusively Gentile matter. However, as my analysis will demonstrate, in Gal 3 Paul discusses righteousness as a Jewish matter. Therefore none of these positions has got the ethnic framework of Paul's argument in Gal 3 right. But in order to see that, we must first consult a Stoic understanding of 1 Cor 15:45.

2 A Stoic understanding of 1 Cor 15:45

In my book *It Is the Spirit That Gives Life: A Stoic Understanding of Pneuma in John's Gospel* (2010), I demonstrated how the Fourth Gospel could be seen as a narrative version of Paul's conceptual theology. I argued that Paul's statement in 1 Cor 15:45 – "the last Adam became a life-giving spirit (ὁ ἔσχατος Ἀδὰμ εἰς πνεῦμα ζῳοποιοῦν)" – consists of two intimately related events: (i.) Christ becoming a spirit, and (ii.) the giving of life by this spirit. In addition, I demonstrated how key concepts in Stoic physics and cosmology – ἀναστοιχείωσις and κρᾶσις – proved helpful for our understanding of the cosmological and physiological/psychological processes involved in these events. Let us first consider the spiritualization of Christ.[33]

Christ becoming a spirit and the Stoic idea of ἀναστοιχείωσις

According to Paul's argument in 1 Cor 15, the transformation of Christ into a spiritual body (σῶμα πνευματικόν, cf. 15:44) involves the whole person including his fleshly body and psychic soul. Consequently, this process differs from the separation of (the highest part of) the soul from the fleshly body which was the traditional understanding of what took place at death according to popular

---

[33] For an exposition that also includes detailed references to the ancient material, see *It Is the Spirit That Gives Life: A Stoic Understanding of Pneuma in John's Gospel*. For an introduction to Stoic cosmology and the processes of ἀναστοιχείωσις and κρᾶσις, see Chapter 2 (59–89). For "Christ becoming a spirit" in the world of the Fourth Gospel, see Chapter 7 (389–404). For the same approach to the Pauline material, see Engberg-Pedersen (2010, 8–38). Whereas the Philonic material is in focus in my analysis of John, in his analysis of Paul, Engberg-Pedersen focuses primarily on Cicero's *De Natura Deorum*. For "the giving of life by this spirit," see Engberg-Pedersen's discussion of the "Bodily Pneuma in Paul" (2010, 39–74).

beliefs, but also among philosophically minded people – Platonists and Stoics alike. However, in Philo's writings a similar phenomenon is found. Instead of an ordinary death, outstanding holy men like Moses, Enoch and Elijah may be transformed or ascend – Philo uses both verbs – into a higher place (*QG* 1.86: μεταβολή, ἀνάβασις).³⁴ In his biography on Moses, Philo goes into more details and explains the scriptural statement that Moses' grave was never found with a reference to this kind of transformation. Philo describes the process with a technical term borrowed from Stoic physics; he speaks of the ἀναστοιχείωσις that befell Moses in place of death (*Mos.* 2.288) (Engberg-Pedersen 2010, 33).³⁵

In Stoic cosmology, the term ἀναστοιχείωσις represents the transformation of the four elements into one another: earthly solids into water, water into air, air into fire. This transformation is possible, because the Stoics did not see the four elements as stable entities, the way they were in Plato's cosmology as described in the *Timaeus*. Instead, the Stoics understood the four elements as being made up of the same amorphous prime matter, but characterized by different states of movement or energy. The πνεῦμα, which permeated prime matter, provided matter with its different qualities. Consequently, by addition or removal of heat – or: by fusion with other pneumatic bodies – the elements were capable of changing into one another. During the Stoic world cycles, the processes of elementary transformations differed; in the phase of creation or reconstruction (διακόσμησις), matter circulated continuously, and the upward motion balanced the downward one. But in the phase of conflagration (ἐκπύρωσις), the upward transformation of the more dense elements of earth, water and air into pure fire prevailed. Whereas the Stoics used the idea exclusively in relation to cosmic phenomena, primarily the conflagration (ἐκπύρωσις), in Philo's writings it is applied to individual characters, too.

I must admit that the technical term of ἀναστοιχείωσις is used neither by Paul nor by the fourth evangelist. Origen, however, uses the term for the risen Christ's transformation in his commentary on John's Gospel (Book 1.276).³⁶ Thus, it seems reasonable to suggest that the idea of a cosmic transformation of the whole person was not foreign to the milieu of intellectual Judaism and Early Christianity. Paul appears to think that something like the Stoic ἐκπύρωσις had begun in Christ, who had – as the first fruit – already passed through the spiritual transformation which was to absorb all believers at Christ's second

---

34 Philo, *Questions and Answers on Genesis. Philo Supplement* I. LCL (Cambridge, Massachusetts: Harvard University Press, 1953).
35 Philo, *Moses* 1 & 2 (*De vita Mosis* I & II). LCL (Cambridge: Harvard University Press, 1935).
36 Origen, *The Commentary of Origen on St. John's Gospel* (Cambridge: Cambridge University Press, 1896).

coming (Engberg-Pedersen 2010, 34–37). In fact, this process had already begun, since Christ's spirit reworked believers from within. This idea leads us to the second event of 1 Cor 15:45, namely the giving of life by Christ's spirit. Again we must have recourse to Philo and Stoicism in order to get a better understanding of Paul's ideas.

The life-giving spirit and the Stoic idea of κρᾶσις

In Philo's treatises, the divine enthusiasm of prophecy with which outstanding persons like Moses and Elijah were empowered is interpreted in terms of a second and divine regeneration. By the down-breathing of God's spirit (*Plant.* 23: καταπνεῖν), the womb of the human mind is fertilized. The regeneration of the prophetic person brings forth virtuous behavior and truth (*Migr.* 33–35).[37] In this way, prophecy opens a short cut to wisdom that, according to Philo, even surpasses the virtue pursued by pagan philosophers. In the case of Moses, the divine regeneration – Philo speaks of Moses' δευτέρα γένεσις (*QE* 2.46) – befell him on the seventh day when he mounted the Sinai. Again, a brief look at Stoicism is necessary in order to understand Philo's ideas.[38]

Although the Stoic monists emphatically argued in favor of the unity of the human being, it was still possible to make analytical distinctions between the soul and the body and also between the soul's different faculties.[39] One just had to remember that the pneumatic bodies, in which faculties and qualities were grounded, were united in κράσις; that is a kind of fusion which left no part of the fusing pneumatic bodies void of the other. The ἕξις soul of slow

---

37 Philo, *On Noah's Work as a Planter* (*De plantatione*). LCL (Cambridge: Harvard University Press, 1930). *On the Migration of Abraham* (*De migratione Abrahami*). LCL (Cambridge: Harvard University Press, 1932).
38 Philo, *Questions and Answers on Exodus*. Philo Supplement II. LCL (Cambridge: Harvard University Press, 1953).
39 In the case of animals, the Stoics made a distinction between soul in a general and in a specific sense. In the general case, 'soul' denoted all the pneumatic bodies that pervaded a region of matter and provided it with form, from the cohesive force to the specific intelligible power of higher beings. In the more specific sense, 'soul' designated the two higher powers alone and was as τὸ ἡγεμονικόν opposed to the body, which was shaped by the two lower powers of cohesion (ἕξις) and growth (φύσις). In spite of this – and without compromising their materialistic and monistic approach to 'bodies' – the Stoics operated in practice with a dualism of body and soul. However, even when this distinction was made, the Stoics insisted on the corporeality of the soul. See Anthony A. Long, "Soul and Body in Stoicism," in his *Stoic Studies*,(Berkeley, Calif.: University of California Press, 1996), 224–249 (234–39).

and coherent forces, which humans shared with inert minerals, was responsible for the coherence of bones and bodily organs. In plants – and also in human beings – the φύσις soul, which was responsible for the metabolism of the body, was added to the mineral soul. Human beings shared their ψυχή soul with the animals; it was responsible for sense perception and instinctive reactions. Finally, human beings were also gifted with the λόγος, which was the aspect of the soul that humans shared with the heavenly bodies, e.g. the stars.[40] In the process of generation, the (prime) matter of the fetus, which was provided by the mother through her menstrual blood, was energized and qualified by the fusion with or penetration by the pneumatic bodies of the different souls. The mother herself provided the two lower aspects of the soul; the father was through his semen responsible for the animal faculties; the heavenly aspect of the soul was received only after birth and then developed. In his exegesis of Gen 1, Philo interprets God's activity during the different days as an allegory of the human soul. Each day is assigned to one aspect of the compound soul. He even extrapolates the continuous Stoic generation by that which may take place on the seventh day, namely, God's conception of wisdom or prophecy in the human being. It is this Sabbatical regeneration which constitutes Philo's δευτέρα γένεσις.

When Paul speaks of the "new creation" (καινὴ κτίσις), which makes circumcision an indifferent matter (Gal 6:15), it appears to be this kind of divine regeneration that he has in mind. The divine sonship – cf. υἱοθεσία (Gal 4:5; cf. Rom 8:15) – he promised his Gentile believers in Galatia would happen through the fertilization by Christ's spirit. But this aspect of Paul's material theology is often camouflaged by the translation of the Greek υἱοθεσία with adoption. However, when understood in the light of Philo's use of Stoic cosmology, Paul's καινὴ κτίσις and υἱοθεσία are just as physical and real as the first generation by earthly parents. This brings us back to the first aspect of the events of 1 Cor 15:45: Christ becoming a spirit. Through his transformation, Christ literally became God's seed capable of generating divine children by transforming them from within. But since this particular life engendering spirit also involves the transformation of the human being who as a Jew was *of* Abraham's seed (and *of* David's seed, cf. Rom 1:3), the transformation also makes Christ Abraham's seed – cf. Paul's claim in Gal 3:16: καὶ τοῖς σπέρμασιν, ὡς ἐπὶ πολλῶν ἀλλ' ὡς ἐφ' ἑνός· καὶ τῷ σπέρματί σου, ὅς ἐστιν Χριστός. By their reception of divine sonship through

---

40 In *Legum allegoriae* 2.22, Philo gives a very Stoic account of the faculties of the human soul. See LCL (Cambridge: Harvard University Press, 1929).

Christ's spirit, believers also become Abraham's progeny and Jews, albeit not by the first birth, but through their new and second generation.

3 Rereading Galatians 3 – from the perspective of Stoic cosmology

The rhetorical situation of Galatians

The inherent problem in any analysis of Paul's letters is that each letter is a statement in an ongoing debate between Paul and his opponents. Inevitably, the way we imagine the opponents' position plays an important role in our reconstruction of Paul's stance. But since we neither have access to Paul's gospel as it was initially preached to the Galatians, nor to the objections that this gospel apparently engendered in his churches, the risk of circular argument and mirror reading is always at hand. But since Paul opens his letter to the Galatians with a reference to his own encounter with the risen Christ, it seems justified to attempt a reconstruction of Paul's initial preaching to the Galatians in light of his discussion of the resurrection/ascension in 1 Cor 15. We may then try to imagine the opponents' reaction to this particular version of Paul's gospel. It is this response which constitutes the (imagined) rhetorical situation of Paul's argument in Galatians. However, the proof of this imaginative exercise lies in the pudding: does it illuminate Paul's arguments in a better way than previous interpretations?[41]

But *if* this premise is accepted, it appears reasonable to assume that in Paul's initial preaching, he promised the Galatians that through the reception of Christ's spirit, they would be regenerated as sons of God (due to Jesus' divinization) *and* also as Abraham's progeny (due to Jesus' Jewish genealogy). Since in this way, the Gentiles had become Jews *by faith*, God's promise to Abraham that he would be the *father* of many nations was fulfilled (Gen 17:5). However, *if* this really was the gospel that Paul preached to the Gentiles, he had a problem. His gospel begged the objection: *if* through their baptism Gentile believers were reborn as Abraham's progeny, why shouldn't they follow the example of Abraham – their faithful ancestor, who was once a 'Gentile' – and *also* become circumcised (Gen 17:23–27)? The opponents may be Jews outside or in Christ or

---

[41] The description of Paul's Galatian opponents I am to offer falls within the framework of John Barclay's category: "Certain or Virtually Certain" in his article, "Mirror-Reading a Polemical Letter: Galatians as a Test Case." *JSNT* 31 (1987): 73–93 (88).

Gentile Judaizers, what mattered was that they had Abraham's behavior and Scripture on their side; the more so as Abraham's God warned those who preserved their foreskin: they had broken the covenant (Gen 17:14). Consequently, it seemed reasonable to claim – as Paul's opponents in Galatia may have done – that the Gentiles as Abraham's progeny and members of God's covenant had to obey the Law's commandments, too. This version of Paul's preaching to the Gentiles leaves his opponents with the stronger case. The apostle to the Gentiles had to take his opponents' arguments into consideration and in his letter to the Galatians he defends his case. But *if* the rhetorical situation is understood in this way, the issue at stake in Paul's argument is no longer how the Gentiles are to get into the Jewish covenant; on this Paul and his opponents appear to have agreed. It happened when God sent his Son's spirit into their hearts. The fact that references to the Galatians' baptismal experience frame Paul's crucial argument in Gal 3 (Gal 3:1–5 & 4:6–7) is in line with this understanding.

Instead, the question with which Paul wrestles in Gal 3 is how these new Jews *by faith* are to stay righteous before God, if they do not have to live in accordance with the Law.[42] Apparently, the opponents' case was so strong that Paul had to reframe the issue at stake. After all, the problem of righteousness was not a Gentile matter alone, it also concerned those who were Jews *by birth* (Gal 2:15). As Paul explains his Galatian readers, he and his fellow Jewish-born brothers in Christ agree that "a *human being* does not become righteous through works of [the] Law" (Gal 2:16: εἰδότες [δὲ] ὅτι οὐ δικαιοῦται ἄνθρωπος ἐξ ἔργων νόμου), because "the *flesh* will be not become just through the commandment of the law'" (Gal 2:16e: ὅτι ἐξ ἔργων νόμου οὐ δικαιωθήσεται πᾶσα σάρξ). It is well known that the chiastic structure of Gal 2:16 establishes a poetic parallelism between ἄνθρωπος and σάρξ, but the meaning of this parallelism is disputed. Is σάρξ just a synonymic Hebraism for ἄνθρωπος? Or, does σάρξ accentuate the deplorable fact that in this world, human life is determined by the condition of *flesh?* In the latter case, the chiasm establishes a semantic field which is best understood in light of Paul's more elaborate discussion of the problem of ἀκρασία in Rom 7:7–25.

---

42 Dunn also sees the problem as belonging to the "second phase": "what follows from the beginning once made by the Galatians? How do they think the completion of God's saving work will be achieved?" (Dunn 1993, 16). Sanders, however, sees the debate in Galatians as a *getting-in* issue: "The argument of Galatians 3 is against Christian missionaries, not against Judaism, and it is against the view that Gentiles must accept the law *as a condition* of or as a basic requirement for membership [...] it is against requiring the Gentiles to keep the law of Moses in order to be true "sons of Abraham" (Sanders 1983, 19, Sanders' emphasis).

In Rom 7, Paul creates a *speech-in-character* (προσωποποιία) of a Jew who suffers from weakness of will and whose good intentions fade away when faced with the desire of the flesh.[43] The solution to this problem is given in Rom 8:11: "If the Spirit of him who raised Jesus from the dead dwells in you, he who raised Christ from the dead will give life to your mortal bodies also through his Spirit that dwells in you (εἰ δὲ τὸ πνεῦμα τοῦ ἐγείραντος τὸν Ἰησοῦν ἐκ νεκρῶν οἰκεῖ ἐν ὑμῖν, ὁ ἐγείρας Χριστὸν ἐκ νεκρῶν ζῳοποιήσει καὶ τὰ θνητὰ σώματα ὑμῶν διὰ τοῦ ἐνοικοῦντος αὐτοῦ πνεύματος ἐν ὑμῖν)." Paul's argument in Rom 6–8 can be seen as an elaboration of his condensed reflections in Gal 2. And in reverse, it is possible to read Gal 2:15–17 as a collective *speech-in-character* – parallel to Rom 7:7–25 – which summarizes the Jewish experiences of life under the law, but performed with a Gentile audience in mind.

In his argument in Gal 3, Paul – as part of his rhetorical strategy – turns the issue at stake upside-down. It is because the physiological/psychologicalempowerment by Christ's spirit enables *Jews* to *stay* righteous *within* their covenant that the incorporation of the Gentiles into Abraham's lineage was *foreseen* to take place in Christ (Gal 3:8). Thus, the very fact that the Galatians as Gentiles have received the spirit in their baptism becomes an indirect proof that also the expected covenantal righteousness will be established in Christ. Consequently, the reference to 'faith' in Galatians is a *synecdoche* that also represents God's powerful deeds which are carried out by the aid of Christ's spirit (Gal 3:5).[44]

---

43 As part of their rhetorical training, educated young men had to make *speeches-in-character* in which they were to illustrate different personalities through speech (Stowers 1994, 16–21). The understanding of Rom 7 as a case of προσωποποιία was introduced into the scholarly community by Stanley K. Stowers in his *A Rereading of Romans*. Stowers' book is one of the two-ways paradigm's most influential volumes. Consequently, he understands the character put into speech in Rom 7 as a Gentile caught in the state of ἀκρασία (weakness of will) lamenting his situation "under the Law": "The person in 7:7–25 whom Paul so carefully constructs by means of *prosōpopoiia* [...] represents those caught between two cultures. [...] he cannot submit to a foreign law because his gentile passions will not allow it. Rom 7:7–25 represents the judaizing gentile's ambiguous status. Neither fully Jew nor fully Greek, he is torn between the passions of an idolator and the law of the one true God" (1994, 278). However, it is possible to use Stowers' valuable insights without buying the two-ways thesis. Whereas I subscribe to Stowers' understanding of Rom 7 as a case of ἀκρασία, I disagree with his understanding of the character as a Gentile figure. On the contrary, I see the character as a (stereotyped) Jew who – in spite of the use of the first person – is not to be identified with Paul himself. Thus, my reading is more in line with Engberg-Pedersen (2000, 243).
44 The synecdoche reflects that in Paul's world, the discourse on faith (*cognition*) and the discourse on the spirit (*cosmo-physiology*) represent two non-reductive descriptions of the Christ event – just as was the case in the Stoic discourses on truth and spirit. See note 13.

Rereading Gal 3 in the light of 1 Cor 15:45

The argument in Gal 3:6–29 consists of two thematically and structurally parallel cycles: the issues raised in the first cycle (3:6–14) are elaborated further in the second (3:15–29). Each cycle consists of an argument in three steps. First, Paul demonstrates how Scripture foresaw that the fulfillment of God's promise to Abraham that he would be the father of blessed nations was to take place through Christ.[45] In the next step, Paul reflects on the righteousness expected of the participants *in* the Jewish covenant. Under the Law (without Christ) it was not met. Finally, he demonstrates how Christ – that is, through his spirit – makes up for all this: for the missing covenantal righteousness and for the inclusion of the Gentiles.

In the first step in the first cycle, Abraham – the Gentile believer who became the ancestor of the Jewish nation – is seen as a paradigm for God's present distribution of his blessings *also* among faithful Gentiles (Gal 3:6–9). The next step demonstrates that, in spite of the Law, the promised blessing has not yet fallen on the *Jews*, since Scripture declared those who did not manage to meet the requirements of the Law to be under a curse (3:10–12). Finally, Paul argues – still based on his somehow idiosyncratic reading of Scripture – that Christ is the solution for Jews and Gentiles alike. First, Christ takes away the curse from the Jews (3:13: Χριστὸς ἡμᾶς [Paul's fellow Jews, cf. Gal 2:16] ἐξηγόρασεν ἐκ τῆς κατάρας τοῦ νόμου γενόμενος ὑπὲρ ἡμῶν [the Jews, again] κατάρα, ὅτι γέγραπται· ἐπικατάρατος πᾶς ὁ κρεμάμενος ἐπὶ ξύλου). Because of this, (first ἵνα) the covenant can be opened up for the Gentiles to enter (3:14a: ἵνα εἰς τὰ ἔθνη ἡ εὐλογία τοῦ Ἀβραὰμ γένηται ἐν Χριστῷ Ἰησοῦ) and (second ἵνα) all Christ-believers – Jews and Gentiles alike – have received the promise of the spirit (3:14b: ἵνα τὴν ἐπαγγελίαν τοῦ πνεύματος λάβωμεν διὰ τῆς πίστεως). The genitive construction of the spiritual promise – ἡ ἐπαγγελία τοῦ πνεύματος – can be taken in two ways. As an *objective* genitive (the promise of the spirit), it refers to the reception of the spirit in baptism; as a *subjective* genitive (the promise inherent in the received spirit), it refers to the reworking (rebirth) of believers from within by the spirit.

---

[45] Strategically, Paul displaces the focus from Abraham and his house's circumcision in Gen 17 to the promise of the blessing in Gen 12:3: "In you, all the tribes/nations of the earth are to be blessed (ἐνευλογηθήσονται ἐν σοὶ πᾶσαι αἱ φυλαὶ τῆς γῆς)." Paul's quotation of Genesis in Gal 3:6: ἐνευλογηθήσονται ἐν σοὶ πάντα τὰ ἔθνη· is a mixture of Gen 12:3^{LXX} and the Lord's thoughts in Gen 18:18^{LXX}: Αβρααμ δὲ γινόμενος ἔσται εἰς ἔθνος μέγα καὶ πολύ καὶ ἐνευλογηθήσονται ἐν αὐτῷ πάντα τὰ ἔθνη τῆς γῆς.

In the first section in the second cycle (3:15–18), Paul appeals to the analogy between God's promise to Abraham and a human will. He reminds his readers that the promise was given to Abraham *and* also to his seed (Gal 3:16 echoing Gen 17:7^{LXX}: τῷ δὲ Ἀβραὰμ ἐρρέθησαν αἱ ἐπαγγελίαι καὶ τῷ σπέρματι αὐτοῦ), which he then identifies as Christ – and having 1 Cor 15:45 in mind, we should add: those who are *in* Christ. Often the analogy with a testament is claimed to bypass the Law and sidetrack the Jewish covenant. But the claim that the promise to Abraham only finds its fulfillment in Christ – or more precisely: in the reception of Christ's spirit – does not imply that the Law is no longer valid. Paul is much more modest; he just explains that the commandments of the Law are not allowed to interfere with the fulfillment of the promise to Abraham. The analogy legitimates Paul's distinction within the Law between those commandments which do not interfere with the inclusion of the Gentiles and those which do – above all, circumcision.

As I demonstrated above, Paul's statement in 1 Cor 15:45 – "The last Adam became a life-giving spirit" – referred to two different, but intertwined events. Whereas it is the spiritualization of Christ which constitutes the rationality behind Paul's identification of Christ with Abraham's seed in Gal 3:16, it appears to be the life-generating powers of this spirit that is in Paul's mind in the next step of the argument (3:19–22). It cannot be coincidental that Paul uses the same word for that of which the Law is incapable– cf. Gal 3:21: νόμος ὁ δυνάμενος ζῳοποιῆσαι – and for the qualities that according to 1 Cor 15:45 characterize Christ's spirit: it is a πνεῦμα ζῳοποιοῦν.[46]

The reduction of the 'seed' from the many to the 'one' (Gal 3:16), which is identified with Christ, does not mean that the Jews *as Jews* are excluded from God's Israel (Gal 6:16). When the argument is seen as a discourse on how righteousness is established *within* God's covenant with Abraham, Jews still stand in the covenant as Jews *by birth*. However, the expected state of righteousness is only reached through faith and spiritual empowerment. Consequently, the last step in the argument (3:23–29) picks up on Paul's appraisal of the promise of the spirit in the previous section (3:14) and is concluded in his description of

---

[46] The verb ζῳοποιέω is also used in Rom 8:11. Again we see a parallel between Paul's argument in Galatians and Romans. The juxtaposition of the life-generating spirit and the incapacity of the Law is also the subject of Gal 5:13–26, which has been the subject of analysis in several works by Troels Engberg-Pedersen (see e.g. 2000, 157–177). Readers of Danish may also consult "Galaterbrevets paraenese i brevet som helhed" in *Læsninger i Galaterbrevet* ed. Lone Fatum (København: Fremad, 2001), 149–185. When the discussion in Gal 3 is seen as a debate on how to *stay* righteous *within* the covenant (cf. Sanders' category), chapters 5 and 6 continue and conclude the argument.

the baptismal experience (3:26–29): those who have been baptized into Christ and dressed themselves up in Christ (3:27: ὅσοι γὰρ εἰς Χριστὸν ἐβαπτίσθητε, Χριστὸν ἐνεδύσασθε) have become *one* in him (3:28: πάντες γὰρ ὑμεῖς εἷς ἐστε ἐν Χριστῷ Ἰησοῦ) who is Abraham's *one* seed. Consequently, ἐν Χριστῷ Ἰησοῦ there is no *difference* between Jews and Gentiles, as Paul famously states in Gal 3:28: the Jews are Abraham's progeny *by birth*, the Gentiles *by faith* – but they all only become righteous *by faith* empowered by the spirit.

4 Jesus Christ's genealogy – Rom 1:1–4 reconsidered in the light of Gal 3

If this Stoically informed exegesis of Paul's argument in Gal 3 is accepted, it has implications for our stance in the scholarly dispute about the creedal formula with which Paul introduces his letter to the Romans: was it just a piece of conventional and pleasing rhetoric or did the formula also represent Paul's own Christology? In order to answer these questions, let us reconsider some of the exegetical cruces in Roman 1:1–4 in the light of the above presented reading of Gal 3. *First*, most scholars understand Paul's claim that Jesus was "of David's seed or semen" (Rom 1:3: ἐκ σπέρματος Δαυίδ) as a *metaphor* for his belonging to David's lineage. However, in the patrilinear ideology to which I have drawn attention, the seed connects the generations and makes them into one eternally living organism. Throughout the generations, the ancestor lives on. I have demonstrated that Jesus' Jewish descent is of utmost importance to Paul in his argument in Gal 3; it is because Jesus is a Jew *by birth* and consequently *of* Abraham's and David's seed that he – through the spiritualization that befalls him in the resurrection – becomes the seed of his ancestors. The inclusion of the Gentiles into the Jewish pedigree tree and covenant depends on that. *Second*, we now see how the genealogy of Christ in Romans represents Paul's *story* about his Lord. Jesus Christ's being κατὰ σάρκα and κατὰ πνεῦμα ἁγιωσύνης refer to two stages in his historical being – having the spiritualization in 1 Cor 15:45 as turning point. Consequently, the compact genealogy of Rom 1:1–4 should be seen more as a summary of Paul's narrative about his Lord than as a piece of dogmatic, metaphysical ontology. *Third*, it is a matter of debate what the adverbial preposition κατὰ πνεῦμα ἁγιωσύνης, which precedes the reference to the resurrection, modifies in Rom 1:4: τοῦ ὁρισθέντος υἱοῦ θεοῦ ἐν δυνάμει κατὰ πνεῦμα ἁγιωσύνης ἐξ ἀναστάσεως νεκρῶν, Ἰησοῦ Χριστοῦ τοῦ κυρίου ἡμῶν. Does it qualify the power of God's son? Or does it modify the verb that defines Jesus as Son of God, indicating either that the Spirit of Holiness was somehow involved in the resurrection or, more modestly, that it just declared Jesus to be God's son? In the light of the above presented interpretation of 1 Cor 15:45, we now see how all these options are in play in Paul's use of the creedal formula. Paul's genitive establishes a poetic field which fully encapsulates his theology. The Spirit of Holiness is intimately related to the transforming power that believers experience as result of their reception of Christ's spirit in baptism. To Paul, Christ's death at the cross was an example of the crucifixion of the flesh and the mortification of the desire that were necessary for the final spiritual transformation since – as Paul claims in 1 Cor 15:50 – flesh and blood cannot inherit the heavenly existence of God's kingdom. When seen in this way, the Lutheran economy of the cross as the atonement for our sins is replaced by the assistance that Christ's spirit offers the believer in this process of pre-mortal mortification (cf. Rom 6). This takes us to the *fourth* crux. Scholars find it remarkable that in Rom 1:4 Paul uses the same verb for Christ's divine sonship (ὁρισθέντος) as he did with regard to his own apostolate (ἀφωρισμένος, ἀφορίζω) in Rom 1:1. Does this coincidence mean that Paul puts himself on a par with Christ? Does it imply that Christ's divinization was no more special than it could also befall Paul and his fellow believers? Yes. What happened to Christ as the first fruit (1 Cor 15:20) is already at work in believers (Rom 6:1–11).

5 Gospel openings reconsidered in the light of Pauline cosmology

Luke: The politics of virgin birth

We are now ready to turn our attention to the opening narratives in the Synoptic Gospels. Since it is easier to understand Mark's agenda if we know where Luke will take us, we will first take a brief look at the interaction between Christology and ethnicity in the third Gospel.

In spite of the fact that Luke designates the spirit that fertilizes Mary's womb as the Holy Spirit (Luke 1:35: πνεῦμα ἅγιον ἐπελεύσεται ἐπὶ σὲ καὶ δύναμις ὑψίστου ἐπισκιάσει σοι· διὸ καὶ τὸ γεννώμενον ἅγιον κληθήσεται υἱὸς θεοῦ), the above analysis of Paul's letters to the Galatians and the Romans makes it clear that this would be an error. We are mistaken if we equate Luke's Holy Spirit with Paul's spirit – be it the "spirit of Holiness" (Rom 1:4: πνεῦμα ἁγιωσύνης), the "Holy Spirit" (Rom 5:5: πνεῦμα ἅγιον), the "spirit of God" (Rom 8:9, 11: πνεῦμα θεοῦ) or the "spirit of Christ" (Rom 8:9: πνεῦμα Χριστοῦ). Paul's Stoically inspired argument in 1 Cor 15 makes all the difference. We now see how Luke's virgin birth effectively cuts off the Jewish roots which it was at the heart of Paul's thought to preserve. Luke's Christ is neither of David's semen nor of Abraham's seed; from the very beginning, he is God's uniquely begotten Son. Whereas Paul's Christ Jesus must have had a biologically Jewish human father (κατὰ σάρκα) in order to fulfill the promise to Abraham that the Gentiles were to be blessed in him, Luke's Christ has God as his one and only father. In Mary's womb God creates a brand new beginning and a new γένος – race or family – independent of Judaism and its patriarchs.[47] Consequently, Luke has to make a reservation with regard to Jesus' human genealogy; in Luke 3:23, he emphasizes that it was *according to costume* when it was said that Jesus Christ was the son of Joseph (3:23: ὢν υἱός, ὡς ἐνομίζετο, Ἰωσήφ). Although Luke does not explicitly deny the traditional understanding of Jesus' genealogy, the new beginning which he adds to this genealogy, contradicts and dismisses it. Also Jesus' argument with the Sadducees in the temple expresses a reservation with regard to the Pauline tradition. Referring to one of David's Psalms, Luke has Jesus question the Davidic origin of the Christ: "If David calls him Lord; how can he be his son?" (Luke 20:44). But if the Davidic roots are rejected, Jesus' Abrahamic lineage also vanishes. We may conclude that the narrative of the virgin birth is no innocent story; above all, it is a symbol of the rejection of Israel as God's chosen and privileged nation.

Mark: Divine adoption and imperial ambitions

The questions are now: where are we to situate Mark between these two poles? Which aim does Mark's genealogy of Jesus, which he only gives us indirectly,

---

[47] Or as Justin Martyr later stated in his *Dialogue with Trypho* 135.3, *ANF* 1:267: "Then is it Jacob the patriarch in whom the Gentiles and yourselves shall trust? or is it not Christ? As, therefore, Christ is the Israel and the Jacob, even so we, who have been quarried out from the bowels of Christ, are the true Israelitic race (ὡς οὖν Ἰσραὴλ τὸν Χριστὸν καὶ Ἰακὼβ λέγει, οὕτως καὶ ἡμεῖς ἐκ τῆς κοιλίας τοῦ Χριστοῦ λατομηθέντες Ἰσραηλιτικὸν τὸ ἀληθινόν ἐσμεν γένος)." Consequently, it is of the utmost importance for the Christian identity whose 'spirit' was to be found in Christ's κοιλία: Was it Abraham's semen or God's Holy Spirit? Both, according to Paul; only the latter according to Luke. Allegory plays an important role in patristic argument. In her book *Why This New Race: Ethnic Reasoning in Early Christianity*, Denise Kimber Buell explains: "Glossing Jacob and Israel as Christ, Justin defines Christ as the first ancestor of the people 'Israel'[...]. When competing to be 'Israel,' Justin contends that 'we, quarried from the bowels (*koilia*) of Christ are the true race of Israel' [...]. This striking phrase leads Justin to elaborate why this 'true race' differs from 'your people,' referring to Trypho" (2005, 101). Buell analyses the attempts by the Christian Fathers to establish this "new race." Her analysis takes over where my analysis of the biblical material stops.

serve? Does Mark follow Paul in his strategy for the inclusion of the Gentiles into the Jewish covenant? Or does he see the Christians as a new, divinely generated γένος like Luke? Or is he just as ambivalent as Matthew, who wants both to have his cake and eat it? As we know, Matthew opens his gospel with a genealogy of Jesus which demonstrates his Abrahamic descent through Joseph, but then also annuls this introduction with his narrative about the miraculous conception of Mary by the Holy Spirit. This just does not add up.[48]

Mark features a kind of two-stage Christology like the one we saw in Rom 1:1–4. His intention to make a biography of Jesus Christ's earthly life forces him to come up with an answer to the question which Paul's correspondence left unanswered – namely: how did it all begin? Mark's solution appears to be inspired by Paul's cosmic pneumatology. As Paul had Christ's powerful spirit to assist believers in their spiritual development and transformation, a powerful spirit must – so Mark may have inferred – have been present with Jesus from the beginning of his ministry. Mark projects Paul's understanding of baptism back into his history of Jesus. In the same manner that Paul's believers received Christ's spirit in their baptism, so the Markan Jesus received his powerful spirit at his baptism. Mark makes use of the probably historical fact that the historical Jesus was baptized by John the Baptist, but gives it a special meaning through his narrative staging of the event. Apart from being the fulfillment of Old Testament prophecies, it is also – as Michael Peppard has compellingly argued in "The Eagle and the Dove: Roman Imperial Sonship and the Baptism of Jesus (Mark 1,9–11)" – a divine adoption worthy of imperial leaders. Thus, already in the opening narrative we get a hint that Mark's worldview will differ from Paul's cosmic vision.

Yet more is in wait for Mark's eschatological prophet. Mark also knows the tradition of Jesus' transformation. In the midst of his gospel, Mark tells the story about the transfiguration, in which Jesus meets with the transformed and shining bodies of Moses and Elijah (Mark 9,28–36). We remember that Moses, Elijah – and also Enoch – were also transfigured in Philo's writings (*QG* 1.86). But in Mark's Gospel, Enoch is left out, maybe because Jesus as Mark's 'Son of Man' has replaced Enoch in the triad. Consequently, the dispute in the temple with the scribes about the Messiah's Davidic descent is more ambiguous in Mark (12:35–37) than it was in Luke's Gospel (20:41–44). Mark's narrative is not polemically told; instead, it constitutes a Christological riddle in the vein of the Messianic Secret. As the Jewish Messiah, Mark's Jesus is *of Davidic origin*, but

---

48 It does not add up, unless Matthew thinks that Jesus was *adopted* into Joseph's family.

he is also – as foreseen in the transfiguration – installed as *David's Lord* through the resurrection. The demons, which are cosmic spirits, know what is in wait.⁴⁹

In my analysis of Paul's Christology in Rom 1:1–4, I argued that there was no tension between Christ's being κατὰ σάρκα and κατὰ πνεῦμα ἁγιωσύνης; on the contrary, Paul's argument in Gal 3 presupposed his Lord's Jewish genealogy (cf. Gal 3:16). However, this is not the case in Mark. On the one hand, Jesus' Jewish genealogy is recognized in Mark; Jesus has a mother and siblings (Mark 3:32). On the other hand, Jesus' family is only introduced in order to be redefined by the Markan Jesus; his true family consists of those who are willing to do God's will (3:35). In addition, when Jesus visits his hometown Nazareth, Mark has him declare that "a prophet is not without honor except in his home town and among his *own* relatives and in his *own* household (Mark 6:4: ἐν τῇ πατρίδι αὐτοῦ καὶ ἐν τοῖς συγγενεῦσιν αὐτοῦ καὶ ἐν τῇ οἰκίᾳ αὐτοῦ)." The Markan Jesus distances himself from his Jewish roots. In this light, it appears unlikely that Mark would share Paul's understanding of baptism as an event in which Gentile believers received Abraham's *Jewish* seed through Christ. The Markan redefinition of Jesus' family signals that the Holy Spirit with which Jesus is said to baptize has not been recirculated through his Jewish body. If, instead – as we may surmise – the Markan community modeled their understanding of baptism on Jesus' case, it would be more in line with Pamela Eisenbaum's divine adoption than Hodge's and my own ideas about the incorporation of believers into Abraham's lineage through Christ's spirit. But all this is just guess-work, since – in contrast with Paul – Mark is not interested in developing the meaning of the baptismal rite.⁵⁰

Although Mark has John the Baptist announce that it is Jesus who is to baptize in the Holy Spirit (Mark 1:8), baptism or baptismal imagery plays no role in Mark's Gospel.⁵¹ In Mark, it is the correct faith in Jesus which is valued – namely, that he, in spite of his problematic relationship with Judaism, is the Jewish Messiah and Son of their God. It is this faith which Mark rewards with healings (cf. Mark 5:34: θυγάτηρ, ἡ πίστις σου σέσωκέν σε) and invitations to participate in

---

49 See Adela Yarbro Collins on the Messianic Secret in *Mark*. Hermeneia (Minneapolis: Augsburg Fortress, 2007), 168–172.
50 This also contrasts with the extensive use of water symbolism in the Fourth Gospel, which is a symbol of the spirit that believers are to receive – as stated explicitly in John 7:38.
51 An exception may be Paul J. Achtemeier, "Toward the Isolation of Pre-Markan Miracle Catenae." *JBL* 89 (1970): 265–291. According to Achtemeier, the identified *catenae* had their *Sitz-im-Leben* in the baptismal ritual of an early Christian community characterized by a kind of *theios anêr* Christology. In Mark's use of the two catenae, the Sea of Galilee makes up for the baptismal element in the catenae. Like in Gal 3:28, water annuls the difference between baptized Jews and Gentiles.

Jesus' meals. Apparently, the ritual which defines the Christian community is no longer baptism, but the Eucharist. The miraculous multiplications of bread, which take place first on the Jewish shore of the Sea of Galilee (Mark 6:30–44) and later among the Gentiles on the eastern shore (Mark 8:1–10), foreshadow Jesus' inauguration of the new ritual at the last supper. In order to have Jews and Gentiles join the same table, the Markan Jesus must remove the obstacle that ritualized food constitutes. Before he sets out for the Gentile shore, he declares all food to be clean (Mark 7:19). In Mark's Gospel, Paul's cosmic kingdom, which was to be completed at Christ's second coming (cf. 1 Cor 15:50–53), has been replaced by a social reality that belongs to this world. Now it is the ritualized meal which includes Jewish sinners and Gentiles that anticipate the coming of the kingdom.[52]

To summarize, to a certain degree Mark follows in Paul's footsteps; he projects the Pauline baptism of believers onto Jesus, and he also foreshadows the transformation of Christ into a spiritual light body in his account of the transfiguration. But the recirculation of Christ's spirit – the spiritualized Christ – into subsequent generations of Christians, so crucial to Paul, plays no role in Mark's world. On the contrary, in Mark's Gospel, Paul's charismatic community of spiritually empowered believers has come to an end. The mighty deeds brought about by the spirit belong to a past era when Jesus as a charismatic preacher and powerful healer was still around.[53] Mark's Christ is no longer the first fruit of many believers who long for their cosmic transformation. Instead, the Markan Christ has advanced to the status of being God's *uniquely* beloved – but not yet uniquely *begotten* – son. Probably it was the fall of the temple that caused Mark to reconsider the Pauline heritage. Mark's passion narrative reframes the tradition of the common meal, which Paul claims to have received from the Lord (1 Cor 11:23), in terms of the Jewish Paschal meal.[54] However, Mark's Exodus is no longer from Egypt, but from Second Temple Judaism.[55]

---

52 Some scholars have seen Mark 5:1–8:21 as a narrative version of Gal 3:28 – cf. Tronier 2006, 40, see note 1. But whereas, according to Paul, the unity ἐν Χριστῷ – established through baptism – was engrafted into Abraham's lineage, the Markan community of Christ-believing Jews and Gentiles joined by Jesus' meal represents a new family.
53 And maybe also to the first generation of Jesus' followers, who probably were baptized by Jesus in the Holy Spirit.
54 John's Gospel appears to pick up on Paul's understanding of Christ as "our Paschal lamb" (1 Cor 5:7). The staging of the Lord's supper as a Paschal meal appears to be a Markan invention.
55 My interpretation of the transition between Paul's charismatic era and Mark's Gospel is indebted to the work of my Danish colleague, Geert Hallbäck. Hallbäck has suggested that the German sociologist Max Weber's theory of the social development of authority – from charismatic, to traditional and institutional – may be applied to the New Testament genres. Hall-

In a symbolic way, the movements of the heavenly spirit, which frame Jesus' earthly life in Mark's Gospel, encompass all this. In the beginning, the Holy Spirit tears heaven apart and descends upon Jesus (1:10: εἶδεν σχιζομένους τοὺς οὐρανοὺς καὶ τὸ πνεῦμα ὡς περιστερὰν καταβαῖνον εἰς αὐτόν). In the end, Jesus' final expiration voices a scream (15:37: Ὁ δὲ Ἰησοῦς ἀφεὶς φωνὴν μεγάλην ἐξέπνευσεν) that is capable of tearing the curtain in the temple apart (15:38: Καὶ τὸ καταπέτασμα τοῦ ναοῦ ἐσχίσθη εἰς δύο ἀπ' ἄνωθεν ἕως κάτω). The repeated use of the verb σχίζω invites the reader to interpret these events in the light of each other. The parallelism seems to suggest that just as the Holy Spirit entered into the world with Jesus' baptism, so it left again with his death. The event is semantically complex: with regard to Judaism, it symbolizes that God's presence in the temple has come to an end and, consequently, that Israel's time as God's chosen nation is over. With regard to Christianity, it symbolizes the end of the charismatic era. Of course, future generations of believers can rely on the assistance of the Holy Spirit; they simply have to wait for it (Mark 13:11) or they can pray for it (Mark 9:29). But they no longer possess the spirit themselves. God's gifts are no longer mediated through the work of the spirit, but have become a reward of the faith which has the *right* understanding of Jesus' identity. The two aspects are intimately related. The end of God's engagement with Israel makes Paul's striking solution with regard to the Gentiles' inclusion into the Jewish nation superfluous. Instead, the correct faith can achieve this. The virgin birth in Matthew and Luke is the corollary of Mark's work and ending. Whereas Mark's Jesus *constructs* a new family, Luke *essentializes* Mark's construct. When Luke began to write his gospel, he already knew the conclusion to his stories: in Christ, God has begun a new γένος. Luke's handling of the Holy Spirit may resemble Paul's, but 1 Cor 15:45 makes all the difference.

---

bäck also sees the Eucharist in Mark as a replacement for the Jerusalem temple. Unfortunately, Hallbäck's inspiring work and striking ideas are not published in English. Readers of Danish may consult Hallbäck's introduction to the New Testament, which is structured around this thesis *Det Nye Testamente – En lærebog* (Frederiksberg: Anis 2010) or his *Om Markus, analyser og fortolkninger* (Frederiksberg: Anis, 2002).

Ole Davidsen
Adam-Christ Typology in Paul and Mark: Reflections on a *Tertium Comparationis*

Preliminary Remarks

If an examination of Paul and Mark should reveal that both are portraying Jesus Christ as a new Adam, how would we then typically explain such an agreement? Well, since Paul is writing earlier than Mark, it seems obvious to assume that Mark got the idea from Paul – as the author of and/or as the transmitter of a peculiar Christological tradition. If Paul is the author of such a particular tradition, we could rightfully claim Mark to have been influenced by Paulinism, by Paul himself or by later transmitters of his theology. A further comparison of Paul and Mark could then be performed in order to detect and reveal the full impact of Paul on Mark.

If Paul is only a transmitter of a pre-Pauline tradition, we can at most claim Mark to have been influenced by Paul in a trivial sense, not by Paulinism. But unless Mark is influenced by particular Paulinism, we cannot with any certainty claim Mark to have been influenced by Paul, since Mark could have received the then common tradition from elsewhere. Paul and Mark may simply share an early pre-Markan, as well as pre-Pauline, tradition. In this article I will argue that this is the case as regards the Adam-Christ typology. By way of introduction, allow me to present some theoretical suppositions:

1) We recognize the presence of an undisputed Adam-Christ typology in Paul (1 Cor 15:20 – 22.44 – 49; Rom 5:12 – 21); but do we find something similar in the Gospel of Mark? Let us suppose that we do, and accordingly distinguish between an *explicit* (or manifest) typology in Paul and an *implicit* (or latent) typology in Mark.

2) Is the explicit Adam-Christ typology Paul's theological creation or did he receive it from an already established tradition? Let us suppose Paul received the Adam-Christ typology from an earlier tradition. In that case the presence of an Adam-Christ typology, explicit or implicit, is no sign of particular Paulinism.

3) If we do find an implicit Adam-Christ typology in Mark, did Mark then receive it from Paul or from another transmitter? If we suppose that Mark received his Adam-Christ typology from Paul (or people influenced by/transmitting Paul), we could talk of some Pauline influence on Mark in a trivial sense, but not of Paulinism in Mark. If we suppose that Mark received his Adam-Christ typology from another transmitter than Paul (or people trans-

mitting Paul), we can speak neither of Paul's influence on Mark nor of Paulinism in Mark, at least regarding this theme.

Thus even if Paul wrote earlier than Mark, we should not explain an implicit Adam-Christ typology in Mark as a sign of Pauline influence in any serious sense, if this typology is pre-Pauline. In fact we should not – taking Paul as our standard – speak of this tradition as "pre-Pauline" at all, but rather in a relative sense speak of a common *primal* tradition anterior to both. Mark may have been acquainted with this tradition without knowing anything (or without caring the slightest) about Paul or Paulinism. A common origin of tradition could explain fundamental agreements between Paul and Mark on this point, and I think it does.

In this perspective, we may still compare Paul and Mark in search of similarities, but not in order to support a thesis of Pauline influence on Mark. Instead, in what follows I shall argue that a comparison of Paul and Mark can support the thesis that both of these first-order theologians were influenced by an early Christological tradition centered on an Adam-Christ typology. This tradition may have represented a particular but relatively widespread movement within early Christianity. If we cannot put a name on this primal tradition, we could be looking for a place of origin (in addition to a time), either mentally (Hebrew or Hellenistic tradition?) or geographically (from Jerusalem/Palestine or from beyond?). Since the Adam-Christ typology is to be seen as the basic narrative structure of a composite Adam-Christ myth, the question of origin points to the Hellenistic milieu in Syria (Antioch).[1]

Intertextuality may be a sign of direct influence between texts (in the form of textual causality/literary dependency), but it can also be a sign of the fact that texts refer back to the same narratology shared by and transmitted by different people.[2] I basically agree with Rudolf Bultmann's understanding of Mark's inten-

---

[1] See Gerd Theissen's theory of the development of the four basic currents in early Christianity up to the formation of the canon, *A Theory of Primitive Christian Religion*, trans. John Bowden (London: SCM Press, 1999), 249–261. Theissen places Mark somewhere between Peter and Barnabas, seeing James and Paul as the more radical positions.

[2] This is of course no objection to literary source criticism as a fundamental part of exegesis. However, traditional source criticism based on comparing texts should not be taken as the only procedure in comparative analysis. Sharing narrative traditions is not necessarily the same thing as sharing narrative texts. The surviving primitive Christian texts are not only a part of what once existed in writing, but written versions of parts of even more widespread oral traditions in primitive Christian narratology. Narratology is normally understood as the semio-literary study of narratives. Here I suggest the use of *narratology* in a wider sense similar to the use of *mythology*, which can mean the myths' inherent teaching about the gods' activities, a more or

tion: "die Vereinigung des hellenistischen Kerygma von Christus, dessen wesentlicher Inhalt der Christusmythos ist, wie wir ihn aus Paulus kennen (bes. Phil 2,6 ff.; Röm 3,24), mit der Tradition über die Geschichte Jesu."[3]

Let me finally state as premise a remark about narrativity as a pre-scientific and pre-philosophical way of understanding life. In a well-known passage in his Journal of 1843, Søren Kierkegaard concedes to philosophy that "Life has to be understood backwards". But one forgets, he adds emphatically, the other proposition, "that it has *to be lived forwards*".[4] Kierkegaard is concerned about the future's openness and emptiness. Here I focus on the correlative perspective: that we do have to live our life forwards, but that we can only understand it backwards. Not only afterwards, but *après coup, nachträglich* in a pointed sense, i.e. by a retrospective *narrative* interpretation. Narrative thinking creates prospective narratives, which manifest the result of this retrospective cognitive process and present the succession of events as fatal or embryo-genetic development right from the ἀρχή (cf. Mark 1:1).

As historians, we may say that the Adam-Christ typology presupposes the Adam narrative in Genesis, but we cannot claim that this narrative implies the Adam-Christ typology in a causal sense, any more than we can claim that the Old Testament implies the New Testament, although the latter presupposes the former.[5] It takes a genuine narrative interpretation by a hermeneutical subject to claim such an implication – as we know from biblical texts. In other words: it takes a genuine narrative interpretation to close the openness of history and to turn a succession of events into a fatal process of divine providence.

The most intriguing part of this phenomenon is, perhaps, the seemingly cognitive fact that we can only keep syntagmatic (or diachronic) entities together be-

---

less coherent view of God, Humankind, and World expressed in stories, and the scientific study of mythical traditions. Thus narratology can refer to a community's or a social circle's narrative encyclopedia, the narratively founded and organized collective consciousness of shared beliefs and moral attitudes circulating in the form of oral and/or written identity marking stories – myths, legends, anecdotes – from history and literature.

3 Rudolf Bultmann, *Die Geschichte der synoptischen Tradition* (8. Auflage. Göttingen: Vandenhoeck & Ruprecht, 1970), 372–373. Bultmann agrees with Martin Werner that "Mk nicht von der paulinischen Theologie getragen ist". But he adds to Werner that Mark belongs to "der Typus des hellenistischen Christentums, ... dem auch Paulus zugehört." Thus we would expect Paul and Mark to share at least some parts of a common Hellenistic narratology.

4 *Journalen JJ:167* (København: Søren Kierkegaard Forskningscenteret, 1843); "http://sks.dk/JJ/txt.xml"; 2 July 2011. *Søren Kierkegaards Skrifter* 18 (København: Gad, 2001), 194.

5 See A.-J. Greimas and J. Courtés, *Semiotics and Language: An Analytical Dictionary*, trans. L. Crist, D. Patte, et al. (Bloomington: Indiana University Press, 1982), "Presupposition" and "Implication".

cause of our paradigmatic (or synchronic) way of thinking. As will be shown, the first Adam and the last Adam of time are interrelated only by virtue of a narrative logic of timeless paradigmatic order.

1 Comparative Reflections

Mark and Paul may be compared for various reasons, but basically comparison means looking for similarity and/or difference. Such an enterprise is more than a formal game, since we are compelled to find an explanation for the correspondence and/or discrepancy. But what could form the point of departure for this exercise? Why bother to compare Mark and Paul in the first place?

1.1 Canonical Comparativism

As part of the canonical corpus of texts that we call the New Testament, Mark and Paul are already compared by historical development. Their texts have been critically evaluated by tradition, and have been found to live up to certain general, normative theological standards. Exegesis may not be obliged to accept this corpus of texts as its primary empirical object, but can establish its own corpus of texts, let us say defined as early Christian literature, canonical as well as non-canonical. This can, however, only be done by a comparative evaluation of texts, identified more or less intuitively as Christian. A reflective examination of these texts leads to the establishment of a corpus identified according to a more or less stringent definition of early Christian literature. Such an exegetical canon will, like the theological canon, be based on the assumption of some sort of unity, despite a recognized diversity.

1.2 Specifying and Generalizing Readings

Two extreme points of view can be foreseen. The first one is keenly specifying, claiming every single text to be unique and different from any other text in the corpus. The second one is eagerly generalizing, claiming every single text to be common and identical to any other text of the body. Both points of view are right and wrong. How is that possible?

The answer is, of course, that texts in such a corpus resemble one another in certain respects, while at the same time distinguishing themselves from one another in others. One way to deal with this challenge is to recognize texts as semiotic entities, i.e. macro signs, units combining a plane of expression and a plane of content. Going a step further, we can analyze the plane of content as a structurally organized semantics with different signification-layers of increasing specificity, from the general (or even universal) to the particular (or even singular). Generally speaking: in addition to comparing texts on the plane of expression (which dominates source criticism), we should compare them on the plane of content (as narrative exegesis). In so doing, we should make sure to compare texts on the same pertinent semantic level of generality/specificity. Comparing two texts, we may find similarities on one level of generality/specificity and at the same time differences on another.

Two modified exegetical approaches can thus be foreseen. One approach specifies all information: that is, it interprets any layer of meaning as articulated and governed by the most particular layer of meaning. *Historical philology* is a well-known example of this approach. The other approach generalizes all information: that is, it interprets any layer of meaning as circumscribed and governed by the most general layer of meaning. *Systematic semiotics,* as applied in this article, is an example of the latter. A given text can therefore be read or analyzed in two opposite directions, and we seem to be facing two parallel lines of interpretation. According to old wisdom, parallel lines will never meet – until eternity. If so, we must learn to live with this eschatological suspense, taking seriously that a point of view is a standpoint that reveals and hides at the same time. In practice, however, I think the two approaches can benefit from one another – the more so as we usually blend historical and systematic reflections without even thinking about it. We can, however, distinguish between a historical and a systematic approach.

1.3 Commonness and Uniqueness

A *historical reading* is a specifying reading in search of the unique, as expressed by Heraclitus's saying, "You can't step into the same river twice." For example, each Pauline letter is unique, in that he cannot write the same letter twice. Even if two letters seem alike, says the keen historian, we should not be fooled into neglecting the crucial differences. Even two sentences with almost the same wording in one and the same letter may have a different meaning. Taken to its extreme, however, this point of view cannot identify two letters as written by the same person. We would end up with a fragmented series of "Pauls": Paul 1, Paul 2, Paul 2a and 2b, etc. We would not even be able to categorize two different texts as Christian texts. "Christian" is a category, and, as such, of a certain generality.

A *systematic reading* is a generalizing reading in search of common strands of meaning in different texts, as expressed by Ecclesiastes' saying, "There is nothing new under the sun" (Eccl 1:9). This too is indeed an overstatement, but not without a certain truth if understood correctly. A comparison of two texts is, after all, founded on the assumption that they have something in common, a *tertium comparationis* of a kind which transgresses the claim of absolute uniqueness. We are able to discern differences as well as similarities, and what I am saying in this simple way is only that two exegetical approaches or perspectives are both possible and necessary, the one stressing the differences, the other the similarities.

As part of a canon (whether defined exegetically or theologically), Mark and Paul must have something in common despite their differences, either because of particular influence one from the other or because of general influence from a common tradition. Since Paul writes before Mark, it seems cogent to explain eventual agreements between the two as particular Pauline influence on Mark, either from Paul or Paulinism. But it depends on the particularity of these agreements. It is not merely possible but rather, in the nature of things, a given that Mark and Paul share some general traditions. Although Paul was an early writer, he was not the first Christ-confessor. So Mark could at the same time be influenced by ideas peculiar to Paul and by general Christian ideas from a common tradition.

1.4 Earlier and Actual Debate

In earlier debate about Mark and Paulinism, we find a tendency to categorical opinions. Either Mark has been considered to be totally influenced by Paulinism, as by Gustav Volkmar; or Mark has been declared free of any influence by Pauline theology, as by Martin Werner, who seemed to have settled the matter.[6] How-

---

[6] Volkmar regards Mark as "eine Darstellung vom wahren Wesen Jesu Christi", *Die Religion Jesu* (Leipzig: Brockhaus, 1857), 269, and as "sinnbildliche Darstellung paulinischer Lehre", *Marcus und die Synopse* (Zürich: Schmidt, 1876), 644. In his "Ergebnis" Werner concludes: A comparison of Mark and the undisputed Pauline letters shows that correspondences always concern general conceptions in primitive Christianity and that particular Pauline features are either lacking in Mark or represent opposite standpoints. Therefore we cannot in the least speak of influence of Pauline theology in Mark ("1. Wo Markus mit Paulus übereinstimmt, handelt es sich immer um allgemein-urchristliche Anschauungen. 2. Wo in den Briefen über diese gemeinsame Basis hinaus besondere, charakteristisch paulinische Anschauungen zutage traten, da fehlen entweder bei Markus die Parallelen vollständig, oder Markus vertritt geradezu entgegengesetzte Standpunkte. 3. Von einem Einfluss paulinischer Theologie im Markusevangelium kann daher

ever, the debate has been reopened by more recent scholars, not least by Joel Marcus. In his article "Mark – Interpreter of Paul", he argues that the time has come to attempt "to compare and even to draw lines of influence between these two contentious theologians".[7]

As shown by the title of his article, Marcus advocates the view that any similarity between Paul and Mark is due to Pauline influence on Mark. He suggests that Mark is an interpreter of Paul. I will take this pointed, but less categorical article as the basis of discussion in what follows.

2 Mark and Paulinism

Marcus does find striking similarities between Paul and Mark, which could point to some Pauline influence on Mark. Among other things he mentions that they both "portray Jesus as a new Adam" and "have negative things to say about Peter and about members of Jesus' family".[8] But the crucial test case for Marcus to prove Mark a Paulinist is their common "theology of the cross" (476).

First, Marcus emphasizes a general point: differences found between Paul's theology and Mark's do not rule out that Mark is a Paulinist. Even if "Mark writes a story about the earthly Jesus whereas Paul seems to be relatively uninterested in him – that does not necessarily mean that Mark is unPauline" (477). It is not impossible that a Pauline disciple – Mark in this case – "might have had plausible reasons for doing what Paul did *not* do, namely incorporating the Jesus tradition into his kerygma" (477). As I understand it, Marcus finds it plausible that Mark was influenced by Paul's kerygma (the core of his theology of the Cross), and that his story about "the earthly Jesus" was incorporated into this Pauline framework or perspective. This is at least seen as a possibility. This opinion is close to Bultmann's, except that Bultmann points to a prior common Hellenist tradition, while Marcus believes Mark to be influenced by Paul.

---

nicht im geringsten die Rede sein".", *Der Einfluß paulinischer Theologie im Markusevangelium. Eine Studie zur neutestamentlichen Theologie*. BZNW 1 (Gießen: Töpelmann, 1923), 209). We should not take Volkmar's "allegorical" or "midrashic" Paulinist rewriting of Mark seriously, though he is right in seeing Mark as an effort to present the true nature/essence/being of Jesus Christ. To Werner, on the contrary, we owe full respect, as will be shown below.

[7] Joel Marcus, "Mark – Interpreter of Paul." *NTS* 46 (2000): 473–487, 485.
[8] For a full list of claimed similarities, cf. Marcus 2000, 475.

2.1 Kerygma and Christ Myth

Like many other scholars in the history of exegesis, I see the Markan narrative as a Christ myth, even if it for the most part seems to tell us about the so-called "earthly Jesus".[9] The Markan Jesus narrative is a Christ narrative because his story of the "earthly Jesus" is told from a kerygmatic "death-and-resurrection" point of view.[10] Mark's narrative presentation of Jesus from Nazaret "in the past" is based on his present understanding of him as Christ crucified and resurrected. Mark himself reveals that to the reader from the very beginning in 1:1: Ἀρχὴ τοῦ εὐαγγελίου Ἰησοῦ Χριστοῦ ("The beginning of the good news of Jesus Christ").[11] He even ascribes this insight and understanding to the narrative Jesus in the story world (cf. for example Jesus' predictions of suffering *and* resurrection, Mark 8:31; 9:31; 10:32–34). From the very (prospective) beginning, the story is told (retrospectively) from the end. As storyteller, Mark knows in advance how the narrative ends, and he presents persons and events according to this governing Christ myth. Now the all-important question is: did he receive this Christ myth/kerygmatic schema from Paul, or from an earlier, more general Christian tradition?

---

9 I have argued that Mark's story presents a *narrative* Jesus, which can be divided into a *realistic* Jesus and a *mythical* Jesus, cf. Ole Davidsen, *The Narrative Jesus. A Semiotic Reading of Mark's Gospel* (Aarhus: Aarhus University Press, 1993), 370. Strictly speaking, "the realistic Jesus" is the state of being that the narrative Jesus occupies only until the anointing with divine spirit is accomplished.

10 Bultmann's understanding is still the most plausible explanation: Mark "läßt sich nur verstehen aus dem Charakter des christlichen Kerygmas, zu dessen Ergänzung und Veranschaulichung das Evangelium dienen musste. (…) Der Christus, der verkündigt wird, ist nicht der historische Jesus, sondern der Christus des Glaubens und des Kultes. Im Vordergrund der Christusverkündigung stehen deshalb der Tod und die Auferstehung Jesu Christi als die Heilstatsachen, die im Glauben bekannt und in Taufe und Herrenmahl für den Glaubenden wirksam werden. Das Christuskerygma ist also Kultuslegende, und die Evangelien sind erweiterte Kultuslegenden. Schon 1. Kor 11,23–26 (Herrenmahl) und 15,3–7 (Auferstehung) zeigen, wie die Motive des Kerygmas erweiternde Veranschaulichung forderten; (…) Mk hat diesen Typus des Evangeliums geschaffen; der Christusmythos gibt seinem Buch, dem Buch der geheimen Epiphanien, eine zwar nicht biographische, aber eine im Mythos des Kerygmas begründete Einheit." (1970, 396–397).

11 This is the only time Mark uses this composite name for the story's main character, whereas Paul is using it all the time, with a few exceptions when using "Jesus" only. The composite "Jesus Christ" is itself the minimal sign of the inseparable relationship between "the earthly" or human Jesus and "the heavenly" or divine Christ, between Jesus Christ before and after Easter. However, I find it more precise to distinguish between Jesus as *virtual* Christ before the anointing with the divine spirit, Jesus as *actualized* Christ after this event, and Jesus as *realized* Christ after death and resurrection. Jesus as *actualized* Christ is already a mythical figure.

Marcus writes: "Mark wants to express the conviction which he shares with Paul and other early Christians, that Jesus' death and resurrection were the turning point of the ages" (478). I agree, and unless "other early Christians" are to be identified as Paul's disciples, this statement reveals that Marcus reckons with the possibility of a pre-Pauline Christ myth. This is fully consistent with the account given by Paul himself, who actually tells us he received his kerygma from tradition (1Cor 15:3–4).

2.2 Does Paul Represent a Particular Version of an Otherwise General Kerygma?

Does the Pauline version of the Christ myth have a certain theological tendency, an inclination towards attitudes and beliefs that makes it less general than the one he received? Paul receives a tradition which can be regarded as a Christian sociolect of a particular Christ-confessing subculture. His theological unfolding of this kerygma can be seen as his ideolectal (idiosyncratic) interpretation and proclamation of it. (There is no doubt that Paul himself is convinced that he is only – by what could be termed narrative inference – bringing to light what is already implicitly present in the received tradition.) His body of followers then turn his theology into a Pauline sociolect, which we call Paulinism.

Now, language is on the move, so we are dealing with entities with floating borders around a center of semantic density. We can detect differences, not only between genuine letters and disputed and pseudepigraphic letters, but even between undisputedly genuine letters. To argue for Pauline influence, however, presupposes an identification of the diacritical features that constitute the peculiarity of Paulinism. A specifying reading will tend to regard a Pauline text as a Pauline text throughout, since every item of information is seen as saturated with Paulinism, whatever Paul might have received from tradition having been absorbed and transformed during his reception of it. If so, however, we would not be able to distinguish between general and peculiar features in a Pauline text. But we can.

2.3 Do Paul and Mark Represent an Accentuation of a Common and General Kerygma?

Marcus points out that "both Paul and Mark lay *extraordinary* stress on the death of Jesus".[12] Others too, it is to be understood, lay stress on the death of Jesus, but Paul and Mark do so in an extraordinary way. If so, this is more than a question of sociolectal style; but is it more than an accentuation of a common and general kerygma? While a serious accentuation for sure, perhaps fraught with specific theological consequences, this could still be a matter of emphasis rather than a completely new idea. Does this accentuation or emphasis mark out a particular current among early Christians, a sociolect regarded as controversial for some Christians in at least some localities, as Marcus argues (481–484)? Well, we know that the diversity of texts in the New Testament represents different traditions that are controversial to one another in certain respects. The exegetical challenge is to explain the particular features of these different Christian sociolects, without failing to appreciate their common generality.

What if Paul and Mark, by the way, lay *ordinary* stress on the death of Jesus according to a common Hellenistic tradition, while later traditions soften this interpretation by, for example, loosening the tension between power and weakness in favor of an unambiguously sovereign Christ (as in the Gospel of John); or by downplaying the Cross event as a matter of giving that is necessary to institute the forgiveness of sins (as in the Gospel of Luke, which omits Mark 10:45)?

2.4 Did Paul and Mark Take the Idea of Christ's Death as a Sacrifice from Tradition?

Both Mark and Paul attest the idea that Jesus' death was a vicarious sacrifice for human sin (Mark 10:45; 14:24; Rom 3:25; 5:9; 1 Cor 5:7; 11:25; 15:3). Is this idea a peculiarly Pauline one? Marcus admits that the idea of Christ's death as a vicarious sacrifice was taken up from tradition by Paul (484–485). But the same is true for Mark, so this very idea belongs to an early general Christian viewpoint or layer of tradition. This early tradition may of course have been disputed: not all Christians will have accepted this general layer of tradition. Maybe it

---

12 Marcus 2000, 479; contrary to Werner, who rejects the widespread opinion of his time that "Ein ungeheures Gewicht wird von Markus auf Leiden, Tod und Auferstehung Jesu gelegt" (1923, 61).

was regarded as valid only in certain circles, but then at least in circles which found their spokesmen in Paul and Mark.

This complicates the matter, since we will have to isolate the general in order to find the particular in what has been termed the Pauline *theologia crucis*. This may be a question of accentuation, as when Marcus says, "both Paul and Mark lay *extraordinary* stress on the death of Jesus" (479). But it is difficult to see that "the thesis that Paul influenced Mark receives important support from the comparison of the two authors' theology of the cross", as Marcus concludes (486). Not all in Mark need be due to Pauline influence, whether in the strict sense of literary dependency on the Pauline texts as its source, or in the weaker sense of ideas taken from later traditions of Paulinism. If both Paul and Mark take up the idea of Christ's death as a vicarious sacrifice from tradition, as Marcus too seems to presume, then we are beyond the question of Pauline influence on Mark, at least on this topic. I agree with Werner, who writes (1923, 69):

> Mit den bisher gemachten Feststellungen halten wir nun die Tatsache zusammen, dass Markus gerade in der Sühnetodlehre mit Paulus zusammentrifft. Und da ergibt sich denn ohne weiteres, dass dieses Zusammentreffen niemals als Beeinflussung des Markus durch paulinische Theologie erwiesen werden kann. (...) Markus (...) trifft (...) mit Paulus zusammen, wo dieser in seiner Beurteilung des Todes Jesu aus der urchristlichen Tradition schöpft, dann ist doch der Schlussfolgerung gar nicht zu entgehen, auch Markus gebe 10,45 und 14,24 völlig unabhängig gemeinurchristliche Überzeugung wieder.

We can detect *intertextual relations* between Paul and Mark, but that is no argument for mutual *influence* either way. We may detect similarities between Paul and Mark which might be due to some Pauline influence on Mark, but that does not imply that Mark's theology is saturated with Paulinism and he himself an interpreter of Paul.

2.5 The Hellenist Kerygma Presupposes a Narrative of a Kind

It was not Paul who inaugurated the Christological interpretation of Jesus' death. His contribution to this ongoing interpretation does not begin from scratch, but should rather be seen as an unfolding of its semantic potentials in a specific theological accentuation. Paul hands on what he himself had received, ὅτι Χριστὸς ἀπέθανεν ὑπὲρ τῶν ἁμαρτιῶν ἡμῶν κατὰ τῆς γραφὰς καὶ ὅτι ἐγήγερται τῇ ἡμέρᾳ τῇ τρίτῃ κατὰ τὰς γραφὰς ("that Christ died for our sins in accordance with the scriptures, and that he was buried, and that he was raised on the third day in accordance with the scriptures", 1 Cor 15:3–4). This kerygma – which keeps the death and resurrection of Christ inseparable from one another

– is the central core of a pre-Pauline proclamation of the good news, and it represents the founding Christ myth.

Here it is not least important to call attention to the indeterminate "in accordance with the scriptures". We try to figure out which scriptural passages are in view (for example Isa 53; Ps 16), but cannot come up with completely satisfactory answers. The most obvious reason is that we are looking for scriptures on the plane of expression (phraseology), while the indeterminate reference to scriptures here (and elsewhere in the New Testament) rests upon a general conception of internal correspondence on the plane of content between separate parts of the overarching plot in God's macro-narrative. The reference to the scriptures writes the death and resurrection of Jesus into the one macro-narrative about God's epoch-making actions, not least as a judge sanctioning man's behavior. The Christ myth is in accordance with the former story as known from the scriptures, it is claimed, and rightly so, since a set of narrative correspondences can actually be detected on the plane of content. In fact the Adam-Christ typology functions as a *narrative argument* of this sort (cf. below).

It would be a mistake, however, to identify the proclamation of this Adam-Christ myth with particular Paulinism, since Paul's proclamation seems to be based on a pre-Pauline Christ myth. This does not rule out the possibility of Mark being influenced by Paulinism in some respects – although this is difficult to confirm. But it reveals another reason for comparing Mark and Paul. Instead of looking for similarities in order to detect particular Pauline traits in Mark, we should focus on similarities in order to detect general features pointing to a common primal tradition. As Bultmann pointed out, the most striking general feature seems to be that the Marcan narrative is an *expansion* of the Christ myth's kerygma (cf. also Davidsen 1993: 358–363).

Bultmann's point, however, itself needs to be extended. The kerygmatic Christ myth is not simply a set of motifs (Death and Resurrection), but a narrative structure. Here we should remind ourselves that Paul could not convert Gentiles simply by telling them that Christ had been crucified and raised. He was urged to unfold this kerygma into a narrative of a kind (answering questions like: "Christ? Whom are you talking about?"; "Which god do you have in mind?"; "What happened to whom, when, and where, and how are these events to be understood?" etc.). The kerygmatic proclamation in 1 Cor 15:3–4 should therefore be seen as a *condensed* narrative. The expanded, kerygmatic narrative of Mark seems to presuppose, if not a fully composed narrative, then at least a narratively organized world of concepts related to this condensed narrative, this kerygma of pre-Pauline origin. I have in mind an oral tradition, but one that is very close to written composition. Even oral traditions are composed narratives with stable structures of signification that can function as cognitive models for theological thinking. As written folk literature, the Gospel of Mark is very close to oral tradition. Although I am not suggesting that an early gospel-like text has been lost, it remains the case that just as a meaningful use of "Adam" presupposes that some narrative traditions about this person are called to mind, so we must infer that the meaningful use of "Christ" needed some narrative traditions about this person.

In this perspective the difference between a gospel story (embedded in discourse) and epistolary discourse (embedding a story) is not important. "Jews demand signs", says Paul, "and Greeks desire wisdom, but we [Christians] proclaim Christ crucified, a stumbling block to Jews and foolishness to Gentiles ..." (1 Cor 1:22–23). Jews demand empirical evidence that the crucified Jesus was Christ. Greeks desire sophisticated philosophical argumentation for an otherwise naive religious proclamation. What is the problem for Paul and other Christians? The problem is that the Christian proclamation is substantiated neither from socially acknowledged experience nor from thinking. All Paul can provide is a revelatory narrative, a story about God's action in the world through Jesus Christ. There is no way to see what the death and resurrection of Jesus meant, and means, in God's *Heilsgeschichte* except by the interpretation of it given by such a narrative. Paul's proclamation of God's εὐαγγέλιον" presupposes and can only be based on such a narrative, the core of which is the general kerygma as cognitive paradigm. Therefore it should be no surprise to us if we do find such a narrative (in a condensed form) at the basis of Paul's world of ideas as known from his letters.

3 The Adam-Christ Typology as the Center of Paul's Semantic World

We are accustomed to regard Paul's letters as composed of three interrelated principal stories, all articulated from the time of enunciation, the "now" of the Pauline discourse.

3.1 The Community-story, the Paul-story, and the Salvation-story

The story of the community is made up of information about the founding of the community (if Paul was its founder) and its relation to Paul in the past; but also of information about an actual situation in time and of wishes for its future situation. (This is comparable to a liturgical structure, which here and now recalls the past with an actualization anticipating the coming glory.)

Then we have the story about Paul's own history as an apostle to the Gentiles, his autobiography, concerning his relationship to God and Christ, to communities, to other apostles/missionaries, and to Israel – again articulated by past, present and future.

Finally we have the story of salvation, which tells us how Paul and the community addressed are written into the story of God's salvation. The past of this story is given by the use made of the narrative world of the Old Testament. The recent Christ event marks a turning point or point of no return that defines the actual situation, the present time of the story. And revelation discloses the teleological ending of the story in the nearest future.

3.2 The Basic Narrative in the Pauline Discourse

Here it is all about the salvation story, or what we could simply call the mythical level of the Pauline discourse. I do not identify Paul's letters (not even Romans) as theological epistles per se. The question is whether we can reconstruct a relatively coherent basic myth from his occasional letters. In fact, Paul has already done something like this himself, if we agree that the Adam-Christ typology is the center of that myth.

In an earlier article on the structural typology of Adam and Christ, I had two objectives:[13] first, to emphasize the presence of a basic narrative at the foundation of Paul's imaginary world; and second, to show how modal semiotics could provide us with a more precise understanding of the complex structure of time and aspect to which we often simply refer as "already/not yet". Here I shall take up and further elaborate some elements of my arguments on this matter for the purposes of this article.

---

13 Ole Davidsen, "The Structural Typology of Adam and Christ. Some Modal-semiotic Comments on the Basic Narrative of the Letter to the Romans." In *The New Testament and Hellenistic Judaism*, eds. Peder Borgen and Søren Giversen (Aarhus: Aarhus University Press 1995), 244–262.

3.3 The Concluding Part of the Adam-Christ Typology in Romans

We can paraphrase the concluding part of the Adam-Christ typology in Romans, Rom 5:18–19, by presentic statements like these:
1) The fall of the one man (παράπτωμα; offence; fault) implies condemnation (κατάκριμα) for all human beings.
2) The righteous deed of the one man (δικαίωμα) implies justification of life (δικαίωσις ζωῆς) for all human beings.
3) Because of the one man's disobedience (παρακοή') all human beings become sinners (ἁμαρτωλοί').
4) Because of the one man's obedience (ὑπακοή') all human beings become righteous (δίκαοποι).[14]

The narrative schema given below shows the two processes of interaction between God as Other and Adam-Christ as Subject:[15]

SCHEMA/ STORY	Manipulation Other's doing	Performance Subject's doing	Sanction Other's doing
Adam	Interdiction	Fall/Disobedience	Punishment/Death
Christ	Prescription	Righteous deed/Obedience	Recompense/Life

3.4 The First and the Last Adam

In a syntagmatic perspective Adam is "the first Adam", whereas Christ is "the last Adam" (1 Cor 15:45), and it is evident that the latter presupposes the former. In a paradigmatic perspective, however, these two persons presuppose each other, which explains why Christ can be named Adam. Typological thinking is not syntagmatic, but paradigmatic. Adam and Christ can be opposed to each other because they belong to the same paradigmatic structure:

---

[14] I use *catalysis* in my exegesis in search of the primary meaning of the text. I make the meaning (the semantics) of the text's sentences explicit by using information from other parts of a text. I formulate presentic statements disregarding the temporality of sentences. Furthermore I formulate the statements as categorical statements and only subsequently look for modifications (for example the relationship between "all" and "many" or a possible difference between fatal and possible implications of action).

[15] See A.-J Greimas and J. Courtés, *Semiotics and Language: An Analytical Dictionary*, trans. L. Crist, D. Patte et al. (Bloomington: Indiana University Press1982): "Narrative schema".

1) They are both particular persons, whose epoch-making actions have consequences for mankind.
2) They represent man to God on behalf of all of mankind.
3) We are dealing with the same God in both cases.
4) Both cases concern man's right of admission to eternal life (the opposition Life vs. Death).

So the two events are related to each other in a systematic way, constituting what we may call a structural relationship. The myth or basic narrative in Paul's theo-semantic world is this double story about Adam and Christ. The Christ narrative cannot stand alone, but presupposes syntagmatically the Adam narrative. It is, however, the paradigmatic structure that keeps them together in unity. This sort of Christian proclamation as *angelion* includes a *dysangelion* as well as a *euangelion*.

3.5 The Double Narrative: Adam Myth and Christ Myth

I do not think that Paul invented this Adam-Christ typology. It points to the existence of a double narrative, composed of an Adam myth and a Christ myth, already circulating in early Hellenistic Christianity. Paul refers explicitly to the Adam myth or narrative in Rom 5:12–21 and in 1 Cor 15 (Adam mentioned in Rom 5:14 and in 1 Cor 15:22.45), while 1 Cor 11:8–9 and Phil 2, for example, show us that he can use this narrative implicitly as well.

The opposition of Adam and Christ is clear evidence that Paul, at least, understood Christ in the light of Adam, and Adam in the light of Christ. Though less evident, it is highly probable that Paul received this narrative paradigmatic model from tradition. Thus we face a structural typology wherein Adam and Christ mutually define each other through systematic similarities and differences. This typological opposition is a formalized opposition of two narratives, an Adam myth and a Christ myth, between which an objective connection is stated. The generic paradigmatic structure constitutes the *tertium comparationis*.

From his mytho-historical perspective, Paul would say that there is a historical connection of continuity between the Adam event and the Christ event. To us as exegetes it is sufficient to recognize an established connection between these events in Paul's semantic world, based on narratives and their structural semantics. We may make two observations at this point. First, the death of Jesus is understood and interpreted on the basis of a narrative way of thinking: only a Christ narrative can reveal what his death was all about. Second, the interpretation of Jesus' death is influenced by the Adam narrative. Thus we have reason to assume that the Adam narrative played a decisive role in the birth and formation of the Christ narrative. This thesis seems well founded, since the Christ narrative receives its (scriptural and theological) plausibility from its structural correspondence with the Adam narrative.

Paul is not merely using the Adam narrative as a pedagogical device to explain the Christ narrative, as if the two stories otherwise had nothing to do with each other. On the contrary, the Adam-Christ typology makes plain the narrative rationality that constitutes the most basic layer of his understanding of the Christ event, the foundation of his semantic universe. We have no reason to assume that this Adam-Christ typology was created by Paul. He may have refined or modified an earlier Adam-Christ tradition, and may even have drawn some particular theological conclusions of his own; but he was not the first one to establish a meaningful intertextual relationship between Adam and Christ. His greatest achievement in this respect is the result of his work as a skilled narratologist, his identification of the foundational narrative schemata (the structural typology) of the composite Adam-Christ myth.

4 The Adam-Christ Typology in Mark

We have no explicit reference to Adam in the Gospel of Mark. However, most scholars detect Adam imagery behind the temptation story in Mark 1:12–13. I need not go into detail here with this short text, which I regard as a symptom or token of a broader narrative matter.[16] Instead I shall explain my thesis by taking a narrative analysis of temptation as my point of departure.

4.1 Test: Temptation and Trial

The Greek word πειράζω can mean "to tempt" as well as "to try" somebody. Thus the word πειρασμός can mean a *temptation* or a *trial*. Test can be used as a wider

---

16 Cf. for example Rudolf Pesch, "Anfang des Evangeliums Jesu Christi. Eine Studie zum Prolog des Markusevangeliums (Mk 1,1–15)." In *Die Zeit Jesu. Festschrift für Heinrich Schlier*, Hrsg. Günther Bornkamm und Karl Rahner (Freiburg: Herder 1970), 108–144; Christian Schramm, "Streit um Eden: Paradiesisch-Schöpfungstheologisches in Mk 13? Eine hermeneutische Problemreflexion." *Sacra Scripta* 1 (2010):18–41. And again the clear-sighted Bultmann, who is inclined to see this story as a story which belongs "zu dem Typus der Versuchungen [temptation] heiliger Männer, die (vom Bösen) auf die Probe [trial] gestellt werden und diese siegreich bestehen" (1970, 271).

term for both temptation and trial. It is important to look at the context in the Greek text to establish the exact meaning, since there is a difference between temptation and trial. But on the other hand we find that temptation and trial are always profoundly connected.

4.1.1 Interdiction relates to Temptation as Prescription to Trial

We speak of temptation in the strict sense when an *interdiction* is given which a) one wants to transgress, b) one actually can transgress, but c) one must not transgress. The Adam narrative in Genesis is the scriptural arch-example of a temptation story, where an interdiction is transgressed in disobedience, because one succumbs to temptation.

We speak of trial in the strict sense when a *prescription* is given which a) one does not want to observe, b) one actually is able not to observe, but which c) one is obliged to observe. The story of Abraham's sacrifice of Isaac and the story of Jesus' passion are arch-examples of radical trials where the prescription is followed in obedience (cf. Jesus' crisis in Gethsemane, Mark 14:32–42: Jesus does not want to die a glorious death; he could have fled, as his disciples later did; but the Father demands obedience from him to the point of death – even death on a Cross). The following figure summarizes this ("I have not to do" means "I must not do").

MODALITY TEST	*Wanting to do*	*Being able to do*	*Having to do*
Temptation	I want to do X	I am able to do X	I have not to do X
Trial	I want not to do Y	I am able not to do Y	I have to do Y

4.1.2 The Correlative Status of Temptation and Trial

One can fall to a temptation and one can fail ("fall through") in a trial. In both cases we have disobedience and violation of law. But one can also stand up to a trial and withstand a temptation. Thus we find a structural solidarity between temptation and trial which also reveals itself in the looser or more complex usage of these words. It turns out that there is a temptation at stake in any trial, namely the temptation not to do what one ought to do. In the same way, a trial is involved in any temptation, since one undergoes a trial to see if one can resist the temptation to do what is forbidden. The serpent's temptation of Adam and Eve is at the same time God's (implicit but correlative) putting them on trial. God's putting Jesus on trial is at the same time Satan's (implicit but correlative) temptation of him (cf. Mark 8:33). I summarize the two forms of obedience and the two forms of disobedience in this semantic micro system of signification:

COMMANDMENT ACTION	*Interdiction*	*Prescription*
Obedience	I resist temptation: I want to but do not do what is forbidden POSITIVE NON-DOING	I pass the trial: I do not want to but do what is prescribed POSITIVE DOING
Disobedience	I succumb to temptation: I want to and do what is forbidden NEGATIVE DOING	I fail the trial: I do not want to and do not do what is prescribed NEGATIVE NON-DOING

It is God's commandments (his law) which establish and reveal the conflict between humankind and God, since human beings do not voluntarily (by inclination) share the divine values. The law is the symbolic castration of humankind's dream of limitless omnipotence. From the law arises the challenge to see whether man can govern his spirit and avoid doing what is forbidden, even if he wants to and is tempted to do it. From the law arises the challenge to see whether man can bring himself to do what is commanded, even if he does not spontaneously want to and is tempted not to do it.

4.2 The Markan Temptation Story as a Pre-test to the Trial in Jerusalem

According to the temptation story, it is the Spirit, i.e. God, who drives Jesus into the wilderness to be tempted by Satan. Satan is tempting Jesus; but God is trying Jesus. In the explicit temptation story we have an implicit story about the trial in the wilderness. God is letting Satan tempt Jesus in order to try him.

In the narrative plot of the Markan story this temptation/trial is a *pre-test*, the outcome of which anticipates the result of the later main test of Jesus' obedience to the Father. According to narratology we often find in folk narratives a preparatory account of how the hero demonstrates his competence before the principal test. This seems to be the case here, where Jesus gives a demonstration of his obedience that anticipates his later submission. Satan tempts Jesus to violate an interdiction (which is not explicit), but Jesus resists the temptation.[17] This obedience, it is true, is only a *positive non-doing*, but it is nevertheless an equivalent to the obedience he later demonstrates by his *positive doing*, i.e. the death on the Cross, understood not as the taking of his life by his opponents (seeing Jesus as patient), but as his own sovereign act of giving his life (seeing Jesus as agent; Mark 10:45).

4.3 The Temptation of Adam and the Temptation of Christ

Now, one could argue like this:
1) The wilderness story in Mark thematizes temptation in a way similar to the Adam story. In both stories we meet an opponent of God, a speaking serpent or Satan, tempting a human being.[18] This could be a first sign showing that the two stories should be taken together. But whereas Adam succumbs to temptation (*negative doing*), Jesus resists it (*positive non-doing*). Is that not an important difference? Well, a difference indeed, but a structural difference, a systematic difference claiming a connective similarity between these stories in all their difference. Jesus appears in his identity as the systematic counterpart to Adam.
2) The temptation story as a pre-test to Jesus' obedience is an anticipation of the principal test in Jerusalem. Is this not an indication that not only the temptation story, but *the entire Markan gospel as Christ myth has to be*

---

17 Violating an interdiction (concerning no matter what) implies an offence against the commanding authority. The relationship between the commanding Other and the commanded Subject really deserves to be called *covenantal nomism* in the most fundamental sense, even if neither "covenant" nor "law" is part of the text's vocabulary. We need no occurrence of the word "covenant" (on the plane of expression) to recognize the presence of a covenantal structure in a text (on the plane of content). We need no occurrence of the word "law" to recognize the presence of a commandment, an interdiction or a prescription, in a text. What matters is the matter of content, not of expression. On the other hand we cannot separate covenant from the law, which stipulates the set of mutual rights and obligations between the parties.

18 The serpent is identified with Satan in *Apoc. Mos.* 16:4; 17:4, but this identification is already asserted or assumed in early passages, for example *1 Enoch* 69:6; *2 Enoch* 31:4–6; *4 Macc* 18:7–8; Wis 2:24; Rev 12:9; 20:2; cf. Joel Marcus, "Son of Man as Son of Adam." *Revue Biblique* 1 (2003): 38–61, 54. This is no surprise, since the serpent plays the role as God's diametrical adversary. We need no occurrence of the word "Satan" to recognize the presence of this role. It is the underlying role configuration in narratively organized texts which permits such identification on a more general level. A specifying reading would accentuate the difference between "serpent" and "Satan". A generalizing reading accentuates the similarity, which is given by these actors' common role, their functional equivalence.

seen as the counterpart to the Adam myth? I think it is, and shall present my argument in what follows. Mark is not the interpreter of Paul, but he uses a tradition common to both to create his gospel narrative.

Remark: Jesus represents obedience in two forms, as *positive non-doing* (resisting temptation) and as *positive doing* (standing up to trial). Adam represents disobedience as *negative doing* (succumbing to temptation), while Peter is the outstanding representative of the last possibility: *negative non-doing*. Peter's passionate promise to follow Jesus into death (Mark 14:31) is a self-manipulation – an oath by which he obligates himself to follow a prescription – but he fails this trial.[19] The Gethsemane scene thematizes Jesus' temptation not to do what he is obliged to do, but in the framework of the trial and its prescription. Cf. how the idea of the angel in Luke 22:43 points to the angels in Mark 1:12.

In Mark 14:38 Jesus warns the disciples to watch and pray in order not to enter into πειρασμός temptation or trial. One can accentuate either temptation or trial, but again, trial is the hyperotactic and temptation the hypotactic term. However, a particular problem shines through. *Wanting* is primarily understood as a somatic feature bound to the body. It can be opposed to *willing*, seeing obedience as an act of volition governed by spirit or mind. Would it be correct to say that the disciples fail in the trial because they do not want to stay awake? Well, they may want to intentionally, but are governed by the somatic modality *not being able to*, a condition open to mythological interpretation. The spirit (pointing to God) might indeed be willing, but the flesh or the body (pointing to Satan) is weak, because of the wanting to sleep – in a further perspective, to stay alive. Jesus himself is tempted to remain alive, but surmounts the crisis and resolves the conflict between wanting and willing, between what he wants and what the Father wants. Mark 14:36: The Father's wanting has to be the willing of the Son (obedience and likeness).

We have no explicit Adam-Christ typology in Mark; only a weak suggestion of an implicit one in the temptation story. However, this is not all. Taking a closer look, we realize how the explicit temptation is the obverse of a test story whose reverse is the implicit trial. In the Passion narrative, we meet the opposite: here the trial is the obverse of a test story whose reverse is the temptation. This suggests to narrative exegesis that the founding structures of signification in the gospel narrative will be the counterpart and structural inversion of the corresponding structures in the Adam narrative. In a syntagmatic perspective, the

---

[19] Paradigmatically, Adam's *negative doing* in temptation relates to Peter's *negative non-doing* on trial – as Jesus' *positive non-doing* in temptation relates to Jesus' *positive doing* on trial.

Christ myth presupposes and continues the Adam myth. In a paradigmatic perspective, the Christ myth is a mirroring inversion of the Adam myth. If Christ is the last Adam, Adam is the first Christ. In early Christian proclamation influenced by the Hellenistic Christ myth, *dysangelion* and *euangelion* can be distinguished, but not separated from each other.

4.4 The Adam Myth as a Paradigmatic Preform to the Christ Myth

In this context the question suggests itself whether this narrative Adam-Christ typology represents a feature peculiar to Paulinism that later influenced Mark, or whether it refers to a pre-Pauline and therefore more general tradition. This is still an open question, but I am inclined to see the typology as a pre-Pauline tradition, and am accordingly compelled to draw some consequences.[20]

We have reason to assume that the *mythos* (the plot structure articulating its fundamental semantics) of the pre-Pauline gospel story was brought about, came to mind, was formulated or composed as a counter-narrative to the Adam narrative. The mythical Christ narrative (condensed or unfolded) came into being by and through a narrative process of interpretation, a creative process in which the Adam myth took a formative part right from the beginning. We are not, and never will be, able to reconstruct this narrative process. We can only say that this Hellenistic Christological interpretation of Jesus finds its primary, original or fundamental form – its final, ideal, and "canonical" form – at the very moment when the interpretation of Jesus' death finds itself integrated into a *mythos* which is the exact inversion of the Adam *mythos*. The idea of such a self-leveling (or self-organizing) process of interpretation seeking its balanced and completing form may look like metaphysics of the rhyme. But we

---

[20] Paul may represent a further elaboration of an early strong stream of Christianity in which he was raised, so to speak. Such a tradition would presumably be characterized by features we point to as Pauline (for example a polemical/ambivalent relation to Peter, James, and Jerusalem) simply because we know of this tradition from Paul. However, such a use of "Paulinism" is quite misleading. Paul was surely creative indeed, but he did not create ex nihilo. Werner's methodological remarks have in no way lost their significance and should be kept in mind. He writes (1923, 29): "Sollen zwei Größen miteinander verglichen und das innere Verhältnis, in dem sie zueinander stehen, bestimmt werden, so sollte zunächst die elementare Vorbedingung erfüllt sein, dass Wesen und Eigenart jeder der beiden Größen für sich als eindeutig klar definiert gelten könnten." Anyone who speaks of "Paulinism" should be able to distinguish between, "was in den paulinischen Briefen selbst als eigentlich original paulinisch, und was als allgemein-urchristlich zu gelten hat" (210).

should not underestimate the significance of "cosmic" form when it comes to the question of force in cognitive and rhetorical plausibility and persuasiveness: "cosmic" structure provides inner evidence. Correspondence between (latent) narrative structures in the Old Testament and what later became a dominating part of the New Testament would seem to be a more convincing proof of Holy Writing than the mere use of (manifest) scriptural passages.

4.5 The Thematic Connection between Adam and Christ in the Christian Perspective

However, one could question whether this focus on form over content is not working on a too general level of signification. After all, the generic structure of temptation and trial (general, abstract, and presumably universal) can be found in a great number of narratives. So it needs to be emphasized that the thematic connection between the Adam myth and the Christ myth – *in the Christian perspective* – is established on the basis of three elements of content:

1) It is one and the same God who expelled Adam and raised Christ: these events are part of the same *Heilsgeschichte*, i.e. the same macro narrative about God's epoch-making (modalizing) actions.
2) The actions of Adam and Christ have consequences for all mankind, because God regards them as mankind's representative in a constituting (covenantal) God/Man-relationship. Both Adam and Christ are acting vicariously on behalf of mankind, presumably as Son of Man or Son of Adam (as a consequence of their semantic complexity, they can also both be seen as Son of God).
3) The central and decisive object of value, to be lost or to be gained, is in both narratives "eternal life" (with what this involves of cosmic destruction and re-creation).

The difference between this semiotic perspective and a more formalistic approach is important. We are not dealing with formal structures here, but with structurally articulated semantics. The Adam-Christ typology is not simply a formal abstraction, but the general level of structured semantics presiding over the concrete or figurative level of the narrative.

4.6 Excursus: A Quick Look at Philippians

Allow me to mention some ideas about a possible narrative intertextuality between Mark and Phil 2:6–11, understood as some familiarity between narratively organized semantic worlds, in this case between Mark and what is often acknowledged as perhaps the most primitive kerygmatic formula we know of.[21] What happens if we compare this evidently *narrative* hymn with the account given in Mark? Well, it does make sense to a remarkable degree, which may be worth keeping in mind for potential confirmation through further findings and examinations.

After his quite ordinary baptism by John, something special happens to Jesus, according to Mark: Jesus is endowed with divine spirit from heaven, i.e, with an extraordinary cognitive competence (being able to know as a prophet and a proclaimer) and with a dynamic competence (being able to do as a miracle-worker). This extraordinary competence was not obtained by any form of taking (it was no robbery, no usurpation), but by a divine giving. However, during his trial in Jerusalem, Jesus has to renounce the use of his divine competence to protect or save himself. Hanging on the cross, he is mocked by bystanders and told to come down to prove his divine being (competence) in a manifest way, Mark 15:29–32. Jesus does not come down: either because he is unable to do so or because he is obliged not to do so.

The bystanders opt for the most evident explanation: that Jesus cannot, which to them proves his lack of divinity: Ἄλλους ἔσωσεν, ἑαυτὸν οὐ δύναται σῶσαι ("He saved others [as wonder-worker]; he cannot save himself [disclosed as a pseudo-Christ]." – Mark 15:31). Jesus is seen as just a human being, in appearance as well as in being (competence). But according to the story's overall perspective, Jesus remains on the cross because he is obliged to do so. At this moment Jesus appears to be a powerless human being, who can neither save himself nor others. But in secret he is a divine being, yet still on his way to full divinity, successively to be granted by God's high exaltation of him (God's sanction, Phil 2:9). He who sees Jesus' death as the saving event cannot miss the dramatic irony.

Now, it makes very good sense to claim that when Jesus as prophet/proclaimer and miracle-worker represented God to man (manifestly was "in the

---

[21] Cf. Ole Davidsen, "Filipperbrevshymnens temporalisering. Om hymnens evne til at fortolke sin performer og hans verden." In *Den poetiske litteratur i Gammel og Ny Testamente*, red. Ole Davidsen (København: Collegium Biblicums Årsskrift 1997), 103–114. In English the title would be: "Temporalization in the Philippians Hymn. On the Hymn's Ability to Interpret its Performer and his World."

form of God", Phil 2:6; i.e. manifested divine competence), he did so with divine approval (Jesus was possessing God's holy spirit, not possessed by the unclean spirit of Beelzebul/Satan, cf. Mark 3:22–30). But later on, when he – like Adam – represented man to God (was manifestly "in human form", Phil 2:7; i.e. manifested human competence), he had emptied himself, having renounced the use of his divine competence, and became obedient to the point of death.

This idea seems necessary in order to mediate between Christ's previous strength (*being able to do* and *being prescribed to do* miracles for others) and actual (apparently) weakness (*being able to do* and *being prohibited to do* miracles for his own sake; cf. the temptation story in Matthew and Luke). Furthermore it seems required in order to stress the perspective according to which the death on the Cross is *a giving* by Jesus as an intentional agent (Mark 10:45), *not a taking* of his life by his opponents. The crucifixion as a manifest, empirical scene of taking life (execution) hides a latent reality consisting in the giving of life (self-sacrifice), a reality that is accessible to those who can perceive hidden meaning, but is not to be observed by even the most attentive eyewitness.[22] This hidden meaning, this secrecy and mystery, is to be accessed only through a revelatory narrative interpretation of the death of Jesus. This interpretation must have been established earlier on as a more or less elaborated narrative Christ myth – presumably already connected to some Adamic imagery. Since death and resurrection dominate this Christ myth, we would first think of a pre-Markan Passion narrative. But we need to go a step further back. The Adam-Christ typology in Paul must be seen as a formalized and reduced version of a pre-Pauline Christ myth already explicitly related to a reception of the Adam narrative. It is highly unlikely that Paul could have persuaded Gentiles (and convinced himself) with

---

22 This is accurate despite the fact that Mark in 15:39 allows the centurion to get a glimpse of Jesus' divine being (by his intentional expiration) and to state an unreserved confession. Ἀληθῶς οὗτος ὁ ἄνθρωπος υἱὸς θεοῦ ἦν should be translated "Truly this man was a god's son". Any idea of Jesus' upcoming resurrection is beyond the centurion's mind. Following Rudolf Pesch: His confession – "Jesus *was* a god's son" – is inadequate compared to a valid Christian confession: "Jesus *is* the Son of God" (Davidsen 1993, 355). I find this interpretation more convincing than the traditional one that sees the centurion as the first Christ-confessing Gentile. At most he may be seen as foreshadowing such a Gentile confession – just as Joseph of Arimathea, who entombs the body without any sense of a possible continuation, may be seen as a role model for potential Jewish Christ-confessors. Both the centurion and Joseph negate the official Roman and Jewish understanding of Jesus, by word or by action. As such they represent a first step towards a positive Christian confession. This is relevant information, according to Mark, also for cocksure Gentiles and Jews, who may believe the matter was all settled by the conviction and execution of Jesus.

such a stylized and condensed Adam-Christ kerygma. There is a story to be told for which this kerygma is only a second-order résumé.[23]

5 The Adam Myth and the Christ Myth as One Single Christian Myth

The Gospel of Mark is a complex story. Besides more episodic events, it relates two main stories, which are intertwined but are to be distinguished. The one is the story of the relationship between Jesus and his disciples. It is dominated by a cognitive dimension of Christological instruction and derivative from the other, more pragmatic, story of the relationship between God and Jesus. It is this God/Jesus-story which constitutes the fundamental structure of the Markan story, and it is more exactly this basic storyline which stands as counterpart to the story about God's relationship to Adam (cf. Davidsen 1993, 348–351). In both cases we are dealing with a covenantal relation, not because the word covenant is used, but because covenant is the adequate term for the mutual loyalty and obligation between God and mankind. In both stories, God as Other is the manipulating (prohibiting or prescribing) as well as the sanctioning (punishing or rewarding) party.[24]

Did Mark receive this Christological story-structure from Paul? It is hard to say, but as I see it, he need not necessarily have it from Paul. The Adam-Christ myth seems to have been circulating in several places before Mark and even Paul entered the Christian scene. In his book *Christology in the Making* James Dunn wrote:

> Adam plays a larger role in Paul's theology than is usually realized – and even when that role is taken into account it is often misunderstood. Adam is a key figure in Paul's attempt to express his understanding both of Christ and of man. Since soteriology and Christology are closely connected in Paul's theology, it is necessary to trace the extent of the Adam motif in Paul if we are to appreciate the force of his Adam Christology.[25]

---

23 As a narrative résumé, Phil 2:6–11, for example, is difficult to understand – then and now – for those, who do not know the presupposed and unfolded story. A missionary enterprise based on such kerygmatic formulas alone is not likely to succeed. A modern missionary enterprise based on, let us say, the sole recitation of the Apostolic Creed would not function either. It would need the retelling of the preceding story or stories.
24 The latent Adam-covenant is made explicit in *Apoc. Mos.* 8:2 (διαθήκη) and in the Quran, Sure 20:115.
25 James Dunn, *Christology in the Making. A New Testament Inquiry into the Origins of the Doctrine of the Incarnation* (Cambridge: Cambridge University Press 1980), 101.

But this perspective seems much too narrow. It seems likely that Adam, or, better, the Adam myth – either directly from Gen 2:4b-3:24 or indirectly from later retold/rewritten versions of that text – plays a much larger role in the New Testament semantic universe than is generally assumed. Thus the Adam-story seems quite important for our understanding of New Testament Christology, not least in Paul and Mark.

A search for an Adam motif, however, is not sufficient. Such a procedure of discovering motifs or themes gives us only a list of superficial signs to a deeper correlation. That is why narrative exegesis does not ask for motifs or themes, but for structures of signification, for the narrative forms of organization, which role configuration is deciding which actors/persons can be typologized. It is the narrative schema in the Adam myth and in the Christ myth that constitute the semiotic presupposition for the explicit typology in Paul, as well as for the implicit typology in Mark.

All of this seems to imply that we should perceive the Adam myth and the Christ myth as one single myth ranging from the beginning of Creation to the end of Re-creation. The entire process, consisting of two narrative trajectories, the one to fall, the other to rise, becomes in this perspective an interactive affair between a single covenantal Lord, God, and a single covenantal Servant, Adam/Christ. As representative of mankind, the covenantal Servant is the single mythical man, the Son of Man – which is why Paul can term them both by the name Adam. In this mythical respect, they have the same representative status: the first Adam relates to the last Adam as Alpha to Omega, as beginning to end, as *Urzeit* to *Endzeit*, according to *paradigmatic* thinking.

The Adam-Christ myth (or perhaps the Son of Man myth) consists of two component parts, *dysangelion* and *euangelion*. The Christ component, which dominates Mark, discloses itself to be just one half of the complete process that constitutes the dominant basic structure of signification in New Testament semiotics. The other half belongs to Adam; but the foundational myth of Christian proclamation comprises both and keeps them together in an indissoluble unity. The explicit Adam-Christ typology in Paul simply spells this out.

6 Conclusive Perspectivization

From the perspective of narrative exegesis, it is Adam's and Christ's status as representatives of man before God that supports the need for a re-evaluation of the use of the term "Son of Man". Do we find other traditions using Son of Man in this functional sense, or has this title been strongly re-semanticized in the Gospel of Mark? (Another question concerns Adam's and Christ's other side as mediators, i.e. their corresponding status as God's representatives towards man. This is probably most evident in Jesus, but cf. Adam as "Son of God" in Luke 3:38.)

Joel Marcus' double article, "Son of Man as Son of Adam" (2003ab), gives us a recent survey of the complex and often fragmented Adam imagery that is relevant for such a re-evaluation of the term "Son of Man". Using another approach, Marcus's study nevertheless supports my own to a great extent. Most important is, perhaps, our agreement that, though we are often dealing with a complex and fragmented Adam imagery, this imagery represents receptions of a text very well known to us: Gen 2:4b-3:24. Compared to some more speculative post-biblical receptions, Paul as well as Mark may represent the more rational interpretations, I wish to add. But I agree with Marcus, who writes (2003a, 51):

> Early Christians … seem also to have been profoundly affected by the stories and speculations about Adam. Their influence on Paul's Christology is plain from 1 Corinthians 15, Romans 5, and other Pauline passages. But their influence on the church pre-dates Paul, as is shown by pre-Pauline Adamic traditions such as the Christ hymns in Phil 2:5b-11 and Col 1:15–20 …

Not least the last point seems well taken in regard to the discussion of Paulinism in Mark. The Adam-Christ typology predates Paul, and instead of talking about a pre-Pauline Hellenistic Christ myth, we should rather speak of a pre-Pauline Hellenistic Adam-Christ myth. The mere fact that we may have become acquainted with it from Paul in the first place is no compelling reason to assume that Mark learned this myth from Paul. The Adam-Christ typology was in the air among the Hellenists, and Mark could just as well have been introduced to this narrative thinking by other persons. We should not become hypnotized by Paul just because his letters are written earlier than the Markan Gospel text. The only safe conclusion to be drawn from Paul's temporal priority is that he was not influenced by Mark – at least not by the Gospel text as we know it.

Contrary to the explicit and double-sided Adam-Christ typology in Paul, Mark is concerned solely with the Christ side; but even here we find signs of the fact that the Christ myth presupposes the Adam myth. It does not seem plausible that a Christ story was given first, whereupon Paul or someone else by sheer accident discovered that it could be brought into meaningful conversation with the Adam story. We must rather assume that receptions of the Adam myth were so powerfully present to people's minds that they became determining for the formation and emergence of the Christ myth, prior to both Mark and Paul.

Comparison of Paul and Mark therefore leads in this generalizing perspective to the acknowledgement of the existence of a *tertium comparationis*, the primal Adam-Christ myth, constituted and structured on the basis of the double kerygmatic schema we see manifested in the explicit Adam-Christ typology.

This schema seems to have been formed before Mark wrote his Gospel, and even before Paul's conversion from a Christ-denying Jew to a Christ-confessing Jew took place. Adam points to the Creation and a theology of the Creation, which cannot but be universal compared to a more local Christological theology of revelation. Would it be wrong to assume that it is the universal Adam that universalizes Christ and creates the possibility of a third Way – Christianity – including Jews as well as Gentiles, i.e. all humanity?

Postscript

I foresee that a possible objection to my thesis – that a primal double narrative existed, of which the explicit Adam-Christ typology is no more than the skillfully exposed backbone – will be based on a suspicion of theological or dogmatic *eisegesis*. In so many churches we see altarpieces contrasting Adam and Christ. Have I not just read a later (post-Augustinian and post-Lutheran) Church reception of tradition into Paul and Mark? "Paul displays an explicit Adam-Christ typology, granted, but need it be exaggerated and spread out all over as a unifying cognitive model for New Testament semiotics in danger of failing to appreciate evidence of diversity?" Or, a perhaps more radical objection could sound: "Why do you stick to the narrative Jesus of Paul and Mark, instead of looking at the historical Jesus, who may have proclaimed a message more trustworthy and less offensive to modern man, Christians as well as atheists and agnostics?"

It is hard to tell which of these objections represents the more severe prejudice concerning the question of scientific integrity for narrative exegesis. It ought not to be necessary, but if it is I shall freely and publicly confess myself to be a scholar who regards narrative exegesis as belonging under the science of religion, not normative theology. But such a scientific and critical study of primitive Christian religion should of course be able to describe and explain the rationality of this religion's *theology* as a religious message in an adequate way – though from another standpoint than the religion itself. Needless to say, I find this to be the case for narrative exegesis as presented here.

I raise this concern about scientific integrity only to reassure those colleagues who are inclined to see unclean holy ghosts everywhere the banned word "theology" is used in a scientific work.[26]

---

[26] Heikki Räisänen's first edition of *Beyond New Testament Theology* (London: SCM Press 1990) may mark the peak of the latest radical wave of specifying approaches stressing diversity. In his second edition (2000, 142–146), however, he acknowledges Gerd Theissen's balanced semiotic approach in understanding primitive Christian religion as an autonomous sign world (Theissen,

I myself, however, appreciate the idea of an intimate correspondence between semiotics and theology. The generalizing perspective of narrative exegesis allows a scientific analysis of early Christian mentality and thought forms that is open for dialogue with theology in a normative sense. I see this scientific integrity and solidarity as a strength, rather than a weakness.

A Theory of Primitive Christian Religion, trans. John Bowden [London: SCM Press. 1999]). No doubt Räisänen appreciates this approach because Theissen avoids using the confessional-like "theology of the New Testament", in favor of "a theory of primitive Christian religion", and thus displaces the perspective from theology to the science of religion. But at the same time Räisänen seems to admit, though more reluctantly, that one can deal with the question of unity without failing to appreciate agreed diversity. In any case, I agree with Theissen (1999, 324) when he says: "There is no necessity to work out a uniform kerygma from the primitive Christian writings, although the question of their unity remains a justified historical and religious concern (and by no means just a theological concern)." Theissen is well aware that he "investigates the unity in the plurality far more intensively than the programmatic recognition of the plurality suggests" (1999, 324). In this respect my own generalizing position may seem even more intense. The Adam-Christ typology as a kerygmatic unity plays a decisive role in New Testament semiotics, I do argue. However, the extension of it is still an open question. Presumably we can expect to see an increasing interest in the generalizing approach. We are realizing that narrativity is a way of thinking, and the prolific and promising cognitive studies strongly support a generalizing perspective. In any case, different theories and approaches are possible, but they should all meet the fundamental exegetical challenge: how to explain diversity without neglecting unity, and vice versa.

Jesper Tang Nielsen
The Cross on the Way to Mark

It is almost an unquestioned fact that the oldest texts in the New Testament are the early Christian hymns that Paul included in his letters.[1] Other kinds of pre-pauline devotional language can be included among the traditions that express the earliest known understanding of Jesus Christ.[2] Due to their social setting in the common Christian worship these expressions of faith would be generally known to the earliest Christians. Otherwise the quoted portions of hymns, prayers and other kinds of liturgical language could not have a rhetorical effect in Paul's letters.

Hymns, prayers and other liturgical formulae are general expressions of faith with a devotional intent, but Paul's writings belong to a quite different genre. They are genuine letters written to particular communities with one or more specific purposes in mind. Paul's presentation of Christ is always fundamentally determined by the communicative situation of the letter. Only small parts of his letters concern strictly theological or Christological issues. He takes for granted that his recipients are familiar with a basic understanding of Christ; what they need is to be admonished in the application of this belief in their daily lives.

The Gospel of Mark is a narrative about the earthly Jesus. It tells his story from his baptism to his empty grave as a kind of founding narrative of the Christian community, perhaps written to be read aloud during worship.[3] It served the purpose of assuring the community of its foundational story and confirming the members of its implications. The Markan Jesus illustrates the beliefs and ethics of the community and in this way secures the belief system of the early Christians.

These remarks introduce the problem of an investigation into the relation between Paul and Mark. It is only to be expected that there are several points of

---

[1] See e.g. the NT introductions, R. E. Brown, *An Introduction to the New Testament* (ABRL, New York etc.: Doubleday, 1997), 489–493; B. D. Ehrman, *The New Testament. A Historical Introduction to the Early Christian Writings* (2nd ed., New York, Oxford: Oxford University Press, 2000), 314; W. G. Kümmel, *Einleitung in das Neue Testament* (Heidelberg: Quelle & Meyer, ²¹1983), 214.
[2] Cf. L. W. Hurtado, *Lord Jesus Christ. Devotion to Jesus in Earliest Christianity* (Grand Rapids, Cambridge: Eerdmanns 2003).
[3] L. Hartman, "Das Markusevangelium, 'für die lectio solemnis im Gottesdienst abgefasst'?" In *Geschichte – Tradition – Reflexion*, FS M. Hengel, eds. H. Cancik, H. Lichtenberger and P. Schäfer (Tübingen: Mohr (Paul Siebeck), 1996), Bd. 3, 147–171.

agreement since they are both early Christian writers. If the two authors include motifs that correspond to the earliest expressions of belief in Christ, this may only prove that they both belong to early Christian tradition.[4] Even if they interpret the tradition in comparable ways, this need not prove that Mark has known Paul.[5] Mark's presentation of the Christ event must be shown to be dependent on the *specifically Pauline* interpretation of that same event in order to establish a direct relation. To pursue this objective I will follow the narrative structures in the prepauline material, in Paul's elaboration of them in his letters, and in Mark's presentation of a complete Jesus story in his gospel. If Mark presents a full-blown narrative on the basis of a specifically Pauline interpretation of traditional structures, it should be possible to claim that Mark has been directly influenced by the way Paul has interpreted the traditional material.

The analysis will be undertaken on the basis of a general narratological theory. It conceptualizes the coherence of narratives and defines the components of narrative structures. It is appropriate for detecting narrative features in traditional fragments, rhetorical arguments and complete narratives. On the ground of this theoretical model it will be possible to see if the specific way Paul elaborates the traditional structures forms a plausible explanation for Mark's way of using the same structures.

Narratology

Narratives make sense. Any kind of narrative tells of events and characters in a way that produce an overall meaning. Because the meaning is dependent on abstract structures, which are instantiated in concrete figures, narrative meaning production can be conceptualized in a model with different levels. By including both abstract and concrete levels it is possible to explain how meaning is created

---

[4] This is more or less the quintessence of M. Werner's classical argument against any direct relation between Paul and Mark. M. Werner, *Der Einfluss paulinischer Theologie im Markusevangelium. Eine Studie zur neutestamentlichen Theologie.* BZNW 1 (Giessen: Verlag Alfred Töpelmann, 1923).

[5] In his article against Werner's dismissal of any Pauline influence on Mark J. Marcus argues that both Paul and Mark lay extraordinary stress on Jesus' death. J. Marcus, "Mark – Interpreter of Paul." *NTS* 46 (2000): 473–487 (479). However, it is not in itself a convincing argument that they show the same tendencies in their interpretation of tradition. More convincing are the "peculiar emphases" that are common to just these two writers. Marcus, "Mark – Interpreter of Paul", 481–484.

within a narrative universe.[6] This model will form the basis for describing the development from narrative fragments to a full-blown narrative in a continuing process of interpretation.

In his treatise on poetics, Aristotle defines tragedy as a μίμησις of an action that is whole, complete and of a certain magnitude (1450b24). To be whole and complete the action must take the form of a plot with a beginning, middle and end. This apparently simple requirement establishes the fact that a whole and complete plot involves a narrative transformation. The three positions, beginning, middle and end, cannot be identical and they cannot be unrelated. Something must happen in a narrative. With necessity or a high degree of probability, the middle follows from the beginning and the end is a consequence of the middle. Hence, the plot is the fundamental narrative structure that constitutes the coherence of the tragedy. It is not enough that the actions concern a specific individual (1451a16). They must have an inner coherence to constitute the unity of a tragedy. For this reason a tragedy cannot be a matter of μίμησις of persons but of actions. This is another way of saying that the plot structure is constitutive of the narrative.

In his recommendations concerning the construction of a tragedy Aristotle establishes a hierarchy of textual levels going from abstract basic structures to concrete linguistic expressions and from general ideas to specific forms (1450a7–12). The primary part of a tragedy is the plot. The second is character and the third thought. Its media are diction and lyric poetry and its mode enactment. In the construction of a tragedy the narrative structure must be worked out before episodes fill out the structure and names are attached to the actions. The next step would be to provide characters to the actions in the plot. After character, thought and diction are the next components. They concern the linguistic expression of the characters' motives. At this point in the hierarchy the narrative may result in either a drama or an epic depending on the choice of mode, whether it be enactment or narrative.

Aristotle's understanding of a whole and complete narrative establishes the plot as a coherent abstract structure that generates the concrete levels as instantiations of the basic structure. Furthermore it lies in Aristotle's theory that actions constitute the narrative structure because they transform one situation into another. Therefore a character cannot constitute a narrative coherence but a line of actions can.

---

6 E.g. in A.-J. Greimas' generative text model. See A.-J. Greimas & J. Courtés, *Sémiotique. Dictionnaire raisonné de la théorie du langage* (Paris: Hachette Supéreur, 1979), art. Génératif (parcours).

A.-J. Greimas transforms some of the fundamental insights from the Aristotelian taxonomy into his own generative text model.[7] At the most fundamental level of his model, very general concepts are structured in opposites, such as life vs. death, nature vs. culture etc. At the next level these oppositions are transformed into narrative structures with abstract functions. Any action can on this level be described as an attempt to affect a situation, either the acting character's own situation or somebody else's. The narrative actions constitute a line of core events that establish the trajectory of the story. Greimas terms the narrative phases manipulation, competence, performance and sanction.[8] In the first phase the protagonist receives the task that he must accomplish. In the second phase he wins the necessary competence (qualifying test). In the third phase he performs the action (decisive test). Finally, his success or failure is evaluated (glorifying test). The phases presuppose each other according to the narrative logic *post hoc ergo propter hoc:* if the protagonist succeeds in the decisive test, it must be because he has had the necessary competence, even if the qualifying test does not occur in the narrative. Each test in the narrative trajectory furthermore involves the risk of failure. The protagonist may fail to accomplish his task. The narrative structure belongs at the deep level of the generative text model. Only at the surface level are the narrative structures made concrete by being invested with room (spatialisation), time (temporalisation) and persons (actorialisation). Through this last part of the generative model, the abstract narrative structures are transformed into concrete narratives with persons placed in time and space.

This model will be the theoretical framework for analysing the prepauline traditions, Paul and Mark. It displays the similarities and dissimilarities in the way the abstract structures have been constructed and transformed into concrete narratives and thereby presents the different levels of potential dependence and influence between the three possible stages of narrative development. As it seems, Paul on the one hand combines the narrative fragments contained in the traditional material into a full narrative structure, on the other hand he interprets the story to fit his own communicative purpose. Mark takes over Paul's narrative structure in his own complete narrative and incorporates the specific, Pauline interpretation into it.

---

[7] It is not quite clear to what extent Greimas was directly influenced by Aristotle but some kind of relation is indisputable. See A.-J. Greimas & J. Courtés, "The Cognitive Dimension of Narrative Discourse", *New Literary History* VII (1976): 433–447.
[8] Greimas & Courtés, *Sémiotique*, art. Narratif (schema).

Prepauline traditions

Investigations into the earliest development of theological terms, concepts and structures often build on assumptions and conjecture. No source-critical operation has been able to achieve complete agreement. Only in a very few cases has it been generally accepted that Paul quotes traditional material and even then it is not certain where the tradition ends and Paul resumes his own discourse. The following presentation takes its starting point from those rare instances and includes a few other texts that are often presented as traditional in scholarly literature. In all cases special attention will be given to the narrative structure.

1 Cor 11:23–25: Paul himself explicitly mentions traditions only in two places (1 Cor 11:23; 15:3).[9] He probably received the tradition from the Jerusalem authorities – though he himself downplays this relation remarkably – and passed it on to his communities.[10] The verb παραλαμβάνω functions as an indicator of the passing on of oral tradition.[11] By reminding his readers of something they should already know, he establishes a common ground for his argument. The first quotation concerns the Last Supper. Paul wants to correct the Corinthians' practice of ritual meals and to (re)install what he claims to have been the original way of celebrating the Last Supper probably in reaction to social differences in the community.[12] For that reason he quotes part of the ritual that he has received from other authorities and handed on to the Corinthians:

> "For I received from the Lord what I also handed on to you, that the Lord Jesus on the night when he was betrayed took a loaf of bread, and when he had given thanks, he broke it and said, 'This is my body that is for you. Do this in remembrance of me.' In the same way he took the cup also, after supper, saying, 'This cup is the new covenant in my blood. Do this, as often as you drink it, in remembrance of me.'" (1 Cor 11:23–25).[13]

As a narrative the fragmentary character of this text is evident. The narrative is reduced to traces such as the remark "in the night when he was betrayed (better:

---

9 Paul refers to statements by the Lord in 1 Cor 7:10; 9:14. These cases probably reflect some kind of sayings tradition. Some scholars also take 1 Thess 4:15 to be a reference to an earlier tradition. However, λόγος κυρίου is better understood as a prophetic word that Paul has received from the exalted Lord. See the discussion in A. Malherbe, *The Letters to the Thessalonians* (Anchor Bible 32B, New York etc.: Doubleday, 2000), 267–271.
10 Hurtado, *Lord Jesus Christ*, 168.
11 *ThWNT* IV (1942), 11–15.
12 G. Theissen, "Soziale Integration und sakramentales Handeln: Eine Analyse von 1 Cor 11:17–34." *NT* 16 (1974): 179–206.
13 Translations are from NSRV.

was handed over (παρεδίδετο))". Even though this reference hints at a narrative action involving Jesus and someone who hands him over, it does not come near to being a whole and complete narrative. The main point in the quotation, namely Jesus' institution of the Last Supper, has no narrative traits. As it stands, it is an episode in a barely visible narrative.

1 Cor 15:3–7: The very small fragment of a narrative in the context of the Last Supper does not seem totally disconnected from the second instance of a tradition that Paul quotes in 1 Corinthians. By way of introduction to his extended discussion of the resurrection of the body (1 Cor 15), he introduces another piece of tradition with the same technical verb (παραλαμβάνω) (1 Cor 15:3).

> "Christ died for our sins in accordance with the scriptures, and that he was buried, and that he was raised on the third day in accordance with the scriptures, and that he appeared to Cephas, then to the twelve. Then he appeared to more than five hundred brothers and sisters at one time, most of whom are still alive, though some have died. Then he appeared to James, then to all the apostles." (1 Cor 15:3–7).

In this case it is obvious that Paul does cite a traditional formula in v. 3b-5 but it is difficult to know if the formula continues in the following verses or it is Paul who has taken over. Only in v. 8 is it certain that Paul adds himself to the traditional line of witnesses. Because of the untypical terminology of v. 6–7, these verses could be traditional material that Paul has attached to the formula in v. 3b-5.[14] Otherwise, it is difficult to explain why all on his own he should have included the otherwise unknown 500 brothers and sisters. Furthermore, the plural form of ἁμαρτία seems to be a sign of nonpauline material.[15] Although the quotation may combine two traditions and its social setting cannot be determined

---

14 Cf. W. Schrage, *Der erste Brief an die Korinther (1Kor 15,1–16,24)*, EKK 7.4 (Neukirchen-Vluyn: Neukirchener Verlag, 2001), 18–21.
15 Besides OT-quotations (Rom 4:7 = LXX Ps 31:1; Rom 11:27 = Isa 27:9 [LXX uses the singular]; 1 Thess 2:16 alludes to Gen 15:16) Paul only uses ἁμαρτία in the plural in 1 Cor 15:3.17; Rom 7:5; Gal 1:4. 1 Cor 15:3 is traditional and the formulation in 1 Cor 15:17 is dependent on that. Gal 1:4 could be traditional, as well. Rom 7:5 seems to be the only place where Paul indisputably prefers the plural. In comparison, there are 52 occurrences of ἁμαρτία in the singular in the seven undisputed Pauline letters. For an analysis of the expression ὑπὲρ τῶν ἁμαρτιῶν ἡμῶν in 1 Cor 15:3 see C. Eschner, *Gestorben und hingegeben "für" die Sünder. Die griechische Konzeption des Unheil abwendenden Sterbens und deren paulinische Aufnahme für die Deutung des Todes Jesu Christi. Band 1: Auslegung der paulinischen Formulierungen*, WMANT 122 (Neukirchen-Vluyn: Neukirchener Verlag, 2010), 107–129.

precisely, v. 3b-5, if nothing more, can be defined as an old Christological formula derived from the earliest communities.[16]

The narrative structure of this traditional formulation of Jesus' death and resurrection is, to say the least, fragmentary. The few events mentioned might together constitute some kind of structure, namely, Jesus' death, his burial, his subsequent resurrection and appearance. But these incidents are not combined into a coherent structure with a beginning, middle and end. Jesus' death can hardly be the beginning of a narrative because something must necessarily be presupposed, namely, his life. And the appearances are not fitting for an end, after which nothing should happen with necessity. Something has to follow the appearances of the resurrected Christ, e.g. his ascension. In general the events are only very loosely connected in terms of narrative logic. From Paul's quotation it is not evident why the events follow naturally from one another or why they come to an end where they do. They remain fragments of a grander narrative that is not made explicit in the context.

From these two references to tradition it is possible to reconstruct the contours of a passion narrative. But it is never set out in Paul's writings as a whole and complete narrative. This does not mean that Paul was not familiar with the passion story or even with a comprehensive narrative about Jesus. However, it is impossible to know what this story may have looked like. Other alleged traditional fragments in Paul's letters provide further elements from a possible Jesus narrative, but these parts are not intrinsically coherent.

Rom 1:3–4: One possible tradition, which Paul does not mention as being traditional, may be found in the prescript to the letter to the Romans. Paul presents his gospel

> "concerning his Son, who was descended from David according to the flesh (κατὰ σάρκα) and was declared (τοῦ ὁρισθέντος) to be Son of God with power (ἐν δυνάμει) according to the spirit of holiness (κατὰ πνεῦμα ἁγιωσύνης) by resurrection from the dead, Jesus Christ our Lord" (Rom 1:3–4).

Both the form and content of this passage point to a prepauline character. If the opening "concerning his Son" and the closing "Jesus Christ our Lord" are Paul's additions, the formulation has a striking parallelism of words and phrases.[17] Furthermore, it contains an untypical wording. Only here in the Pauline writings is Christ presented as a descendant from David; and the word σάρξ normally, and

---

16 Schrage, *Korinther (1Kor 15,1–16,24)*, 18.
17 B. Byrne, *Romans*, SacraPagina 6 (Collegeville, Minnesota: Liturgical Press, 1996), 43.

especially in parallel with πνεῦμα, has a pejorative sense in Pauline writings, which it does not have in this formulation. It is not typical of Paul to describe the resurrection as a declaration (ὁρίζειν) of God's Son; and only here do we meet the expression πνεῦμα ἁγιωσύνης. Finally, the presentation of Christ seems to fall in two stages. Prior to the resurrection Jesus was the Messiah due to his Davidic descent; at the resurrection he was appointed or installed (ὁρίζειν) as Son of God. Whether this picture should be called adoptionist or not, it seems clear that contrary to Paul's ordinary understanding of Christ as the Son of God, the formula construes the resurrection as the crucial point for his divine sonship. If Paul has added ἐν δυνάμει to the formula, this may be in an attempt to prevent an adoptionist interpretation.[18] Outside Rom 1:3–4 Paul never refers to a transformation of Jesus' identity at the resurrection. Thus it is likely that in this case, too, the prepauline formula stems from some kind of confessional formula derived from early Christian worship.[19]

The narrative structure of the formula is evident albeit again quite fragmentary: beginning at the birth of Jesus in David's family (manipulation), it ends in the installation of him as Son of God at the resurrection (sanction). The middle is lacking, as the transformation from beginning to end is very abrupt.

Gal 4:4f is one of several other texts that have been proposed as containing prepauline traditions.[20]

> "But when the fullness of time had come, God sent his Son, born of a woman, born under the law in order to redeem those who were under the law, so that we might receive adoption as children" (Gal 4:4f).

If this is a traditional formula, it only states that in the fullness of time God sent his son, born of a woman, born under the law to free those under the law. The description of the divine son as a human being born under the law is certainly presented as a precondition for the redemption that he is going to establish.[21] But the formula presents his redemptive act as having a purpose (ἵνα). As it stands, the tradition only concerns the beginning of a narrative where the sending out (manipulation) takes place. The middle and end are missing.

---

18 Byrne, *Romans*, 44.
19 Hurtado, *Lord Jesus Christ*, 107.
20 On the traditional character of Gal 4:4f see e.g. H.-D. Betz, *Galatians. A Commentary on Paul's Letter to the Churches in Galatia*. Hermeneia (Philadelphia: Fortress Press, 1979), 206f.
21 Cf. J. D. G. Dunn, *Christology in the Making. A New Testament Inquiry into the Origins of the Doctrine of the Incarnation* (second ed., Grand Rapids: Eerdmans 1989), 41f.

1 Cor 8:6: With regard to the alleged, confession-like expression in 1 Cor 8:6, it is not even possible to speak of a narrative fragment.

> "Yet for us there is one God, the Father, from whom are all things and for whom we exist, and one Lord, Jesus Christ, through whom are all things and through whom we exist" (1 Cor 8:6).

The formula states in poetic form the identity of God the Father and Jesus Christ the Lord. Even though the confession itself is grounded in Christ's salvific act, it does not recount any kind of action.[22]

Phil 2:6–11: Only one significant prepauline text contains a complete narrative structure comparable to the fragments of Rom 1:3–4. It has often been proposed that Phil 2:6–11 is a hymn derived from the earliest community which Paul integrates in his letter to support his ethical admonition.[23]

> "Let the same mind be in you that was in Christ Jesus,
> who, though he was in the form of God (ἐν μορφῇ θεοῦ),
> did not regard it as something to be exploited (οὐχ ἁρπαγμὸν ἡγήσατο)
> to be equal with God,[24]
> but emptied himself,
> taking the form of a slave (μορφὴν δούλου),
> being born in human likeness.
> And being found in human form,
> he humbled himself
> and became obedient to the point of death— even death on a cross.
> Therefore (διό) God also highly exalted (ὑπερύψωσεν) him
> and gave (ἐχαρίσατο) him the name
> that is above every name,
> so that at the name of Jesus
> every knee should bend
> in heaven and on earth and under the earth,
> and every tongue should confess
> that Jesus Christ is Lord
> to the glory of God the Father" (Phil 2,5–11).

---

[22] W. Schrage, *Der erste Brief an die Korinther (1Kor 6,12–11,16)*. EKK 7.2 (Neukirchen-Vluyn: Neukirchener Verlag 1995), 242.

[23] Cf. e.g. R. P. Martin, *Carmen Christi. Philippians ii. 5–11 in Recent Interpretation and in the Setting of Early Christian Worship*. SNTSMS 4 (Cambridge: Cambridge University Press, 1967).

[24] Translation adjusted.

The argument for the prepauline origin of the hymn consists of several observations.[25] The context in Philippians does not invite a poetic section. Even though Paul usually presents the background to his paraenesis quite thoroughly, the hymn is exceptionally long and dense if it had been constructed only to argue for internal unity in the Philippian community (cf. v. 1–4). The language contains several *hapax legomena* and unpauline expressions. Not only are the terms uncommon to Paul, the ideas are also unique in his letters, e.g. the expression ἐν μορφῇ θεοῦ used of the pre-existent Christ (v. 6), δοῦλος used of Christ (v. 7), ὑψοῦν used in an almost Johannine way (v. 9), χαρίζειν used of the relation between God and Christ (v. 7), and the tripartite construction of the universe (v. 10). Finally, there are remarkable theological differences between the hymn and Pauline theology: the hymn uses a structure of humiliation and exaltation whereas Paul prefers a scheme of cross and resurrection;[26] the idea of Christ as Lord of the universe is not typical of Paul; and the typical Pauline ὑπὲρ ἡμῶν is completely lacking from the hymn's presentation of Christ's act. To these traditional arguments for the prepauline character of the hymn we may add that it is meant in the Pauline context to have an authoritative function. It aims to establish Paul's ethical admonishment on the ground of Christ's own identity (v. 5). The rhetorical impact of this would be much more significant if the Philippians already knew and accepted this presentation of Christ. If Paul does not give the Philippians any new information in this paragraph, he is simply admonishing them to recognize the Christ they already knew as a paradigm for the proper 'Christian' attitude and behaviour.[27] These observations all point to the traditional character of the hymn. And if it is traditional, it must have had its social setting in worship in the form of some kind of devotional expression (cf. v. 10–11).

The hymn contains a whole and complete narrative in a highly condensed form. The beginning is found in the description of the divine being who is legitimately equal to God (v. 6). Because of the obedience motif that follows, a commissioning can be presupposed in this phase (manipulation). From this starting point the narrative middle phase consists of the divine being emptying himself when he takes on human form and subjects himself. His obedience culminates in death (v. 7–8). According to the narrative logic it is possible to see the transformation into human form as the qualifying test that he must pass in order to carry out the decisive test. The incarnation provides him with the proper compe-

---

[25] E.g. J. Gnilka, *Der Philipperbrief*, HThKNT 10 (Freiburg, Basel, Wien: Herder, 1968), 131–133.
[26] According to several advocates of a prepauline hymn, the phrase θανάτου δὲ σταυροῦ (v. 8) is Paul's addition to the traditional formulation, cf. e.g. Gnilka, *Philipperbrief*, 124.
[27] Cf. L. W. Hurtado, *How on Earth Did Jesus Become a God. Historical Questions about Earliest Devotion to Jesus* (Grand Rapids, Cambridge: Eerdmanns, 2005), 87.105.

tence. In human form he is able to fulfil the task he was given by being obedient unto death (performance). His death is the culmination of the middle phase from which the narrative moves into the end. Because of (διό) his obedient self-subjection, the divine being is vindicated by God, over-exalted and given the ultimate name of honour (v. 9). In the end God recognizes the protagonist's performance (sanction). The final verses connect this fundamental Christological narrative to the cultic situation behind the hymn by letting the community's devotion take place in the name that is attributed to the divine being as a consequence of the narrative trajectory (v. 10–11). In so far as the transition from middle to end, which is expressed as an 'over-exaltation', covers the resurrection from the dead and the ascension into heaven, the hymnic structure is a complete version of the narrative structure that was also involved in the traditional material from Rom 1:3–4.

It is characteristic of the traditional material that has been analysed so far that it primarily concerns the identity of Christ and only indirectly mentions his function. The main focus in the traditional fragments is on the vertical structure of Christ's story, i.e. his relation to God in his descending and ascending movement, and seldom on the horizontal structure, i.e. his relation to human beings in his act of salvation. This may be due to the devotional character of the fragments and their setting in early Christian worship that was centred on the relation to the exalted Lord.[28]

Gal 1:4: However, a few traditions take up Jesus' function, e.g.

> "who gave himself for our sins to set us free from the present evil age, according to the will of our God and Father" (Gal 1:4).

The arguments for taking this expression to be at least partly prepauline build to a large extent on the fact that 1 Cor 15:3 is explicitly traditional. The plural form of ἁμαρτία points to a nonpauline formulation.[29] Furthermore, the simplex form διδόναι seems to be unpauline.[30] But if the first half of the verse is traditional, the second half may be Paul's own interpretation of the traditional formula in

---

28 Cf. the expression "binitarian worship". Hurtado, *Lord Jesus Christ*, 134–153.
29 Cf. Betz, *Galatians*, 41f.
30 Compare Gal 2:20 and Rom 4:25, which are influenced by Isa 53, although they may be traditional themselves, cf. e.g. Dunn, *Romans 1–8*, Word Biblical Commentary 38 A (Dallas: Word Books, 1988), 224.

line with the way he formulates Christian hope in 1 Thess 1:10.[31] But even without the apocalyptic scheme Christ's self-sacrifice has a salvific effect. The motive of the act is expressed in the ὑπέρ (or according to some important MSS: περί) -sentence, that is, the self-sacrifice is meant to take away sin.[32]

In this context it is not decisive how much of the verse is prepauline and how much is Pauline. It contains a traditional formulation of Christ's action, which in a narrative structure is his decisive test (performance). But only the middle of the potential narrative is explicated. Both beginning and end are left out although the last paragraph ("according to the will of God our Father"), which is probably Pauline, hints at a commissioning that belongs to the narrative beginning (manipulation). This tradition remains a narrative rudiment.

There may be much more traditional material in Paul's letters. It is impossible to recover all the traditions that Paul may have had access to. But on the basis of the analysed passages, it is possible to summarise the characteristics of some devotional traditions that Paul was acquainted with. In the explicitly traditional statements (1 Cor 11:23–26; 15:3–4) there are no narrative structures but only the contours of a passion story mentioning the handing over, the Last Supper, the death and the resurrection. The only full-blown narrative structure to be found in the prepauline material is the one contained in the Philippians Hymn (Phil 2:6–11). It contains all phases of a narrative about a divine being who is transformed into a human being, crucified as a consequence of his obedience and finally vindicated and made lord. A number of other alleged traditional formulations contain rudiments of a narrative structure. They concern only one or two of the narrative phases and do not set up a whole and complete narrative. That God's son was born in David's tribe according to the flesh and at the resurrection was determined as God's son in power according to the spirit (Rom 1:3–4) follows a certain narrative structure but leaves out the middle part. God's sending of his son in the form of a human being born by a Jewish woman to redeem humans (Gal 4:4) is the beginning of a narrative that lacks both middle and end. Jesus' death for the sake of human sins according to his Father's will (Gal 1:4) is the narrative middle with a hint of a beginning but the end is absent. All these rudiments may fit a narrative structure but they apparently were not integrated into a single one in the earliest literary stratum. The reference to Christ's present heavenly Lordship (1 Cor 8:6) illustrates this. It could

---

[31] For an analysis of the involved traditions and their integration, see J.T. Nielsen, "The Cognitive Structures in Galatians 1:4." In *Cognitive Linguistic Explorations in Biblical Studies*, eds. J. B. Green, B. G. Howe, Cognitive Studies of Sacred Texts (Berlin: Walter de Gruyter (forthcoming)).

[32] For a thorough exegetical analysis of Gal 1:4 see Eschner, *Gestorben und hingegeben*, 383–413.

be the end phase of a narrative (cf. Phil 2:9), but as it stands in 1 Corinthians, it is detached from any narrative structure.

In conclusion, the hymnic structure is the only whole and complete narrative that it is possible to recover from the prepauline traditions. Since the protagonist is a divine person both at the beginning and the end of the narrative and since focus is on his relation to God, this structure may be called 'vertical'. The crucifixion marks the culmination of the divine being's human existence at the narrative middle and at the same time forms the turning point to his final vindication at the narrative end. But its precise function is not logically explicated. In the hymn itself it is not explained why the divine figure had to die on the cross or what effect his death had. A few other traditional fragments present Jesus as giving his life for the sake of sins. In these texts he appears as a saviour and his performance is presented as a salvific act that saves humans from their otherwise hopeless situation. This story, which could be called 'horizontal' because it focuses on Jesus' relation to humans, is never explicated in a whole and complete narrative.

Jesus' 'vertical' relation to God and his 'horizontal' function as a saviour of man do not seem to be connected in any narrative structure in the prepauline traditions. This may be due to the fact that the traditional phrases are all to be found in devotional texts (a hymn, a confession, a prayer etc.). Argumentative structures and theological reflections do not belong to this genre. It is different, though, in letter writing. Therefore, it is to be expected that longer passages in Paul's letters will integrate the two distinct dimensions of the traditional material.

Paul

It goes without saying that a detailed and comprehensive exegetical analysis of Paul's use of tradition is beyond this contribution. The purpose of this part of the essay is to observe how he transforms the traditional structures into his own foundational narrative. The traditional expressions of faith in Jesus Christ open up for an almost limitless number of possible elaborations, expansions and theological reflections. Paul transforms them into narrative structures for rhetorical purposes. The narrative structures are meant to support his arguments and admonitions. On the abstract narrative level Paul just explicates and elaborates the fragmentary structure contained in the traditional material. But in doing so with a specific purpose in mind he forms the figurative level of the narrative in a specifically Pauline manner. This configuration of the textual surface in Paul's interpretation and elaboration of the traditional structures connects the Gospel of Mark with Paul.

The investigation will be conducted on the basis of a few central texts that include a narrative structure. Paul does not recount a whole and complete Jesus story but he transforms the 'vertical' Jesus structure into a basic theological narrative. This reconfiguring of the traditional material is Paul's contribution to the continuing interpretation of the cross.

Romans 5: The fifth chapter of the Letter to the Romans can be read as Paul's interpretation of the traditional understanding of Jesus' death as being "for the sake of our sins" (ὑπὲρ τῶν ἁμαρτιῶν ἡμῶν). In the opening five verses he introduces the new situation that has arisen for the believers who are made righteous by faith (v. 1). They have peace with God, they are accepted into his mercy and enjoy the hope for his glory (v. 2), a hope that will not fail despite present sufferings (v. 3–5a) because God's love has been poured into their hearts by the spirit that was given to them (v. 5b). The presence of the spirit is a sure sign of their inclusion into a community with God.[33]

In the following paragraph (v. 6–11) Paul explains how this new situation arose by connecting Jesus' death directly to the human condition. As humans were in a dire situation, weak as they were, idolaters, sinners and even enemies of God, God showed them his love by letting Christ die for human sinners (v. 6–8). Jesus' death for the sake of human sin establishes a transition from their old situation as sinners to a new situation as righteous ones (v. 9). Here Paul adds an interpretation of another aspect of the Christ event. As his death produced righteousness, so his life will produce salvation (v. 10). The righteous will be saved from the eschatological wrath. For this reason they may boast already now as they have received reconciliation through Christ (v. 11). Both Christ's death and his resurrection are connected to the human situation so that humans participate in the Christ event. They benefit from his death and life. Paul interprets Jesus' death "for the sake of our sins" as the means for bringing reconciliation to God's enemies so that they may be both righteous and saved. This is a proof of God's love (v. 8), which the believers participate in through the spirit (v. 5). But even though the presence of the spirit connects the believers to Christ, it is still not evident how Paul conceives of the interrelation between the two stories, the human story and the Christ story. This is the topic of the next paragraph (5:12–21) as indicated by the introductory διὰ τοῦτο.

The Adam-Christ typology (v. 12–21) is meant to answer the questions that arose from 5:6–11: Why are human beings unrighteous, and how has Christ changed that situation? It is possible to argue that in his answer Paul elaborates

---

33 Byrne, *Romans*, 167.

the motif of obedience that was present in significant parts of the traditional material (v. 19; cf. Phil 2:8). Paul solves the problem by constructing two opposing corporate personalities: Adam and Christ. Their stories run in parallel but with opposite results: Adam is disobedient and so introduces sin and death into the world; Christ is obedient thereby introducing righteousness and life. As Adam's sin had consequences for all, so does Christ's righteousness. At the bottom of this comparison lies a narrative.[34] Its abstract structure corresponds to a model narrative: In the beginning the protagonist is presented with a task that he must carry out (manipulation). In the middle he tries to fulfil his duty (performance). At the end his success or failure is evaluated (sanction). The structure is invested differently in the Adam story in comparison with the Christ story but the two stories are nevertheless parallel insofar as God gives both persons a command that should lead to life. Here Adam fails; but Christ succeeds. Both cases have collective consequences. In the first case the sanction is the introduction of sin, death and condemnation into the world. Hence the structure may be called a *dysangelion*. In the second case the result is righteousness and mercy. This story is consequently an *euangelion*.[35] The next paragraph concerns the individual's connection to the foundational theological structure through the ritual inclusion into the death of Christ (6:1–11).

Against the background of the proposed traditional material, three aspects of Paul's interpretation merit attention. First of all he explicitly connects Christ's death for the sake of sins with a transformation of the human situation. Secondly, he elaborates the obedience motif to become the central element of a Christ narrative that is parallel to the Adam narrative. Christ is successful in the very narrative structure in which Adam failed. At this point he implicitly connects the obedience motif with the "death for the sake of our sins". Thirdly, for both features it is significant that Paul is concerned with the connection between the fundamental Christ narrative and the individual human being. He relates the two stories by the idea of participation. The believer is incorporated into Christ's narrative through a ritual repetition of Christ's death in the individual's baptism. And as the relation between 5:5 and 5:8 demonstrates, the presence of God's spirit is proof that the believer participates in God's love that was presented in the Christ event.

---

34 O. Davidsen, "The Structural Typology of Adam and Christ. Some Modal-Semiotic Comments on the Basic Narrative of the Letter to the Romans." In *The New Testament and Hellenistic Judaism*, eds. P. Borgen, S. Giversen (Aarhus: Aarhus University Press, 1995), 244–262.
35 Davidsen, "Structural Typology of Adam and Christ", 250.

1 Cor 1:18–2:16: Another significant text for Paul's interpretation and rhetorical use of Jesus' death is the first two chapters of 1 Corinthians. They do not include a whole and complete narrative but rather highlight the one point that Paul focuses on: the cross. But Paul's interpretation of the cross presupposes an understanding of Christ as the one who is being crucified. It is essential to Paul's argument that Christ is understood as a divine being; otherwise Paul's argument will not work.

Paul constructs his argument on the 'vertical' Christological structure that was present in the Philippians Hymn: Christ descends from his divine position to suffer the infamous death on the cross and returns to his heavenly abode. This structure contains a radical opposition between the high status position in heaven and the lowly status position on the cross (1:18–25). The fact that the most elevated phenomena – God's power and God's wisdom – are revealed in the most disgraceful object – the cross – is at the very core of Paul's argument in central parts of the Corinthian correspondence. It means first and foremost that all value systems are turned upside down.[36] What is good, fair and right on earth is the very opposite as seen from a heavenly perspective. And also the other way around: what is rejected and unwanted in the human world has the opposite character in the divine world. Or in even fewer words: here we meet an "Umwertung aller Werte". Because of its general character this interpretation has been made a headline of Pauline theology to be understood as a theology of the cross.

This understanding has two immediate consequences. It creates a social dualism based on cognitive competence.[37] Human beings are divided into two groups according to their perception of the cross. Either they understand it as a revelation of God's power and wisdom; or else they see it as foolishness and a scandal (1:18). Secondly, it overturns ordinary hierarchies. Economic, social, rhetorical etc. hierarchies should not be allowed in the community (1:26–31). Both these consequences are fundamental for the argument of both 1 and 2 Corinthians.

The background to this Pauline interpretation of the cross seems to be the 'vertical' Christological structure to be found, for instance, in the Philippians Hymn. Remarkably, Paul focuses solely on the cross as the fundamental part of the foundational Jesus narrative. Of course, he presupposes the resurrection;

---

[36] Cf. e.g. D. B. Martin, *The Corinthian Body* (New Haven, London: Yale University Press, 1995), 59–63.

[37] H. Tronier, *Transcendens og transformation i Første Korintherbrev*, Tekst og Tolkning 10 (København: Akademisk Forlag, 1994), 68–75.

but it is never explicated. The cross is the main event in the Jesus narrative according to this Pauline interpretation (cf. 2:2).

A *conclusion* concerning Paul's interpretation of tradition must divide the Pauline reception of the traditional material into two lines of interpretation. From Romans 5 we may conclude that Paul interpreted the traditional understanding of Jesus' death as being "for our sins" in a narrative structure. The death is an act of obedience that constitutes the protagonist's performance and consequently corresponds to the preceding manipulation and the subsequent sanction. Included in this interpretation is the question of how the believer participates in the Christ event. Paul's answer refers to the presence of the spirit and the ritualistic repetition of Christ's death in baptism. These main foci in this line of interpretation, namely, the Christ event as an *act of obedience* and the *individual's participation* in Christ's accomplishment, can be found in e.g. Rom 3:21–26; 2 Cor 5:18–19 and Gal 2:15–21.

In the second line of interpretation Paul uses the event of the cross as a model for Christian behaviour. 1 Corinthians 1–2 unfolds the cross as the basis for the *reversion of value hierarchies*. The Pauline context of the traditional hymn in Philippians brings the *paradigmatic function* of the Christological structure to the fore (Phil 2:5). And in 2 Corinthians the paradigmatic structure of the Christ event lays the ground for large parts of the argument (e.g. 2 Cor 2:14–17; 4:3–4; 10:3–6; 11:30–33). In this interpretation of traditional formulations Paul focuses on the application of the paradigmatic value reversing structures of Christian life.

Whereas the formulae derived from Early Christian worship both present Christ in a 'vertical' structure and refer to his 'horizontal' function as saviour by dying "for the sake of our sins", Paul connects these traditions and explicates their content in coherent theological arguments. The obedience motif and the salvific understanding of Jesus' death are united in his explanations of the Christ event in a whole and complete narrative structure (Romans 5). In this way he combines the 'vertical' structure of the Christ myth with the 'horizontal' structure of the salvific death. In the other line of interpretation he incorporates the 'vertical' Christology into a 'horizontal' paraenetic context (1 Corinthians 1–2). Both the Adam-Christ typology and the theology of the cross represent a second-level reflection since Paul is here concerned with the logical coherence and consequences of the belief that is expressed in devotional terms in the celebrations of the community.

Mark

The Gospel of Mark is a whole and complete narrative. It has a beginning, middle and end, and the different parts follow each other in a logical and coherent way. It is, of course, also a deeply theological work, but its theology is neither presented in devotional statements nor in rhetorical arguments but in narrative structures placed in time and space with acting persons and figures. I will present the structure briefly.[38]

The Markan Structure: At the beginning of the Markan narrative, Jesus receives the task he is going to fulfil in his earthly life. At the baptism the divine voice announces to him that he is "my son, the beloved" (1:11). But at this point the announcement includes an obligation (manipulation). Jesus must perform his identity as Son of God by proclaiming, healing and saving (performance). Before he can complete the obligation in the narrative middle, he must prove that he has the proper competence (qualification). He does this when the Spirit brings him into the desert and Satan tempts him (1:12–13). Next the narrative turns into the middle phase, in which Jesus is expected to fulfil the roles that belong to his identity as Son of God. At two significant points in the narrative the Markan Jesus explicitly directs the reader's attention to the task he must accomplish. At 10:45 he defines the purpose of the coming of the Son of Man as that of serving instead of being served and of giving his life as a ransom (λύτρον) for many. In the Gethsemane garden the conflict between his obligation and his own will is played out in the repeated prayer about being liberated from his duty (14:32–42). In the Gospel of Mark the role of Son of God includes the obligation to give his life for the sake of others. The narrative plot is constructed around the question whether or not Jesus will fulfil his obligation as Son of God. When the Roman officer at the foot of the cross announces that he in truth (ἀληθῶς) was Son of God (15:39), the text indicates that in his death on the cross Jesus has successfully fulfilled the task that he was given at his baptism. The empty tomb and the implied resurrection and ascension at the end of in the narrative are to be understood as the divine recognition of the accomplished mission (sanction). In this structure Jesus' status as Son of God is dependent on his role as saviour. The failure or success of the protagonist is decided with regard to his ability to carry out the salvific action, because his obedience is defined as his death as a

---

38 Cf. O. Davidsen, *The Narrative Jesus. A Semiotic Reading of Mark's Gospel* (Aarhus: Aarhus University Press, 1992).

ransom for many. The act of obedience concerns not only Jesus' identity but also his function.

The Gospel of Mark has a perfect narrative structure. It places the cross event as the decisive test in the narrative middle. It furthermore establishes a course in which the protagonist successfully performs his obligation and on that account achieves a divine identity. Structurally, this corresponds to the hymnic structure of the Philippians Hymn except for the fact that Mark tells a 'horizontal' story about the earthly Jesus whereas the Hymn presents a 'vertical' story about a divine character. In accordance with Paul's reconfiguring of the devotional material Mark attributes a purpose to the infamous death on the cross: it serves as a ransom for many. Even if this formulation presents another interpretation of Jesus' death than the traditional formula "for the sake of our sins", both statements let the story of Jesus affect the believers' situation. His death on the cross initiates a new human existence. By letting Jesus' death have this function Mark connects two dimensions in his story. Jesus' relation to God, i.e. the 'vertical' relation in which he fulfils his obligation, is combined with Jesus' relation to human beings, i.e. the 'horizontal' relation in which he serves as saviour. Both Mark and Paul interpret the most infamous point in the life of the earthly Jesus as the narrative culmination and a salvific act and hence insert human beings into Jesus' story as beneficiaries of his deed.³⁹

The passion predictions in the gospel (8:31; 9:31; 10:26) support this interpretation and add other aspects to the understanding of Jesus' death.

Mark 8:31: Jesus teaches his disciples about the passion after they have realized that he is Christ (8:29). The idea that the Christ should suffer an infamous death by the hands of the Jews is, of course, a scandal to Peter (8:31). Jesus' reaction (8:33) corresponds to the overall obedience motif as already presented. But the next paragraph offers another interpretation of Jesus' death (8:34–38). It is depicted as a model for the proper Christian behaviour. Not only must Jesus' adherents imitate Jesus' attitude by following him and metaphorically taking up their own cross, they are also expected to accept a reversal of ordinary values.⁴⁰ One

---

39 If the formula in Mark 10:45 is traditional (so e.g. M. Hengel, *The Atonement. The Origins of the Doctrine in the New Testament* [Philadelphia: Fortress Press, 1981], 34), the interpretative strategy of Paul and Mark is even more alike.
40 It is a matter of dispute whether or not the expression "to take up one's cross" is metaphorical. Fundamental for the concrete interpretation that sees some kind of persecution as the social setting for the text is E. Haenchen, "Die Komposition von Mk VII 27-IX 1 und Par." *NT* 6 (1963): 81–109. But see also, e.g., A. Y. Collins, *Mark: A Commentary*. Hermeneia (Minneapolis: Fortress Press, 2007), 409. However, it is not altogether convincing that Mark refers to an actual

has to lose one's life to save it. And one does not get any profit from gaining the whole world, if one's soul is lost. It is necessary to reject one's ordinary life to guard the community with Jesus. Only the relation to Jesus leads to eternal life. The paradigmatic status of Jesus' death on the cross includes a complete reversal of ordinary value systems.

Mark 9:31: The context of the second passion prediction confirms the interpretation of the first one.[41] After Jesus has repeated the prophecy of his death and resurrection, he takes up the theme about being superior (μείζων) (9:33–37). In the narrative this had been the topic of a conversation between the disciples (9:34). Jesus responds that the one who wants to be the first must be the last and everybody's servant (διάκονος) (9:35). He illustrates his point by placing a child in the midst of the disciples (9:36) and claiming that by receiving one of the children in Jesus' name one receives Jesus himself (9:37). As was the case with the first passion prediction, the second is followed by an invitation to reverse the ordinary value hierarchies. Jesus' own disgraceful death is paradigmatic of the fact that his adherents should reject customary markers of status. The child and the servant are to be considered as prototypical for people with a superior status within the Christian community because they are normally placed on an inferior level in the social hierarchical system.

Mark 10:32–34: The third passion prediction is also set in a context where the topic is social status. The conversation with the rich man (10:17–22) and the conversation that follows with the disciples about the conditions for being saved (10:23–27.28–31) precede the prediction. The conversation with Peter even ends in the pregnant statement "many of the first shall be last, and the last first" (10:31). After Jesus' statement about his future death and resurrection there follows a discussion with the sons of Zebedee (10:35–40) which explicitly concerns the question of status. In his final answer (10:41–45) Jesus reverses the hierarchies and places the slave (δοῦλος) at the top of the hierarchy. The Son of

---

context of persecution (cf. Mark 13:13). On the contrary, Paul's use of terminology of cross and crucifixion (e.g. Gal 2:19–20; 6:14) points to a metaphorical understanding. Cf. T. Engberg-Pedersen, "Hvorfor tager Geert Hallbäck fejl om Markus og Paulus?" In *Den store fortælling. FS Geert Hallbäck*, eds. S. Holst, C. Petterson (København: Forlaget Anis, 2012), 29–44 (33f). See also Engberg-Pedersen's contribution in this volume.

41 The relation between the passion prediction and the following instruction is normally not noted by commentators, not even when 9:30–37 is read as a single paragraph, e.g. by B .M. F. van Iersel, *Mark. A Reader-Response Commentary*, JSNTSS 164 (Sheffield: Sheffield Academic Press, 1998), 305.

Man with his special obligation illustrates this (10:45). Just as is the case with the two earlier passion predictions, so the context of the third one makes Jesus' death paradigmatic for the reversal of values in the Christian community. But Jesus' dialogue with the sons of Zebedee adds another aspect to Mark's presentation of Jesus' death. In his answer he refers to the chalice and to baptism. In the narrative they are symbolic references to Jesus' death.[42] When Jesus remarks that the sons of Zebedee will drink the chalice that he will himself drink, and be baptised with the baptism that he will himself be baptised with, there probably is a reference to their death as martyrs. However, seen in a somewhat broader perspective the reference to baptism and the Last Supper also point to the individual repetition of Jesus' death in the Christian rituals. This ritualistic participation in Jesus' death is necessary in order to benefit from his obedience.[43]

The Gospel of Mark contains an interpretation of the cross that mainly focuses on two aspects. First of all Jesus' *obedience* is presented as part of a narrative structure that constructs his death as the task he as Son of God has to carry out. Furthermore, in this narrative structure Jesus' death is interpreted as a ransom for many. It has a salvific character. The narrative structure combines the 'vertical' role as Son of God with the 'horizontal' function as saviour. Secondly, the contexts of the passion predictions present Jesus' death as *paradigmatic* for the *reversal of value hierarchies* that is expected to be characteristic of Christians. The believers constitute a cognitive community based on an understanding of social hierarchies and value systems. A third aspect may be the *ritual repetition* of Jesus' death as a means of being included in the Christ event and enjoying its effect.

In the Gospel of Mark the interpretation of Jesus' death takes the form of a whole and complete narrative. The narrative structure with a beginning, a middle and an end constitutes the basis for the presentation of Jesus' death as the fulfilment of a task he has been given. But the narrative genre also demands that the events take place in time and place. Theological structures are presented as narrative actions performed by narrative persons and figures. For that reason the understanding of Jesus' death is played out in the basic narrative structure and the other interpretations are added on through the discourse at the narrative surface.

---

42 Cf. Collins, *Mark*, 496 f.
43 This would correspond to Paul's interpretation of eucharist and baptism (1 Cor 11:17–34; Rom 6:1–14), cf. Engberg-Pedersen, "Hvorfor tager Geert Hallbäck fejl", 36.

Conclusion

This investigation has been concerned with three genres. Prepauline fragments present an understanding of the death of Christ in devotional language. The most complete prepauline narrative conceived of Christ as a divine being who in complete obedience descended to suffer an infamous death on the cross and afterwards returned to the heavenly world. Other traditions were not concerned with the divine starting point but stated that the Son of God died for the sake of our sins. Because of the devotional language, the theological logic of these representations of the Christ event was not explicated.

Paul, on the other hand, elaborates his understanding of Jesus' death in a rhetorical context. His presentation of the cross often forms the basis for his arguments in the letter. He develops the traditions into theological structures in order to create the most convincing arguments. His main focus is on the salvific effect of Jesus' death, and he establishes a connection between Christ's obedience and his death for the sake of our sins. Furthermore, he points to the paradigmatic character of Christ's death on the cross for a reversal of ordinary value hierarchies.

Mark's interpretation of Jesus' death takes place in a whole and complete narrative. The understanding of Jesus' divine identity as including his role as saviour is played out in a narrative in which Jesus must fulfil his obligation and give his life as ransom for many. At the same time this act of obedience is a model for the reversal of values in the Christian community.

On the basis of these observations, the tentative conclusion is that Mark builds on and continues Paul's interpretation of the earliest traditions about Jesus' death. He constructs his narrative on the basis of Paul's interpretation of Christ's obedience as a willingness to give his life for the sake of our sins. This obligation constitutes the narrative core in the Gospel of Mark. At the same time, Mark just as Paul sees this event as constituting an "Umwertung aller Werte". Mark cannot elaborate this theologically but he integrates it into his narrative by placing references to the cross in contexts that concern status and hierarchy.

Finn Damgaard
Persecution and Denial – Paradigmatic Apostolic Portrayals in Paul and Mark

Introduction

In the introduction to his article on the author of the Gospel of Mark (hereafter, Mark) as a Paulinist, Joel Marcus argues that the negative things Paul and Mark write about Peter and the members of Jesus' family are among a number of 'striking similarities' between Paul's letters and Mark. Though the figure of Peter is not in focus in Marcus' article, in his conclusion he does suggest that a study of Paul's and Mark's attitudes to Peter would support his thesis, since "not everyone was as negative as Paul about Peter and Jesus' family – but Mark was".[1]

Mark's picture of Peter is notoriously complicated, and there is no scholarly consensus about it. In this article I aim therefore to consider the basic question of how Mark portrays Peter and to discuss the consequences of my findings for the general question of the relationship between Paul and Mark. Since many of those scholars who argue for Mark's dependence on Paul often assume that Mark's negative portrait of Peter is influenced in one way or the other by Paul's attitude to Peter,[2] an examination of the specific relationship between Mark's portrayal of Peter and Paul's letters is needed. Scholars disagree strongly about whether the negative portrayal of Peter in Mark is polemical or sympathetic. As Robert W. Herron has shown,[3] redaction critics in general support the polemical interpretation of Mark's presentation of Peter, while literary critics main-

---

[1] Joel Marcus, "Mark – Interpreter of Paul." *NTS* 46 (2000): 473–487, esp. 487. In his commentary on Mark, however, Marcus modifies this statement. Though he still finds a parallel between the negative things said about Peter in Paul and Mark, he acknowledges that the polemic against Peter is somewhat different in the gospel, since it is not linked to the issue over Law observance, as it is in Galatians 2, see Joel Marcus, *Mark 1–8*, Anchor Bible 27 (New York: Doubleday, 2000), 74.
[2] Most noticeably Joel Marcus (see above) and Michael Goulder in his "A Pauline in a Jacobite Church." In *The Four Gospels 1992. Festschrift für Frans Neirynck*, vol 2, eds. F. Van Segbroeck, C. M. Tuckett, G. Van Belle & J. Verheyden (Leuven: Leuven University Press, 1992), 859–875, esp. 875, and in *A Tale of Two Missions* (London: SCM Press LTD, 1994), 16–23.
[3] Robert W. Herron, Jr., *Mark's Account of Peter's Denial of Jesus. A History of Its Interpretation* (Lanham, New York & London: University of America Press, 1991), 8–9, 89–115.

ly interpret the negative portrayal as a literary device:[4] though Peter is portrayed negatively, the listeners would still identify and sympathize with him. Redaction critics, by contrast, have viewed Mark's portrayal of Peter as a case of polemic either against a theology supported by an alternative tradition within the community of Mark or against specific historical persons.[5] It is hardly surprising that different approaches produce different interpretations: while a literary analysis is interested in the sophisticated narrative world, redaction criticism is hunting for intriguing relations between the text and the world behind the text, i.e. the author's agenda and the community to which the text was originally addressed.

In this article, however, I shall seek to combine the two approaches to Mark. While I agree with those literary critics who have argued that Mark's negative portrayal of Peter is actually sympathetic, I shall also search for the historical and theological agenda that may have brought about Mark's portrayal of Peter. I disagree with the view that Mark's portrayal of Peter is polemical as turned against someone or something. Neither does the portrayal, in my view, reproduce a Pauline polemic against Peter (in fact, Peter is not just portrayed polemically in Paul's letters, Paul's attitude to Peter is much more complicated). Though there may be some similarities between Paul's and Mark's portrayals of Peter, I do not find these similarities very significant. In both portrayals, Peter is a kind of leader of or spokesman for the apostles (Gal 1:18; 2:7–9; 1 Cor 9:5; Mark 1:36; 8:29–30; 9:5; 10:28; 14:37) and is the recipient of a resurrection appearance (1 Cor 15:5; Mark 16:7). In both portrayals, Peter also somehow changes his behaviour (Gal 2:11–14, Mark 14:29–31, 66–72). However, in contrast to Paul's criticism of Peter's changed behaviour in Galatians, Peter's failure is not the last word that is said about Peter in Mark. Peter remembers, breaks down and weeps, and the readers will assume that his experience of grief at his own failure will lead to a positive change of behaviour more or less of the type we find in Paul, who changed his opinion of the Christians, abandoned his persecution of the church and became what he had been predestined to be from his mother's womb: an

---

[4] See, for instance, Robert C. Tannehill, "The Disciples in Mark: The Function of a Narrative Role." *JR* 65 (1977): 386–405, Ernest Best, "Peter in the Gospel According to Mark." *CBQ* 40 (1978): 547–558, idem, *Mark: The Gospel as Story* (Edinburgh: T & T Clark, 1983), and Augustine Stock, *Call to Discipleship: A Literary Study of Mark's Gospel* (Wilmington, DL: Michael Glazier, 1982).

[5] See, for instance, Alfred Kuby, "Zur Konzeption des Markus-Evangeliums." *ZNW* 49 (1958): 52–64, Joseph B. Tyson, "The Blindness of the Disciples in Mark." *JBL* 80 (1961): 261–268, Theodore J. Weeden, "The Heresy That Necessitated Mark's Gospel." *ZNW* 59 (1968): 145–158, idem, *Mark – Traditions in Conflict* (Philadelphia: Fortress, 1971), and Werner Kelber, "Mark 14:32–42: Gethsemane, Passion Christology and Discipleship Failure." *ZNW* 63 (1972): 166–187.

apostle (Gal 1:15). While interpreters have usually searched for parallels between the portrayals of Peter in Paul and Mark, I will pursue another parallel – to my mind a far more interesting and significant one – between the Markan Peter and another apostle in Paul's letters, namely Paul himself. Mark's ambiguous portrayal of Peter might be read as reproducing another ambiguous apostolic portrayal, namely Paul's self-portrayal in his letters[6].

Mark as an interpreter of Peter?

In a recent article, Joel F. Williams claims that inside views are a pervasive narrative feature in Mark. "Mark's gospel", he argues, "often takes on a point of view that is internal to the characters themselves, by portraying the perceptions, thoughts, and emotional reactions of various characters"[7]. Though Williams is primarily interested in the inside view in relation to the story about the rich man in Mark 10:21, he also notices that Mark's picture of Peter is unique in that Peter is the only character who remembers (Mark 11:21; 14:72). Mark frequently narrates what different characters see and hear, but the act of remembering is only attributed to Peter – the leading disciple. Williams' observation is interesting since it might explain how the tradition known from Papias came into being. As is well known, there existed a tradition at the beginning of the second century that connected Mark (which was of course originally written anonymously) with Peter himself. According to the well-known fragment from Papias of Hierapolis, which is preserved in Eusebius' *Ecclesiastical History* (3.39.15), the author of this gospel, by the name of 'Mark', was present when Peter taught about Jesus. According to Papias, Mark became Peter's ἑρμηνευτής when he wrote down his gospel. Although in itself the theory is unlikely to be true,[8] it is quite interesting

---

[6] I am grateful to Geert Hallbäck and Anne Vig Skoven for having suggested this idea to me during a research seminar on *Paul and Mark beyond the Letter/Gospel-Divide* in Copenhagen, 24–27 August 2011.
[7] Joel F. Williams, "Jesus' Love for the Rich Man (Mark 10.21): A Disputed Response toward a Disputed Character." In *Between Author & Audience in Mark. Narration, Characterization, Interpretation*, ed. Elizabeth Struthers Malbon, New Testament Monographs 23 (Sheffield: Sheffield Phoenix Press, 2009), 145–161, esp. 150. I am grateful to Elizabeth Struthers Malbon for this reference.
[8] However, Martin Hengel has argued in favour of the reliability of the theory in his article, "Probleme des Markusevangeliums." In *Das Evangelium und die Evangelien. Vorträge vom Tübingen Symposium 1982*, ed. Peter Stuhlmacher (Tübingen: J. C. B. Mohr [Paul Siebeck], 1983), 221–265, esp. 252–257. Recently, Richard Bauckham has also supported the authenticity of the Papias tradition in his *Jesus and the Eyewitnesses: The Gospels as Eyewitness Testimony* (Grand

that the Gospel of Mark had been connected with Peter at an early stage (the fragment of Papias is normally dated to c. 120–130). It is also likely that the Papias fragment may reflect an even earlier tradition given the fact that Papias is rather critical of Mark's work, which "makes it more likely that he inherited the tradition of the apostolic authority of Mark and had to come to terms with it, rather than that he invented it".[9] The last chapter of the Gospel of John also seems to presuppose a tradition in which Peter is connected with other written traditions. The notion that the beloved disciple has testified "to these things and has written them" (John 21:24) should probably be read in the context of the chapter's portrayal of Peter and might indicate that the author was familiar with a tradition that identified a written gospel with Peter. Rather than 'domesticating the gospel', as Richard M. Hill has suggested,[10] I would suggest that those interpreters who later saw a close connection between Mark and Peter actually based their identification on a careful reading of the gospel.[11]

My aim in this article is not to propose any historical relationship between Mark and Peter. Mark probably was *not* an interpreter of Peter. Instead, I shall claim that the author used the figure of Peter – albeit rather implicitly – to connect his gospel to an apostolic authority in order to acquire authority for his own account.

The figure of Peter in Mark

It may be helpful to begin with a quantitative analysis in order to get an impression of how many times Mark actually refers to Peter in comparison with the other synoptic gospels. Whereas both Mark and Matthew refer to Simon/Peter

---

Rapids: Eerdmans, 2006), 202–239. See also the article by Michael F. Bird that claims that the Gospel of Mark is an early synthesis of the theology of Peter and Paul, "Mark: An Interpreter of Peter and Disciple of Paul." In *Paul and the Gospels: Christologies, Conflicts, and Convergences*, eds. Michael F. Bird & Joel Willitts, Library of New Testament Studies (London: T&T Clark, 2011), 30–61, esp. 32.
9 Adela Yarbro Collins, *Mark: A Commentary*. Hermeneia (Minneapolis: Fortress Press, 2007), 4.
10 This is argued by Richard M. Hill in *The Role of Peter in the Gospel of Mark: A Study in Authority in the Early Church* (Unpublished dissertation, Drew University, 1994), 220.
11 Justin Martyr's repeated references to the gospels as "memoirs" (ἀπομνημονεύματα) of the apostles may also derive from Mark's use of the language of remembering in relation to Peter (see *Dial.* 100.4; 101.3; 102.5; 103.6, 8; 104.1; 105.1, 5, 6; 106.1, 3, 4; 107.1 and *1 Apol.* 33.5; 66.3; 67.3). At one place in the *Dialogue with Trypho*, Justin even refers to Peter's memoirs (*Dial.* 106.3) which seem to refer to the gospel of Mark, cf. Claus-Jürgen Thornton, "Justin und das Mk-Evangelium." *ZNW* 84 (1993): 93–110.

25 times, Luke refers to him 30 times. However, if we compare these numbers with the number of words in the three gospels, we see that the word Simon/Peter occupies 1/443 of Mark against 1/648 of Luke and 1/722 of Matthew.[12] Even though Matthew, for instance, adds the story about Peter's walking on the sea (Matt 14:22–33), Mark refers more frequently to Peter than do Matthew or Luke. My aim is not to compare Matthew (or for that matter Luke) and Mark here, but as readers of Mark we should take care not to read Peter through the lens of Matthew. Matthew's unique narratives about Peter were probably invented by Matthew himself.

However, it is not only in quantitative terms that Peter appears to be important in Mark. If we go into detail about Mark's use of Peter, we find that he is a recurring figure who is important both at the beginning, in the middle and at the end of the narrative. Peter (Simon) is Jesus' first disciple (Mark 1:16), he is selected as one of the twelve apostles and his name appears first on the list of the twelve (Mark 3:14–19). His name is also the last name to be mentioned in the gospel, and it seems to be especially emphasized in the speech to the women at the empty tomb (Mark 16:7). Thus his name forms a kind of *inclusio* for the entire work. As Richard Bauckham has argued, an *inclusio* may have been a literary device that indicated eyewitness testimony according to the conventions of popular biographical works (Bauckham 2006, 124–127 and 132–145).[13] According to Bauckham, Lucian and Porphyry also used the *inclusio* of eyewitness testimony in their biographies of *Alexander the False Prophet* and *Plotinus*. In Lucian's account, the name of Rutilianus, a Roman aristocrat and supporter of Alexander, forms the *inclusio*, and in Porphyry's work, it is Amelius, one of Plotinus' most prominent disciples, who has this function. Though Lucian and Porphyry wrote their biographies considerably later than Mark wrote his gospel, their use of the device may well attest to a literary convention that belonged to the tradition of Graeco-Roman biographies.

Peter also fulfils an important narrative function in the gospel's plot: he is the first human being in the gospel to confess Jesus as Christ. The confession appears almost in the middle of the gospel in the episode at Caesarea Philippi (Mark 8:29) which leads to Jesus foretelling his suffering, death and resurrection.

---

12 I take the quantitative analysis from Reinhard Feldmeier, "Die Darstellung des Petrus in den synoptischen Evangelien." In *Das Evangelium und die Evangelien*, Vorträge vom Tübinger Symposium 1982, ed. Peter Stuhlmacher (Tübingen: J. C. B. Mohr [Paul Siebeck], 1983), 267–271, esp. 267.
13 Bauckham argues that Mark really used a Petrine testimony in his gospel, whereas I am more inclined to the view that the author wants his readers to believe that he had used a Petrine testimony.

The episode is followed by an extended passage concerning discipleship (Mark 8:27–10:52) which is characterized by a tension between Jesus' understanding of his mission and the disciples' – including Peter's – misunderstanding of it. However, Peter is not only a plot functionary, as in the case, for instance, of the figure of Judas. The audience is given more knowledge about Peter than is strictly necessary for the plot (for instance, we are told that he has a mother-in-law, which means that he either is or has been married; it is also said that he has a house together with Andrew, see Mark 1:29–30) and he is from time to time transformed into a rounder character, for instance in the denial story. Also the fact that he is first named Simon and then even renamed Peter (Mark 3:16) encourages the audience to construct him as an individual. In addition, the omniscient narrator presents Peter's thoughts on several occasions (Mark 9:6; 11:21; 14:40, 72). This also encourages the audience to take an interest in him and perhaps even to take a sympathetic view of him. The audience may also recognize a development of Peter's inner personality, when he finally breaks down and weeps after his three denials of Jesus (Mark 14:72). His tears may be seen as indicating a growing self-knowledge, and the audience may assume that he now sees clearly his own failings and shortcomings. He remembers that Jesus had predicted that he would deny him and that he had himself asserted that even if everyone else would become a deserter, he himself would not (Mark 14:29). Indeed, Peter is again and again singled out because of his failings. He is called Satan because of his rejection of Jesus' teachings concerning his suffering, death and resurrection (Mark 8:32) a moment after he has confessed Jesus' true identity. He also misjudges the situation in the transfiguration scene (Mark 9:1–13) and falls asleep in the Gethsemane scene (Mark 14:32–42). In both these scenes, however, the omniscient narrator uses an inside view in order to gain the audience's sympathy for Peter.[14] Though Peter fails in his endeavours, the result is not, in my

---

14 In the transfiguration scene, the omniscient narrator himself cuts into the narrative and explains Peter's inappropriate suggestion by claiming that: "He [Peter] did not know what to say, for they [Peter, James and John] were terrified" (Mark 9:6). As in other places of the gospel, the inside view is here used to arouse the audience's sympathy for Peter. Just as we usually sympathize with people we find amusing, the audience would take an interest in Peter, because of his failure in finding something to say in this extraordinary situation. The inside view is also used in order to arouse the audience's sympathy for Peter in the Gethsemane scene in which Peter is again singled out because of his failings. Just like James and John, Peter cannot keep awake but repeatedly falls asleep while Jesus is in agony a little way off. When Jesus returns and finds the three disciples sleeping, he addresses not, as we might expect, all three of them, but only Peter: "Simon, are you asleep? Could you not keep awake one hour?" (Mark 14:37). As we know, Peter does fall asleep again, and here too the narrator cuts in: "[...] their [Peter, James and John] eyes were very heavy; *and they did not know what to say to him*" (Mark 14:40). The

view, that the listeners dissociate themselves from him. On the contrary, it seems to me that they become painfully aware of how difficult it is to be Peter.

At the end of the gospel the narrator also shows that there is continuity between the readers' sympathy for Peter and Jesus' final assessment of him. In the final reference to Peter the suspense (if there ever was such a thing) concerning his fate is resolved. Peter is not cursed; on the contrary, he is, once more, singled out from among the other disciples (Mark 16:7) and asked to follow Jesus, who is headed for Galilee. The reference to Peter in Mark 16:7 could also be read as a subtle reference to Peter's function as the first witness to the resurrection (compare 1 Cor 15:5 and Luke 24:34). Though Mark's portrayal of Peter primarily focuses on his mistakes, the narrator does not turn his readers against Peter, nor does he portray Jesus as someone who parts company with Peter. In addition, Peter seems to have been important for Mark as a purveyor of tradition. Thus the last reference to Peter in Mark 16:7 might be seen not only as a rehabilitation of Peter after all his denials, but also as a loose suggestion to the readers concerning the chain of tradition.[15] In this way, Mark might actually exploit Peter in order to gain authority for his gospel in much the same way as Paul does in Galatians when he portrays himself as standing toe-to-toe with the apostolic authority, Peter, and rebukes him for his inconsistent behaviour.

But if the author really wanted his readers to see Peter as a purveyor of tradition, why did he focus so much especially on Peter's failings? In what follows, I shall examine Paul's portrayal of himself in the letters, since one may find a striking similarity of those autobiographical remarks of his with Mark's picture of Peter. Just as Mark focuses on Peter's mistakes, so Paul focuses on his own

---

observant listener will recognize that earlier in the transfiguration scene the narrator had attributed almost the same motivation to Peter. Even though the narrator here also includes James and John, the listener will probably first of all think of Peter, since he was singled out at the beginning of the scene. Just as in the transfiguration scene, Peter fails in his endeavours, but that does not necessarily mean that the listener becomes estranged from him. In my view, the author's use of the inside view has exactly the opposite effect: the listener will now begin to sympathize with Peter.

15 Against John Drury who, on the contrary, claims: "Indeed, he [Mark] presents them [the disciples] as so obtuse and wrongheaded that it is extremely difficult, within Mark's own terms, to account for his having any coherent or dependable tradition to use at all", John Drury, "Mark." In *The Literary Guide to the Bible*, ed. Robert Alter & Frank Kermode (Cambridge, MA: Belknap, 1987), 402–17, esp. 404. So also Theo K. Heckel, who claims that Mark portrays all the disciples including Peter in a negative light and in this way prevents "daß bestimmte Menschen in der Vergangheit zu Garanten der kirchlichen Tradition werden können", Theo K. Heckel, *Vom Evangelium des Markus zum viergestaltigen Evangelium*, WUNT 120 (Tübingen: Mohr Siebeck, 1999), 62.

mistakes in his portrayal of himself as a persecutor of the church. I shall argue that Mark focused especially on Peter's failings because he wanted to create a paradigmatic apostolic portrayal comparable to Paul's self-portrayal.

Paul's self-portrayal as a persecutor of the church and later developments of this portrait

In three of his letters, Paul claims that he persecuted the church (Gal 1:13, 23; Phil 3:6; 1 Cor 15:9). Though the claim does not serve an autobiographical purpose, but rather an argumentative one, Paul actually himself indicates that he became well known in his own time as one "who was then (ποτε) our persecutor, [but] now (νῦν) proclaims the faith that he then (ποτε) was trying to destroy" (Gal 1:23). Paul's reference in Galatians to his former lifestyle is his way of defending the point made in Gal 1:12 that his gospel did not come from a human source, but from direct revelation of Jesus Christ. The contrast between "then" and "now" – between Paul as persecutor and Paul as preacher – is a crucial thought figure behind the letter. The temporal contrast prepares for the important antitheses later in the letter between flesh and Spirit, law and grace, and slavery and freedom. The contrast is also applied to the Galatians themselves in 4:8–11: between the past, when the Galatians did not know God, but were enslaved to idols, and the present, when they have come to know God. But the temporal contrast is not only a contrast between "then" and "now", but also between the present and the future. If the Galatians will accept the need to be circumcised as the Galatian troublemakers want them to, they will actually return to the former state of slavery, according to Paul. Paul's "then and now contrast" in his autobiographical remarks thus serves "a paradigmatic function, to contrast Paul's conversion from Judaism to Christianity with the Galatians' inverted conversion".[16]

While in Galatians there is no sign of a guilty conscience in Paul's reference to his persecution of the church (see also Phil 3:6), in 1 Corinthians Paul claims that he is "the least of the apostles, not qualified to be called an apostle" precisely because he has persecuted the church (1 Cor 15:9). This contrast in Paul's attitude may even be found in his use of figurative language in the two letters: in Galatians he claims that God separated (ἀφορίσας) him as an apostle from his mother's womb (Gal 1:15), whereas in 1 Corinthians he calls himself an abortion (ἔκτρωμα) to whom the Lord appeared as the last of all (1 Cor 15:8). In 1 Corin-

---

16 George Lyons, *Pauline Autobiography. Toward a New Understanding*, Society of Biblical Literature (Atlanta: Scholars Press, 1985), 150.

thians Paul also makes the opposite claim of the one he makes in Gal 1:12 to the effect that the gospel came through a revelation. In 1 Corinthians, by contrast, he claims that he did receive his gospel from tradition (1 Cor 15:3). As Jack T. Sanders has argued, it is most likely that the discrepancy is to be explained from the situational context against which Paul argues in either case.[17] While according to Paul, his opponents in 1 Corinthians were rejecting the tradition,[18] it is acceptance of tradition (namely, circumcision) that poses the problem in Galatians. In order to defend his position in the two letters, Paul accordingly claims in 1 Corinthians that his gospel was not transmitted apart from tradition, but in Galatians that it was in fact transmitted apart from tradition. The discrepancy in the two letters in the way Paul describes his persecution of the church should be read in this light. While in Galatians Paul may defend his authority by referring to his personal revelation of Jesus Christ, he cannot claim a unique personal revelation in 1 Corinthians while at the same time arguing for the necessity of tradition. Instead he stresses the fact that he was actually the last to whom the Lord appeared. However, in portraying himself as "the least of the apostles" and "not qualified to be called an apostle", Paul does not refer to any guilty conscience because of his persecution of the church. Instead, his portrayal is meant to present himself in accordance with the fundamental theme of the letter, namely that "what is low and despised in the world" was chosen by God (1 Cor 1:28).

As is well attested, Paul's "biography of reversal"[19] was developed further in later Christian literature such as Ephesians, Colossians, and the Pastorals. As Martinus C. de Boer has argued, the picture of Paul as the "redeemed persecutor" becomes paradigmatic for all Christians in these letters.[20] In 1 Timothy, for in-

---

[17] Jack T. Sanders, "Paul's 'Autobiographical' Statements in Galatians 1–2." *JBL* 85 (1966): 335–343, esp. 339.
[18] Most noticeably in relation to the resurrection of the dead (1 Cor 15:12–58). Paul's stress on the tradition can also be found in 1 Cor 7:10; 9:8–10, 14; 11:23.
[19] John Howard Schütz, *Paul and the Anatomy of Apostolic Authority*, SNTSMS 26 (Cambridge: Cambridge University Press, 1975), 133.
[20] Martinus C. de Boer, "Images of Paul in the Post-Apostolic Period." *CBQ* 42 (1980): 359–380, esp. 371. In later times, the image of Paul as a redeemed sinner became extremely influential. For Augustine, for instance, Paul became "his prototype of the sinner saved despite himself because of God so willed", cf. Paula Fredriksen, "Paul and Augustine: Conversion Narratives, Orthodox Tradition, and the Retrospective Self." *JThS* 37 (1986): 3–34, esp. 26. Luther, too, found in Paul's biography his own autobiography: "Paul's life experience interprets Luther's life experience. This reflects an exegetical back-and-forth between text and interpreter where Luther's sense of identity and mission are being formed and confirmed", cf. Mickey L. Mattox, "Martin Luther's Reception of Paul." In *A Companion to Paul in the Reformation*, ed. R. Ward Holder (Leiden: Brill, 2009), 93–128, esp. 121.

stance, Paul is portrayed as the prototypical sinner and receiver of God's grace (1 Tim 1:16). Paul's self-portrayal as a persecutor of the church has here been generalized. It is never specified what it is that he had persecuted and there is no mention of his Jewish past. Instead, it is claimed that Paul was a "blasphemer" and a "violent man" (1 Tim 1:13), both of which are common entities in catalogues of vices. By transforming Paul's offence, his persecution of the church, into more general vices, the author made Paul's story applicable to his Gentile readers. Paul became a model with whom they could identify. For just like Paul, the converted Gentiles had to abandon their wicked ways and give their lives to the service of virtue.

The author of Acts (hereafter, Luke) also exploited Paul's self portrayal as a persecutor of the church. Acts often draws a contrast between Saul the persecutor and Paul the missionary to the Gentiles, and in each account of Paul's 'conversion', his role as the great persecutor is emphasized (Acts 9:4, 6, 13–14; 22:7–8; 26:14–15). Paul's persecution is here used as a foil to display God's miraculous intervention. According to Luke, Paul was engaged in acts of violence against his victims. He had Christians imprisoned (Acts 8:3; 22:4; 26:10) and voted for the death penalty against them (Acts 9:1; 26:10). As has been stressed by several scholars, Luke seems, however, to exaggerate Paul's brutality probably in order to highlight all the more his later missionary activity. According to Hultgren, "Paul does not understand persecution as a procedure which ends in the death of the victim".[21] He does not himself claim that he persecuted the church "violently" as καθ' ὑπερβολὴν (Gal 1:13) has been translated in the NRSV. The expression probably refers not to the intensity of the persecution, but rather to the intensity of Paul's zeal (see also Phil 3:6). Luke not only exaggerated Paul's brutality in order to emphasize God's transforming power, the exaggeration also creates an important contrast between Saul the persecutor (Acts 9:1–2) and Paul the persecuted (Acts 9:23–29): from now on Paul is persecuted for the same reasons as those for which he had himself persecuted.[22] While in the first account of Paul's 'conversion' Luke focuses on the transformation of Paul: his change from persecutor to persecuted, Luke turns to an autobiographical discourse in the two other accounts of the 'conversion'. As Jean-François Landolt has empha-

---

[21] Arland J. Hultgren, "Paul's Pre-Christian Persecutions of the Church: Their Purpose, Locale, and Nature." *JBL* 95 (1976): 97–111, esp. 108.
[22] Concerning the portrait of Paul as suffering in Acts, see Jens Schröter, "Paul the Founder of the Church: Reflections on the Reception of Paul in the Acts of the Apostles and the Pastoral Epistles." In *Paul and the Heritage of Israel*, eds. David P. Moessner, Daniel Marguerat, Mikeal C. Parsons & Michael Wolter (London: T&T Clark, 2012), 195–219, esp. 206–212.

sized such a turn indicates "a stronger focus on Paul's character".[23] Paul here recalls the circumstances of his own 'conversion' in order to appeal to his listeners to recognize the need for repentance (Acts 26:19–20, 29). Luke thereby turns Paul into a paradigmatic figure by making his journey of conversion "representative of the conversion of all believers" (Landolt 2012, 307).

A parallel between Mark's portrayal of Peter and Paul's biography of reversal?

As we have seen, Paul pictured himself as persecuting the church in order to back up different arguments in his letters. By using the contrast between "then" and "now", he created an effective self-portrayal that he then applied to the Galatians. And in 1 Corinthians he characterized himself as "the least of the apostles" because of his persecution in order to go on from there to assert his apostolic authority. Later writers, too, applied Paul's biography of reversal to their own readers, and Paul's self-portrayal became paradigmatic for later Christians as a model for those who had turned away from the evils of the world. Paul was the redeemed persecutor, the great sinner whose life had been completely transformed. In light of Paul's own use of his autobiographical remarks of persecution, and given that the picture of Paul as a former persecutor was well known not only in his own time but also became extremely popular after his death, I would suggest that Mark created his ambiguous portrayal of Peter in imitation of Paul's biography of reversal. Paul's autobiographical remarks not only exerted an influence on how later Christians wrote his biography, they also had an impact on the way Peter was portrayed in Mark. By imitating Paul's popular biography of reversal, Mark created a paradigmatic portrayal of Peter. Of course, Mark could not portray Peter as a persecutor of the church, but he could picture him as a coward in his denials of Jesus and thereby pave the way for a Petrine version of the biography of reversal, which had been shown to be so effective in the case of Paul. This suggestion may explain why the author focused on all Peter's failures although he also wanted his readers to believe that Peter was a transmitter of tradition. The negative portrayal of Peter was not meant to be polemical against him; rather, it was a literary device.

---

23 Jean-François Landolt, "'Be Imitators of me, Brothers and Sisters' (Philippians 3.17): Paul as an Examplary Figure in the Pauline Corpus and the Acts of the Apostles." In *Paul and the Heritage of Israel*, eds. David P. Moessner, Daniel Marguerat, Mikael C. Parsons & Michael Wolter (London: T&T Clark, 2012), 290–317, esp. 303.

Just as Paul claims that the intention behind his former persecution of the Church was to honour God, so Mark either portrays Peter's words or actions as having a positive intention even though they are often corrected or rebuked, or else portrays Peter as being weak in the denial scene, but in a way that eventually leads to his self-realization of his failure and presumably to his change. In contrast to Paul's rebuke of Peter in Galatians, which only gives the readers a negative impression of Peter since he is portrayed as acting inconsistently out of fear (Gal 2:2), Mark's account of Peter's denial actually seems to indicate that Peter got the better of his fear. Thus the readers would probably imagine that Peter's grief had its source in self-recognition. Though we have seen that Paul's self-portrayal in 1 Corinthians as "the least of the apostles" and "an abortion" was probably more an expression of sophisticated rhetoric than of a genuinely guilty conscience, the expressions were very likely read as painful autobiographical remarks. Mark may therefore have constructed his portrait of the tearful Peter on the basis of Paul's autobiographical remarks in 1 Corinthians. By attributing Paul's biography of reversal to Peter, Mark became able to make use of the highly effective pattern of a biography of reversal also in relation to the story he was primarily interested in telling, namely that of Jesus' earthly ministry.

It is of course impossible to decide if Mark *intentionally* constructed his picture of Peter by imitating Paul's biography of reversal. But as we shall see, later Christians did read Peter's biography as a biography of reversal[24] and they also found his biography to be comparable to Paul's autobiography. For instance, while Mark had not found it necessary to develop in detail how Peter turned to Christ after the resurrection, Luke hints at Peter's reversal at the end of his gospel (Luke 24:12, 34) and when Peter appears again at the beginning of the Book of Acts his reversal has been completed (Acts 1:15–26). As often noted, there is also a parallel portrayal of Peter and Paul in Acts.[25] Both men are led

---

24 See now Markus Bockmuehl, *Simon Peter in Scripture and Memory* (Grand Rapids: Baker Academic, 2012), especially 153–163.
25 As is well known, this parallel portrayal was especially important for Ferdinand Christian Baur's view of early Christianity. Baur argued that the parallel portrayal was composed in order to reconcile the Petrine and Pauline parties in early Christianity. See F. C. Baur, *Paulus, der Apostel Jesu Christi* (Stuttgart: Verlag von Becher & Müller, 1845), 1–14. For recent studies of the parallels between Peter and Paul in Acts, see, Susan Marie Praeder, "Miracle Worker and Missionary: Paul in the Acts of the Apostles." *Society of Biblical Literature Seminar Papers*, 1983 (Chico: Scholars Press, 1983), 107–129, esp. 114–120, Andrew C. Clark, "The Role of the Apostles." In *Witness to the Gospel: The Theology of Acts*, ed. I. Howard Marshall & David Peterson (Grand Rapids: Eerdmans, 1998), 169–190, esp. 185–189 and Jürgen Becker, *Simon Petrus im Urchristentum*, 2. edition (Neukirchen-Vluyn: Neukirchener Verlagsgesellschaft, 2011), 120–121.

by the holy spirit (*Peter:* Acts 2:4; 4:8; 10:19, 44–46; *Paul:* Acts 13:4, 9; 16:6–7, 20:22), and learn about God's plan through visions (*Peter:* Acts 10:3, 17; *Paul:* Acts 16:9–10; 18:9), their gospel message is very similar and both of them believe that the Jews as well as the Gentiles are co-heirs (*Peter:* Acts 10:34–48; 15:7–11; *Paul:* 13:46; 17:22–31). They both have a miraculous aura (*Peter:* Acts 5:15; *Paul:* 19:11–12), perform miracles (*Peter:* Acts 3:1–11; 5:12–16; *Paul:* 14:3, 8–10; 28:3–6), exorcisms (*Peter:* Acts 5:16; *Paul:* 16:16–18), resurrections (*Peter:* Acts 9:32–43; *Paul:* Acts 20:7–12) and miracles of punishment (*Peter:* Acts 5:1–11; *Paul:* Acts 13:6–12). Both speak with παρρησία (*Peter:* Acts 2:29; *Paul:* Acts 9:28; 13:46; 14:3; 26:26; 28:31), are successful (*Peter:* Acts 2:41; 4:4; *Paul:* Acts 13:42–43) and act courageously before the Jewish council (*Peter:* Acts 5:26–33; *Paul:* Acts 23:1–10). They are both imprisoned (*Peter:* Acts 4:3; 5:18; 12:3–5; *Paul:* 16:19–24; 21:33) but experience a miraculous release (*Peter:* Acts 5:19–25; 12:6–19; *Paul:* 16:25–40) and have a tense relationship with parts of the congregation in Jerusalem at some point in their career (*Peter:* Acts 11:2–3; *Paul:* 15:1–6) (cf. also Becker 2011:120–121). The most important parallel for our purpose, is, however, the portrayal of both men as preachers of repentance, which is one of the most repeated themes in Acts (*Peter:* Acts 2:38; 3:19–26;[26] 5:31; 8:22; 11:18; *Paul:* Acts 13:24, 38–39; 17:30; 20:21; 26:20). Luke moreover claims that both men experienced a change or reversal prior to their new ministry as preachers of repentance. Luke's Jesus even addresses them in a similar way when he twice calls them with their former name in the crucial narratives about their 'turning' (*Peter:* "Simon, Simon", Luke 22:31; *Paul:* "Saul, Saul", Acts 9:4; 22:7; 26:14). Just as later Christian authors often found Paul's story to be paradigmatic for their readers, so they also explicitly applied Peter's biography of reversal to their readers.[27] In the *Acts of Peter*, for instance, Peter's biography of reversal appears next to Paul's, and both apostles portray themselves and their biographies as paradigmatic for the Roman Christians. Though Peter is the main protagonist in the *Acts of Peter*, the author begins by introducing Paul. The readers learn that Paul has recently been living among the Roman Christians, but he is now about

---

[26] Peter's speech in Solomon's portico is characterized by Robert Tannehill as "the repentance speech *par excellence*", cf. Robert C. Tannehill, "The Function of Peter's Mission Speeches in the Narrative of Acts." *NTS* 37 (1991), 400–414, esp. 406, italics in original.

[27] Just as the image of Paul as a redeemed sinner gained new importance in Protestantism, so did the similar image of Peter. See for instance Karen Bruhn, "Reforming Saint Peter: Protestant Constructions of Saint Peter the Apostle in Early Modern England." *The Sixteenth Century Journal* 33 (2002): 33–49. A modern example of Peter as the exemplar of the forgiven sinner can be found in Daniel J. Harrington's book, *What are we hoping for? New Testament Images* (Collegeville: Liturgical Press, 2006), 30.

to leave, as he will be headed westward for Spain, and to be replaced by Peter. As we shall see in a moment, Paul's and Peter's respective biographies of reversal are portrayed as being quite comparable, differing mainly due to their different roles as a missionary on the one hand and as someone who reconverts the Roman Christians on the other hand. While in his farewell discourse to the Romans Paul is portrayed as using the "then and now contrast", which is in fact not particularly suited to the Romans' situation (it seems more to anticipate a missionary speech which the author might expect him to deliver in Spain),[28] Peter's introductory speech to the Roman Christians is more to the point. For just as the Romans had been led astray by Simon the Magician, so Peter argues that he was also led astray when he denied Jesus:

> You men who are here, hoping in Christ, you who suffered a brief temptation, learn why God sent his Son into the world, or why he begot him by the Virgin Mary, if it were not to dispense some mercy or means of salvation. For he meant to annul every offence and every ignorance and every activity of the devil, his instigations and powers, by means of which he once had the upper hand, before our God shone forth in the world. Since with their many and manifold weaknesses they fell to death by their ignorance, Almighty God had compassion and sent his Son into the world, and I was with him. And I walked on the water and survived as a witness; I confess I was there when he was at work in the world performing signs and wonders. Dearest brethren, *I denied our Lord Jesus Christ, not once, but thrice*; for those who ensnared me were wicked dogs, just as the prophet of the Lord said. *But the Lord did not lay it to my charge; he turned to me and had mercy on the weakness of my flesh, so that I wept bitterly; and I mourned for my little faith, having*

---

[28] "And Paul lifted up his voice and said, 'Eternal God, God of heavens, God of the unspeakable majesty, who has established all things by your word, who has broken the bond fixed to man, who brought the light of grace to all the world, Father of your holy Son Jesus Christ, we jointly beseech you through your Son Jesus Christ to strengthen the souls who were once unbelieving but now believe. *Once I was a blasphemer, but now I am blasphemed; once I was a persecutor, now I suffer persecution from others; once I was an enemy of Christ, now I pray to be his friend. For I trust in his mercy and promise; for I believe that I am faithful and have received remission of my former sins.* Therefore, I also exhort you, brethren, to believe in God the Almighty and put all your trust in our Lord Jesus Christ, his Son. If you believe in him, no man will be able to uproot you from his promise. Likewise you must bend your knees and commend me to the Lord, who am about to go to another nation, that his grace may go before me and my journey be prosperous, that it may receive his holy vessels and that the believers, thanking me, who proclaimed to them the word of the Lord, may become firmly established in the faith.' And the brethren wept for a long time and with Paul they implored God and said, 'O Lord Jesus Christ, be with Paul, and bring him safely back to us, for we know our weakness which is still in us.'" (*Acts of Peter*, ch. 2, p. 47.12–34). The translations of the *Acts of Peter* are taken from James K. Elliott, *The Apocryphal New Testament* (Oxford: Clarendon Press, 1993). The page and line numbers after the chapter numbers refer to Lipsius' edition, R. A. Lipsius & M. Bonnet, *Acta Apostolorum Apocrypha*, Pars I (Leipzig: Hermann Mendelssohn, 1891).

been deceived by the devil and disobeyed the word of my Lord. And now I tell you, men and brethren, who are convened in the name of Jesus Christ, Satan the deceiver sends his arrows upon you too, to make you leave the way. But do not be disloyal, brethren, nor fail in your mind, but strengthen yourselves, stand fast, and doubt not. *For if Satan has subverted me, whom the Lord esteemed so highly, so that I denied the light of my hope, causing me to fall and persuading me to flee as if I believed in a man, what do you think will happen to you, who have just become converted? Do you imagine that he will not subvert you to make you enemies of the Kingdom of God and to bring you by the worst error into perdition? For every one whom he deprives of the hope in our Lord Jesus Christ is a child of perdition for all eternity. Repent therefore, brethren whom the Lord has chosen, and be firmly established in the Almighty Lord, the Father of our Lord Jesus Christ, whom no one has ever seen nor can see except he who believes in him (Acts of Peter, ch. 7, p. 53.20 – 54.23).*

If in his portrayal of Peter Mark had intentionally wanted to create a paradigmatic apostolic portrayal comparable to Paul's, such as I have suggested, he very much succeeded, as we may judge from the *Acts of Peter*. While the author of the *Acts of Peter* provides the readers with only a glimpse of Paul's biographical "then and now" preaching, since already at the beginning of the work Paul is on his way to Spain on his neverending missionary tour, it is Peter and his biography of reversal which are in focus.[29] The author seems to have found Paul's biographical preaching extremely effective in a missionary context, whereas he saw Peter's biography as being more advantageous for deluded or lapsed Christians. This has probably to do with the different times when Paul and Peter are portrayed as committing their 'errors'. The author probably found Paul's biography to be more valid in a missionary context, since he had obviously not believed in Christ prior to his change of heart in contrast to Peter's denial and subsequent repentance which happened while he was a disciple (though Paul had himself used his biography of reversal in a non-missionary context in Galatians in order to exhort the Galatians not to accept circumcision).

Conclusion

As has been pointed out by literary critics, Mark's negative portrait of Peter is primarily a literary device. Redaction critics have accordingly, to my mind, been wrong to identify the portrait of Peter with Mark's portrait of Jesus' family,

---

29 According to Bockmuehl, "the author of the *Acts of Peter* presents the figure of the apostle [Peter] as a graphic embodiment of his own message of repentance and conversion". Bockmuehl interprets the story of Peter's *return* to Rome to face martyrdom as a "redemptive reversal" of his previous denial (Bockmuehl 2012:161).

which is thoroughly negative. However, if Mark did not produce his portrait of Peter as part of a polemic, we will need, as redaction critics, to look for other reasons for Mark's ambiguous portrayal of Peter. As I have argued, Mark might have focused especially on Peter's failings because he wanted to create a paradigmatic apostolic portrayal comparable to Paul's self-portrayal. But the author also does use the figure of Peter to make a persuasive connection back to the disciple tradition (a move that eventually succeeded, as the Papias tradition demonstrates). For all his criticism of the disciples and Peter in particular, Mark actually employed the figure of Peter to connect the gospel to an apostolic authority. In so doing, he probably rescued his gospel from just being absorbed into Matthew, Luke and John and thereby consigned to oblivion.

Mark may indeed have been a Paulinist, as Joel Marcus has argued in reopening the debate about Mark and Paul, but if he was, it was in spite of Paul's negative attitude to Peter. Instead, it was under the influence of Paul's complicated portrayal of himself.[30]

---

[30] I would like to thank Professor Troels Engberg-Pedersen for reading and commenting on a draft of this study. I also wish to thank the participants in the New Testament Velux seminars, University of Copenhagen, for their constructive suggestions for improvement.

List of Contributors

Eve-Marie Becker is Professor for New Testament exegesis at Aarhus University

Gitte Buch-Hansen is Professor at the University of Copenhagen

Finn Damgaard is a Post Doctoral student at the University of Copenhagen

Ole Davidsen is Associate Professor at Aarhus University

Jan Dochhorn is Associate Professor at Aarhus University

Troels Engberg-Pedersen is Professor of the New Testament at the University of Copenhagen

Kasper Bro Larsen is Associate Professor at Aarhus University

Joel Marcus is Professor of New Testament and Christian Origins at Duke University

Mogens Müller is Professor of the New Testament at the University of Copenhagen

Jesper Tang Nielsen is Professor at the University of Copenhagen

Heike Omerzu is Professor at the University of Copenhagen

Anne Vig Skoven (†) was a Ph.D. student at the University of Copenhagen

Gerd Theissen is Professor em. at Heidelberg University

Oda Wischmeyer is Professor em. at the University of Erlangen-Nuremberg.

Index of Subjects and Names[1]

A fortiori argument 154, 160
Abjathar 154
Abraham 223, 224, 225, 226, 230, 231, 232, 234, 235
Achimelekh 154
Acts of the Apostles 58
Adam 31, 56, 161, 162, 163, 286, 287, 289
– myth 258
– Christ myth 269
– covenant 268
Adamic connotations 161
Adamic motifs 167
Adoption 218, 225
Adscriptions 97
Allegoresis, allegorization, allegory 21, 25, 52, 60, 115, 116
Allegorists, radical 174, 180, 182
Ambassadorial letter/epistle 129, 134, 136
ἀναστοιχείωσις 227, 228
Anonymity 102
Anthropological distinction (inside/outside) 179–180, 183
Antioch 140, 174
Apocalyptic 32, 36, 40, 43
Apocalypticism 195–196
Apology 52
Apophthegma 148, 153
Apostle 136
Apostolic council 174, 182
Aristotle, Aristotelian 190, 275, 276
ἀρχή 72, 77
Audience 87, 127, 135, 137, 138, 139, 140, 141
Author 87, 133, 135, 136, 137, 138, 141, 145
Authority 126, 127, 137, 138, 139, 187
Author-oriented expectations 95
Authorship 127, 136, 139

Baptism 240
Barnabas 74, 80, 81, 82, 83, 84, 86
βασιλεία 104

Baur, Ferdinand Christian 13, 15
Biography 97
Biography of reversal 303, 306
Book 141, 142, 143, 145
Brevitas 138
Bridegroom 154
Bultmann, Rudolf 244

Catalogues of vices 56
Christ 287
– myth 250, 258
Christological titles 150
Christology 54, 57, 60, 114, 149, 154
– Adamic 162
– Davidic 154, 165, 166
– God 159, 166
– high 158, 166
– implicit 151
– two-stage 217, 218
Christusmythos 245
Cicero 90
Circumcision 46
Claudius 69
Clean and unclean (food) 57
Cluster of literary activity 88
Cognitive distinction (knowledge/ignorance) 180
Communication 127, 130, 136, 137, 146
Community-letter 97
Comparativism 246
Competence 276, 282, 288, 290
Conceptual variations 100
Condensed narrative 254
Congregation 107, 108
Constructivism 59
Contemporary literary activity 142
Conversion in Mark 198, 207
– in Paul 203
Corinth 140, 142
Covenant theology 111
Covenantal nomism 220, 221, 262

---

1 The index of subjects and names is compiled by stud. theol. Anna Bank Jeppesen (Aarhus).

Cross   36, 37
Crucifixion   31, 36, 37, 38

Dan   35
David   151, 155
Death, of Jesus   36, 38, 40, 42, 57, 284
Decomposition   153
Demonic powers   42
Demonic responsibility   42
Demons   19, 43
δευτέρα γένεσις (second generation)   229, 230
Deutero-Pauline letters   58
Deutero-Pauline tradition   178, 183, 186
Devil   43, 162
Dibelius, Martin   107, 116
Divorce   56
Dualism, dualistic   31, 56
Dunn, James   268
Dysangelion   258

Early Christian literature   145
Early principate   98
Earthly Jesus   34
Einmalig   35
ἐκκλησία   57, 102
ἐκπύρωσις   228
Elijah   114
Elisha   114
Emotionality   95
Engberg-Pedersen, Troels   115
Epistemology   38
Epistolary theory   94
Epistolography   93
Ethnicity   26, 214, 226, 237
εὐαγγέλια   63, 64, 68, 71, 77
εὐαγγελίζεσθαι   63, 65
εὐαγγέλιον   31, 56, 63–76, 80, 102, 258
Eucharist   240
Eusebius   114
Exorcism   31, 38, 43
Exorcistic technique   150
Expanded narrative   254
Expansion   254

Faith   31
Family, Jesus'   31

Fasting   150
Flesh   165
Foods   48, 49
Formgeschichte   114, 153

Gan Eden   163
Gattungsbezogene Erwartungen   91
Genealogy   223, 224, 226, 231, 236, 240
Generalizing readings   246
Generation   225, 230
Generic expectations   101
γένος   239, 242
Genre   87, 93, 141
Genre-building   134
Genre-theory   131, 132
Gentile Christ believers   170, 174, 182, 187
Gentiles   32, 44, 46
Gethsemane   40
Getting-in   220, 222, 223, 226
Gospel   137
– genre   130, 190
– of Luke   114
– of Mark   113, 114, 115, 116
Grundtvig, Nikolaj Severin   107

Halakah   170, 186
Hallbäck, Geert   115
Hand-washing   46, 48, 172
Hardening of the heart   56
Hartman, Lars   113, 114
Harvesting   152
Hellenists   181
Herodians   149
Herrschaftsrhetorik   67, 68–71, 77
Hidden author   146
Historical Jesus   21, 22, 25, 172–174
History of literature   102
Holy Spirit   237
Homer   60
Horizontal   285, 289, 291, 293
House-churches   57, 139
Human condition   100
Hypocrisy   179

Influence   253
Initium   123, 125
Intentio auctoris   122

Interdiction 260
Intertextual relations 253
Intertextuality 59, 60, 244
Jerusalem 141, 175–176
Jesus 35, 137, 138
Jewish covenant 234
Jewish dietary customs 45–49, 180–182
Jews 32, 44, 45
Jezebel followers 174
John the Baptist 17, 19
Josephus 178
Judaizers 187

καί 160
Kerygma 103, 245, 249
Kierkegaard, Søren 245
κληρονόμος 161
Koine 101
Koinos 176
Kosher/Kashrut 45–49, 180–182
κράσις 229
κύριος 151, 158

Last Supper 277, 278, 284
Law 32, 38, 234
Leben-Jesu-Forschung 16, 25
Lectionary hypothesis 113
Letter, genre of 190, 208
Letter-hermeneutics 96
Literacy 93
Literal and metaphorical reading 191–193, 195, 196–197, 198
Literary
– activity 87, 88, 143
– communication 90
– criticism 59
– culture 144
– function 141
– genre 93
– milieu 99
– strategy 127, 130, 141
– text 127
Literaturszene 87
Lord 160
Love command 57
Lucian 299
Luke-Acts 58

λύτρον 56

Man from heaven, the 162
Manipulation 276, 280, 282, 284, 287, 289, 290
Marcion 114
Matthew 174
Mark/Markus (author) 83–86
Messianic secret 26, 217, 239
Messianology 149, 164
Meta-historical 100
Method 171–172
– of comparing *Mark* and *Paul* 189–190, 201
Miracles 34, 35
Missionary propaganda 103
Modality 260
Mosaic Law 20
Mythos 264

Narrative 127, 133, 141, 190, 207, 208, 254, 275, 276, 278, 279, 281
– comments 100
– criticism 133
– exegesis 271
– interpretation 245
– *Jesus* 250
– literature 134
– and philosophy 190, 207
– thinking 245
Narrativity 245
Narratology 244, 274
New covenant 110
New Perspective on Paul 26, 214, 221, 222, 226
Nicolaitans 174

Obedience 287, 289, 291, 293, 294
Obligation 290, 291
Ontological distinction (god/human beings) 177–178, 180
Opening 127
Opening clause 124
Oral performances 135
Oral proclamation 96
Orality 94
Order of creation 157

Papias of Hierapolis 29, 297, 298, 310
Paradigmatic 246
Paradosis 104, 177
Paraenesis 59, 108, 115
Parody 132
Parousia-motif/Parusie 65, 68, 69, 94
Participation 293
Participation paradigm 220
Passion narrative 34, 279
Patrilinearity 224
Pauline Christianity 167
Paulinism 51, 52, 57, 58, 60, 61, 249
Performance 276, 283, 284, 287, 289, 290
– criticism 89
Pesch, Rudolf 267
Peter/Petrus 56, 65, 67, 70, 73, 74, 78–86, 291, 298
Pharisees 149, 152, 174–176, 179
Philo 174, 176, 180, 182–83
Phraseology 254
Plane of content 247
Plane of expression 247
Plot 275
Plutarch 90
πνεῦμα 166
Posteriority 92
Pragmatics 141
Pre-historiographical literature 105
Pre-Markan traditions 104
Pre-Pauline traditions 39
Prescription 260
Pre-test 261
προσωποποιία 233
Pseudepigraphy 102
Public recitals 135
Publication 94
Purity/impurity 46, 47, 48, 170, 176, 181–182
– ethical 182–186

Q hypothesis 199–200, 206
Qumran 179
Quotations 142

Recitatio 88
Redaction criticism 54, 60, 168
Religious literature 134, 136

Repentance 307
Resurrection 31, 36, 284
– appearances 37, 40
Revelation 177–178
Reversal, of ordinary values 291, 292
Reversion, of value hierarchies 289, 293, 294
Rewritten Bible 117
Roman historiography 99
Rome 140

Sabbath 151, 152, 155, 156
Sacrifice 43
Salvation story 256
Sanction 276, 280, 283, 287, 289, 290
σάρξ 165
Satan 261
Satire 179
Scripture 143, 144
Semiotics 247
Septuagint 60, 141, 143, 145, 176
Sermon 107
Shma Jisrael 158
Simon the Magician 308
Sinners 56
Sitz im Leben, of Mark 191–193
Social distinction (insider/outsider) 177, 180
Social practice 89
Son
– of Adam 265
– "of David" 151
– of God 265
– of Man 18, 20, 149, 150, 161, 162, 163, 165, 167, 265
Soteriology 56
Specifying readings 246
Speech-in-character 233
Spirit 165, 225, 227, 228, 229, 230, 241
Staying-in 220, 221, 223, 226
Stoic cosmology 214, 219, 222, 227
Strauss, David Friedrich 15
Suetonius 87
Superscriptions 97
Synoptic tradition 104
Syntagmatic 245

Tabellarii 94
Temple 241, 242
– curtain 36, 38, 44
Temptation 259
Tenement churches 139
Tertium comparationis 115, 258
Test 259
Theologia crucis 76, 83, 243
Theologizing in Mark 208–209
Theology of the cross 36, 39, 44, 56, 57, 170, 249, 288
Thucydides 91
Tiberius 64, 70, 77
Timothy 160
Titulus 102
Torah 46, 157
Torah-observance 45
Tradition 42, 104
Transfiguration 20
Trial 259
Tronier, Henrik 115
Tun-Ergehen-Zusammenhang 194
Two-ways paradigm 223

Typology 243
– explicit 243
– implicit 243

υἱὸς ἀνθρώπου 161, 165
Umwertung aller Werte 288
ὑπομονή 56

Value systems 288
Vertical 283, 285, 286, 288, 289, 291, 293
Vespasian 63, 70, 71
Vicarious sacrifice 252
Vice lists 183–186
Virgil 91
Virgin birth 237, 242
Volkmar, Gustav 116, 248

Weber, Max 115
Werner, Martin 24, 25, 248
Worship 113

Zebedee, Sons of 293

Index of References[1]

Mark
1:1–15   31
1:1–8   17
1:1–4   18, 143
1:1–3   122, 125
1:1   31, 56, 66, 70, 72, 73, 76, 102, 114, 122, 123, 124, 245, 250
1:2–4   124
1:4–13   122, 123
1:7–8   18
1:9–15   31, 56
1:9–11   217, 239
1:10   242
1:11   35, 290
1:12–13   43, 259, 290
1:12   263
1:13   162, 164
1:14–8:26   19
1:14–15   19
1:14   56, 66, 70, 72, 100, 102, 145
1:16–20   19, 149
1:17   197
1:18   197
1:20   197
1:21–3:6   149, 150
1:21–28   19, 149
1:23–28   56
1:23   176
1:24   43
1:26–27   176
1:26   43
1:27–28   165
1:29–34   20
1:32–39   56
1:35–39   20
1:40–45   20
2–3   55
2:1–3:6   148
2:1–28   149, 150
2:1–12   20, 22, 158
2:5   154

2:7   158
2:10   149, 154
2:13–17   20, 22
2:15–3:6   55
2:16   149, 153, 175
2:17   32, 56, 149, 154
2:18–3:5   20
2:18–20   150
2:18   175
2:19–20   149, 150, 154
2:19a   154
2:19b-20   150
2:19b   154
2:20   36, 154
2:23–28   147–168 passim
2:23   152
2:24   153, 155, 175
2:25–26   151, 155, 164, 165
2:27–28   147–168 passim
2:27   156
2:28   149, 158
3:1–5   150
3:6   36, 42, 175
3:7–19   149
3:7   20
3:11   176
3:20–35   20
3:20–21   32, 56
3:22–30   267
3:22   176
3:30   176
3:31–35   32, 56
3:32   240
3:35   240
3:36   198
4:1–34   20
4:10–20   48
4:10–12   31, 56
4:10   181
4:11–12   37
4:12   38

---

[1] The index of references is compiled by stud. theol. Anna Bank Jeppesen (Aarhus).

4:20   198
4:21–25   37
4:35–41   20
5:1–8:21   241
5:1–20   20, 56
5:2   176
5:7   43
5:8   176
5:13   176
5:21–43   20
5:34   240
6:1–6   20
6:4   240
6:7   176
6:30–46   20
6:30–44   241
6:45–52   159
6:47–52   20
6:53   175
7   55
7:1–23   20, 45, 46, 47, 169–187 passim
7:1–5   46
7:1–4a   172
7:1   175, 176
7:2   176
7:3–5   177
7:3–4   172
7:5   176, 177
7:6–13   177
7:6–7   173, 179
7:6   178–180
7:8–9   177
7:8   177, 178
7:9   156, 179
7:11   172, 177
7:13   177
7:14–23   57, 179
7:14–19   173
7:14   175
7:15   46, 47, 48, 55, 170, 173, 174, 176, 179, 187
7:16   179, 180
7:17   47, 180, 181
7:18   46, 47, 48, 176, 179, 180
7:19   32, 44, 46, 48, 172, 173, 179–181, 241
7:19c   46, 47
7:20   46, 47, 176
7:21–22   183–186
7:21   56, 179, 180
7:23   46, 47, 48, 176, 179
7:24–30   20, 173
7:25   176
7:27–29   32
7:27   56
7:28   44
8–10   44
8:1–10   241
8:1–9   20
8:14–21   20
8:22–26   20, 35
8:27–10:52   208
8:27–33   208
8:29   291
8:31–33   32, 56, 151, 163
8:31   31, 198, 250, 291
8:33   261, 291
8:34–9:1   189–209 passim
8:34–38   291
8:35   66, 70, 73, 74, 75
9:1–13   300
9:2–8/13   208
9:2–8   25, 208
9:6   35
9:9   35
9:22   43
9:25   176
9:26   43
9:28–36   239
9:28–29   48
9:29   150, 242
9:30–37   292
9:31   31, 250, 291, 292
9:33–37   292
9:34   292
9:35   292
9:36   292
9:37   292
10:2–9   157
10:5   56
10:10–12   56
10:10   181
10:11   104
10:12   175
10:17–22   292

10:23–27   292
10:26   291
10:28–31   292
10:29–30   195
10:29   66, 73, 74, 75
10:30   57
10:31   292
10:32–34   250, 292
10:33   176
10:34   31
10:35–40   292
10:41–45   292
10:45   32, 42, 56, 198, 204, 209, 252, 262, 267, 290, 291, 292
10:52   151
11:12–14   25
11:15–18   176
11:18   43
11:21   297
12:1–9   44
12:13–17   57
12:13–14   175
12:28–34   57, 198
12:35–37   151, 159, 167, 239
12:36   164
13:3–37   48
13:3   181
13:9–13   195
13:9–11   197
13:10   66, 70, 74, 75, 80, 114
13:11   242
13:13   56, 291
13:14   141
13:24–25   43
13:26   162
13:33–37   154
14:9   66, 70, 74, 75, 114
14:22–24   104
14:24   42, 198, 252
14:31   263
14:32–42   260, 290, 300
14:33   40
14:36   263
14:38   263
14:62   161, 164
14:65   38
14:65a   38

14:65b   38
14:72   297, 300
15   36
15:15   38
15:16–19   38
15:17   48
15:19–20   38
15:21   197
15:24   38
15:29–32   266
15:30   197
15:31   266
15:32   38, 197
15:33   36, 43
15:34   38, 43, 44
15:37–39   38, 44
15:37   41, 43, 242
15:38   38, 242
15:39   35, 37, 267, 290
16:6   37, 40, 66, 76, 78, 79, 85
16:7   301
16:8   40
16:15–16   18
16:19–20   18

Pauline and deutero-Pauline letters
Rom
1:1–7   125, 126, 127, 136
1:1–4   216, 217, 236
1:1   56, 237
1:2   143
1:3–4   31, 54, 156, 165, 166, 279, 280, 281, 283, 284
1:3   65, 69, 72, 76, 80, 85, 166
1:4   237
1:5   129
1:8–15   136
1:14–16   206, 207
1:15   145
1:16–17   31, 56
1:16   32, 56, 206, 207
1:18–3:20   129
1:29–31   183–186
1:29   56
2:5   56
2:7   56
2:28   179

2:29   179, 180
3:21–8:29   129
3:21–26   289
3:21–22   31
3:24–25   56
3:24   54, 245
3:25   32, 42, 252
4:7   278
4:15   32, 56
4:25   283
5   286, 289
5:1   286
5:2   286
5:3–5a   286
5:5   286, 287
5:5b   286
5:6–11   286
5:6–8   286
5:8   32, 56, 286, 287
5:9   42, 252, 286
5:10   286
5:11   286
5:12–21   31, 56, 243, 258, 286
5:18–19   32, 56, 257
5:19   286
6   111
6:1–14   204, 293
6:1–11   287
6:6   39
7:5   278
7:7–25   232, 233
8:2   110
8:11   233, 235
8:15   230
8:38–9:1   56
8:38–39   31
9–11   27
11   32
11:7–10   31, 56
11:7   214
11:25–32   32
11:27   278
13   134
13:1–7   57
13:8–10   46, 57, 109, 110, 182
13:13   183, 185
14   170

14:1–23   57
14:1–2   180
14:3–11   182
14:13–23   181
14:14–23   46
14:14   46, 49, 176, 181, 182
14:20   32, 46, 48, 49, 181
15:14   258
15:16   56
15:31   176
16   126, 139
16:1–16   57
16:16   94

1 Cor
1–2   36, 44, 289
1   94
1:13–17   111
1:17   39
1:18–2:16   287
1:18–25   288
1:18   35, 39
1:22–23   255
1:23   37, 39
1:26–31   288
2:2   37, 39, 288
2:4–5   112
2:4   35
2:6–16   31, 56
2:7–8   38
2:7   26
2:8   42, 43, 54
3:22–23   163, 164
4:8–13   39
4:10   39
5:7   42, 241, 252
5:9   95
5:10–11   183–186
6:9–10   183–186
6:12   112, 181
7:1   95
7:10   56, 104, 109, 277
7:19   109, 182
8   170
8:1   181
8:6   159, 182, 281, 284
8:7   180

8:8   181
8:9   180
8:10   180
9:14   277
9:19–22   45
9:21   23, 110
10   170
10:23   112, 181
10:25–30   180, 181
10:26   182
11:8–9   258
11:17–34   277, 293
11:23–26   284
11:23–25   104, 109, 277
11:23   241, 277
11:25   42, 111, 252
14:37   109
15   31, 219, 258, 270, 278
15:3–7   278
15:3–5   64
15:3–4   69, 251, 253, 254, 284
15:3   42, 64, 66, 72, 78, 80, 85, 252, 277, 278, 283
15:3b-5   278, 279
15:6–7   278
15:8   302
15:9   302
15:14   220
15:17   278
15:20–22   243
15:20   237
15:21–22   31, 56
15:22   162, 258
15:23–28   162, 163, 164
15:24   31, 42, 56
15:27   162
15:28   163
15:35–41   220
15:44–49   243
15:45–49   31, 56
15:45   226, 227, 229, 230, 235, 236, 242, 257, 258
15:47   162
15:50–53   241
15:50   237

2 Cor
1:5–7   38
1:12–14   95
2:14–17   289
3   111
3:5–6   111
4:3–4   289
5:12   179, 180
5:17   109
5:18–19   289
10:3–6   289
10:9–11   96
10:10   95
11:1   39
11:30–33   189
12:20–21   183
13:4   37, 39

Gal
1–2   177
1:1   177
1:4   204, 278, 283
1:6–9   31, 56
1:7   179
1:10–12   177
1:13–17   177
1:14   177
1:15–16   177
1:23   302
2   32, 56, 170, 174
2:1–4   175, 176
2:2   178
2:9   23
2:11–14   23, 46
2:11   22
2:12–14   174
2:12   176
2:13   179, 180
2:15–21   289
2:15–17   233
2:15–16   177
2:15   23, 232
2:16   232
2:19–20   202, 203, 291
2:19   39
2:20   178, 204, 283
3:1   39, 179, 180

3:3   180
3:4   35
3:5   233
3:6–9   234
3:8   233
3:10–12   234
3:13   38, 39, 234
3:14a   234
3:16   230, 235
3:21   235
3:27   236
3:28   214, 236, 236, 241
4:1   284
4:4   280, 284
4:5   230
4:10   174
4:25   176
5:6   109, 182
5:11   37, 39
5:13–26   235
5:14   46
5:19–21   56, 183–186
6:3   110
6:12–13   179
6:12   39, 174, 179
6:14–15   110
6:14   36, 39, 202, 203, 291
6:15   109, 182, 230
6:16   235
6:17   179

Eph
1:21   42
4:31   183–185
5:3–5   183–185
6:12   43

Phil
1:27   95
2   37, 258
2:1–4   282
2:4–5   109
2:5–11   158, 281
2:5   282, 289
2:5b-11   270
2:6–11   54, 108, 266, 268, 281, 284
2:6   245, 267, 282

2:7–8   282
2:7   267, 282
2:8   39, 41, 287
2:9   158, 266, 282, 283, 284
2:10–11   282, 283
2:10   282
2:12–13   109
2:12   95
3:2   179
3:3–4   179
3:5–6   175
3:6   302
3:7–8   205, 206
3:10   38, 204
3:18   39

Col
1:15–20   270
2:8   178
2:11–15   111
2:14–15   42
2:16–23   181
2:20–22   177
2:22   178
3:5–8   183–186
3:16   113

1 Thess
1:5   68
1:10   284
2:2   56
2:9   56, 68
2:15   43
2:16   278
4:15   277
5:27   94

Old Testament Writings/Septuagint
Gen
1:1   125
1:26   163
2:4b-3:24   269, 270
3   162
6:5   183
12:3   234
15:16   278
17:5   231

17:14   232
17:23–27   231
18:18   234

Exod
16:29   152
31:13   157
34:21   152

Lev
11:46–47   47
11:47   48, 49
15:2   47
24:8   155
24:9   154

Deut
14:3–20   47
21:23   38
23:10   47
23:13   47
23:26   152

1 Sam
21:2–7   154, 155
21:7   155

1 Macc
1:47   176
1:62   176

Ps
2:7   164
8   162, 163, 164
8:5–7   161, 164
8:5   161, 162, 165, 167
8:7   162, 164
31:1 LXX   278
110:1–2 MT/109:1–2 LXX   162
110:1 MT/109:1 LXX   151, 158, 159, 164

Job
9:8   159

Wis/Sap Sal
2:23–25   162
2:24   262

14:25–26   184–186

Hos
1:2   137
1:2b   125
6:6   173

Amos
5:21–24   173
8:9   36

Isa
1:10   173
27:9   278
29:13   173, 177–179, 187
40   125
53   283
58:1–14   173

Jer
31:31   111
31:33   180
38:31–34 LXX   110

Ezek
11:19–20   111
28:13   31
36:25–27   180
36:26–27   111

Dan
7:14   161

Early Jewish texts/Non-canonical writings
Apoc. Mos.
16:4   262
17:4   262

Apoc. Sedr.
3:2–4   157
6:2   161

2 Bar.
14:8   157

3 Bar.
4:8   163

4:17   184–186
8:5   184–186
9:7   163
13:4   184, 185

1 En.
69:6   262

2 En.
10:4–6   184
31:3–6   162
31:4–6   262

Jub.
7:20   184
23:14   184
50:12   152

Let. Aris.
305–306   172
315   176

4 Macc.
7:6   176
18:7–8   262

T. Ab.
10.5   184, 185

T. Ash.
2.5   184–186

T. Benj.
6.4   185
8.1   184

T. Gad
5.1   184, 185

T. Iss.
7.2–4   184, 185

T. Levi
14.5–6   184–186
17.11   185

Vit. Ad.
13   161, 163, 164
44 (15–21)   162
44 (15)   163
44 (16)   164

Dead Sea Texts
1QS
3:15–4:26   43
IV, 9–11   180, 184–186
IV, 20–21   180

4Q169 3–4
II, 2   179

CD
10:22–23   153
11:5–6   152

Early Jewish Authors

Josephus
   Ant.
3.181   176
4.234   152
11.346   176
12.320   176
13.297   177
13.4   176
13.408   177
20.169   152

Philo
   Agr.
83   185

   Cher.
71   185
93   184

   Conf.
90   185
117   184, 185

   Decal.
170–171   184, 185

Her.
173   184, 185

Leg.
2.22   230

Migr.
33–35   229
89–93   173, 174, 180
90   180

Mos.
2.22   153
2.288   228

Plant.
23   229

Post.
93   184, 185

QE
2.46   229

QG
1.86   228, 239

Sacr.
32   185

Spec. Laws.
1.281   184
4.48   185

New Testament (excl. Mark and Pauline as well as deutero-Pauline letters, s. above)

Matt
1:1   166
5:17–20   174
5:20   175
10:33   199, 207
10:38–39   199, 200
12:23   166
15:1–20   173
15:19   183
15:20b   48
16:16   40
16:17–19   137
16:24–28   199
16:24   200
16:26   200
21:9   166
21:15   166
23   175
23:13–15   179
23:23   179
23:25   179
23:27   179
23:29   179
26:37   40
27:50   41
27:51–53   40
27:54   37, 41

Mark (see above)

Luke
1:1–4   100
1:32   40, 166
1:34   40
1:35   237
3:23   238
9:23–27   199
9:23   197, 200
9:25   200
12:9   199, 207
13:33–35   176
14:27   199, 200
17:33   199, 200
20:41–44   239
20:44   238
22:3   42
22:31   307
22:41   40
22:43   263
23:27–31   41
23:39–43   41
23:46   41
23:47   37

John
1:3   157
1:49   40
1:51   162

5:1   176
5:27   162
6:70   42
12:31   42
12:42   175
13:2   42
13:27   42
14:30   42
18:6–9   41
18:36   41
19:11   41
19:26–27   41
19:28–30   41
21:15–19   137

Acts
1:12   152
4:5   176
6:1–8:3   181
9:4   304, 307
9:6   304
9:13–14   304
10–11   174, 182
10   187
10:11–15   48
10:14–15   176
10:15   181
10:28   176
10:36   182
11:8–9   176
11:20   174
15   174
15:5   174, 182
15:23–29   88
21:25   174
21:28   176
22:7–8   304
22:7   307
26:5   175
26:14–15   304
26:14   307

Rom – 2 Thess (see above)

1 Tim
1:9–10   183–185
1:13   304

1:16   304
4:2   179
6:4–5   183, 185

2 Tim
2:8   166
3:2–5   183, 185

Titus
1:7   183
1:14   178
1:15   181
3:3   183, 184

Heb
1:1–2:9   161, 164, 167
1:2   164
1:3b   164
1:6   161
2:2   164
2:3   164
2:5   164
2:6   161
8:8–12   110
9:10   178
9:13   176
10:29   176
12:23   161
13:9   181

Jas
3:14–16   183

1 Pet
2:1   183, 185
4:3   183, 185
4:15   183, 184

2 Pet
3:15–16   112

1 John
3:9   225

Rev
1:1   16
2:12–21   174

2:20   174
9:21   183, 184
12:9   262
14:14–26   162
20:2   262
21:8   183, 184
21:27   176
22:15   183, 184

Early Christian texts/Extra-canonical writings
Acts Pet.
2.47.12–34   308
7.53.20–54.23   309

Barn.
12:10   166

Gos. Thom.
14   174

Ignatius
    Eph.
18:2   166
    Smyrn.
1:1   166

Early Christian authors
Eusebius
    Hist. eccl.
3.39.15   29, 297
3.4.7   114

Jerome
    Epist.
57:9,4–5   154
121:10,20   152

Justin
    Apol.
66   112
67   112

    Dial.
103.8   113
135.3   238

Origen
    Comm. Jo.
1.276   228

Rabbinica
Aboth de Rabbi Nathan
1:11   163

b. Menaḥ.
95b   155

Gen. Rab.
18:56   31
20:12   31

m. Avot.
1:1   177
4:9   185
5:22   185

m. Bek.
1:2   49

m. Ḥul.
8:4   49

m. Joma
8:6b   157
85a   157

m. Šabb.
7:2   152
12:2   152
23:3–4   152

m. Soṭah
9:15   173

Maimonides
    Hilkhot Shabbat
    8:3   153

Pirqe R. El.
14   31

t. Bek.
1:6   49

t. Ḥul.
8:11   49

Tg. Ps.-J.
Gen 3:4   163

Tg. Yer. I
Gen 3:7   31
Gen 3:21   31

Yerushalmi Tractate Berakhot
  1:2   180

Greco-Roman authors
Aristoteles
  Gen. an.
15.735b10 – 36a30   225

  Poet.
1450a7 – 12   275
1450b24   275
1451a16   275

Cicero
  Fin.
5:51   103

  Verr.
2.5.66   37

  De or.
8.24   90

Corp. herm.
1.23   184, 185
13.7   185

Dio Chrysostom
  Fel. sap. (Or. 23)
7   185

  Invid. (Or. 77/78)
39   185

  Virt. (Or. 8)
8   185

  Virt. (Or. 69)
9   184, 185

Diogenes Laertius
6.85   184

Plutarch
  De aud. poet.   90

  Sera
555E   185
565C   185

  Tranq. an.
468B   185

Pseudo-Phocylides
228   173

(Pseudo)-Plutarch
  Lib. ed.
13 A   185

Sib. Or.
2.256   184, 185
3.591 – 3   172

Stobaeus
  Ecl.
2.93.1   184, 185

Suetonius
  Gramm. et Rhet.
3.4   87

www.ingramcontent.com/pod-product-compliance
Lightning Source LLC
Chambersburg PA
CBHW070606170426
43200CB00012B/2604